our savage art

Also by William Logan

POETRY

Sad-faced Men (1982)
Difficulty (1985)
Sullen Weedy Lakes (1988)
Vain Empires (1998)
Night Battle (1999)
Macbeth in Venice (2003)
The Whispering Gallery (2005)
Strange Flesh (2008)

CRITICISM

All the Rage (1998)
Reputations of the Tongue (1999)
Desperate Measures (2002)
The Undiscovered Country (2005)

OUR SAVAGE ART

Poetry and the Civil Tongue

WILLIAM LOGAN

COLUMBIA UNIVERSITY PRESS   *New York*

COLUMBIA UNIVERSITY PRESS
Publishers Since 1893
NEW YORK   CHICHESTER, WEST SUSSEX

Library of Congress Cataloging-in-Publication Data

Logan, William, 1950
  Our savage art : poetry and the civil tongue / William Logan.
    p. cm.
  Includes bibliographical references and index.
  ISBN 978-0-231-14732-3 (alk. paper)—ISBN 978-0-231-51961-8 (e-book)
    1.   American poetry—20th century—History and criticism. 2.   Criticism—United
States—History—20th century.   I. Title.
  PS323.5.L644 2009
  811'.509—dc22

                                          2008036414

Columbia University Press books are printed on permanent and durable acid-free paper.
This book is printed on paper with recycled content.
Printed in the United States of America

c 10 9 8 7 6 5 4 3 2 1

For Jane Alpert and Judith Vecchione

Contents

Acknowledgments

No man who writes for money fails to owe a debt of gratitude to the editors who sign the checks; and I am grateful to the gentlemen who considered my opinions worth the trouble, even at a discount. Many of these editors made my debts the greater by pointing out my errors and infelicities, which more often than not I labored to correct. I'm grateful to the editors of the *New Criterion, New York Times Book Review, Parnassus, Poetry, Southwest Review, TLS, Virginia Quarterly Review,* and *Wall Street Journal,* as well as to Garrick Davis, the editor of *Contemporary Poetry Review,* who conducted a placable interview with me.

I have placed two reviews of Thomas Pynchon in a volume otherwise about poetry because there is something, as there was for Melville, intrinsically poetic about the way he writes. They are also here for comic relief.

It was my intention to reproduce, in the essay "Frost at Midnight," eight passages from Frost's notebooks in photofacsimile, so that the reader might judge for himself the flaws in the editor's transcriptions. The Frost estate, unfortunately, refused permission.

"Those mountains certainly do, my lord," rejoined the Countess, pointing to the Pyrenées; "and this château, though not a work of rude nature, is, to my taste, at least, one of savage art." The Count colored highly. "This place, madam, was the work of my ancestors," said he.
—Ann Radcliffe, *The Mysteries of Udolpho* (1794)

Yet, notwithstanding all the attention which these people bestow upon this savage art, for which they have public schools, they are outdone by savages. When one of the English squadrons of discovery was at Tongataboo, several of the natives boxed with the sailors for love, as the phrase is, and in every instance the savage was victorious.
—Manuel Alvarez Espriella, *Letters from England*, 3rd ed., vol. 3 (1814)

The cavalcade had not long passed, before the branches of the bushes that formed the thicket were cautiously moved asunder, and a human visage, as fiercely wild as savage art and unbridled passions could make it, peered out on the retiring footsteps of the travellers.
—James Fenimore Cooper, *The Last of the Mohicans* (1826)

The more a man studies savage art, the more is he struck by the almost universal good taste which it displays. Every chair, stool, or bench is prettily shaped and neatly carved. Every club, paddle, or staff is covered with intricate tracery which puts to shame our European handicraft.
—G. A. "Cimabue and Coal-Scuttles," *Cornhill Magazine* (July 1880)

A remarkable peculiarity of their pipe-carvings is that accurate representations are given of different natural objects, instead of the rude caricatures and monstrosities in which savage art usually delights. Nearly every beast, bird, and reptile indigenous to the country is truthfully represented, together with some creatures now only found in tropical climates, such as the lamantin and toucan.
—Hubert Howe Bancroft, *The Native Races* (*The Works of Hubert Howe Bancroft*, vol. 4, 1886)

This is just what I was told by a carpet manufacturer who was perfectly aware of the ugliness of his wares, who laughed at it, and regretted that it was a necessity. He illustrated it by showing me the kinds of carpets and rugs which "sold like hot cakes." It was pitiful, for no Red Indian and no savage negro would ever have designed aught so repulsive. Savage art is never half so savage as that produced by the most enlightened nation on the face of the earth, and English carpets are little better.
—Charles G. Leland, *Practical Education* (1888)

I also got from another fellow a very pretty model of a New Guinea canoe. . . . It cost me no less than three sticks of trade tobacco to become the possessor of this masterpiece of savage art, for its owner evidently valued it highly, though of what use it could have been to him I cannot conceive.
—E. E. Ellis, *Cassell's Picturesque Australasia*, vol. 3 (1888)

[The aboriginal's] place in art—as to drawing, not color-work—is well up, all things considered. His art is not to be classified with savage art at all, but on a plane two degrees above it and one degree above the lowest plane of civilized art. To be exact, his place in art is between Botticelli and De Maurier. That is to say, he could not draw as well as De Maurier but better than Bot[t]icelli.
—Mark Twain, *Following the Equator* (1897)

Some men were even relapsing from the point that art had reached on the earlier stage of "rim ram ruf"—on the rhythmical prose of alliteration either simple of itself or awkwardly bedizened, like a true savage art, with feathers and gawds of inappropriate stanza and rhyme.
—George Saintsbury, *A Short History of English Literature* (1898)

our savage art

The Bowl of Diogenes; or, The End of Criticism

A man must serve his time to every trade
Save censure—critics all are ready made.
—Byron

He was so generously civil, that nobody thanked him for it.
—Johnson

The more criticism I write, the more I'm asked to write about criticism; and, the more I'm asked to write about criticism, the less I want to write about anything at all. Samuel Johnson once said, "When a man is tired of criticism, he is tired of life," or words to that effect; but at times I'm just tired of criticism. Then something gets under my skin. The other day, I was sent the proofs of a book of poetry, introduced by a letter from the publisher. "The real trouble with most contemporary poetry," the letter said, "is that it is piled high, mostly unread and gathering dust, in the attic of its own obscurity." Imagine someone thinking contemporary poetry too obscure, when it isn't half obscure enough! Just as I was feeling rather blue, there was a man handing me an ax to grind; and before I knew it I was writing criticism again. (Readers who persevere with this volume will eventually discover whose publisher wrote such rubbish.)

In the first edition of his great dictionary, Johnson defined a *critick* as a "man skilled in the art of judging of literature; a man able to distinguish the faults and beauties of writing." Later he added a new definition. What was a critick, on second thought? "A snarler; a carper; a caviller." As a snarler in good standing (with oak-leaf clusters for carping and caviling), I would argue that a critic is a man—skilled, perhaps, in the judging of literature—*who can't resist the chance to criticize.*

There have always been poetry critics. I imagine that when Homer had sung the last lay of the *Odyssey* and laid down his lyre, some scruffy fellow in the corner said, "Oh, come on! Why would anyone drag a wooden horse into Troy? What were they thinking? And who's going to believe that stuff about the sailors? Those pigs must be more of a metaphor or whatever. Then that bit about the one-eyed guy—that, now *that*, was a little hard to believe. I liked a few lines, I guess; but your earlier work, that battle kind of a thing, was much, much better."

Critics are insects, as everyone knows, one of the plagues that poets have to bear. When Coleridge complained that the "meanest Insects are worshipped with a sort of Egyptian Superstition, if only the brainless head be atoned for by the sting of *personal* malignity in the tail," he was talking about critics. We laugh now at the critics who, reviewing the Romantics, got things so horribly wrong—Francis Jeffrey on Wordsworth, say, or John Wilson Croker on Keats. How dare they! Why, William Wordsworth could lick his weight in wildcats, if there were any wildcats in the vicinity of Dove Cottage; and John Keats's little finger could write better poems than any of the poetasters hurtling around London. Yet the poets who are giants to us often seemed to their peers no taller than anyone else—and sometimes rather shorter. Time is the great discoverer of quality, and the great magnifier of difference.

When you read Jeffrey's and Croker's actual reviews, rather than rumors or opinions about them, you think those critics were blinded by their prejudices, certainly; but they saw clearly that such poets had their faults. Take Jeffrey's infamous *Edinburgh Review* article on *The Excursion*, a review that starts, "This will never do."

Why should Mr. Wordsworth have made his hero a superannuated Pedlar? What but the most wretched and provoking perversity of taste and judgment, could induce any one to place his chosen advocate of wisdom and virtue in so absurd and fantastic a condition? Did Mr. Wordsworth really imagine, that his favourite doctrines were likely to gain any thing in point of effect or authority by being put into the mouth of a person accustomed to higgle about tape, or brass sleeve-buttons? . . . A man who went about selling flannel and pocket-handkerchiefs in this lofty diction, would soon frighten away all his customers.

This is hilarious, in part because it is at someone else's expense, someone whose poetry we admire. (Do we secretly resent those we love? I leave that to the psychiatrists.) Hilarious, too, because its strictures are so misplaced. Two hundred years later, we scarcely care whether Wordsworth chose a retired peddler, or the parish pauper, or the wife of a poor weaver, or a retired army chaplain (all of whom he *did* choose, and all of whom put the critic's nose out of joint). We don't care, because such occupations are almost as obscure to us as the doctrines Wordsworth put into their mouths. To us, it's merely literature; and we enjoy it for what it is, as well as for what it is not. To Jeffrey, Wordsworth's peddler was an affront to taste and to the plain evidence of a man's eyes. Even Coleridge, though he indulged in a good deal of special pleading on behalf of that peddler, was willing to admit that "whether this be a character appropriate to a lofty didactick poem, is perhaps questionable. It presents a fair subject for controversy."

Reading such critics now, we laugh, and the world laughs with us; but we have the advantage of two hundred years of the slow grinding of critical analysis and the fine filtering of taste (however wildly mistaken in the short term, in the long run taste is as delicately tuned as analysis). We read, with our modern, sensible eyes, in the easy chair used by readers before us. Who cares about all the insignificant wretches who suffered when Jeffrey or Croker turned the screw? The difficult thing would be to like *our* Keats and *our* Wordsworth, if we have them, to scour out from anonymity *our* Hopkins and Dickinson, to call *our* Whitman a genius, instead of saying, as a critic of 1856 did, that Whitman must be "some escaped lunatic, raving in pitiable delirium" (another said he was "as unacquainted with art, as a hog is with mathematics"). Critics get things wrong all the time; if a critic ever suffered insomnia, it would be because he had dismissed the Emily Dickinson of his day. Yet critics know the future may pluck up some writer they think a nonentity and say, "Here, here, the critics were blind to genius!" Randall Jarrell said something similar fifty years ago, but Randall Jarrell often said fifty years ago the very things I want to say about poetry now.

I once suggested to an interviewer that a critic could best be compared to a district attorney. "You mean *judge*," he said, a little shocked. I took his point. A critic longs to be a Solomon, disinterested and wise, pronouncing impartial sentence upon the poetry of the age—the good, the bad, and the indifferent (many critics despise the age they were born in and look back with ill-concealed fondness to an earlier one, where they would have been equally miserable). Perhaps the critic starts by believing himself a judge, an incorruptible dispenser of justice; but there is so much bad poetry, and so little good, that often he ends by becoming an overworked prosecutor, presenting the case where the only crime is against art.

A critic is, nonetheless, the most optimistic man alive, living in perpetual hope, like a Latter-day Saint. No matter how many times he is disappointed, he opens each new book with an untarnished sense of possibility. If, amid the dust heaps of mediocrity, he does find a few books rich and strange, such is the essential generosity of this peculiar craft that his first impulse is to call everyone he knows and to buttonhole strangers on the street. It's his duty, however, to hold up weaker books to public scorn. Bad books *do* drive out good ones—it's the Gresham's law of literature. The shock is not how often critics are wrong; it's how often they prove to be right. The first reviewers of Whitman, however wrongheaded they were, often saw clearly the weaknesses of the good gray poet; and we can only nod now in respect.

However, if out of antiquarian curiosity we open the book reviews of the past, two things may surprise us: that often the harshest criticism was not nearly harsh enough and that mediocrities were praised to the skies (read some of the reviews Robert Southey received, and you'll know what I mean). When critics get it wrong, it is usually in how *kind* they are. Open the old quarterlies and see how charitable the critics were to Harry Brown and Howard Baker and Winfield Townley Scott, poets of whom most readers today will never have heard, yet all had books in the classiest publishing project of the 1940s, James Laughlin's Poet of the Month series. Read the benevolent reviews of Robert Horan, Rosalie Moore, and Edgar Bogardus, all chosen in the Yale Series of Younger Poets by the best judge the series ever had, W. H. Auden—and he chose them with the same eye that chose Adrienne Rich, John Ashbery, James Wright, and W. S. Merwin. Jarrell said it better: "When we read the criticism of any past age, we see immediately that the main thing wrong with it is an astonishing amount of what Eliot calls 'fools' approval'; most of the thousands of poets were bad, most of the thousands of critics were bad, and they loved each other."

The critic's besetting vice is generosity. (His telling virtues—well, I'm not sure he *has* telling virtues, because the critic is a mythological creature, a monster with the jaws of a shark, the heart of a lawyer, and the eye of a pawnbroker.) The critic's vice compares very favorably with a poet's deadly sins, pride and paranoia. Many an author, stung by his bad reviews, nevertheless believes his work so original it cannot be appreciated by more than a happy few. (Sooner or later, every artist finds his few.) No doubt such a fairy tale warms the poet's heart, for what author ever felt his reviews, no matter how larded with praise, were ever good enough? Indeed, many an otherwise sensible poet is certain a conspiracy of critics is out to get him. (Of course, such a conspiracy exists. We e-mail each other to arrange bad reviews and plan the blood rituals for our annual convention in Salem.) But how often does a poet, by the pool of Narcissus where he dwells, actually listen to what a critic says? What a critic sees as a poet's sins are often the very signs, to the poet, of his saintliness.

Coleridge claimed, according to John Payne Collier, that "reviewers are usually people who would have been poets . . . , if they could: they have tried their talents . . . and have failed; therefore they turn critics, and, like the Roman emperor, a critic most hates those who excel in the particular department in which he, the critic, has notoriously been defeated." Words like that are painted on the wall over every poet's desk, to console him. Things have changed since Coleridge's day, however, because the twentieth century offered one long string of poets who turned their hands brilliantly to criticism: Eliot, Pound, Empson, Auden, Blackmur, Jarrell, Berryman, and Lowell. For these poets, who had not been defeated (except for Blackmur, who, though a brilliant critic, was a dreadful poet), criticism was high-minded, an attempt to explain the art to itself. It might seem wise to make a distinction between those who practice criticism in its drier and more erudite forms and those who take off their gloves for a bare-knuckle brawl. Yet most of these critics were bare-knucklers, some of the time.

Coleridge's own career gives the lie to his statement; but a critic is often a snarler when young. By the time he turns thirty, someone has usually taken him aside and explained the way things work in the land of Cockaigne that is poetry; and soon he has muffled his barks and muzzled his bites. In most arts, indeed, there is a guild rule against writing criticism. One looks in vain for the ballet reviews of Twyla Tharp and the film reviews of Angelina Jolie. In poetry, as in few other arts (fiction is a partial exception), the critics are the artists themselves—even though many poets, and wise poets they are, have sworn an oath of *omertà* never to breathe a word of criticism against a fellow of the guild.

When R. P. Blackmur called criticism the "formal discourse of an amateur," he flattered those of us who like the amateurishness of criticism, the implied distrust of professionals, even if a professional is sometimes just an amateur who has hung around too long. (Still, *professional critic* ought to be an oxymoron, like *military intelligence* or *friendly fire*). Poets grumble that there are too many critics, while editors complain all the time that there aren't enough of them, that if only a few pale young poets could be convinced to write criticism the world of poetry would be a better place. Should we have camps for critics, then, the way we have music camps? (I'm sure some wit will think I mean prison camps.) Should a rising generation of critics sit at the feet of aging veterans, with their brutal scars and war stories? Is criticism something to be encouraged at all?

Part of me says we should leave things as they are, though that unhappily implies that once upon a time someone left things as they were so they could become things as they are now—and who is satisfied with the way criticism is now? Perhaps criticism ought to remain a private vice, unmentioned in polite company, quite possibly illegal in Georgia, and written for reasons obscure, because the critic can't help but write it. I turned to criticism myself, not out of messianic instinct or the will to martyrdom, but out of the terrible knowledge that I was a better reader when I read for hire, that I read more intently when driven by necessity. I teach poetry for the same reasons—I don't really know a poem until I scribble all over it.

I started writing book reviews thirty years ago, at the end of the great age of newspaper criticism. Poetry was still covered in major papers and even in quite a few smaller ones. My first book of poetry, published in the early eighties, was reviewed in the *Washington Post, Boston Globe, Chicago Tribune, Chicago Sun-Times, Los Angeles Herald-Examiner, Worcester Sunday Telegram*, and—in a review spread over half a page, with a large photograph of the long-haired, pasty-faced poet—*Winston-Salem Journal*. The list reads like an elegy; today a book of poetry reviewed in one or two papers is fortunate. My students, when they take up criticism, publish their reviews on the Web, which is no doubt the future. It's like the earlier swashbuckling era of newspaper publishing (in 1876 the tiny village of Plattsmouth, Nebraska, had three newspapers, one of them in German; Fargo, a city of only ten thousand in 1883, boasted eight). The problem with the Web is that everyone and his sister has a poetry blog, and you need a critic to tell you which critics to read.

I won't presume to ask what the benefits of criticism are for the reader, though there may be few beyond being provoked to sympathy or *Schadenfreude*. Devoted readers often feel, not that criticism drives them toward reading books, but that it drives them away. For every review that has led me to pick up a book, a hundred have convinced me not to bother—and, worse, I've been grateful. Even glowing reviews sooner or later end up quoting from a poem or two, presumably something that glows; the curious thing is, the quotes so rarely deserve the praise. Being a critic has meant, for more years than I care to count, reading a hundred books of new poetry a year and leafing through the pages of at least twice that number. When poetry books arrive at my door, they come singly like spies or in droves like petitioners. I look at them as I can, somewhat lazily and haphazardly, and sometimes after ten or twenty pages I put one down with a sigh and turn to another—there are so many waiting and so few I can review. In truth, if a poet doesn't catch your eye in twenty pages, he probably never will. Life is too short, and poetry books, however short, are too many.

What are the benefits of criticism for the critic? (The critic must derive some benefit from his vice.) First, criticism has forced me to read books I would otherwise have ignored. I've read far more contemporary poetry than most people and far more than I would have, left to my own devices. I've probably read more dreary and ordinary books of verse than is healthy; and I have learned more, speaking selfishly, speaking artistically, reading the sermons of John Donne. Yet, on rare occasions, I've felt like Balboa staring out across an unknown sea or Herschel seeing Uranus swim before his telescope (or the Japanese marine biologists who recently saw a living giant squid): I've found a book that reminds me, not just why I write criticism, but why I write poetry. The second benefit of criticism is that it has taught me, more often than I care to admit, how to think about this minor art.

There are often subsidiary comedies to amuse the critic as he works. I've been threatened by a few poets and told by two newspapers never to darken their doorways again. Years ago the editor of *Poetry*, rejecting a review he had commissioned, warned me never to publish it, because it would harm my reputation. I published it elsewhere, of course; but during his tenure the magazine never asked for another review. A well-known journal recently asked me to review any poet I chose, as long as I chose only a poet I liked. A poet I'd ever whispered a critical word against—no, that would never do. Why? Because I might be prejudiced against him.

When Plato banished the poets from his Republic, did he banish poetry critics, too? As he was himself a poetry critic in a big way, he'd have been forced to banish himself. His idea of utopia must have been, instead, a place where all the poetry critics stood inside the walls and all the poets outside. (Even the poets might have appreciated that.) Let us imagine a different world, the opposite of the Republic. Let us imagine a world where poetry critics *are* forbidden. Bad poets would continue to publish and be read, good ones to publish and be ignored, and occasionally vice versa. In that utopia without critics, authors would go about comfortable in the rich cloth of their illusions. I'm sure poets would think that a very good thing, for who does not like to be alone with his illusions, except those who want everyone else to share them?

Is there a place, then, for criticism? A critic looking for a classical hero usually thinks, all too flatteringly, of Hercules cleaning the Augean stables. I have cleaned a few stables in my time, but I've never felt like Hercules. Let me propose a different model. Diogenes, famed for his austerity, lived for a time in a terra-cotta tub in the Athens marketplace. ("What can I do for you?" asked Alexander, having come a distance to see this unusual philosopher, something dictators and presidents do all too rarely these days. Diogenes looked at him and said, "You can get the hell out of my light.") In his frugality, the cynic reduced his possessions one by one, until he owned only the cloak he wore, a pouch, and a drinking bowl. One day he saw a boy drinking from a stream with his hands, and threw away the bowl. Diogenes here is the reader. The bowl is criticism. And the water . . . the water is poetry.

"For I am nothing, if not critical," said Iago, the patron saint of modern critics. Every now and then, I try to throw away my bowl and stop writing criticism (then I can drink the pure waters of poetry from my bare hands). But something happens, like that publisher's letter, and I'm dragged back again. There are even now publishers and readers and even poets who think poetry far too obscure, who think poetry ought to be so simple it hardly needs to be read at all. I won't castigate the poets who exemplify this age of prose. Their publishers say such poets open the door to poetry; but readers who go through that door don't want poetry any less wooden than the door itself.

The best poetry has often been difficult, has often been so obscure readers have fought passionately over it. The King James Bible comes closer to poetry than faith usually dares: I Corinthians used to say, "For now we see through a glass, darkly," and then along came someone to improve it. Until a century ago, a mirror was called a glass, so the meaning is not as obscure as it seems, though the Jacobeans were already updating their source—the literal meaning of the Greek is to see one's face in the haze of a bronze mirror (Corinth specialized in bronze mirrors). One recent translation reads, instead, "For we see now through a dim window obscurely," which is far from the literal sense and lousy prose as well. (What the hell is a "dim window"?) In bowing to the prose literacies of our day, the translators have scrubbed out the rhythm and the poetry, leaving little for the ear and less for the eye. If they'd wanted to translate I Corinthians into modern English, they should have said, "For now we see ourselves as in a tinted windshield."

For two centuries, well-meaning vandals have been trying to dumb down Shakespeare, wanting to make him common enough for the common reader, in the doltish belief that, introduced to poetry this way, the common reader will turn to the original. Yet the reader almost never does. He's satisfied with a poor simulacrum of poetry, never realizing that Shakespeare without the poetry isn't Shakespeare at all. The beauty of poetry is *in* the difficulty, in the refusal of the words to make the plain sense immediately plain, in the dark magic and profound mistrust of words themselves. Does it surprise anyone that there is a Web site, Shakespeare Online, that translates the Bard's sonnets into modern English? Or that "When in disgrace with fortune and men's eyes," the opening of sonnet 29, is rendered, "When I've run out of luck and people look down on me"?

Surely we read poetry because it gives us a sense of the depths of language, meaning nudging meaning, then darting away, down to the unfathomed and muddy bottom. Critics, generations of critics, have devoted themselves to revealing how those words work, to showing that each sense depends on other senses. Not every poem has to be as devious and shimmering as Shakespeare (there is room for plain speaking, too); but the best poetry depends on the subtlety and suggestiveness of its language. If we demand that poetry be so plain that plain readers can drink it the whole plain day, we will have lost whatever makes poetry poetry. (This plainest of plain poetry often goes, "Once upon a time, blah, blah, blah . . . ha! ha! ha!") It's curious that complex or difficult poets of the previous generation, Robert Lowell and Anthony Hecht and Richard Wilbur, are still praised for the elegance and intransigence of their words, while young poets are told, in not so many words, that subtlety is old fashioned.

It is notoriously difficult to define poetry, because any definition leaves out something (it's almost a definition of *definition* that it leaves something out); but I like Michael Oakeshott's idea that the poet "does *one* thing only, he imagines poetically." And the critic? The critic is someone who imagines *critically*, for what is good about good criticism is that it imagines with the same sympathies as the poet—and then, of course, decides whether he is worth a damn. If critics, all of them, threw away their bowls, it might be a very good thing—for the critics, that is. (Artists are said to suffer for their art, but I don't recall anyone saying a critic ought to suffer for his criticism—no one except the poets he criticizes.) If it is too much to believe that criticism can alter the taste of the age, a critic may at least whisper to the future that not everyone *agreed* with the taste of the age.

The critic, if he is to be a critic, must risk being wrong, must say what seems right to him, though it makes him a laughingstock for generations afterward. A critic who does his job must be a good hater if he's to be a good lover, because if he likes everything he reads he likes nothing well enough—and the critic lives for the moment when he discovers a book so rare his first instinct is to cast such a pearl before readers (some of whom will be swine who ignore it; others, the real readers, simply people with a taste for pearls). The daily job of the critic, what he does in the meanwhile, is to explore the difficulty of poetry, not for other readers, but for himself, because who is the critic critical *for*, if not himself? This may seem to make a minor craft more a moral virtue than a moral failing; but a critic needs no deeper philosophy or impulse than that criticism is what he does—it is, in Blackmur's phrase, his "job of work." When Diogenes threw away his bowl, in other words, he made a mistake.

Verse Chronicle

Out on the Lawn

Billy Collins

I should have reviewed Billy Collins's *Nine Horses* months ago, but I couldn't stand the excitement. Collins is that rarity, a poet with popular appeal, easy to read as a billboard, genial as a Sunday golfer, and not so awful you want to cut your throat after reading him. Many readers complain that poetry is difficult to understand, the way they grumble when an opera is sung in Italian or resent a Czech film with subtitles. Art isn't supposed to be such hard work, is it? Billy Collins writes poetry for those people, and they appreciate it.

Collins specializes in goofy, slightly offbeat subjects. If you want a poem about mice who play with matches, or about that song incessantly repeating in your head, or about feeling sorry for Whistler's mother, he's your man. *Angst* is not a word he's learned, or *Weltschmerz* (he may have learned *Schadenfreude*, but he's forgotten it). What he loves is the cheesy sentiment of the everyday: "I peered in at the lobsters//lying on the bottom of an illuminated/tank which was filled to the brim/with their copious tears." *To the brim*! Or worse, if anything could be worse than weeping lobsters, he loves everything—he's got a heart big as all outdoors:

> This morning as I walked along the lakeshore,
> I fell in love with a wren
> and later in the day with a mouse
> the cat had dropped under the dining room table.
>
> In the shadows of an autumn evening,
> I fell for a seamstress
> still at her machine in the tailor's window,

> *and later for a bowl of broth,*
> *steam rising like smoke from a naval battle.*

You want to stop him before he becomes a public hazard. It's tough to read a poet who has overdosed on some mood elevator, who is every goddamned minute "cockeyed with gratitude."

Collins has been called a philistine; but you can read a lot of contemporary poetry without coming across references to William Carlos Williams, Coventry Patmore, Walter Pater, or *Clarissa*—they're all in Collins, and more. He's something worse, a poet who doesn't respect his art enough to take it seriously. Once or twice an image makes you stop: a dead groundhog, say, like "a small Roman citizen,/with his prosperous belly, // his faint smile,/and his one stiff forearm raised/as if he were still alive, still hailing Caesar." Then it's back to a kind of NPR commentary on contemporary mores, like the use of trompe l'oeil in your kitchen. Collins makes cheap art for the masses, like posters of a Monet. Once you've seen a real Monet, posters can't compare.

The best poem here is about the afterlife. The skies there are sulphurous, the dead souls crowded into boats, bent over writing tablets, under the gaze of hellish boatmen. What are the dead working on? Poetry assignments.

> *how could anyone have guessed*
>
> *that as soon as we arrived*
> *we would be asked to describe this place*
> *and to include as much detail as possible—*
> *not just the water, he insists,*
>
> *rather the oily, fathomless, rat-happy water,*
> *not simply the shackles, but the rusty,*
> *iron, ankle-shredding shackles—*
> *and that our next assignment would be*
>
> *to jot down, off the tops of our heads,*
> *our thoughts and feelings about being dead.*

In Collins's last book, the best poem was also about a poetry assignment—why can he be hilarious about them and merely droll about everything else?

Collins never gets worked up over things—even faced with death, he makes winsome jokes, the kind morticians tell at undertaking conventions. He's the Caspar Milquetoast of contemporary poetry, never a word used in earnest, never a memorable phrase. The moral revelation toward which his poems saunter always seems to be "See? I'm human, too." I read this as not joy but contempt. If such poems look embarrassing now, what are they going to look like in twenty years?

Yet readers adore Billy Collins, and it feels almost un-American not to like him. Try to explain to his readers what "The Steeple-Jack" or "The River Merchant's Wife" or "The Snow Man" is up to, and they'll look at you as if you'd asked them to hand-pump a ship through the locks of the Panama Canal. Most contemporary poetry isn't any more difficult to understand than Collins—it's written in prose, good oaken American prose, and then chopped into lines. Perhaps it's self-absorbed, downbeat, even self-pitying, where Collins every morning throws open the drapes to greet the dawn, taking a deep breath of good suburban air. (You can imagine him hosting a health and fitness show.) If once in a coon's age there's a dark cloud on the horizon, if he gets a trifle gloomy or down in the mouth, then, well, he's rueful with a *twinkle*, damn it, the way a poet ought to be.

Rosanna Warren

Rosanna Warren has a warm, classical sensibility (if she has a chip on her shoulder, it's a chip of Greek marble); and some of her poems are an atlas of Greek temples, a phone book of Greek gods. Though *Departure* is her fourth book, her imagination is not highly distinctive—she does what a lot of other poets do, often a little better, sometimes a little worse. There's a poem contemplating a Hellenistic head, poems about her dying mother, poems about gardening or a story by Colette or a landscape seen from a plane, even a poem that almost makes Boston a classical ruin (in a book that invokes the *Iliad*, it's amusing to come across the lines "By beer bottles, over smeared/Trojans").

Warren has the disadvantage of being the daughter of two once well-known writers—when she mentions her father, it's hard not to think, "But that's Robert Penn Warren." When her mother is ill, you're tempted to cry, "But of course—Eleanor Clark." Warren never drops names, but then she doesn't have to. The children of writers must be aware that in their work biography intrudes more dramatically than for poets whose parents are anonymous.

The poems about her mother's last years ought to be among the most moving; yet, however carefully coddled, however dryly observed, they seem merely dutiful. Not dutiful toward her mother—dutiful toward poetry.

> *Your purpled, parchment forearm*
> *lodges an IV needle and valve;*
> *your chest sprouts EKG wires;*
> *your counts and pulses swarm*
>
> *in tendrils over your head*
> *on a gemmed screen: oxygen,*
> *heart rate, lung power, temp*
> *root you to the bed—*
>
> *Magna Mater, querulous, frail,*
> *turned numerological vine . . .*

With that sudden nod toward grandiloquence, all the heart leaks out of the poem. The description is as good as such descriptions are, but with nothing stirring in the phrases—it's life worked up into art; yet, while the strangeness of life has gone, the intensity of art has not arrived.

The most curious work here is a series of translations from the notebooks of a young French poet, Anne Verveine, who disappeared while hitchhiking in Uzbekistan. The poems themselves are stale and unprofitable—they seem, like so many translations, just the translator wearing a different suit of clothes. At times the Frenchwoman sounds more like Warren than Warren. This would be unremarkable if Verveine were not completely imaginary. Having admitted as much in the notes, Warren oddly tricks her out with a dry biography ("She lived obscurely in Paris, avoiding literary society and working as a typographer") and then smartly packs her off to her death.

It's hard to know what to make of this convoluted business. W. D. Snodgrass published a book of poems under the pseudonym S. S. Gardons (a cheerful anagram), making his alter ego a gas-station attendant. The British poet Christopher Reid, twenty years ago, published translations of an imaginary Eastern European poet named Katerina Brac—some readers were convinced she was real. In recent decades, there have been examples enough of literary imposture, authors winning awards by impersonating an Australian aborigine or a Jew who survived the Holocaust. Warren's "translations" give no special insight into Paris or the lives of young women. It's strange that she went to so much trouble.

In her own poems, Warren uses all the right devices—similes, metaphors, allusions, lists—in a slightly mechanical way. Her favorite method of construction is a violent turn or peripeteia; but such swervings often seem nervousness, not nerve. What salvages this book of intelligent, well-meaning poems, most of them conventional as cottage cheese, are one or two that rise from some dark source even the poet seems unsure about:

> *For six days, full-throated, they praised*
> *the light with speckled tongues and blare*
> *   of silence by the porch stair:*
> *honor guard with blazons and trumpets raised*
> *still heralding the steps of those*
> *   who have not for years walked here*
> *   but who once, pausing, chose*
>
> *this slope for a throng of lilies:*
> *and hacked with mattock, pitching stones*
> *   and clods aside to tamp dense*
> *clumps of bog-soil for new roots to seize.*
> *So lilies tongued the brassy air.*

This has the intensity missing elsewhere (the densities required by rhyme seem partly responsible). Whatever ritual the poet incanted, however she prepared for description so coolly rehearsed and a transcendence effortlessly reached some lines later, she ought to do it again and again.

Howard Nemerov

Howard Nemerov, who died in 1991 at the age of seventy-one, wrote dry philosophical poetry with an air of maundering discontent and surly introspection (you can almost smell the martinis being drunk). Though his *Collected Poems* (1977) won both the Pulitzer Prize and the National Book Award, he never enjoyed a commanding critical reputation—sometimes as the honors pile up a poet's reputation withers. Nemerov is doomed to be remembered for the accident of birth that made him the older brother of the photographer Diane Arbus.

The Selected Poems of Howard Nemerov is an honorable attempt to make a case for a connoisseur of margins and glooms, of grand illusions and middle-class mortgages. Nemerov came to poetry almost fully formed, for a long while writing pentameter so stiff it seemed to be wearing a neck brace:

> The dry husk of an eaten heart which brings
> Nothing to offer up, no sacrifice
> Acceptable but the canceled-out desires
> And satisfactions of another year's
> Abscess, whose zero in His winter's mercy
> Still hides the undecipherable seed.

Abstractions were Nemerov's best friends (and therefore worst enemies)—he could cram so many into a poem, they looked like frat boys stuffed into a phone booth. The language here has congealed into a diction and pace all too familiar in the thirties and forties (Yeats was responsible, but what for him was banker's marble was linoleum for anyone else). Yet the lines above were published not in the forties but in 1960, just after *Life Studies* had made that style as out-of-date as a velocipede.

Nemerov's poems grew more colloquial as he aged, though he was never comfortable with what the age demanded (he roared against it like the last tyrannosaur), withdrawing into rote performance—like a singer forever giving his farewell concert, Nemerov perfected the dying fall. Misanthropes are agreeable enough, if you share their misanthropy (no one has ever founded a Misanthropes' Club, because they'd murder each other trying to write by-laws). Nemerov's poems suffered, not because they were forbiddingly deep or abstruse, but because he couldn't end them without buttonholing the reader with stilted, crackjawed observations:

> To translate the revolving of the world
> About itself, the spinning ambit of the seasons
> In the simple if adamant equation of time
> Around the analemma of the sun.

Was *analemma* really the best word available? A poet who wants above all to be taken seriously usually ends by pricing himself out of business.

Though Nemerov managed to temper his bad habits (the passive constructions, the cholesterol of "to be" verbs, the curiously submissive speakers), he couldn't avoid a moral coldness. Writing sourly of Christmas, he refers to the "alien priest/Who drenches his white robes in gasoline/And blazes merrily in the snowy East." The image is appalling—irony has crossed into hatred. (If this is Vietnam, why the snow?) Two decades later, the poet writes of the *Challenger* disaster, "The nation rises again/Reborn of grief and ready to seek the stars;/Remembering the shuttle, forgetting the loom." To end a poem of mourning with dreadful puns reveals a tone deafness that would have crippled even a great poet.

The pleasures of reading Nemerov are fugitive and coarse (even in his grander poems something is withheld): a poet of bilious emotion and narrow technique is better off writing epigrams, where dyspepsia is a recommendation, even an advantage.

> *Their marriage is a good one. In our eyes*
> *What makes a marriage good? Well, that the tether*
> *Fray but not break, and that they stay together.*
> *One should be watching while the other dies.*

The fondness here has been cloaked, but then misanthropes are often misanthropic because of a sentimental streak.

A few war poems not included here, all published forty years after VJ Day, suggest the poet he might have become had he been willing to write more about the combat missions he flew in World War II. As belatedly as Anthony Hecht, he could have been an exception in a war where the best verse was written by men who did not see combat (Randall Jarrell, Richard Eberhart, Henry Reed). Nemerov was one of the most intelligent poets of his generation; yet, for all the austere and noble lines, his high-sounding phrases (and occasional low jokes), the verse is mostly dead to its language, as strewn with salt as the ruins of Carthage.

Sherod Santos

Sometimes a poet of whom the world has taken only minor notice begins to write more provocatively in middle age, as if it took decades to rub away the burrs of apprenticeship. (What remains is a glimmer of youth irretrievably lost, rather than the glare of youthful hubris.) Sherod Santos, a mild-mannered poet now in his midfifties, at first seems a bard of the suburbs, a poet of domestic certitudes and muted despairs (few Americans admit to being middle-aged; fewer confess to living in the suburbs—our prejudices are as shallow as the Great Salt Lake). In *The Perishing*, his idea of a wild time is waking to what sounds like a rain shower but turns out to be a neighbor's sprinkler:

> *Across the street, our recently widowed neighbor*
> *Had left her garden sprinkler on, its standing water*
> *Here and there welling up over the concrete curb*
> *In loose, collected rivulets of wet, a moon-lit runoff*
> *Less like spilled water than the dispossessing ghost*
> *Of water sluicing down the gutters and away.*

There's nothing wrong with this, and nothing very right, either—it's an instant well described, touched with the music of sadness and a twitch of regret, the sort of thing John Updike must do a thousand times in every novel. Santos loves such moments, which hover between sentiment and sententiousness. After a dozen of them you want to put your hand into a lawnmower blade.

Not all Santos's suburban poems hedge like hedge-clippers, as dull as a sack of mulch; but they love garden-variety transcendence almost as much as they'd love, say, Irish peat moss. Santos's life doesn't lend itself to drama (most lives don't—they'd sell themselves to drama for pocket change). There are love poems of a dispiriting sort, homages to his wife's naked body, things a mature poet can write almost without thinking, but with what Henry James called "finish." Such poems live the way cakes do behind the plate-glass window of a bakery—they live in plaster.

Many poets now write of domestic routines, which may take the adage "Write what you know" to the point of fallacy, or suicide. In the odd limbo of the suburbs, that zone once merely the spillage of city into country, now a center of its own, what's lacking is intensity (many suburban poems seem muffled or padded). I can imagine the poems Larkin would have written had he lived in Levittown—they'd have been just as morose as those he wrote in Hull. Americans seem unable to catch the rage at the heart of Larkin's verse. Perhaps as a country we're not repressed enough.

You have to go a long way in Santos to find the mildest fracture in his suburban pastoral; but then he's another poet altogether. When he was thirteen, a woman entered his bedroom during a party and, opening her blouse, drew his hand first across her breast, then across her mastectomy scar. Instead of becoming a paean to an older woman's beauty and need (the seduction that follows seems almost incestuous), the poem questions all the love he has known since. Santos has seen certain abysses and not drawn back from them.

Most of the poet's past work has been easy-going as conversation, colloquial as a coat of paint; but the new poems sometimes require a different register:

> When my father broke his family's counsel
> And re-upped for the airlift into Germany,
> He stormed the black capital like Ecgtheow's son,
> His tonnage downgraded to anthracite
> From Amatol and TNT, such payloads
> As custom still meted out to a city Grendeled
> In the underworld of incendiary smoke.

This growls out Germanic myths like an Anglo-Saxon scop, the savage names—Amatol and TNT—sounding like Beowulf's companions-in-arms. In half a dozen poems, Santos portrays a world the suburbs try to forget—the world where people starve, or are beaten and tortured.

> One evening, for the benefit
> Of three mothers who'd been summoned
> To watch through the open window
> Of a barber shop, a badly beaten
> Milicias youth was carried inside, stripped
> Of his clothes, and bound spread-eagle
> To a tabletop. They'd thought, at first,
> He might be the one-armed riverman's son,
> The one who trapped chameleons
> He'd then sell for coins in the village square.

That note of irrelevance, even of mild comedy, rescues what might remain of the human. Santos does not yet have Anthony Hecht's brutality or grace; but, in a time when poems are more politicized than political, he accepts the homeliness of evil. If he sometimes makes his points too plainly (there's an egregiously silly poem about dictators), if he doesn't quite know how to finish what he's started, beneath the surface of his tranquil suburban tracts something brutish has begun to stir.

Carolyn Forché

Carolyn Forché writes hushed, whispery, numinous lines, the kind that emerge from a blank page held over a candle flame. *Blue Hour* is ghost-ridden, stained with the salts of European poetry (Forché loves Desnos, Char, Jabès); and it's possible to let her poems mesmerize you for a time.

> *In the blue silo of dawn, in earth-smoke and birch copse,*
> *where the river of hands meets the Elbe.*
>
> *In the peace of your sleeping face,* Mein Liebchen.
>
> *We have our veiled memory of running from police*
> *dogs through a blossoming orchard, and another*
>
> *Of not escaping them. That was—ago—(a lifetime),*
> *but now you are invisible in my arms.*

Such death-hunted lines pay homage to half a century of poetry wounded into speech by Fascists, Nazis, Communists, and many a murderous government since. That poetry is inadequate to such politics is a commonplace: the tormented phrases of Paul Celan were almost a suicide note. That does not make the attempt to speak against injustice less noble, however ignoble most poems about politics are. Forché once wrote poems passionate with righteous (and self-righteous) anger; but, in her last book, *The Angel of History* (1994), she lost her taste for lyric or narrative and took up a style of tesserae and ostraka, Eliot's "fragments I have shored against my ruins."

The Angel of History was an original work, pretentious and disturbing, opportunistic, vampirish, soiled in its own sorrows and everyone else's. Forché's new poems, if poems they are, continue this disjoint, fragmented manner in ways sometimes alarming. *Blue Hour* consists of eleven poems, ten short and one immensely long, less a poem than a shopping list of images. Her shorter pieces establish the atmosphere of, the sense of foreboding in, secrets kept and pain suffered. Forché wants to do something different from her contemporaries without sacrificing the beauty of lyric. (The death of the lyric is announced as often as the death of the novel, the press release usually read out by someone who wouldn't know a lyric if it ate him.) What this means in practice is vague and portentous lines by the barrelful, lines whose gestures toward meaning are rhetorical nudges. When the poet writes, "An abandoned house, after all, will soon give itself back, and its walls become as unreadable as symbols on silk," something beautiful has been said, but said in half-thoughts.

That such partial, undecoded meanings are in essence religious is nowhere clearer than in the forty-page poem that closes the book. The notes inform us that it is based on "Gnostic abecedarian hymns" that "date from the third century A.D." These thousand lines are meant to render the last images passing through the mind of someone dying—that's the dust jacket's opinion (how it can tell, I'm not sure).

> *bone child in the palm a bird in the heart*
> *bone-clicking applause of the winter trees*
> *bones of the unknown*
> *bones smoothed by water*
> *book of smoke, black soup*
> *born with a map of calamity in her palm*

A stanza of this is unsettling, a page tiresome, forty pages nearly unbearable agony. I don't know if thoughts like these will pass through my mind as I die (though I hope not), but I'm sure they won't pass through alphabetically. (I'll probably be thinking of the unpaid gas bill and the cock I owe Asclepius.) I read every line, as a reviewer is obliged to do; and I must report that I shouted with delight when I got past the letter *a*. Whatever the gnostics saw in this form, it must have been one of the reasons they died out.

Religions love to call tedium ritual, and I see advantages to using repetition to numb the chanter to the torments of his day. It's hard to know what to make of such lines as a poem—you get snapshots of horror, fresh as the daily news; lines that hint at secrets, searches, refugees; and images that might have come from Freud's secret dreams. It's as if the poet had for a decade stored up surplus images in a carton and one night dumped them out and arranged them in alphabetical order. The problem with these contextless phrases is, not that they don't let tragedy in, but that they don't keep comedy out. This poem is the graveyard where unused lines go to die.

I can't resist quoting some of the blurbs, which take a kinder view: an "uncanny mixture of peace, beauty, and cruelty. If you ask, 'Which country is it?' the answer is, 'This country called earth'"; a "masterwork for the twenty-first century"; "wise beyond any possible taint of a false or assumed innocence"; "Carolyn Forché, my hero." Even in this country called blurbdom, these have drunk too long at the bar. Forché wants to write a wisdom book, gilded by all the misery that is the world. I had complaints about her early poems, chiefly that they were sentimental; but I have more complaints about poems that aren't poems, just do-it-yourself kits of New Age gnosticism, some assembly required, batteries not included.

James Fenton

James Fenton, the best poet of his generation in Britain, is still too little known in our country. He has spent long periods of his life not writing poetry at all, having been, at various times, a foreign correspondent in Europe and on the Pacific rim, a London theater critic, an explorer in Borneo, and the Professor of Poetry at Oxford. He grew rich, it is said, writing the lyrics for *Les Misérables*, though his songs were never used (this suggests the importance in life of having a good agent). If Fenton wrote a novel on the back of cereal cartons or made a model of St. Paul's from matchbooks, the results would be worth seeing; but, if a man does some work brilliantly and the rest half-heartedly (his Oxford lectures on poetry, for instance), shouldn't he do only what he does well? The same question hovered over the late career of a greater poet, T. S. Eliot.

The Love Bomb consists of two libretti and an oratorio, all commissioned, labored and fretted over, but only the last performed. Fenton has a witty introduction lamenting the librettist's life ("Nobody would believe that the dog ate my homework. But that the dog ate my opera house—*twice*—might well be believed"). *The Love Bomb* starts with a terrible handicap: to enjoy a libretto properly, the reader ought to have a recording of the music—or, better, at an appointed hour a tenor, a soprano, and a man with a boom box should show up on your doorstep. On the bare page, words are stripped of much that would have made them interesting on stage—costume and voice, gesture, the emotive color of music, all the things that clothe the naked word. Without them the emperor is often, well, naked.

In "The Love Bomb," a young man tries to rescue his former girlfriend from a religious cult. The cult plots to recruit him, as well as—here's the twist—his boyfriend. This began in a reading of the Orpheus and Eurydice myth, and soon enough you wish it had stayed there. Even the most awful opera plot can be rescued by words and music, but the words here aren't doing a very good job:

Don't go down the towpath, Anna.
Don't go along the canal.
That's where all the accidents happen.
Treat me to an accident. Be my pal.

'Cos one door opens on love
And one door opens on death.
And one door opens on the lift shaft.
Turn the handle. Hold your breath.

The Audenesque strain isn't nearly strong enough. Where Auden was clever, Fenton is callow and cliché-ridden—it would be hard to sit through a performance without snickering. The first act is much worse than the two that follow; yet the whole is leaden, not because it has ideas (as Auden's work so often did), but because it lacks them. Everything about colloquial language that Fenton has turned to advantage in his poetry has turned against him here.

The second libretto tries to make an opera from *Haroun and the Sea of Stories*, the children's book by Salman Rushdie. A storyteller loses his wife and, with her, his ability to tell tales—without his stories, soon he may lose his tongue. His son must journey to the Sea of Stories to set things right. (Rushdie was working some typically inventive if irritating turns on Eastern folktales.) It's hard to imagine this as opera, and not just because the tale has such sentimental notions of storytelling—it's a fantastic childlike adventure with Arabian Nights effects, including water genies and floating gardeners and talking hoopoes, as well as a kidnapped princess about to be sacrificed by the Prince of Darkness and Arch-Enemy of All Stories.

The poetry is no better than before (it's a pity Fenton didn't take more delight in names like Snooty Buttoo, Prince Bolo, and the Shah of Blah). There's a moment, late in this silly business, when W. S. Gilbert seems to come to the rescue. It's only one song, and wouldn't seem much if quoted; but, after eighty or so pages of chewing shoe-leather, it tastes like caviar. You realize then that Gilbert took sillier ideas and made genius of them.

All that can be said for Fenton's oratorio, "The Fall of Jerusalem," is that it contains some passable light verse and some awful free verse: "God it was who gave us our minds,/Minds that scorn death,/Scorn to live in slavery/Under a Roman yoke." Fenton was once able to handle both with dexterity and wit—he has written some of the most sensitive war poems of the last half century. In this long and wearying book, I felt his talent engaged by a single couplet: "Something better than those nefarious gymnastics/With coked-up blokes in various elastics." Cole Porter and W. S. Gilbert and even Auden might have smiled over such lines, but there's nothing else like them. Readers who want to know what this remarkable poet can do should read his early collection of poems, *Children in Exile*; his book of theater criticism, *You Were Marvellous*; his essays on art, *Leonardo's Nephew*; or his book of reportage, *All the Wrong Places*—and then send Fenton a postcard pleading with him to get back to work.

Verse Chronicle

Stouthearted Men

George Oppen

George Oppen was one of the minor literary figures of the thirties. Friend of Pound, employer of Zukofsky, collaborator with Williams and Reznikoff, an animating spirit of the objectivist movement, he was a young man with ideals and a little money who with more money or fewer ideals might have become as useful as James Laughlin. In 1935 Oppen joined the Communist Party, concealing his bourgeois past as a poet (this might have told him something about the party, if Stalin's purges did not). For the next twenty years or more, Oppen swore off poetry; when not training for party leadership, he organized the poor, fomented strikes, and protested against monopolies, though the aim of any union is to exploit a monopoly of labor. During World War II, he was wounded while serving in an antitank unit in Europe. After the war he built furniture, attended art school in Mexico on the GI Bill, and added to his swollen FBI file.

In the late fifties, Oppen began writing again, in the starved, cruelly compressed style abandoned decades before. This resurrection of a poet so long out of touch, and even out of date, proved irresistible to young writers influenced by William Carlos Williams. The minor figure of the thirties became a minor figure of the sixties. Before the decade was over, he had won the Pulitzer Prize.

Oppen's spareness was like that of a Zen master with a migraine:

> *Never to forget her naked eyes*

> *Beautiful and brave*
> *Her naked eyes*

> *Turn inward*

> *Feminine light*
>
> *The unimagined*
> *Feminine light*
>
> *Feminine ardor*

Paring away his poems until they were nearly skeletons, he was often left with just a few ribs and some knucklebones. His critics, who have frequently been his disciples, have made high claims for Oppen's minimalism, which he pursued more aggressively than Williams, though it could seem pinched and hectoring, a telegram from Moscow instructing you that everything you thought yesterday is wrong. (When Oppen confused his poetry with his politics, the results were disastrous.) In Pound or Williams, you see details refined until they glow with the spectral light of imagism; but in Oppen you seem to get farther, down to the sludge at the bottom of the glass.

Oppen's poems are plain as a brown paper bag, slightly depressing, maudlin about people in a thirties way (which was also a sixties way), often tone-deaf to the virtues of language (that *is* his virtue, say his critics).

> *We want to say*
>
> *"Common sense"*
> *And cannot. We stand on*
>
> *That denial*
> *Of death that paved the cities,*
> *Paved the cities*
>
> *Generation*
> *For generation and the pavement*
>
> *Is filthy as the corridors*
> *Of the police.*

The world of Oppen's poems has removed all that might qualify or enrich it, all that might make it more various than some shopworn Platonic form.

Michelangelo chiseled away the marble until he freed the figure—but what made him a genius was knowing when he'd *reached* the figure. In other words, he knew when to stop.

Oppen's ambition often seems in excess of the words he left behind. At best his sketchy, expressionist method pays homage to the shudders and hesitations of thought; but this is fiendishly difficult to do well—otherwise H.D. and Edith Sitwell would be geniuses (the attempt to compare Oppen to Paul Celan is ludicrous). Oppen lived for pretentious observation and barnyard wisdom—"How much of the earth's/Crust has lived/The seed's violence!" His reviewers have used phrases like "stunning, elliptical," "one of the twentieth century's most dazzling makers of lines," "verse that sparkles like broken glass." Such opinions seem quaint as antimacassars.

Oppen offered an alternative to bland academic verse, as well as to the garrulous and self-absorbed Beats (the disorganized long essay included in this edition of *Selected Poems* comments drily on the difference), though his minimalism couldn't conceal how desolately inward his poems became, like clippings from a freshman philosophy textbook or the empty thoughts of mannequins. You can't wholly dislike a poet whose main villains are Romans and shoppers; but, when a poet writing of poetry invokes Gethsemane, you wonder if his mind doesn't turn to betrayal a little too easily. How much more telling about the lives of the poor are the photographs of Helen Levitt or Walker Evans. You wonder what Oppen would have written about that anti-tank company, but the lines he devoted to the war were gauzy and general.

This poet stopped writing for reasons as noble and laughable as Laura Riding's. Once a man has quit poetry to show class solidarity or his despair at the tragedy that is the world, how does he start again without seeming a hypocrite? Yet Oppen ground on at his minor craft until the dry rot set in, a man at odds with his art, which ought to have benefited the art more than it did (art often thrives on contraries or arrested impulse). His poems wanted to be a poem, which wanted to be a line, which wanted to be a word, which at last wanted to be just a single letter, perhaps "I" or "O!"

Franz Wright

Americans are suckers for self-pity—they order their mawkishness by the yard. We're still at heart a Puritan country: since we can't throw sinners in the stocks any more (unless it's done on prime time), we'll settle for the humiliating public apology followed by the spectacular relapse. Franz Wright's poems may be rancid and repetitive, but he's perfected a confessional tone angry and apologetic at once. *Walking to Martha's Vineyard*, which recently won the Pulitzer Prize, is the latest installment of this fragile, self-obsessed author's stony path to grace.

Most of Wright's poems are nasty, brutish, and short—it's an old joke, but Wright really *is* Hobbesian man, consoling himself with secondhand religious formulae and the salve of salvation:

> *Oh build a special city*
> *for everyone who wishes*
>
> *to die, where*
> *they might help one another out*
>
> *and never feel ashamed*
> *maybe make a friend,*
>
> *etc.*

Maybe make a friend! (This is how Mr. Rogers would talk, if he were an ex-junkie.) Yet for all the tabloid-style anguish, Wright's minimalism is deft and effective, with the emotional pressure of Louise Glück. These damaged and tormented poets (if they were to collaborate on *Passive-Aggression for Dummies*, I'd hardly be surprised) have refined the poetic act into short prosaic sentences, brimful with resentment, seething with a rage for which words are inadequate. Behind every poem stands an entourage of nurses, shrinks, and self-help counselors.

Like few other poets in our pulse-taking age, Wright has solved the problem of how to reclaim the confessions of Lowell and Plath without falling victim to the *tableaux vivants* of a Sharon Olds (whose poems look, next to Wright's austerity, like the wildest fin de siècle dandyism). The pain is so raw, it's like watching documentary footage; but, if you make a competition of suffering by having nails driven through your wrists, one day someone will tear out his own tongue, pluck out his eyeballs, and call it art. Wright has a gift for sneered gratitude, for invoking God with the wheedling piety of a three-time loser before a parole board:

Thank You for letting me live for a little as one of the
sane; thank You for letting me know what this is
like. Thank You for letting me look at your frightening
blue sky without fear, and your terrible world without
terror, and your loveless psychotic and hopelessly
lost
    with this love

Wright clings to his newfound religion the way men cling to the raft in Géri-cault's "The Wreck of the Medusa." He's so self-abasing, he reminds us that con artists are usually conning themselves along with everyone else. I see why some poets like his work—he's a sad-sack punk, a fifty-year-old who pisses and moans like a depressive teenager. Hell, you want to adopt him.

When Wright offers the crude, unprocessed sewage of suffering, it's nasty stuff. Yet this poet is surprisingly vague about the specifics of his torment (most of his poems are shouts and curses in the dark). He was cruelly affected by the divorce of his parents, though perhaps after forty years a statute of limitations should be invoked. His father was the poet James Wright, which seems to make the son twice damned—his poems whisper about an aban-doned son of his own and hint repeatedly at attempted suicide. Just when I decide to dislike him for his truculent theatrics, his prima-donna moroseness (when have we had a poet more devoted to Our Lady of the Eternal Victim?), he'll write something so ruefully funny it's hard not to forgive him: "Now she is going to put on some / nice cut-your-wrists music" or "What an evil potato goes through / we can never know, but / I'm beginning to resemble one." (And it's true—he *does* resemble one.) We need a modern Beddoes, and I wish Wright would apply for the job.

A few such lines are not enough, however, and soon he's back to the drudgery of self-loathing. Self-loathing is a meager thing for a poet to offer as his only medium, even if here and there he's able to turn his brutishness to account. "The Only Animal," the most accomplished poem in the book, collapses into the same kitschy sanctimoniousness that puts nodding Jesus dolls on car dashboards. Wright's religious angst, just the right stuff for our shallow, shopping-mall culture, makes his poems the Hallmark cards of the damned.

Tony Hoagland

You meet a lot of Tony Hoagland's friends in Tony Hoagland's poems. *What Narcissism Means to Me* names more names than you can shake a stick at— there's Alex and Greg and Boz and Rus, Susan and Margaret, Kath and Peter and Mary, Neal and Sylvia and Ann and Ethan, Carla and Jerry and Peter, and these just in the first half-dozen poems (it would be easier if they were all named George, like George Foreman's sons). Frank O'Hara used to give his friends walk-on roles, and many a young poet now stuffs his acknowledgments with what seems to be his entire address book. Hoagland's friends merely slouch around the house making smart remarks, which their Boswell dutifully records.

> *Alex said,* I wish they made a shooting gallery
> using people like that.
>
> *Greg said,* That woman has a Ph.D. in Face.
> *Then we saw a preview for a movie*
>
> *about a movie star who is*
> *having a movie made about her,*
> *and Boz said,* This country is getting stupider every year.
>
> *Then Greg said that things were better in the sixties*
> *and Rus said that Harold Bloom said*
> *that Nietzsche said Nostalgia*
> *is the blank check issued to a weak mind,*
>
> *and Greg said . . .*

But enough! This is all very agreeable, as far as it goes—the lines suggest that Americans have become couch potatoes who get their Nietzsche second- or thirdhand. Yet when poem succeeds poem of these nattering chums, you realize how little you care about them—if the poet stopped hanging out with them, he might have something more interesting to write about. They come and go with all the anonymity of Eliot's women talking of Michelangelo—except, four generations later, they're no longer talking of Michelangelo.

It's no secret that America is overrun with "RadioShacks and Burger Kings, and MTV episodes," that we have supersized our egos with our appetites—Hoagland isn't improving here on the wit and wisdom of Thorstein Veblen. What's peculiar is that the poet has chosen, not to analyze the condition, but to embody it; and his poems are full of droll banalities—they reduce everything to the lowest common denominator and smirk about it. If Dante's *Inferno* were populated by Hoagland's buddies, they'd look around and not be able to think of a single complaint.

O'Hara wrote his I-do-this, I-do-that poems half a century ago. These days they seem, most of them, pretty trivial; but Hoagland aspires to go him one better, or one worse. The poems here are cozy but forgettable, no harder to swallow than a dose of aspirin. If the younger poet ever feels any unease—and he does, sometimes, for a minute or two—it's best to assuage it with a wisecrack and drift back to that waking dream we call television (he spends a lot of time watching television and wants the privilege of whining about it).

> How did I come to believe in a government called Tony Hoagland?
> with an economy based on flattery and self-protection?
> and a sewage system of selective forgetting?
> and an extensive history of broken promises?
>
> What did I get in exchange for my little bargain? What did I lose?
> Where are my natural resources, my principal imports,
> and why is my landscape so full of stony ridges and granite outcroppings?

These lines are deceptively good-natured, and they're as deep as he gets. There's nothing terrible about such poetry—Hoagland has a ready-to-wear style, the kind you can throw into the washer when it's dirty and take out half an hour later, wrinkle free. Such a style can take on any subject, yet never put two words together in a meaningful way. If he can reduce the awful heritage of slavery to a TV tennis match, world peace should be a snap.

Perhaps it's enough to write such mild, self-conscious, smugly unambitious poems. Hoagland's subject is the late, declining American empire; and he intends to watch the fires from the comfort of his sofa. You don't ever get the feeling that he reads, or is affected by anything he can't shut off with a remote control—he's made so uncomfortable by AIDS he calls it "one of those diseases/known by its initials." Despite the yammering presence of myriads of Hoagland's friends, I've rarely read a book that seemed lonelier. Even Narcissus wasn't that lonely—he had himself for company.

Spencer Reece

The Clerk's Tale was written by the assistant manager of a Brooks Brothers store in Palm Beach Gardens, Florida, a world as distant from poetry as Wallace Stevens's office in the Hartford Accident and Indemnity Company. How unlikely (and unlike anyone else's), however, Stevens's poems were. Spencer Reece's confident, stagy, slightly occluded first book proves that poetry not written by academics can be just as academic as any assistant professor's.

It cheered me up to think the title poem might have a little Chaucer in it, but "The Clerk's Tale" is rather the *cri de coeur* of a man who works in a clothing shop, a man perhaps a little like the author. Though verging on self-pity, it portrays the lives endured blankly on the other side of the counter, reminding us how much the customer must mask out just to buy a shirt. (That, indeed, was the whole point of keeping servants faceless presences—when you start to sympathize with them, someone somewhere starts sewing mob caps.)

Reece's mature if slightly overheated voice shows how much can be gained by waiting a few years to publish a first book. He's in his early forties, about the age when Frost and Stevens published theirs. I'm not drawn to all parts of Reece's talent—he has a taste for short declarative sentences, sometimes half a dozen in a row, that sound like tabloid reportage. Elsewhere the touches of artistry, and even aestheticism, offer transcendence on the cheap:

> *when the maple sweats and saps at the corners of his mouth*
> *and when the oak shakes his leaves like a thousand horseshoes*
> *   is the time my heart bangs with barn-joy and I breathe in the subtle*
> *approbation of death coming as I recognize the Byzantine look*
>
> *of the trees emptying themselves of themselves.*

Barn-joy, eh? The poet's exuberance seems heartfelt but somewhat demented, and he can't help himself from busting out into lines like "encircled by a halo of rocks, trees, crops, rivers, clouds— /by every blessed thing conspiring together to save my life" or "I've been waiting for the tulip bulbs, those necessary ambulances, /to come and sound the emergencies of the world. Nothing so far." There's only so much a reader can take before wanting to crawl under a blanket to shut out the neon signs.

Reece includes two sequences of ghazals that aren't ghazals at all (they're scraps from John Ashbery's wastebasket: "Tra la la la. Lovers fling their arms open like medicine cabinets, / offering their baptized scalps to fun new people like thesauruses"). Some young poets can make new selves from their influences, but Reece gets into his influences' skin the way he might throw on a Halloween costume. The book ends with an overlong sequence of unpunctuated poems that sound more like late Merwin than Merwin.

It's easy to catalogue the problems in these poems—their preciousness and exaggeration of feeling; their news-at-eleven opportunism; their taste for freakish similes, as if W. H. Auden's executors were having a fire sale (a severed tongue "in her hand like a ticket," "fish disappear like keys," "hydrangeas shift in their pitcher like wigs"). Indeed, though a few poems possess a beautiful modesty, many are afflicted with a boorish loudness, as if they had caught Dylan Thomas disease—Reece's *diminuendi* might be other poets' *crescendi*.

Yet if Reece makes some mistakes young poets make, and some winningly his own, there are enough moments of raw talent and character to make those promises young poets are known for.

> *Inside everything was Episcopalian—*
> *the wicker chaise lounges, the small spotted mirrors,*
> *the rattan dining room set, the tears.*
> *No one saw tears. We hid them—*
> *especially the men, who buried their tears*
> *in the sea, or so I once dreamed and wrote down,*
> *until the dream became what I believed and what I wrote.*
> . . . .
> *There was a yacht club meeting every summer*
> *with a cannon that went off—*baboom!
> *Women arrived in their thin Talbots belts,*
> *carrying wicker purses shaped like paint cans*
> *with whalebone carvings fastened on top,*
> *resembling the hardened excrement seagulls drop.*
> *Occasionally the purses would open,*
> *albeit reluctantly, like safe-deposit boxes.*
> *Men wore cranberry trousers and Brooks Brothers blue blazers.*

There's product placement for you! Many of the descriptions are rendered with similar lightness, only occasionally coming too close to the tears the poet always seems on the verge of shedding. In his best poems his modesty becomes suffering and his discontinuity, rage. His portraits are reminiscent of those by the elderly Rembrandt, pushing paint this way and that, almost from pure joy, until the painting has been thumbed into life.

Charles Wright

Buffalo Yoga is the silliest title in a body of work that gives it close competition in *Zone Journals* and *A Short History of the Shadow*. Charles Wright, who turns seventy next year, has for a long while been among our best poets. My complaint has been that lately he hasn't written any *poems*, just bundles of lines, loose as kindling, offered to the reader with a crooked country grin, as if to say, "Why, you can't hardly find so nice a bunch of kindling in fifty mile." And you couldn't, if what you were after was kindling.

Wright is a master of the natural image—he exemplifies what Pound wanted when he said the "natural object is always the *adequate* symbol."

> *The sun has set behind the Blue Ridge,*
> *And evening with its blotting paper*
> > *lifts off the light.*

Indeed, if they didn't sometimes have the air of a later day, Wright's images would seem pilfered from Pound's notebooks. The problem in Wright's work has been that he gets beyond such gorgeous images only to indulge in garden metaphysics. He has read the Chinese poets Pound was so influenced by—the new poems often resemble ancient Chinese scrolls, otherworldly but static. At times he's like some bearded sage crossed with Mammy Yokum, puffing on a corncob pipe:

> *God's ghost taps once on the world's window,*
> > *then taps again.*
> *And drags his chains through the evergreens.*
> *Weather is where he came from, and to weather returns,*
> *His backside black on the southern sky,*
> *Mumbling and muttering, distance like doomsday loose in his hands.*

The silliness here doesn't quite outweigh the pleasure, the calculation and risk; when Wright pulls off such pretentious humbuggery, you're glad he took his chances. Yet the poems are too often saddled with maundering esoterics, Sunday school phrases like the "stained glare of angel wings," and moments when the poet waxes philosophic about his work, having perhaps read more of late, apologetic Pound than is good for a man: "I tried to give form to the formless, / and speech to the unspeakable. / To the light that shines without shadow, I gave myself." Pound earned the right to say similar things at the end of his life; here there's just the sound of a man patting his own back.

Wright has been writing fragments for too long; the new poems that make the most impression hold their form in narrative or reminiscence, corrupted by memory (and the defaults of memory), by old dreams and desires. The poems are haggard and loose-hipped, sometimes winning in their refusal to force a story into shape, yet often collapsing into a banal gloss on memory and narrative—they're so affectless and cool, it's hard not to grow irritated when they pass off as profound the most appalling cornbread platitudes: "Imagination is merely the door. / All we can do is knock hard / And hope that something will open it." The poet's lyric fragments are an admission that telling a tale is beyond him.

By his fifties or sixties a poet has taken out a certain number of patents (perhaps all he is likely to), and these he defends to the death, whether or not they're worth it. The best poets may take out hundreds, scattering them across the public domain, secure that no one will be able to use them quite as well. Like most older poets, Wright has sunk into a mire of self-imitation, and sometimes self-flattery. Yet here and there, broadcast through this self-indulgent book, are stanzas of astonishing freshness and needle-eyed vision:

> Shadows are clumsy and crude, their eggs few,
> And dragonflies, like lumescent [sic] Ohio Blue Tip matchsticks,
> Puzzle the part-opened iris stalks,
> > hovering and stiff.
> New flies frenetic against the glass,
> Woodpeckers at their clocks,
> > the horses ablaze in the grained light.

You'd have to go a long way to find a poet who does these things so well (though where was the copy editor when Wright tried to strike the match of "lumescent"?). It's like finding a man who makes brilliant origami out of *Playboy* centerfolds—you love them, but you wonder if it's an art worth pursuing.

Philip Larkin

When Philip Larkin died in 1985, he was the most beloved poet in Britain; only the year before, he had turned down the invitation to become poet laureate. Anthony Thwaite, his old friend, edited the *Collected Poems* (1988; U.S., 1989) by placing Larkin's poems in chronological order and infiltrating scores of uncollected poems among the published verse. This might have been a sensible procedure for another poet; but the earlier volume, which this edition replaces, concealed the strengths and diluted the intensity of the most important British poet between Auden and Geoffrey Hill.

Larkin's reputation has been in free fall since the publication of Thwaite's *Selected Letters of Philip Larkin* (1992) and Andrew Motion's literary biography *Philip Larkin: A Writer's Life* (1993), which revealed that behind the poems' miserable loner lay a real loner, one nasty and misogynist and racist to boot. Why were people surprised? Yet they *were* surprised. Many readers apparently thought that Larkin's morose self-hatred concealed something lovable, that a man so wise about inadequacy and foible must have been exaggerating the ugly part of his personality. Few thought he might have toned down his opinions out of embarrassment or shame, that instead of a shy librarian he might be an alcoholic who kept porn magazines in his office closet.

Larkin was "one of those old-type *natural* fouled-up guys." The world had changed around him, and what he disliked was that it had changed. The repulsive opinions appear in his letters, not the poems; but there are worse things than concealing private intolerance behind public respectability (think how despicable the reverse is). Whether he's referring to Morocco as "coonland," or calling the government "decimal-loving, nigger-mad, army-cutting," or saying, "The Slade is a cunty place, full of 17-year-old cunts," we have no idea what Larkin felt when he wrote such things. He may have been indulging in matey blokishness (the remarks are made mostly to old school chums), proving himself immune to new public manners, or merely revealing the lethal prejudices he'd learned to keep private. It might have been a mixture of these things; but it is crude to assume he was moved only by hatred, just as it would be exculpatory to believe his impulses were without trace of hatred.

In a tell-all age all must be told, but it's crucial to remember how recently such language was common. If we're going to call Eliot an anti-Semite and Larkin a racist, we ought to start drawing up an indictment of Sylvia Plath, who noted in her journals a girl's "long Jewy nose"; or Wallace Stevens, who wrote, "I went up to a nigger policeman"; or Marianne Moore, who mentioned in a letter that a "coon took me up in the elevator"; or William Carlos Williams, whose letters are peppered with references to wops, niggers, and Jews. Until very recently such remarks were so prevalent in Britain and America, we do ourselves no credit by turning into scapegoats the writers who merely succumbed to the bigotry of the age.

We are no better if we condemn such opinions without seeing where Larkin rose above them, sometimes merely by exposing the insecurity and self-loathing at their heart. His poems may be the record of how a man converts his basest feelings to something more humane; and we read him, not because he is less base, but because the flaws reveal his pathos. In all their quiet generosities, their humility despite themselves, the poems make clear they were not simply a way of concealing from the public taste his gruesome prejudices.

Indeed, why should we assume that letters are any more trustworthy than poems? If I lie about myself in my poems, trying to appear wiser or more charitable, in my letters I may make myself seem dumber and more intolerant. People who don't want to be known in public don't necessarily drop their trousers in private. The current taste for *meae culpae* is no more laudable than the self-criticism Communist governments used to demand of prisoners before standing them against a wall. Will later generations value so highly the poets who quoted only the approved opinions of our day or preached only the pieties the age demanded?

Anthony Thwaite, no doubt stung by the protests raised by critics, has now done more or less what he ought to have done originally, kept the poems in the order Larkin wished (few poets constructed their books so carefully), with appendices to collected the strays. The new introduction is, alas, defensive and unapologetic. Having omitted any poem the poet failed to publish, Thwaite has thrown some of the babies out with the bathwater. Almost a hundred minor poems no longer appear here—though few will be missed, two or three (among them, "An April Sunday . . . ," "The Dance," and "Love Again," all of which Thwaite laments not including) deserve a place in Larkin's collected works.

Larkin ought to be considered (though the idea would have given him the heebie-jeebies) a confessional poet *avant la lettre*, revealing himself as brutally in his way as Lowell and Plath in theirs. He's our great poet of mixed feelings, of disappointment and self-doubt (and as good as Frost—who was also something of a monster in private—on the complexities of human nature). Larkin's poems catch the tension between impulse and reserve (reserve always winning out), proclaiming, not in the least ironically, the virtues of ordinariness—"May you be ordinary," he wrote to a new baby.

Though his early poems were influenced by Yeats and Auden, the model for Larkin must be Housman. They share the same taste for moral observation, the wry and somewhat sour demeanor, the preference for the memorable phrase over the clever one. In other ways they could not be more different—Housman looked for classical virtue and often gave way to sentiment, while Larkin pursued only his own unsentimental muddles amid the bric-a-brac of English life. His most heartbreaking poems fear that life is going on somewhere else—he's a wonderful poet of nothings ("Nothing," as he said, "like something, happens anywhere").

The list of Larkin's best poems must include "I Remember, I Remember," "Mr Bleaney," "The Whitsun Weddings," "MCMXIV," "Talking in Bed" (has there ever been a better poem about the bedroom?), "Dockery and Son," "Church Going," "An Arundel Tomb," "The Trees," "Going, Going," "Homage to a Government," "This Be the Verse," "Sad Steps," the great swansong "Aubade," and dozens scarcely less fine. In the past century, no British poet except Housman and Auden has written verse as memorable, or better suited to public memory. The virtues of Larkin's ordinariness have never been more necessary—every age needs to be reminded that the ordinary sometimes requires a kind of heroism.

The Most Contemptible Moth
Lowell in Letters

I n the spring of 1936, Ezra Pound received a letter of introduction from a
young poet.

> I am 19, a freshman at Harvard, and some relation, I don't know what, to
> Amy Lowell. All my life I have been eccentric according to normal stan-
> dards. I had violent passions for various pursuits usually taking the form
> of collecting: tools; names of birds; marbles; catching butterflies, snakes,
> turtles etc; buying books on Napoleon. . . . At 14 I went to St. Mark's and
> never mixed well or really lived in the usual realities. . . . I was proud, some-
> what sullen and violent.

This raw bundle of nerves wanted to sail to Italy and sit at the master's feet.

> I began reading Homer thru the dish-water of Bryant's 19th century transla-
> tion. . . . A poor translation is an ugly photograph.
> Last spring I began reading English poetry and writing myself. All my
> life I had thought of poets as the most contemptible moth.

The young man hoped to drop out of college (instead he just quit Harvard)
and claimed, not very convincingly, "I am not theatric, and my life is sober
not sensational." Intimate, blustering, full of cheerful blarney and the roaring
bonfire of ambition, this extraordinary letter turned phrases that few nineteen-
years-olds could.

A man's letters have a different claim on privacy than his poems and there-
fore a different claim on truth. Letters lie in the uneasy realm between writ-
ing published (the words, if not anonymous, a writer must stand by) and writ-

ing meant for no one else's eye (the best diaries are often those published from the grave). Letters are usually directed to one person alone, like a whisper, though in some centuries they have been passed around like dime novels (when Nelson captured letters in which Napoleon grumbled over Josephine's infidelities, he published them). The inky page, the homely sheet of paper itself, becomes the property of the receiver; but the words remain the writer's, not to be published except where leave is given—in this way letters follow a peculiar byway of property law.

A letter writer may tattle his secrets only to find, when coat is turned or heart broken, that his words hound him like revenants. (Many a lover has demanded the return of his billets-doux or paid hard cash for the privilege. Better, perhaps, to follow the iron words of the Iron Duke—threatened with exposure by one of his mistresses, Wellington is said to have thundered, "Publish and be damned!") Since the letter's words are sounded for private ears rather than the mobbish ears of the public, how much can we trust them? Rare is the writer who doesn't play to his audience, seduce by his gossip or gossip of seductions, use discretion to be indiscreet, salt his pages with what must be taken with salt.

Nothing a writer writes can be trusted (there's no gospel truth even in the Gospels)—facts are altered by will or whim, to make a point or a joke, to comfort a friend or confuse an enemy. Writers are guilty in letters of their share of pettifoggeries and persiflage, of white lies and red herrings, humbling themselves before their elders, bowing when they should be brazen, praising to the skies some book meant for the sties. Yet for all their insecure facts and intransigent fictions, indeed in part because of them, letters seem to draw us closer to the devious imagination behind them.

The letters in *The Letters of Robert Lowell* are peculiar not least for their antic honesty. A young man trying to wheedle his way into Pound's household might be inclined to flatter. Although Lowell praised the *Cantos* in the letter following ("like lily pads on a lake: a flat surface swaying with vigorous and beautiful images"), he wrapped a nettle of criticism inside a question: "Can the main current of English literature float such a vast quantity of spondées [*sic*] and compound nouns?" Lowell could be candid to the point of cruelty, especially during his bouts of mania (he learned tact from the Tartars); but the dry, harried scruples and homely truths of these letters were, without being prickly or petty, the sort few writers dare—he even criticized Pound's definition of poetry. "I don't flatter," Lowell wrote Robert Frost some years later, while praising Frost's poems. However graciously praise falls when it doesn't fall like fawning, in such rectitudes there's a thorn waiting.

A poet begins in the threats and responsibilities of language (Auden claimed to be far more interested in a young poet who liked "hanging around words listening to what they say" than one who claimed to have "important things" to express). In Lowell's college letters, we hear the earliest scratchings, the casual densities of expression, before he had written a memorable line of poetry—Lowell told Pound he felt "choked with cobwebs" and his parents that he didn't want work as a "comma-pruner for *Atlantic Monthly* or head pencil sharpener" for his father's brokerage firm. Compare this to the adult whose adjectives sometimes strike like rattlers. On solitude: "It doesn't *drug* me, but I get fantastic and uncivilized." Florence "is gray and sand-colored, Boston-ish, compact, very unvegetable." *Bostonish! Unvegetable!* When his third wife suffered nervous depression, she nevertheless remained "quite lively, oxlike and functioning"—*oxlike* conveys the deadening lethargy of nervous illness better than any diagnosis.

It would be too simple to suggest that Lowell's talents lay in such virtuoso brushwork, the comic and adjectival touches akin to the finishing strokes by which the master leaves his imprint on an apprentice's canvas. Lowell's poems are littered with brilliant phrases, phrases that learned to let syntax not just marshal thought but be twisted into it, like the fibers of a rope. The muscle-bound rhythms of his early verse were never entirely banished—even his free verse is full of metrical angles and wounds—but he learned the appearance of ease, even when the verse was uneasy. In the late poems, there's still a sense of violence ready to break out—Lowell never found the sweetness and grace he admired in Elizabeth Bishop. When he imitated her in "Skunk Hour," he could manage only rueful, poisoned self-regard.

After a long bout of reading, Lowell complained, "My head rocks, as though it held the lantern-slides of the world." Such images landscape an inner realm, the realm from which the poems came. What in poems entertained a certain severity, in a letter could be merely entertainment (in poems, Lowell's seriousness darkened the glint of humor). Of a pair of his father's hairbrushes: "On my own hair, their action has been perplexed, like clearing a swamp with a toy-lawn mower." This genial self-mockery Lowell rarely dared in poems, but in letters his character is bulked out by a joking, genuine humility. Lowell's eye for frailty makes him seem exposed and fragile, perhaps because we are most vulnerable to our own comedies if not armed against those of others. After his mother visited Lowell and his second wife, Elizabeth Hardwick, in Florence, he wrote,

> *She is a very competent, stubborn, uncurious, unBohemian woman with a genius for squeezing luxury out of rocks. That is, she has a long memory for pre-war and pre-first-world war service; and thinks nothing of calling the American ambassador if there's no toilet-paper on the train.*

Robert Traill Spence Lowell IV was born to a minor branch of an important New England family—his mother's ancestors had come over on the *Mayflower*, and his relatives included Jonathan Edwards, the astronomer Perceval Lowell, and the Revolutionary War general John Stark. Lowell's parents, the crippled familiars of his memoir "91 Revere Street," were a study in mutually corrosive insecurities (they destroyed each other from the inside out). Even as a boy, he found himself at odds with his mother—armed like a first-rate with self-indulgent grandeurs and casual cruelties—as well as with his hen-pecked, emasculated father, who left the navy as a commander (that middling rank for timeservers) for a dry-dock career in business. He became, to his wife's disdain, a minor executive selling soap. This family of long heritage and good connections, which Lowell's mother was never slow to use (a distant cousin was president of Harvard), was living on borrowed capital. In their ruined and fractious household, during a steamy argument over a girl he longed to marry, at nineteen Lowell knocked his father flat. His mother wanted him committed to a mental hospital.

Merrill Moore, her psychiatrist, a minor member of the Agrarian movement, tried to heal this breach in the family by channeling Lowell's literary ambitions. He drove the brutish young man south to Vanderbilt (a significant distance from home, before the interstate highway system) and introduced him to John Crowe Ransom and Allen Tate. Soon Lowell had bulled his way into pitching a tent on Tate's lawn, the southern poet too genteel, or too astonished, to turn the gangling youth away. Following Ransom to Kenyon College, Lowell roomed at different times with Randall Jarrell and Peter Taylor.

Lowell was a peculiar example of a type familiar to teachers: the wayward and insufferable student, harboring the worm of ambition without a thing yet to show for it, convinced of his own genius but with something cracked or missing in his makeup. He was, however, a young man to whom things happened—eight years after the letter to Pound, Lowell published *Land of Unlikeness* (1944), the chapbook that first won him attention. His first book,

Lord Weary's Castle (1946), won the Pulitzer Prize; soon after, he was named poetry consultant to the Library of Congress (the position we now call poet laureate). The peculiarity was that Lowell amounted to something.

Lowell's search for a father figure forms the underlying drama of these letters. The father's inadequacy left the son eager to transfer his filial devotion; his relation to the ideal parents of the literary world marks off the limits of his discontent and the measure of his ambition. His letters to the philosopher George Santayana, for example, are full of untroubled and abashed fondness. By then elderly, cared for in a Rome hospital run by nuns, Santayana had been attracted to the Catholic piety in *Lord Weary's Castle*. The poet was forced to confess that he had since lost faith and become "something of a mild, secular quietist—usually in trouble though—and an anarchical conservative." This may have appealed to Santayana, the "Catholic atheist." He was so drawn to the young man that on Lowell's marriage to Elizabeth Hardwick he sent a gift of money, to the poet's embarrassed gratitude. Arriving in Rome after many thwarted plans (Lowell's conviction as a conscientious objector during the war, a felony, made it difficult to secure a passport), he had a touching meeting with the half-deaf philosopher. Returning a couple of years later, Lowell was crushed to find that Santayana had died only weeks before.

Lowell became a model and attentive son, visiting Pound in his confinement at St. Elizabeths in Washington, corresponding with Robert Frost and William Carlos Williams and T. S. Eliot, confiding but confident, critical but not captious. He was never deceived about the needs of his fathers. It moved Lowell that Williams once kissed him goodbye after a visit, saying, "You're my son. That's what I do to them." (Surrogate fathers sometimes have no sons of their own or troubled relations with those they have—a son searching for a father may find a father searching for a son.) When his own father died, Lowell said, "He was not a suffering or heroic man, but rather . . . always smiling or about to smile—and deep under, half-known to him: apathetic and soured." The difference in susceptibility is marked.

Lowell showed impeccable taste in choosing fathers, and even more impeccable taste in leaving them behind—when his devotion fell away, they were outgrown and sometimes simply discarded. At nineteen, he wrote Richard Eberhart, only recently his teacher at St. Mark's, that one of the older man's poems was "effective enough as a tour-de-force, but only an etymological fanatic armed with a Webster's dictionary could read through it." Later, during a manic episode, Lowell gave Tate's wife the names of her husband's lovers. Having arranged the publication of *Land of Unlikeness* and written the preface, then gone to pains to find Lowell a job, Tate remained bewildered by his former disciple. Their earliest breach seems coincident with the moment Lowell had drawn all he could from Tate's poems. How odd, then, that Lowell so rarely committed the Oedipal betrayal, writing respectfully to his literary fathers into their great age (the modernist generation was spectacularly long lived).

Lowell had a gift for friendship the poems scarcely reveal (he needed friends the way some people need food). Wounded, at times self-righteous and hectoring (he was not always a stranger to his mother's noblesse oblige), Lowell had a personality held together with baling wire. Like many men who are a difficult proposition, he was grateful to those who bore his assaults and forgave his affronts. (It's easy to suggest that in madness the shackles of behavior are discarded, but often madness steals the shackles of our affections instead.) Throughout his life, Lowell stayed close to two friends made at St. Mark's. It is with hilarity that one reads, in Ian Hamilton's biography, of the monastic discipline Lowell imposed on them the summer before he entered Harvard (ideal followers, they proved all too compliant to his will)— their regimen included a course of improving reading bound to an improving diet of eels as well as some awful cereal laced with honey.

Though like most dictators he was blind to his dictatorial bearing, Lowell pricked down the names of friends for jobs, shoved their careers forward, responded with boyish delight when they wrote something remarkable. Friendship is an act of taste as convincing as criticism—his close circle included, apart from Jarrell and Taylor, Elizabeth Bishop, Mary McCarthy, Hannah Arendt, John Berryman, J. F. Powers, Flannery O'Connor, and Theodore Roethke. (Lowell once said that Delmore Schwartz, a man whose friendship it was not hard to mislay, was the only literary friend he'd ever lost.) These friendships were often uneasy (the letters to Mary McCarthy after Hardwick's harsh and pseudonymous review of *The Group* show one source of strain). The poet complained of his friends, perhaps forgetting his earlier boast about flattery, that "it's like walking on eggs. All of them have to be humored, flattered, drawn out, allowed to say very petulant things to you," while admitting that he probably behaved no better. Perhaps, like many devotions (especially in a man who has lost faith), Lowell's went a little too far.

Most of his friends remained indefatigable in return, Peter Taylor rescuing him during a particularly gruesome manic episode. The poet's relations with Jarrell were cooler, one of many things these letters reveal—Lowell often felt like a spurned suitor for Jarrell's affections. The older poet's lavish reviews of *Land of Unlikeness* and *Lord Weary's Castle* had done much to establish Lowell's reputation. Even the slightly brutal review of *The Mills of the Ka-vanaughs* (1951) contains some of the fondest things one poet has ever written about another:

> *I cannot think of any objection at all to "Mother Marie Therese" and "Fall-ing Asleep over the Aeneid," and if I could I would be too overawed to make it. "Mother Marie Therese" is the best poem Mr. Lowell has ever written, and "Falling Asleep over the Aeneid" is—is better.*

Still, Lowell was unsure of his ground:

> *I'm boiling mad at Randall. . . . He gave a tremendous Philippic at Har-vard against our culture that has no time or taste for poetry—something that would have made Jonathan Edwards sound like Montaigne. Then what with his tennis tournaments, swimming and new enthusiasms had no time to read my poem and never apologized. Ah me!*

Jarrell's wife suggested, "You and Elizabeth are the kind of people that make friends." Randall, she said, just wasn't. Lowell bore this well, but it rankled— Jarrell was the man whose literary judgment he most respected and whose praise he most desired.

From adolescence, Lowell suffered episodes of nervous distress or ela-tion; his first full-blown manic outbreak occurred when he was thirty-one, and he endured more than a dozen in the three decades remaining to him. There have been arguments enough about the diagnosis. The editor of these letters, Saskia Hamilton, believes the illness was what is now called "mixed mania," where mania and depression appear in tandem, the patient "simulta-neously elated and lethargic." (I'm not sure this accords with the evidence of the letters—Lowell seems all too wild at the onset of his attacks.) Her attempt to gauge the precise stage of mania in which Lowell wrote certain letters is comically obtuse. Since many letters written between the hailstorms of his illness sound little different, you'd need a theodolite and his doctor's charts to distinguish one mania from another.

Lowell's "enthusiasms," as he sometimes called them—they were also christened "excitements," "crack-ups," "mix-ups"—affected his friendships, his ability to write, and most spectacularly his love life. When the shad-ows came, the first sign was a talking jag, usually with mention of Hitler or

Napoleon. (It was also a bad sign if he began rewriting the classics.) The brilliant talk became too brilliant, a dense and crazed monologue that scared people—those who weren't aware of his illness sometimes thought it a magisterial performance, just how a Romantic genius was expected to act. Friends who knew the signs could sometimes wrestle him into care; but, if the illness found him among strangers, he could be dangerous—Lowell stood over six feet and could have wrestled a bull. He tried to strangle one lover in an argument over Shakespeare and once ran the streets of Bloomington, Indiana, hollering about the evils of homosexuals and devils, convinced he was the reincarnation of the Holy Ghost. Lowell's third wife, Caroline Blackwood, grew so nervous around him that any mention of Hitler set her antennae waving.

Over the years, there were attacks of the most baroque character. The first episode began in 1949 at Yaddo, where he accused the director of harboring Communist spies; continued in New York, where Lowell held Allen Tate at arm's length out a second-story window while reciting, in a bear's voice, Tate's "Ode to the Confederate Dead"; and ended in the unfortunate events in Bloomington. In 1963, while eating lunch at the presidential palace in Buenos Aires, Lowell insulted the general who was about to be made president. Later, having insisted on touring the city's equestrian statues, Lowell undressed and clambered up beside the bronze horsemen, a half-naked emperor himself. He sent telegrams to the pope and President Eisenhower, anointing himself Caesar of Argentina. Long stays in mental hospitals were the usual result, accompanied by straitjackets, shock therapy, large doses of Thorazine, then slow recovery and remorse. Or, as Lowell put it, "short weeks of a Messianic rather bestial glow, . . . then dark months of indecision, emptiness etc."

Often there was a woman involved, the attacks attended by Lowell's crush on some girl and an impulsive decision to leave his wife. More than once, he set up his new inamorata in an apartment and moved in. Whenever he fell for someone, he was eager to begin housekeeping, a mock marriage with a mock picket-fence around it—Lowell was of a domesticating strain that suggests certain discomforts in childhood. The only child hated being alone. Lowell's poems are the residue of the complications of modern love—For Lizzie and Harriet (1973) and The Dolphin (1973) are as close as the twentieth century came to the distracted sonnets of George Meredith.

Lowell seems to have been a serial monogamist, though his monogamy was geographic (one city, one woman at a time). As for wives, he preferred novelists, three of them. The strains on his marriage with Hardwick, during which many of these attacks occurred, were heartbreaking. She once said, he reported, that the "only advantage of marriage is that you can be as gross, slovenly, mean and brutally verbose as you want." Lowell apparently did not recall half what he'd done during his "enthusiasms," so his letters are short on incident but long on excuses—he wore the battered piety of a good apologist. This worked longer for him than for most.

There was, however, a lot of human wreckage in the aftermath. Girlfriends had to be dismissed, at least once by a cool letter from his lawyers. Those who know of Lowell's many amours, of his seduction of young women, often enough his students, will find little more than sidelong references in the letters, usually at the back end of a manic episode. It's hard to believe Lowell did not write more to his lovers, he wrote so often to his wives when they were apart (long-distance phone calls were once prohibitively expensive—in 1952, a three-minute call from Seattle to New York cost $2.50, the equivalent of $20 in 2008). Whether for diplomatic reasons or because letters were unavailable, this collection has numerous missing presences. We sense too infrequently the overwhelming eros that came with Lowell's madness, like an ill-mannered guest.

Given what he was capable of writing when lovesick, perhaps the omission isn't to be regretted:

> There's a scene. White sheets. Salt air from the Mediterranean, far below. Sound of waves. Then you in your bridal dress. Nothing very fancy, for such wouldn't do for us. Maybe some stiff, close-fitting brocaded dress. And I am undressing you. WE are together, our mouths are together, our hair is together. Ah, there! I speak of mysteries, and I kneel now and throw salt, or whatever one throws, over my shoulder to prevent ill omens. All is humbleness and joy.

We do have, fortunately, Lowell's letters to Elizabeth Bishop, for whom Lowell felt a deep friendship he at times mistook for another of his passions—during his manias he would bemuse her with mad declarations of love. (His poem "Water" took shape in regret over the affair they never consummated.) Bishop had enjoyed flings with men when younger, but by the time she met Lowell her sexual affections were reserved for women. His letters to her are otherwise boyish and relaxed; yet, even in his saner periods, Lowell's fondness seems slightly inflamed, decent but suspect—she was perhaps fortunate to live in Brazil. Bishop's poems were influential in the development of his style, possessing a vulnerability and tenderness beyond the brooding intensities of his—she was the poet of his generation of whom he was most in awe. Only near the end of his life did a little testiness leak out. He wrote to Hardwick,

> *The dog must be sent away because of her asthma but will that be enough?*
> *. . . Then so many things she can criticize, the disheveled garden, the care-*
> *free garden man, our care of Sheridan. Should he be sent away too? So*
> *many things down to my not writing meter, making errors in description.*
> *Of course no one is more wonderful, but so fussy and hazardous now.*

Bishop by then was a raging alcoholic—theirs was a generation whose letters bear the sins of too many martinis.

The Lowell of these letters is not the harassed, hounded wreck of the poems, though he was hounded and harassed enough. The poems bear scars of his long-suffered suffering, the madness that recurred like bouts of malaria; but they seem the recognitions of a man slipping toward the maelstrom, or emerging battered from it. The mania seemed to inspire him, yet the poetry Lowell wrote during his episodes proved almost worthless afterward. Only occasionally could he harry it into form. Though he rejected the term, the poems in *Life Studies* (1959) soon attracted the word "confessional"—the poet seems to know he's done wrong, the necessary condition for confession and repentance. Like many during the heyday of Freud's influence, Lowell put his trust in psychotherapy, and in ever more stringent courses of it, a regimen that seemed to do him no good whatever. The lithium treatment developed in the late sixties stabilized his condition for a good while, folding Freud's complexes into a salt deficiency. This lets his parents off the hook.

The partial and prejudiced record of a writer's letters proves more valuable than its fly-by-night form—but history often lies in the richness of the ephemeral. Lowell was a chatty, indulgent, fraternal correspondent, turning his eye to domestic mishaps, amusing anecdotes, family matters, more eagerly than to the poems lying on his desk. His comments in passing on a poet's labors (even when writing fluently, he could make the task sound Sisyphean) rarely give deep or thorough analysis of his intentions. The reader has to work from stray evidence, like a forensic investigator at a crime scene.

This might not be much of a loss, as poets are famously bad at analyzing their work. Lowell, however, could be wittily and painfully insightful about the toils of the workshop. He understood the creepy narcissism poems entailed: "As you overlook the black keyboard of your typewriter, it's as though you were facing yourself in the mirror and trying to hold the attention of what you see there by what you see there." When a poet writes letters he's not doing the one thing he should be, writing poems—yet a poet can't spend all day on poems, lest the world be overrun with them. He's lucky to spend a productive hour or two scratching out lines. Lowell knew too well what could happen; he remarked of one book that "none of the poems are the kind of empty thing one writes to write poetry."

Lowell was no prose writer. There's something too arch and crabbed about his formal prose, too "poetic," and he knew it: "Prose is hell. I want to change every two words, but while I toy with revisions, the subject stinks like a dead whale and lies in the mud of the mind's bottom." He often made things worse by revising: "I've been . . . trying to write prose—a hell of a job, it starts na-ked[,] ends as fake velvet." If his intensities were rarely trained on prose, and rarely repaid there, Lowell's criticism was nevertheless original, unexpected, mandarin with the touch of a magus. The autobiographical fragments are overrich as French gâteaux but brilliant, full of the "magical detail, that at first you mistake for a misprint." What kept his prose too calculated made his letters fizz with offhand remarks, sly adjectives, the banter of intelligence. His faults made him a letter writer of no common ability, who might have been forgiven the vanities of craft, had he been aware of them.

Lowell lived by revision and knew his poems sometimes withered because of it—revision was the vice of his virtues. Writing the poems in *Notebook* (1968), he had a trusted young friend, Frank Bidart, to respond to his endless tinkering—this may not have been an advantage: "I think I've spent more futile hours trying to perfect something satisfactory—always pressing and in-visible, the unimagined perfect lines or ending, for there it usually falls. Of-ten I've given up, and wondered why I ever found fault." The letters, which were never choked into such lifelessness, reveal that teasing, implacable intel-ligence that so seduced his friends. A reader is grateful merely for his casual, causal opinions, for the flypaper that letters become. Lowell on form:

> *The intoxicating thing about rhyme and meter is that they have nothing at all to do with truth, just as ballet steps are of no use on a hike. They are puzzles, hurdles, obstacles, expertise—they cry out for invention, and of course in the end for truth, whatever that is.*

The loophole glimpses into his workshop are welcome enough; but the letters allow us to eavesdrop on his nervy, indiscreet table talk—it's for the things unsaid in his poems that we value these letters. A writer may not be expert on the delicate suspensions of his ambiguities, but he's the only expert on his literary opinions. They fix him in the constellation of his peers while being, in Lowell's case, an intensive course in practical criticism of the most personal kind. Lowell never styled himself a critic, but the force and character of his remarks are as cunning as Jarrell's. He sketches other writers with a breezy deftness that isn't gossip, not exactly, though gossip is the highest form of criticism many writers will venture.

[On Dylan Thomas] *Somehow he was kept on beer most of the time . . . no meals except breakfast. About the best and dirtiest stories I've ever heard—dumpy, absurd body, hair combed by a salad spoon, brown-button Welsh eyes always moving suspiciously or fixing on the most modest person in the room . . . a great explosion of life, and hell to handle.*

[On Robert Browning] *How he muffed it all! The ingenious, terrific metrics, shaking the heart out of what he was saying; the invented language; the short-cuts; the hurry; and (one must say it) the horrible self-indulgence—the attitudes, the cheapness!*

[On an art colony] *No use describing Yaddo—run down rose gardens, rotting cantaloupes, fountains, a bust of Dante with a hole in the head, sets called* Gems of Ancient Literature, Masterpieces of the World, *cracking dried up sets of Shakespeare, Ruskin, Balzac, . . . pseudo Poussins, pseudo Titians, pseudo Reynolds, pseudo and real English wood, portraits of the patroness, her husband, her lover, her children, lit with tubular lights, like a church, like a museum.*

[On T. S. Eliot] *He's maimed somehow, but not dull, not untrustworthy. . . . There are many layers to be gotten under, when you do there's something wonderfully warm and human.*

[On Amsterdam] *Our apartment is right now full of half-filled half open suit-cases, leaves are beginning to hide the canal, the sun is shining, the radio is playing a sort of Indian summer Mozart minuet, and each [of] us knows that if he can only stall long enough the other will do the packing.*

[On Delmore Schwartz] *Delmore in an unpressed mustard gabardine, a little winded, husky voiced, unhealthy, but with a carton of varied vitamin*

bottles, the color of oil, quickening with Jewish humor, and in-the-knowness,
and his own genius, every person, every book—motives for everything,
Freud in his blood, great webs of causation, then suspicion, then rushes of
rage. . . . [I]t was like living with a sluggish, sometimes angry spider.

[On Virgil] It's comforting to think of Vergil, working all the time, casually
and steadily—and turning out a line a day! Comforting till you realize
what that line was!

The reader feels at times like that reader of Virgil. Lowell's portraits betray, like the rapid pencilings in the little albums Rembrandt carried with him on the street, a deft and vital interest with a fondness for foible, the tolerant amusement of a man who knew that all too often he had to be tolerated himself. When he says that Pound's "voice of anti-semitism is like the voice of a drunkard telling people in cars to drive through the pedestrians" or that Jarrell is like a "fencer who has defeated and scarred all his opponents so that the sport has come to be almost abandoned," you feel you've seen through Lowell's eyes. Then there are the anecdotes: Pound saying, "Cal, God be with you, if you like the company," or, after listening to Alice Longworth chatter away ("ending with a synopsis of two 1880 novels she'd read as a girl"), "You like reading more than I do." Or Allen Tate saying sweetly to Lowell's daughter, "You will be dear to me when you are older." She looked at him and slowly replied, "If you are still alive."

Lowell's poems, his letters, his criticism, his memoirs, it's increasingly clear, were all part of one ramshackle enterprise, in some ways forming the most naked and ravaged autobiography, the most artfully artless, the most rational in its embarrassments, since Rousseau's. It was a life in fractions. The memoirs, thumbed into shape, were fired, then shattered. There are, most consequently, the poems. Even the earliest, read now through the lens of *Life Studies*, reveal private incidents, coded and forced into the symbolic life of a Noh play. ("I'm a fisherman myself," he wrote in a letter, "but all my fish become symbols, alas!") Lowell's major contribution to poetry was to open it to the privacies that poets for a millennia or two had smuggled in on poetry's terms. Lowell made poetry accept his life on its own terms—mortifying, myopic all too often, full of familiar sins and a few unfamiliar ones. Philip Rahv, reading some of the poems that became *Life Studies*, knew exactly what they were: "Diss is da break-through for Cal and for poetry. The one real advance since Eliot."

The vagrant events of the day became the certain events of poems, while not sacrificing (as the Beats did) the symbols, metaphors, verbal acuteness, ambiguity, and even meter of poems more traditional. In 1954 Lowell remarked about his students, "They write about letting dinner burn while they dream of writing lousy poems." Only a few years later he made it possible, even attractive, for them to do just that (we have been reading about burnt dinners ever since). There was a cost. A roman à clef offers the decent veil of fiction; Lowell's poems were less discreet. He felt qualms enough about *Life Studies*, whose poems did not even *seem* like poems to Allen Tate. Shown a draft of *The Dolphin*, which incorporated scraps of Hardwick's angry letters, Bishop felt Lowell had gone beyond the bounds of decency. He continued to revise, fictionalize, but this only made things worse—the poems violate the fiction of privacy husband and wife usually maintain. It's one thing for a man to show you his diary, another for him to show you his wife's—or her lingerie. Hardwick was indomitable, and forgiving past the point of sanity or good sense. That after the divorce, after *The Dolphin*, after Lowell's further breakdowns, after everything, she was still ready to take him back tells us much about the "original moment that his presence always was."

These letters remind us that the career was not without pain to others, nor without pain to Lowell himself. He welcomed the rigors necessary to art, the monastic discipline imposed—he had to work for his inspirations. Hardwick said, "Since he was . . . not the sort of poet, if there are any, for whom beautiful things come drifting down in a snowfall of gift, the labor was merciless." (In the sediment of many poems lay a foreign original—"half my pieces come from something," he wrote.) No sooner had Lowell mastered a style than he grew bored with its limitations and cold to its virtues. The free verse of *Life Studies* caused a mass stampede of younger poets away from fifties formal poetry, but soon enough Lowell was writing the octosyllabic couplets of *Near the Ocean* (1967). Like many of the moderns, he drove himself to ever new impositions, to any change as long as it was change, his work the record of artistic restlessness, a "dread of more of the same."

After the prose and the poems, each inventing a different Lowell, there is now Lowell's autobiography in letters—this Lowell is fonder and more amused, a man at the center of complex loyalties, one sometimes broken by the tactical skirmishes of his marriages, the endless string of girlfriends. Saskia Hamilton must be congratulated on her painstaking labor and meticulous instincts—she has muscled a large chore into submission. Making a life out of such letters is like trying to rebuild a smashed vase out of half the shards (how much we miss the letters to his first wife, Jean Stafford, which she burned or tore to shreds). A collection of letters gives a skewed view of time, lingering in some years and skimming over others, sometimes at center stage and sometimes—the letters lost or unwritten—missing important events entirely. The editor's notes are instructive, thorough without being overbearing (having only casual discursive notes, Robert Giroux's edition of Bishop's letters is far less useful). In her somewhat unfocused introduction, Hamilton offers impressionistic, amateurish readings of passages of Lowell's prose (very Eng. Lit. 101); but about his life she is to the point while rarely missing the point. The criticisms I offer are lost among the larger pleasures bestowed.

Though this selection of letters is generous enough, the list of correspondents is top heavy with famous names. (Beginning with the letter to Pound, however dramatic, means suppressing the prep-school letters quoted by Ian Hamilton.) Lowell was at the center of a brilliant circle, admittedly; but letters to former students or editors (fragments published elsewhere suggest these would have been of value) are too rare. The life recorded here is played out for his literary friends—he was a different person to his Cousin Harriet, and the reader deserves to know better the Lowell outside literature.

An editor who believes Lowell's letters possess the "very thing he revised away in his poems" doesn't have much sense of the way writers compose. They don't revise only on the page—they revise before the words reach the page. Lowell once wrote to Bishop, "You seem to have a loose seemingly careless style . . .; but of course I know all [the] fierce labors you really go through." About his own work:

> The Life Studies *poems were meant to be entirely art, yet they are meant to give a sort of notebook effect, an impression of truth and a fragmentary naturalness, that would lose all its point if too worked up.*

It was freshness he revised *toward*—his most graceful touches seem absent from letters composed off the cuff. What lies charged on the page may have been third or fourth thought. I believe the editor when she says that Lowell rarely revised his letters (though I don't see how she knows he "typed as fast as he could think"), but she also says they were "glancingly corrected" and "visually messy" and that the "paper often looks like a worksheet." That sounds like revision to me.

Lowell was a perfectly miserable speller, one of fantastic principles. The editor has left a few misspellings on purpose (the notes provide corrections to, for example, "electricuted"), but others unnoted call into question her editorial eye: "she can bare to contemplate," "Prince Metterich," the "whole caste will turn up," "somesort," "promess" (for "promise"), "high-fy," "Dixi" (for "Dixie"), "Havrd" (for "Harvard"), a "good pare" (for "pair"), and "embassadoress." (Her own spelling is not beyond criticism when she writes of the "British Navel Reserve.") Further, it seems unlikely that George Santayana wrote "taking the low into its own hands" or Hannah Arendt, "Your poem . . . was such a consolated," or that Paul Valéry's translators rendered his most famous remark as a "work is never *complete* . . . but *abandoned*." (I don't know where the editor found the translation she uses, but it is radically different from the one cited.)

Some of the editor's errors betray an insecure knowledge of twentieth-century literature. It's only mildly odd to call George Santayana a "Spanish American" or Edmund Wilson a "critical essayist" (rather than a critic—of course he also wore other hats); but who would describe Nathanael West as the "author of *A Cool Million*" rather than *The Day of the Locust* or *Miss Lonelyhearts*? Yaddo is an artists' colony, not merely a writers' colony; and the proper spellings are the Iowa Writers' Workshop and St. Elizabeths Hospital. Death dates should have been provided for Alan Dugan, Mona Van Duyn, Charles Tomlinson, James Ross, and Robert Creeley—other writers of note are given no dates at all, which rather maroons them in literary history. Sometimes figures in the letters go unmentioned in the notes—you don't know whether the editor missed them or simply couldn't find out a thing about them.

Slips of the eye, like slips of the tongue, are often telling—who wouldn't want to know that Lowell once referred not to Heathrow but to Heathcliff Airport? However much I admire the method and resourcefulness of the editor, however, writers want to be saved from their accidentals—Hamilton sinks to pointless trivia in printing "d reams," then noting that "Lowell's typewriter skipped." If that's the only such typo in seven hundred letters, he was a lucky man. (The editor might have paid more attention to her own occasional slips, like the misnumbering in the notes to letters 439 and 545.) The notes have been left unindexed, which makes it almost impossible to find anything mentioned there; and the index, which suffers some of the usual problems, has a few peculiar to itself. Enough cavils.

Lowell was the most brilliant poet of his generation, the most extraordinary America has had since the moderns, those fathers he chose so eagerly. (How fortunate he was to live at a moment when it was clear whom to choose.) With the publication of his letters, the general reader has most of the private

evidence of his life. A complete edition of the Bishop and Lowell correspon-
dence is in the works, and one day someone will embark on an edition of all
his letters (the mills haven't even started to grind out the proposed complete
edition of Henry James's letters, so perhaps we can expect Lowell's in a cen-
tury or so). As letters, these fall only a little short of the finest examples—
Byron, Keats, Lear, Carroll, and Shaw, among literary men (though Lowell is
more like Byron than perhaps any poet since), with Coleridge not far behind.
They created an entire world in their letters, a world that answered more than
the questions posed by the life. Lowell's world is smaller, bound more closely
by its social gravities, philosophical only in the sense of stoic, his remarks
sometimes uttered through gritted teeth. The mania kept Lowell's gaze too
much on the mirror, or thumbing the rosary of apology. When you finish the
letters, however, you know his world much better; and you know the man
without feeling you have exhausted him. It was a life lived in the swagger of
language.

Forward Into the Past

Reading the New Critics

G reat poetry is not a matter of memorable snippets and gobbets; but, without snippets worth remembering, poetry does not exist. The critic must give meaning to memory, yet there has long been an argument about what that job of work requires. If you walk into college classrooms now, you'll meet two armed camps of critics. In a poetry workshop, discussion turns on the poem's meaning and how meaning becomes lodged through metaphor, image, meter, symbol, allusion, argument (what Pound called the *"art of getting meaning into words"*). In a literature class, the poem will be analyzed, often as not, as a "text" that mirrors the world of its making, as if it had been written not by a poet but by Sir History or Dame Sociology. The professor will employ the cryptic jargon of methods that to their promoters reveal hidden tensions in language but to their detractors tar and feather poems for the sins of another day and force very different poets to sing the same tune. To the Marxists, the sins remain those of class; to the feminists, gender; to the scholars of ethnic literature, race—they wave over poems, mere poems, a Geiger counter that detects the decaying radioactivity of racism, sexism, and class hatred. "Sir!" says the critic, accusingly. "I have discovered a swarm of phonemes in your poems." "Aye, sir," the poet replies, "the damned lines are infested with 'em."

Perhaps there was a prelapsarian era, before the flood of "theory," as it is so unhappily called, when men were men and women were women and critics were critics. There may also have been an exact hour in the seventeenth century when, as Eliot declared, a "dissociation of sensibility set in" or a specific day, "on or about December 1910," when Virginia Woolf noticed that "human character changed." My quarrelsome reading of history, however, suggests that men were never simply men, women never simply women, and critics never simply critics.

There did exist, however, a golden age of modern literary criticism, roughly from the early essays of Eliot and Pound to the end of the heyday of *Partisan Review*. Call it fifty years when a reader could pick up certain magazines and be gratified, provoked, or happily infuriated by the discussion of poems—of course it didn't seem a golden age then. It never does at the time (Jarrell once said that "people who live in a Golden Age usually go around complaining how yellow everything looks"). We are rarely so stimulated or flabbergasted today (when infuriated now, we're not happy about it)—if readers have grown no less intelligent, the time must no longer be ripe for critics. One of the ways a time is not right is if it falls after an age of such criticism.

I've known poets who kept runs of the old *Partisan* or *Hudson* or *Kenyon Review* at arm's reach, just to browse the stray essays of an Empson or a Blackmur. I'm speaking of criticism proper, not reviewing—for reviewing is always its own fashion, its pleasure the Force 9 gales of the reviewers themselves, whether George Bernard Shaw and Bernard Haggin on music, James Agee and Pauline Kael on film, Mary McCarthy on fiction, Randall Jarrell on poetry, or Robert Hughes on art. A good reviewer is both of his time and beyond his time—we can read his charities and condemnations with delight, even if we haven't the faintest notion of the book or play or painting judged. A good *critic*, however, must say something, not just about a particular work of art, but about the structures of art itself; and to understand him you need to know the work criticized.

Great critics have a long afterlife, but sometimes a long beforelife. When Matthew Arnold at last gave them a name, "touchstones" had lain ready for a millennium or two in the teaching of schoolboys—among ancient grammarians, a similar idea rescued lines from the lost plays of Athenian drama. It's good to be reminded of exactly what Arnold wrote:

> *Indeed there can be no more useful help for discovering what poetry belongs to the class of the truly excellent, and can therefore do us most good, than to have always in one's mind lines and expressions of the great masters, and to apply them as a touchstone to other poetry.*

Arnold was not without subtlety, for he went on:

> *Of course we are not to require this other poetry to resemble them; it may be very dissimilar. But if we have any tact we shall find them, when we have lodged them well in our minds, an infallible touchstone for detecting the*

presence or absence of high poetic quality, and also the degree of this qual-
ity, in all other poetry which we may place beside them.

Behind Pound's gists and piths and Eliot's vaunted gift for quotation lies the
touchstone. Though Arnold has often been disparaged, I caught a critic re-
cently referring to the touchstone with approval; a century or two from now it
will not be dead to critics yet. We think of criticism as transient, as à la mode
and all too soon outmoded; but the name and nature of criticism have some-
times proved more durable than what was criticized. (Though I hesitate to
accept it, the reviewers of one day may inherit the outmoded critical practices
of the day before—reviewers are often conservative in their technique, even
when radical in their tastes.)

Criticism never starts over; yet sometimes it suffers a forgetfulness, an ill
nature, an ignorance of its soundings. There's no going back, but there is a
going forward that does not fear looking back. The complaint about "theory"
is that it treats literature with the dispatch of a meat grinder—if you know the
method, long before the poem has been dragged in by the tail you can pre-
dict whether the butcher will sell you the sausages of Derrida, or Foucault, or
Lacan. It's disheartening to see a poem raided for evidence of sins long de-
funct or treated with a forensics kit, as if it were a crime scene. I therefore find
it hard to work up enthusiasm for the latest announcement of racism in *Oliver
Twist* or *Huckleberry Finn* (there are scholars who would ban both books, and
gladly), or elitism in Shakespeare, or sexism in, well, in just about everything.
There have been sophisticated and revealing studies on these subjects, but in
the classroom what you tend to get is a professor who counts penis symbols—
this reduces criticism to something like trainspotting. If even teaching Shake-
speare is elitist, what of the professor who uses a jargon so pompous, tortured,
and harrowingly opaque the man on the street would stand scratching his
head about it for a month of Sundays?

Seventy or eighty years ago, what we now call criticism was forbidden in
literature classes—English professors clerkishly confined their studies to liter-
ary history or philology. John Crowe Ransom recalled the head of graduate
English studies at a prestigious university telling a student, "This is a place
for exact scholarship, and you want to do criticism. Well, we don't allow criti-
cism here, because that is something which anybody can do." (Ransom re-
marked that it was easy for a professor of literature "to spend a lifetime in
compiling the data of literature and yet rarely or never commit himself to a

literary judgment.") What passed for "criticism," where it existed at all, was an amateur course in appreciation, the instructor like some hereditary retainer rambling the halls of a stately home, pointing out the heroic cast of a rusty suit of armor or the hollow eye of some time-darkened portrait, as well as the cupful of finger bones dubiously from the Battle of Towton—the professor, in his own house of literature, repeated the plot; muttered respectfully over artistic touches of language; and enthused, if not on the nobility of character, then on its iniquity.

New Criticism was created by a divided and often embattled group of American poets (they were almost all poets) born between 1888 and 1907—John Crowe Ransom, Allen Tate, Robert Penn Warren, Cleanth Brooks, W. K. Wimsatt, R. P. Blackmur, Yvor Winters, and Kenneth Burke, less a close-knit family than a quarrel of cousins and perfect strangers. To them may be added their precursors and influences, the expatriate poets Ezra Pound and T. S. Eliot, the English literary critic I. A. Richards, and Richards's brilliant student William Empson. The age in which they practiced most fruitfully, from about 1913 to 1963, was an age newly scientific, the age of Einstein's relativity and Bohr's quantum mechanics (the equations of Maxwell half a century earlier came from a ruder mechanic age). New Criticism grew up partly to justify modernist literature—the novel's novel experiments in consciousness or chronology and the rejection of meter in vers libre were the literary correlatives of the repudiation of figure in painting and sculpture (English use of *avant-garde* for art rather than armies dates only to 1910). The tension between Eliot's resistance, in "The Perfect Critic," to the "vague suggestion of the scientific vocabulary" in criticism and his wish to cultivate an Aristotelian intelligence that might "see the object as it really is" dramatized the ambivalence toward science in much of the New Criticism. (When Ransom writes that "criticism must become more scientific," he means "precise and systematic," not something using beakers and Bunsen burners.)

The New Critics reacted violently against the impressionistic criticism of the previous generation, which favored books like A *Thousand and One Gems of English Poetry* and Palgrave's *The Golden Treasury*—such criticism longed for the moral suasion of art. (The moral appeal has been smuggled back into literature in the self-righteousness of the "poetry of witness.") The comprehensions of art a century later live within the climate that reaction established; even when our arts are more conservative, or at least tolerant of conservation (figure has returned to painting; fiction has abandoned experiment in wholesale fashion; meter occasionally worms its way back into poetry), they are created on the foundations of the moderns, and often with the moderns in mind—in fiction the sense of belatedness is especially compelling.

According to René Wellek, there were four major objections to New Criticism: it was (1) merely aestheticism by another name; (2) a method profoundly unhistorical; (3) an attempt to make criticism a science; and (4) a deracinated imitation of the French schoolboy's *explication de texte*. In the American volume of *A History of Modern Criticism, 1750–1950*, he vigorously refutes these accusations. Even so, if a shiver of suspicion regarding history or the whiff of aestheticism infects New Criticism (any criticism so fond of literature must have some taste for the aesthetic), the bill of complaint betrays the prejudice of critics dubious in their own practice of history and flagrantly hostile to aesthetic concern—which has meant, among other things, hostile to the notion that some poems are better than others. As Winters wrote some seventy years ago,

> The professor of English Literature, who believes that taste is relative, yet who endeavors to convince his students that Hamlet is more worthy of their attention than some currently popular novel, is in a serious predicament.

The resolution to this dilemma is that the professor has stopped trying.

Critics cannot be blamed for every wrong turn taken by art; but a less frantic approval of the modish and "original," of gesture over craft, of idea over execution might have spared visual art in the past half century from fashions dizzying in their rapid and rabid succession. (This is not to deny that an artist as rich in character as Richard Serra may emerge from a sometimes trivial movement; but the rage for novelty that produced the broken crockery of Julian Schnabel, now almost forgotten as a painter, has replaced it with the formaldehyde-drenched sharks of Damien Hirst.) To look back at the New Critics is to indulge in a nostalgia for the days when books were books and not "texts" (when critics blather on about "dialogic intertextuality" in *Batman*, my eyes glaze over). Beyond the holy trinity of race, class, and gender; beyond the murder of the author (hardly the death of him); beyond jargon-ridden, vatic, riddling "methodologies" fond of sophomoric wordplay and genial mystification (recall how Pound despised "critics who use vague terms to *conceal* their meaning"); contemporary theory remains largely inoculated against the way poems work. In the end, it is a very dull way to look at poetry.

Despite its pretense of dispassion, theory—which often lies in a fog of unfinished philosophy—turns out to be surprisingly judgmental, for behind the mask of tolerance, the love of the "free play of the signifier" and respect for the "other," the "valorization" of relative values, it wallows in the age's prejudice: for female over male, black over white, poor over rich, gay over straight, Palestinian over Jew, colonist over empire, native over colonist, anarchy over order. It little matters where one's sympathies lie in such oppositions, if they require sympathies at all (rather than, say, curiosity, or regret); but you can't pretend to moral relativity, as theorists do, and embrace such prejudices. Theory often mingles, in a way Orwell would have noticed, the language of revolutionaries with that of prison guards—who will "subvert" these subversives or "interrogate" these interrogators? For a criticism that prizes nonconformity and "difference," theory proves alarmingly fond of orthodoxy. (In the classrooms of theory, all readings are tolerated, except the wrong ones—the morally absolute masquerades here as the morally relative and manages to be high-minded about it, too. Kafka would have smiled in recognition.) Having deprived the author of "agency," reduced him to the victim or weathervane of his time, the smug discriminations of theory are exactly those New Criticism set out to disturb. To the New Critics, the poem struggles to escape its time; the interest lies in the rare poem that succeeds, not the mass that do not. (The importance of some poems, especially in the modern period—*Howl*, for example—may *be* largely sociological. That is their failure.)

Poets become poets by making sense of the poets who came before them. As literature classes were slowly dyed in the blood of theory, New Criticism retreated to writing workshops. Like all schools of criticism, the New Critics have been derided by their successors; but they retain an extraordinary influence on the daily practice of criticism (this division between practice and theory is more than peculiar just now). It's not surprising that the close reading of poetry has remained the method of choice in workshops, which are— lamentably, no doubt—more concerned with craft than capitalism. They still believe, with Allen Tate, that "literature is neither religion nor social engineering." The New Critics developed a mechanics of poetry that any poet would love—by attending to the words. Such critics did not treat poems in ignorance of what literary history or biography reveals; but these became the means of criticism, not the end. This turned topsy-turvy the academic study of the day—it would be no less radical now.

Wellek reminds us that close reading was a late development in New Criticism—it was not the point but the tool developed to prove the point. The method was secured by the textbook *Understanding Poetry* (1938), which became a mainstay of college classrooms for two generations. The editors,

Cleanth Brooks and Robert Penn Warren, tried to dissect what a poem said, not reveal the poet as a dolt, a closet racist, a chauvinist, a snob, or a prig. New Criticism takes as its task to understand how meaning and feeling are invented in language (theory flinches as much from the neural itch of feeling as from aesthetics) and to judge if some poems are better than others—not simply better at kowtowing to the mores and manners of our day, but better in aesthetic terms. If New Criticism seems a bit like a henhouse built by foxes, the foxes sometimes walked and talked like hens themselves, out of respect—or because they were secretly hens.

T. S. Eliot is often accused of writing the criticism necessary to read his own poetry (this is like a man rich in nails inventing the hammer); his taste for Donne and antipathy to Milton did clear-cut a few square miles of metaphysics for *The Waste Land.* (It might be more accurate to say he was working out in prose the apprehensions about his predecessors that animated his verse line.) Many of Eliot's insights, however, apply to poetry generally and can be read against his notions of taste. Taste is always more narrow than criticism, at least if it is at all interesting *as* taste. However much Ezra Pound's promotion of the troubadours licensed his poems in pseudo-medieval English (he labored like a man trying to drag Edwardian England back to a world of sackbuts and krummhorns), in the end Provençal lyrics have proved one of the standards against which his poems are measured. Meanwhile, it did not harm the troubadours to be dragged to the century's attention. Pound's later drumbeating for Li Po, the Anglo-Saxons, Chaucer, and Dante opened a few dusty parlors for *The Cantos* in the House of Fame; but, judged against such poetry, *The Cantos* look less than dominating. The tastes have endured, but criticism abides even when taste goes astray—criticism creates values, taste often vices, though that is no reason not to have taste.

What happened to New Criticism? Even the best critical method may run out of things to say, may become arthritic in its response to new work, may reduce itself merely to method. (Though New Critics analyzed some kinds of poetry more brilliantly than others, any universal criticism might be universally suspect. New Criticism works well for a poetry of logical and defensible meaning, even modernist work where ambiguities have been strained to the limit—but there *is* a limit.) By the sixties, a sense of routine and exhaustion had set in—most of the New Critics still alive had stopped writing criticism (though Empson was scribbling combative reviews until the end), and younger critics were not, most of them, nearly so talented. Nor were they poets (the poets—Jarrell, Berryman, Lowell—made better reviewers than they did writers of critical essays). The founders, a cleverer lot than their followers, grew old in their understandings; but discoverers always claim the richest land in terra incognita. New Criticism did, eventually, grow tired of itself. Its legacy lies in the craft revealed and the clarity gained.

Most contemporary poetry is written in a tradition, a tradition more susceptible to New Critical readings than to any criticism that has followed. New Criticism remains our basic critical language—the reader schooled there is best placed to return to Matthew Arnold, or David Masson, or Coleridge, or Dr. Johnson and extract the most from them. (I suspect that New Criticism was largely founded on the footnotes of editors of Shakespeare, beginning with Johnson, if not before.) The good doctor says little in *The Lives of the Poets* about how poems actually work; but he illustrates the value to the critic of generous knowledge, a robust sensibility, and a style like a battery of cannon.

If I have been unfair to the natural disaster of theory, I have grown weary of hearing my students complain that professors don't like literature very much—indeed, they seem to prefer truffle hunting the sins of the authors. (Of course, I'm interested in the effect of his time upon the poet and vice versa—but I'm not interested only in that.) Theory has reduced literature largely to what Winters calls the didactic function—but the poems, in their poor, poetic way, serve theory almost entirely as a storehouse of negative examples. A generation of students, having chosen English because they love books, has graduated bemused that anyone would read such debauched and offensive trash—the brightest wonder why studying literature seems no different from political indoctrination and why their professors have turned into grim-faced, razor-beaked theocrats. (It's past time to launch a new *Dunciad*—where is Pope when you need him?)

I used to think things would get better; but too many young Ph.D.'s now learn no way but theory's way of discussing poetry, if they discuss poetry at all (they also know little about grammar and less about meter, but those are complaints for another hour). We might instead think of what was lost when the New Critics were cast into the shadows and, as Eliot said of the metaphysical poets, "consider whether their virtue was not something permanently valuable, which subsequently disappeared, but ought not to have disappeared."

Verse Chronicle

One If by Land

Gary Snyder

Gary Snyder was a marquee poet in the sixties, when his eco-Buddhist paeans to nature were read in every commune from Maine to Baja. Decades later, their misty imagism, indebted equally to Ezra Pound and Japanese haiku, seems cloying and sentimental, dependent on the *Zeitgeist* for its effect. The poetry of the day is passé when the day is past, its beauties no longer beautiful; and even a style stronger than Snyder's may sooner or later seem obsolete, like the picket fences of Augustan couplets after the hurricane of Romanticism swept through.

The poems of *Danger on Peaks*, Snyder's first volume of new verse in twenty years, are a throwback to those heady days of Haight-Ashbury, free love, and Volkswagen buses painted in Day-Glo colors, though what used to be poems are now mostly half-hearted diary jottings followed by a snippet of verse. Snyder has been influenced by the travel journals of Bashō (the style of poetry mixed with prose is called *haibun*); but, if prose is to have the force of poetry, it can't be as badly written as poetry.

In 1945 Snyder climbed Mt. St. Helens and on coming down learned that the United States had dropped atomic bombs on Hiroshima and Nagasaki. The awful contrast—the tranquil splendor of the mountain, the hideous deaths of innocent civilians—brutally affected him:

> *Horrified, blaming scientists and politicians and the governments of the world, I swore a vow to myself, something like, "By the purity and beauty and permanence of Mt. St. Helens, I will fight against this cruel destructive power and those who would seek to use it, for all my life."*

It's easy to forgive the pretensions and naïveté of the young man, harder to bear the self-satisfied maunderings of the older one. Thirty-five years later, the mountain erupted with far more violence than a mere A-bomb—and, reader, guess what! The explosion reminded him of Hiroshima! The Romantic sublime ended not with a whimper but a bang. As Snyder says elsewhere, in an argot revealing that the sixties never died, "West Coast snowpeaks are too much!"

Snyder has long been a guru for the ecology movement, his poems reflecting the woodsy self-reliance, the Emersonian search for knowledge, that forms an appealing part of his character. He studs his poems with a geologist's lingua franca—*doab, schrund, tephra, lahar, cirque*—and has a cheerful disregard for the small formalities of English. Fortunately most of his wilder notions were corrected, between the proofs I read and the finished book, by some cigar-chewing copy editor of the old school, one who still cares for the distinction between "lay" and "lie" and has no love for idiosyncrasies like "fistfull" and "millenia" (though he missed the animal whose neck had been "ate out"). *Oh, man!* you can hear Snyder say, *don't be so uptight!* None of this would matter if the poems weren't like the disconnected thoughts of a man trying to make verse with magnets on a refrigerator door:

> *white-hot crumbling boulders lift and fly in a*
> *burning sky-river wind of*
> *searing lava droplet hail,*
> *huge icebergs in the storm, exploding mud,*
> *shoots out flat and rolls a swelling billowing*
> *cloud of rock bits,*
> *crystals, pumice, shards of glass*
> *dead ahead blasting away—*
> *a heavenly host of tall trees goes flat down*
> *lightning dances through the giant smoke.*

That's the volcano erupting, and it looks as if it erupted in Miss Purple Prose's eleventh-grade English class. The words couldn't have been thrown onto the page with more juvenile abandon if the volcano had hurled them there.

The reader is left with desultory scraps from journals, even when Snyder's not writing journals ("I'm 63 now & I'm on my way to pick up my ten-year-old stepdaughter and drive the car pool. / I just finished a five-page letter to the County Supervisors"). At one point he tells us, in case we're interested, that he's going to try an ostrich burger and then that he's busy eating it— "The Ostrich burger is delicious. It's big, with lots of lettuce, onions, hot mustard . . ." *Stop!* you want to say. The poor poems, when they can get a word in edgewise, would embarrass even a county supervisor:

> *Earth spirit please don't mind*
> *If cement trucks grind*
> *And plant spirits wait a while*
> *Please come back and smile.*

This compassionate, benign, grizzled patriarch, supporter of just causes, sensitive to the land around him, a Buddhist (more or less), is the sort of man you'd call if you had to overhaul a tractor engine or drag a cow out of the mud (he's also the sort who asks a mountain for help and thinks that it answers). If you want someone to write you a decent poem, however, you'd better look elsewhere. A lot of readers buy poetry books because they agree with the author's character or politics and like to be thought of as people who read such things—perhaps they don't mind too much when the writing has grown slovenly (a dozen or more poems end with a cute three-word tag like *twitchy pine boughs* or *velvet-dusty pigs*). Books like Gary Snyder's should come free in a box of granola.

Rita Dove

To read a lot of criticism these days, you'd think the most important thing about a poet was his ethnic identity or sexual proclivities and the most important thing about a poem was *its* ethnic identity or sexual proclivities. This is a recent notion, as well as a bad one; but it isn't bad because who our ancestors were and whom we sleep with have no consequences. (To treat people badly because their skin has a different hue, or because they don't share our lusts, or because they're lame, halt, or blind is a despicable way of behaving. It is also impolite.) The notion is bad because poems of identity offer only a narcissistic, needle's-eye view of the world—when poetry is used merely to build self-esteem, it's time to make Larkin required reading. Thank goodness Homer didn't go on about being blind and Ionian.

Even so, Rita Dove's *American Smooth* reminds us how important it is never to ignore the sins of the past or to pretend the past hasn't afflicted the present. Dove has a natural interest in the history of blacks in America, a history she has labored into verse. It's curious that it so often *seems* a labor. A long section of poems consists of accounts by black soldiers of their service in World War I. Unwelcome in the segregated American forces, they served overseas because France asked for them and there fought furiously and bravely. One poem, however, consists of eleven pages of diary entries about life aboard a troop ship; and for tedium it rivals building the Eiffel Tower out of matchsticks. Worse, the poet's note to the sequence bristles with resentment.

Blacks in America have a lot to be resentful about, but I'm not sure the poetry of resentment is the best way to deal with it. The scene is a country club, and some thoughtless white woman has just complimented Dove on her dress by telling her she looks "good in every color."

> *For once I was not the only*
> *black person in the room*
> *(two others, both male).*
> *I thought of Sambo; I thought*
> *a few other things, too,*
> *unmentionable here. Don't*
> *get me wrong: I've always loved*
> *my skin, the way it glows against*
> *citron and fuchsia, the difficult hues,*
> *but the difference I cause*
> *whenever I walk into a polite space*
> *is why I prefer grand entrances.*

"Don't/get me wrong" suggests the poet worries that we might think, for a moment, she's ashamed of being black. Something hidden and mortifying is touched here, but like those "unmentionable" things it's skated over in favor of a swish of indignation and a self-satisfied nod of triumph.

Very occasionally you get a hint of the angers and sharp-toothed motives that swim like great predators beneath the tranquil waters of these poems. Dove instead tries to fob the reader off with sentimental rubbish—say, about the heart: "I can't wear it/on my sleeve,/or tell you from/the bottom of it/how I feel." You read that and you know the price of saccharin just fell through the floor. Or perhaps you'd prefer some love couplets, tossed off seemingly on the spur of the moment:

I could choose any hero, any cause or age
And, sure as shooting arrows to the heart,
Astride a dappled mare, legs braced as far apart
As standing in silver stirrups will allow—
There you'll be, with furrowed brow
And chain mail glinting, to set me free:
One eye smiling, the other firm upon the enemy.

It's like something scribbled on the table of a medieval-theme restaurant, where men in armor are bashing away at each other a few feet from your table. The inflated language, the sloppy pun on "sure as shooting," the dappled mare, and that ridiculous smiling eye! Sir Walter Scott can take the blame for the props, but the ugly composition (almost every line desperate for its rhyme) and ungainly meter (now too many iambs, now too few) are all Dove's own.

No matter what subject she touches, it turns to lead in her hands: Salomé, Hattie McDaniel, chocolate, Adam and Eve, a drive-in, dance lessons. Dove rarely does more than what's expected (she's steady as a gyroscope and twice as dull, though always whirring away) and increasingly writes as if lecturing a class of third graders:

Don't
hold your breath. Don't hold
anything, just stop breathing.
Level the scene with your eyes. Listen.
Soft, now: squeeze.

Is that another love poem? Yes, about owning a handgun (Glock or Keltec seems to be the choice). If this conflicts with her liberal values, she makes no mention of it—then she writes in the voice of a bullet: "o aperture o light let me off / go off straight is my verb straight / my glory road." *My glory road*!

In her best work, the former poet laureate catches some residue of black experience; but she scarcely realizes that in herself lie the tensions that reveal the long sorrows of race in this country. Even when a poet doesn't trade in confessions, the reader wants some sense of the private world behind the mask. Dove's poems have become so superficial, so lacking in felt life, they might have been ordered from some poem sweatshop in a third-world country. After a series of banal commissioned poems, written to be carved on the backs of twelve marble chairs in a federal courthouse (Dove's poetry has invited more commissions than a corrupt police department), you wonder if this is what the end of her poetry will be: all public spirit and no private life.

Two Versions of *Gilgamesh*

The ancient heroes who slashed and burned their way into epic were the bully boys of their time, tearaways, real roarers, greedy and careless, their deeds so exaggerated they'd overwhelm any kernel of fact if we didn't have historical examples like Alexander and Caesar to remind us how much a man might accomplish without fiction. If Achilles and Odysseus, Beowulf and Gilgamesh never existed, they were lucky in their poets. Derrek Hines's knockabout version of *Gilgamesh* shakes some of the dust off a poem too often translated with white gloves (a 1946 version modestly rendered the dirty bits in Latin), as if simply by being the oldest of western epics it must be treated with the courtesy due some doddering relict wearing the family jewels. This is disastrous for that venerable antique, which can be made to sound more like a monumental inscription than a poem.

If there was once a king named Gilgamesh, he ruled the Sumerian city-state of Uruk nearly five thousand years ago (from Uruk the name Iraq is derived) and was worshiped as a god longer in his culture than the Holy Trinity has been in ours. The tales that accrued around him have come down to us in Sumerian, Akkadian, Babylonian, Elamite, Hurrian, and Hittite, the tablets that bore them salvaged from the great rubbish dumps of ruined cities across the Middle East. The standard text consists of eleven tablets (with a twelfth misfit), all of them damaged or fragmentary, in a version edited in Nineveh in the seventh century B.C. Anyone attempting to bring this old yarn to life has a lot of broken crockery on his hands.

Hines has thrown the cuneiform back onto the scrap heap and started fresh:

> Here is Gilgàmesh, king of Uruk:
> two-thirds divine, a mummy's boy,
> zeppelin ego, cock like a trip-hammer,
> and solid chrome, no-prisoners arrogance.
>
> Pulls women like beer rings.
> Grunts when puzzled.

> *A bully. A jock. Perfecto. But in love?—*
> *a moon-calf, and worse, thoughtful.*

Not all readers will care for a translation that takes such liberties ("two-thirds divine" violates any sensible genetics; but that's the ancient poet's fault, not the translator's), though Hines is hardly the first poet to retailor the past to the fashions of the present. Dryden long ago saw the value of what he called "imitation," where the translator aims, not for the vanities of fidelity, but for the violations of license. Hines's *Gilgamesh* is only the latest in a long line that descends from Samuel Johnson's "The Vanity of Human Wishes" and Pound's translations of "The Seafarer" and the Chinese poems in *Cathay* down to Robert Lowell's infamous *Imitations* and Christopher Logue's peculiar and muscular versions of the *Iliad*, which have carried the tradition farther than Dryden might have imagined.

Since Hines has learned many of Logue's virtues and a few of his vices (no one would want Logue's mannerisms to become the default style for the classics), you have to be prepared for a jazzy tone and language that careers slangily across the centuries. Here one of Gilgamesh's soldiers lodges a complaint during the campaign to cut down the cedars of Lebanon:

> *So, we figured, no snatch for medals in this caper.*
>
> *A month now, desert-yomping in full kit.*
> *Scorpion wind in the face, crotch rot, boils.*
> *Not helped by our great King, who wakes each morning*
> *from dreams like multiple car crashes.*

Yomping in full kit, for British squaddies, is what GI's call *humping full packs*. (American readers may find a few references bewildering, such as the "toff's precious Hooray Henrys"—this may be a good thing in a translation from Babylonian.) The language, though often hopped-up and bug-eyed, carries some of the strangeness of the shattered text.

At the outset Gilgamesh is a royal monster who takes full advantage of *jus primae noctae* (the right to sleep with a man's bride on his wedding night). The gods answer his subjects' pleas by creating a musclebound wild man, Enkidu, who is soon civilized by the sexual gymnastics of a temple prostitute—this suggests the Fall might have been more interesting if caused not by food but by sex (the original *Gilgamesh* sometimes reads like Akkadian porn).

Enkidu fights the king to a draw and they become great friends; but, after they kill the wizard Humbaba, who guards the famous cedars, and then for good measure the sacred bull of heaven (the heroes are like two WWF wrestlers on a tear), the gods decide that as punishment Enkidu must die. Afterward, in mourning, and in terror at his own mortality, Gilgamesh travels to the underworld; but the herb of youth he brings back is stolen by a snake. (The relations between *Gilgamesh* and Old Testament myths are a minor scholarly industry.) He must then prepare for his own death.

Hines will do most anything to get the reader's attention—though not as much as Logue, who introduced helicopters to the weaponry available in the *Iliad*. Point of view descends from on high to the common grunt; and the language has, not the priestly rhythms of a poem once sung to a lyre or intoned like prayer, not the panoply of tedious repetitions, but the density of modern poetry.

> *Euphrates' airy, fish-woven halls,*
> *a sleep of reed beds, the éclat of date palms,*
> *wind-glossed corn. And in the distance*
>
> *desert—the sun's loose gunpowder.*
> *Green rolls up*
> *and rasps along it like a tongue*
> *wetting sandpaper.*

Hines makes vivid what might have died as a dusty footnote: his temple prostitutes strut like fashion models, "striding down / the cat-walk of Uruk's high street / in the designer gowns of Paradise." The night is "soft-mouthed as a gundog," the sound of ghosts drinking blood like that of "surgical tape ripped off skin"; and a goddess "pulses into focus before him: // breasts taut as airships / from hangars nosing." The mannerisms are the manner here, but line by line you have a poem hauled fresh from the sands again.

Such radical revision loses much the old epic had to offer; yet even the King James Bible, with its learnèd committee of translators, had to make occasional accommodation to its own world, if it was not to lose the meat with the method. Indeed, it would have been interesting to see what the committee would have done with Gilgamesh, written in the same broad culture that produced the Old Testament and scattered with parallels to the Bible, including its own version of the Flood, which Hines unfortunately omits.

It's disconcerting to have a Gilgamesh who plays backgammon and drinks ouzo, who dresses in silks and apparently suffers the attentions of paparazzi; but then it is disconcerting to read in a history of Babylon that in 600 B.C. Nebuchadnezzar asphalted the streets. The past is stranger than we imagine; if a translation like *Gilgamesh* does not get us closer to the past as it was, it gets us closer to something almost more important—the past that must exist continually in the present. If you want Juvenal, you don't go to Johnson—you go to Johnson to see what the eighteenth century made of the second, what post-Augustan London thought of post-Augustan Rome. At best you find that the modern teases out some nuance asleep in the old lines, like Hines's evocation of Gilgamesh waiting for death, "swallowing this fist of fear in a quayside café/beside these old men/like rows of buttons waiting to be undone." When men try to update Shakespeare, what they usually get is Bowdler; when they try to modernize Homer's Achilles, they get Brad Pitt (Logue's *Iliad*, though scrappy and intermittently awful, is a fine exception). We are fortunate to have a new version of *Gilgamesh* that makes the ancient world another world altogether.

By contrast, Stephen Mitchell's earnest, forelock-tugging new version of the epic is homely as a mud fence, which shows how fidelity can make this gaudy and musclebound artifact merely workmanlike. Mitchell's translation, which has a longwinded high-schooler's introduction, drags a heavy sledge of notes; and his attempt at four-stress accentual meter is a foot-dragging failure. If you want the incidents Hines cuts in his fast-forward version and some of the nuances (or even contradictions) of behavior, you have to read Mitchell: in the original, Gilgamesh beats Enkidu in their wrestling match, and no army accompanies them in the attack on Humbaba, who is a terrible monster, not some distant ancestor of the Wizard of Oz. The beautiful Babylonian tale of the Flood is here, as is the full story of Gilgamesh in the underworld, which he reaches by ship, using three hundred punting poles! Though Mitchell's is more cheerfully vulgar than previous versions, other than those in Latin, he has no particular gift for language. His *Gilgamesh* might have been better translated by a team of U.N. bureaucrats.

Derek Walcott

Derek Walcott's *The Prodigal* is a valedictory book, the long poem of a man who has seen the world and been left with a handful of airline-ticket stubs.

For half a century Walcott has been one of the great stylists of English verse, in an age when style has been more and more a badge of shame, when sentences grow ever shorter and the confession of sins ever longer. The poem begins as a whistle-stop tour of cities and countries, dashing through Pennsylvania, New York, and Massachusetts, flitting now to Zermatt and Geneva, now Florence and Abruzzi, Pescara and Genoa, then to Spain, Germany, America again, Colombia, all before the poem is half spent—it's hard to keep track without an itinerary and a GPS device. This is a book of transit, of voluntary exile, of almost pathological restlessness, the travel conducted with a bored melancholy that infuses even the poet's wandering eye, for this is also a book of erotic liaisons, sly glances, closet desires—in short, of wanting to screw anything that walks. As a man ages, his romantic opportunities shorten with his odds. Walcott seems at times a character in Henry James, waiting and waiting for his moment, until he realizes the moment has passed.

The prodigal son "wasted his substance with riotous living," according to St. Luke, but at last returned home to be fêted as someone dead returned to life. The divided racial heritage of St. Lucia, Walcott's home island, shadows his uncomfortable and wary relation to the traditions of English poetry. To what extent, his poems have asked, is a man born in the colonies a traitor if he adopts the language and literature of his masters? Walcott has instead become a "vague pilgrim," never at home even at home, a man for whom all frontiers become one.

The poet has never flinched from what he saw as his duty to the tradition; reading his long, elaborate sentences is like watching a master goldsmith fashion a coronation crown and decorate it with rubies, diamonds, and amethysts in bold array.

> Chasms and fissures of the vertiginous Alps
> through the plane window, meadows of snow
> on powdery precipices, the cantons of cumuli
> grumbling or closing, gasping falls of light
> a steady and serene white-knuckled horror
> of speckled white serrations, inconceivable
> in repetition, spumy avalanches
> of forgetting cloud, in the wrong heaven . . .

Cantons of cumuli! The passage is lovely, but the sentence is scarcely begun. On and on it goes—in this new book Walcott does what he has always done, except now he overdoes it with an old man's desperation. The figures are as boldly formed as ever; but when reading them you think, "Didn't a bird *arrow* by just a few pages ago? Hasn't Walcott often described the ocean as like *tinfoil* or glistening water as like minted *coins*? Haven't the island days often been compared to hot *zinc*?" The sentences seem endless; and, if the reader on occasion gets tangled in their complex syntax, so at times does the writer.

This long poem reads like a pendant to Walcott's precocious verse autobiography *Another Life* (1973), published when he was just forty-three. (*The Prodigal* is what the poet of Dove Cottage might have called *The Postlude*.) Walcott is remarkably honest about his priapic instincts (he even manages to give a woman soldier his bedroom gaze), though he succeeds only in making himself ridiculous:

> *Past the stalagmites of the Duomo*
> *the peaches of summer are bouncing*
> *on the grids of the Milanese sidewalks*
> *in halters cut close to the coccyx.*
> *I look and no longer sigh for the impossible,*
> *panting over a cupidinous coffee*
> *like an old setter that has stopped chasing pigeons.*

The *peaches of summer*? Oh, you think, he means *breasts*. But what is that setter doing panting over a *cupidinous coffee*? Too often, as the cities come and go like buses, the poem lounges there, drowsy and fractured, the buttery lines of Walcott's descriptions so rich they're worse than a diet of chocolate icing. Besieged by the deaths of strangers, of friends, of family, the poet already feels like a "name cut on a wall that soon/from the grime of indifference became indecipherable." This has the doomed grace of lines by Keats; but then it's back to the flood of purple passages, the gouts of adjectives and fatty verbs, until the poem becomes a kind of numbing mad mutter. There was a time when Walcott gave his style point, a time when his poems didn't just finger his memories like fragments of the True Cross.

Czeslaw Milosz

The death of Czeslaw Milosz at the age of ninety-three deprived us of one of the most interesting exiles of the twentieth century. Born in Lithuania to a

Polish family that once owned great estates, as a boy he traveled with his parents across Russia and Siberia (his father was a highway engineer for the czar's army). After university he lived in Paris, where he came under the influence of his uncle Oscar, a French poet of an eschatological and mystical temper. (Milosz notes wryly that, when he received the Nobel, some French newspapers wrote "that it had been given to the wrong Milosz.") During World War II, the young poet served as a radio operator, after the fall of Poland living in Nazi-occupied Warsaw, where he wrote for the resistance. He later became a minor diplomat in Washington and then in Paris, where he sought political asylum in 1951. From 1960 he taught at Berkeley, though not until the late sixties were translations of his poetry available in English.

Being an exile under such conditions hardly compares to the banishment of Ovid to the Black Sea; yet Milosz's poetry, darkened by war and memories of the Holocaust, more and more took on an elegiac cast, until in this book he is surrounded by throngs of ghosts, like Odysseus in the underworld. The question that troubles him is the source of evil. As a skeptical believer, a Christian with a rational tongue (his faith tended to be sturdy but gentle, unlike Emily Dickinson's barely controlled passions and distastes), he could not help echoing the Epicureans: "If God is all-powerful, he can allow all this only if he is not good." This made his poems a fruitless search for redemption and consolation.

The poems in *Second Space* at times seem muted by their journey from Polish. For the latter part of his career, the poet was fortunate to have as his translator the talented Robert Hass, whose own poetic gifts allow him to ride herd on Milosz's work without feeling it necessary to put his brand on every line. The best of the poems offer visions with a retrospective burden:

> *An English horn, a drum, a viola making music*
> *In a house on a hill amidst forests in autumn.*
> *A large view from there onto bends of the river.*
>
> *I still want to correct this world,*
> *Yet I think mostly of them, and they have all died.*
> *Also about their unknown country.*
> *Its geography, says Swedenborg, cannot be transferred to maps.*

Translation, if we're lucky, leads us out of the conventions and proprieties in which our own poetry is mired (poetry in another language suffers conventions, too; but at least they're not ours). A poem in translation is like a newspaper report of a ballet—the only thing lost is the dance. Even when a translation has been cast in the same form, it may have different weight or bearing—Dante's terza rima is nothing like terza rima in English. It's surprising, therefore, how much of Milosz's personality—his scratchy wit, his wry pessimism, his joviality ("I should be dead already, but there is work to do")—comes through the baffles and cofferdams of English. For the poor translator, finding the equivalents for a foreign language can be like wandering through a fabric store trying to match the pattern of the sofa Aunt Matilda reupholstered in 1937.

The shorter poems here often consult rather than confront problems of faith and belief—they're mild-mannered, meditative poems that perhaps wish to be darker and danker. The book ends with four long poems, two so tangled in religious themes they're like cats lost in a great ball of yarn. The others cut deeper into conscience, one a portrait of Uncle Oscar, the depressive romantic who once shot himself in the heart but survived to become an honored French poet. Belabored with footnotes, which prove surprisingly helpful in setting the poem in history and explaining references that might otherwise be lost (opacity is rarely a virtue in translation), the poem is an homage to a great spirit, the "master of alchemy" from whom Milosz received his sense of vocation. As the younger poet counts his debts, the poem turns rather dry and Swedenborgian, echoing the only rational thing one can say about the past (as well as the only irrational thing), Goethe's words: *"Respect! Respect! Respect!"*

The final poem opens with a witty portrait of Orpheus at the gates of hell:

> *Standing on flagstones of the sidewalk at the entrance to Hades*
> *Orpheus hunched in a gust of wind*
> *That tore at his coat, rolled past in waves of fog,*
> *Tossed the leaves of the trees. The headlights of cars*
> *Flared and dimmed in each succeeding wave.*

Here the problems of faith and trust that have harried Milosz find their way to antique myth. For a man who seemed to hear footsteps behind him most of his life, there is a terrible pathos when Orpheus turns, having led Eurydice almost out of hell, and no one is there.

Verse Chronicle

The Great American Desert

John Ashbery

John Ashbery was born when Pola Negri was still box office, yet his poems are more in touch with the American demotic—the tongue most of us speak and few of us write—than any near-octogenarian has a right to be. He has published more than a thousand pages in the last fifteen years, almost twice as many as Wallace Stevens wrote in half a century—and Stevens was no slouch. Ashbery's poems are like widgets manufactured to the most peculiar specifications and in such great numbers the whole world widget market has collapsed.

Where Shall I Wander (a title lifted from the nursery rhyme "Goosey, goosey, gander") begins with a typical piece of Ashberyian folderol:

> *We were warned about spiders, and the occasional famine.*
> *We drove downtown to see our neighbors. None of them were home.*
> *We nestled in yards the municipality had created,*
> *reminisced about other, different places—*
> *but were they? Hadn't we known it all before?*

Ashbery's poems revel in such intimations of disaster (they're a tease without a strip), a disaster curiously similar to the nameless wars and borders and betrayals of Auden's early poems. In the middle of these Egyptlike plagues, punctuated by small touches of absurdity and big doses of nonsense, the reader may wake wondering if he hasn't read this poem before. Almost all Ashbery's poems, those dead-ends of déjà vu, offer the dream of meaning endlessly deferred—the deception finally becomes the expectation. "There's a sucker born every minute," said a banker involved in the hoax of the Cardiff giant, and in Ashbery there's a sucker born every line.

When the contract between writer and reader is so fragile, the poet can pretend to fulfill it with no more than the chaff and loose ends of sentences, fragments that never grow up to be wholes. In general, the more of Ashbery there is, the less there is (the worst poems here are prosy and interminable). Much of the book, despite its local fireworks, is the exhausted repetition of his old vaudeville routines:

> Attention, shoppers. From within the inverted
> commas of a strambotto, seditious whispering
> watermarks this time of day. Time to get out
> and, as they say, about. Becalmed on a sea
> of inner stress, sheltered from cold northern breezes,
> idly we groove: Must have
> been the time before this, when we all moved
> in schools, a finny tribe, and this way
> and that the caucus raised its din.

And so on and on. Here we have the embrace of American idiom, whether high-stepping or lowbrowed (Ashbery's range is as broad as Whitman's), the steep descent of tone, the enjambment almost as flirtatious as Milton's. Ashbery offers some things few other poets do (including the patented double take and stop-on-a-dime *volte-face*) while being incapable of offering what most think absolutely necessary. This makes him not just a slapstick artist for our fallen times—no, it means that when you read Ashbery you have to forget much of what you know about reading poetry. You have to take satisfaction where pleasures are rarely given and never let yourself wish for what isn't there. (There's so much that isn't there.) Ashbery undermines many of the axioms on which poetry rests—he's smiling, not like Carroll's cat, but like Schrödinger's, neither dead nor alive but always already both.

Some of the most engaging passages here comment archly on parties or clothes. They make you wish that, instead of writing poems like a man with an attention-deficit disorder, Ashbery were capable of writing a novel as long as *Remembrance of Things Past*. Though sometimes it's a perverse pleasure to see large issues reduced to candy floss, there's a devious moral world, largely untapped, beneath his nonsense—Ashbery is a man not afraid to write whatever rattles into his head (if he had an internal censor, one logical as a lawyer, he'd lose all that devil-may-care charm). Alas, it's no use asking this poet to be something he isn't—and sometimes no use trying to like the something he is. When you read his poems, you sigh with pleasure to see a thing so odd done with such panache, such savoir-faire, such élan, such . . . well, whatever the word is, it would be French, in order to apply to that ultimate boulevardier of American poetry, Mr. Ashbery.

Ashbery has inherited the mode of attention that gave us Baudelaire but also Walter Benjamin's archives project and Roland Barthes's *Writing Degree Zero*. He finds America in its hither-thither diction, much as Whitman (who scrawled down examples of American slang in his notebooks) did in its American scenes. An outsider sees things too common for us to notice or too strange for us to admit; and for his whole career Ashbery has been an American outsider, though a much honored one. He is now rapidly going, even so, from elder statesman to venerable antique (as once he went from Peck's Bad Boy to elder statesman)—all you can do with such Victorian whatnots is dust them off once in a while and wonder what people ever saw in them.

Dean Young

The quality of whimsy is not strained. It falleth from Ashbery like the gentle rain—and it falleth on a lot of young poets now, students in the School of Goofball Poetics, boys who cut their teeth on Ashbery and Charles Simic and James Tate and now show little interest in any poems written before Dada came to town. Dean Young's sixth book, *Elegy on Toy Piano*, is fairly representative of the younger generation, full to the gills with gewgaws and thingamabobs and dojiggers; but one tradition embraced is a lot of tradition rejected.

> *What happened?*
> *shouts the hero rushing into the study room.*
> *Mung magph naagh, replies the heroine*
> *still in her gag. Insert flap A*
> *into slot A. X-rays inconclusive.*
> *Want to hear me count to 1,000 by 17s?*
> *Beep hexagonal, my puppeteer.*
> *I hate your dog.*

Huh? Well, now that you mention it, fella, I don't want to hear your times table, after all. Not every Young poem is quite this scatterbrained, but he uses non sequiturs the way a snake uses mice. (Not that non sequiturs seem to like *him* very much.) Reading Young is like watching a stand-up comic on a cable channel, unsure of his audience, staring at the crowd like a gazelle surrounded by a pack of hyenas and bombing like a B-17. The problem with comedy of this trivial sort is that, rather than shock or provoke, it manages merely to irritate (the reader is reduced to muttering *Uh-oh* or *Ho-hum*). A poet who wants to get laughs begins to write for the joke, and when he can't nail that he just lays down a laugh track.

Poets find it hard to be serious now, unless they're writing about their lives (on which they tend to be all too grave, as if working up a pathology report). At best, Young's poems mock themselves as well as poets of more serious temper. At worst, they're the poems of someone who took a mail-order course in surrealism:

> *One walking a lobster on a leash.*
> *One who knew the functions of 14 different forks.*
> *Something there is that does not love*
> *a constructor of roller coasters.*
> *When Lung Zu looked at the wall, he saw no wall.*
> *When Po Chu walked east, she also walked west.*
> *The symphony opens with heroic proclamation disclaimed by a*
> *   hush of liquid paper.*

Forever late like the White Rabbit, such helter-skelter lines seem in a headlong hurry to be elsewhere. In one poem, Young mentions setting an alarm clock for five A.M., "to write fast without thinking"; and a lot of these poems must have been written that way. He grooves along like a scat singer, not really caring if he's blithering (not caring is, after all, the point). Sometimes his poems have delightfully loopy premises (one consists of a hundred true/false statements; another juggles the complicated mathematics involved in liking a married couple), but sooner or later they run out of steam—he's not a poet who knows when he's overstayed his welcome.

Young's poems want so badly to be loved, after a while you're willing to buy them a ticket to Lapland, just to be rid of their shining, eager faces. On the rare occasion that this poet does think about something serious, he jokes about it for a couple of lines, then scurries off in embarrassment. *Elegy on Toy Piano* shows what happens when a poet inherits a difficult, contradictory tradition (the uses of surrealism are almost as various as the uses of lyric) and can make nothing out of it but trash.

Jorie Graham

Jorie Graham loves big ideas the way small boys like big trucks. Her books start with some notion just the far side of grandiose ("What does it mean," the dust jacket trumpets, "to be fully present in a human life? How—in the face of the carnage of war . . . —does one retain one's ability to be both present and responsive?") and end up grinding the Himalayas down to gravel. In *Overlord*, her tenth book, she visits Omaha Beach, attempting to see beyond the placid sands—where children play along the shore, where the rusting landing craft have become tide pools—the indiscriminate slaughter of June 6, 1944:

> *others meant for Easy Green or Easy Red also thrown at Dog—mostly*
>   *all still*
> *alive—off-schedule—including the*
> *sweepers—all dragged down, freezing, waves huge—meant to land*
> *where gun emplacements were less thick and channels between lines*
>   *of tracer-fire*
> *could be* read through *the surface of*
>   *the beach*

This odd shorthand—historical flotsam and jetsam swept up along the tide line of verse (she employed no fewer than seven researchers, though she still can't tell a bomb squadron from a bomb group)—recreates some of the frenzy, the helpless panic, of those first moments of D-Day (the code name for the invasion was Overlord). Yet the bullying italics and the knowing use of "reading," as if the sands were simply another text, drag us away from the helpless soldiers (the most telling passages in these poems are snippets from their letters and interviews) to the mastering presence, the overlording, of the poet herself.

For a long while, Graham's poetry has suffered this grotesque immodesty. No matter where her poems start, sooner or later their subject becomes the poet's hyperkinetic awareness of her own senses (reading some of her poems is like tripping on LSD); and this too easily turns into the blank stare and lapel grabbing of the quietly mad—"I'm actually staring up at/you, you know, right here, right from the pool of this page./Don't worry where else I am, I am here."

Graham has reduced the poetry of meditation to navel gazing; the minute attention to her yammering thoughts, to the violence of her vision (at one point she gets down to photon level), merely reworks, in stilted fashion, the stream of consciousness Dorothy Richardson pursued in the twenties. If Graham had concentrated on the accident and contingency of war, had honored the men whose deaths she casually invokes, *Overlord* might have become the sort of serious meditation that produced Geoffrey Hill's *The Mystery of the Charity of Charles Péguy* (1983).

Graham is so busy taking everything back to first principles, hurling Plato and Zeno into the breach, she's in danger of forgetting that poems embrace dullness only at great risk.

> [when your work sells for][millions of dollars][you][can]
> indulge yourself. You can paint to prove that painting is dead. You can
> paint as a true believer in painting. [Oh I should][I really should][you said
> it was there][truly there][I only had to take the photograph]
> [and that only one thing exists][no . . . not death!][this!]

In the wrack and wreckage of her current work (did she buy a box of brackets at a discount?), it's hard to remember the difficult pleasures of *Erosion* (1983) and *The End of Beauty* (1987), high-voltage moments in the poetry of the eighties. Unfortunately, the powers a poet harnesses for a book or two may eventually prove so unruly that what was once an imagination in tension becomes a stampeding coach and six.

Graham's lack of any sense of proportion reduces the argument of *Overlord* to something like "On the one hand, my kitty has AIDS; on the other, a whole lot of guys died on Omaha Beach." (If you think the poet can stoop no lower, that her high-mindedness can't be more unintentionally hilarious, you haven't read the poem in which she buys a homeless man a meal and practically kills him.) Halfway through the book, the poor soldiers have been forgotten; and Graham, like a mini-U.N., begins deliberating on the idea of nations:

> Time of the flags is long past—how
> strange—a Flag! Of what? Are you a
> nation, you, you there. Are you in a nation. Is one in you?

Are you at war or at peace or are war and peace
playing their little game over your dead body?

Such hectoring, humorless lines, trite as tar paper, are worse than the propaganda Marianne Moore wrote during World War II. For years, Graham has scoured the bushes for finches, has pried loose every stray barnacle she has come across; there was long hope that these scattered minutiae (one man's junk being another man's scientific collection) might one day prove the coral accretion of a grand poem or two. Alas, the method has long since become her meaning: she scrapes and shuffles and observes her grains of sand, but in the end all she has to show for it is the scraping and shuffling.

Almost everything Graham writes offers the swagger of emotion, pretentiousness by the barrelful, and a wish for originality that approaches vanity—she's less a poet than a Little Engine that Could, even when it Can't. If I close her later books disappointed, it's never a disappointment in their boldness but rather in her inability to bring these huge engineering projects to successful conclusion. Will that stop her? Like hell it will!

Kevin Young

There's this skirt, dig, named Delilah Redbone, see, and this dick in Shadowtown named Jones, and the sap falls for her. The frail's maiden name was Trouble; and the dick, his middle name is Danger. If you've never gotten your fill of alibis, gunsels, snitches, paybacks, hideouts, and hooch, Kevin Young drags in the whole cast and a police van of props in *Black Maria*, his homage to hard-boiled fiction and the great *films noirs* of the forties. The trappings of a new genre often refashion an old one (though in new feathers even a good poet may look ridiculous). Almost two decades ago, Nicholas Christopher's detective novel in verse, *Desperate Characters* (1987), showed how impossible the genre can be for the dilettante; but then almost a century and a half ago another amateur proved that brilliant things could be done—what is *The Ring and the Book* but a detective novel? (Some might claim *Paradise Lost* is a police procedural.)

Young, whose last book was a misdirected and sentimental reworking of the blues, is an ambitious young poet with quirky ideas. *Black Maria* is meant to be a film, its sections, called "reels," composed of poems that straggle down the page half starved for punctuation:

I didn't have a rat's chance.
Soon as she walked in in

That skin of hers
violins began. You could half hear

The typewriters jabber
as she jawed on: fee, find, me,

poor, please.
Shadows & smiles, she was.

Strong scent of before-rain

Her pinstripe two-lane
legs, her blackmail menthol.

The occasional phrase reveals what delights await a genre transformed; but the rest is jazzed-up jawing and sidelong remarks that niggle their way toward wisecracks ("pinstripe two-lane/legs" must refer, clumsily, to the dark seam in old nylons). Young loves wordplay more than any contemporary except Paul Muldoon; he'll go to great lengths to fetch a pun, and even greater ones to drag back a bad joke. The poems here are addicted to internal rhymes, winsome glances at the reader, and a diction that slides from the most perfumed poeticism to ghetto dialect (the language at times suggests that Jones and Redbone are black, though it's not entirely clear).

Such frenzied invention might be just the thing to invigorate contemporary poetry, which often can't see past the third-rate traumas of private life (the vampire in Sylvia Plath turned out to be—Plath). Think how Auden's urban-renewal projects unsettled the thirties and forties—"Letter to Lord Byron," "New Year Letter," "For the Time Being," and "The Sea and the Mirror" razed some of the settled assumptions of modernism. Young has seen that *noir* can capture, as critics have been saying for decades, the anxieties of the age—and what age is more anxious than ours?

Young's *vers noir*, alas, has none of the suspense of film or novel. Narrated in a slack-jawed style where all characters talk alike, it meanders along without much by way of plot, the incidents democratically clichéd, the denizens proud to be stereotypes, only the language working overtime. Young is devoted to his dumb jokes; and by the time you've been sledge-hammered by "my entrenched coat," a "well-minxed martini," "here comes the bribe," "two eggs,/over queasy," an "ashtray full of butts/& maybes," "she played/soft to get," and "case clothed" (all right, I admit a fondness for "older ladies // . . . thought his shinola // didn't stink"), you're punch-drunk and ready to cry "Uncle!" You might forgive as merely high spirits such punishing punning, such quarrelsome quibbles; but the poet's archness falls prey to far too much blowsy sentiment (genre is doing a lot more for Young than Young is doing for genre): a can "whose jagged lid//opens your hand/as if charity," "smelling of catharsis/& cheap *ennui*." Bullets are made of lead, and so is the repartee.

Black Maria is set in the thirties or early forties (there are references to a tommy gun and a decoder ring, one that might come in handy for deciphering the poet's system of capitalization), but somehow the modern age of the bikini (a word first recorded in 1947), the Saturday night special (1968), and paparazzi (1981) keeps sidling in. Then there are the wobbly writing, the misdemeanors of spelling and grammar, the dog's dinner of punctuation, the dialect that often goes on the lam. As the story inches forward, repeating some scenes as if we hadn't gotten the idea, the whodunit becomes the who gives a damn? After some two hundred pages, though we're no closer to knowing these characters (or having any idea what's going on by way of plot), there's a passage of science fiction that seems to have fallen out of another novel on the paperback rack.

Young has tried so hard to make this a tour de force, he's forgotten, not just the ontology that makes *film noir* so haunting, but the suspense that makes it entertaining. There seems no world beneath the clamoring surface of his language, which lacks the philosophy of form on which genre depends. This giddy be-bop poet hasn't yet found the right back alley for his gifts.

Ted Kooser

Ted Kooser is a prairie sentimentalist who writes poems in an American vernacular so corn-fed you could raise hogs on it. Kooser never met a word he didn't like, unless it was a long one, or one derived from Latin, or Greek, or French—in the new poems of *Delights & Shadows*, which recently won the Pulitzer Prize, as well as the older ones in *Flying at Night*, he stands for a foursquare, hidebound American provincialism that, by gum, has every right to write poems and, by golly, means to write them, too. His poems tend to be short, dying for air, afraid to do more than tell you what happened on the porch, or right out the window, or maybe, just once, down the block.

William Carlos Williams may be responsible for the strain of American individualism that, in our poetry, took the multitudes of Walt Whitman and squeezed them into a shoe box (think of the mop-haired words Whitman loved, not just foreign but American, too). It seems odd that poets should be drawn to plain-talking yokelism in a country clapped together out of immigrant ways and migrant tongues, but it doesn't take long for a country to establish its own traditions and begin to hate everybody else's. In Williams, and Creeley, and Kooser, you see the wish to make poetry out of the American language, meaning any word that can be spoken down at the corner grocery without making the clerk furrow his brow (when Kooser gets stuck for an adjective, he slaps in "old" and keeps on going, so after a while he's got old men, old ladies, old dogs, old moles, old coats, old stoves, old snow, old thunder, old No Hunting signs, and much old else). It doesn't matter that the grocery is now a Starbucks and the clerk is called a barista.

Kooser wants a poetry anyone can read without shame and understand without labor, because he thinks poetry has too long been in the hands of poets who "go out of their way to make their poems difficult if not downright discouraging." This would come as a surprise to Shakespeare and Milton, Pope and Browning, and other poets who thought poetry was for those who loved it enough to spend time educating themselves—indeed, who felt that learning to read poems was itself an education. (Folks like Kooser want to render Shakespeare or the Bible in kitchen-sink English, without a difficulty or a discouragement in sight.)

The current poet laureate, like many of his countrymen, doesn't like anything that seems tough going. (It's fortunate he isn't in charge of teaching music, which has all those pesky notes.) Kooser prefers a poem whose meaning can be plucked from a dry streambed like a nugget of gold.

A Glimpse of the Eternal

Just now,
a sparrow lighted
on a pine bough
right outside
my bedroom window

and a puff
of yellow pollen
flew away.

It's not much of a fight, but the monosyllables beat the disyllables hands down. There's nothing awful about a poem that ends in mystic nothingness (at times you feel Kooser practices a kind of prairie Zen), slathered in sentiment like corn on the cob with butter; but, to outdo it, the next poet off the farm will have to write in grunts.

Maybe you'd like to get into this poetry racket yourself. Kooser's *The Poetry Home Repair Manual* is full of down-home charm and genial misinformation (the poet laureate is folksy as an old rain barrel). He dispenses dollops of homespun wisdom to folks who want to write poems but have never had the gumption to try—they've been scared off by, of all people, poets themselves, who apparently spend most of their time advancing their careers and worrying about literary critics and making their poems so tangled up that, well, they're just nonsense to an ordinary Joe: "most of us learned in school that finding the meaning of a poem is way too much work, like cracking a walnut and digging out the meat." If Shakespeare knocked on his door for advice, Kooser would scratch his head and say, "Why, Bill, I guess these *look* like poems, but they're way too much like walnuts for me." Among all the poets of the past, who inspired our poet laureate? Whom does he use as an example? Why, Walter de la Mare!

For Kooser, poetry's main selling point is that it doesn't have any rules, because rules are apparently very bad things to have. He doesn't much like rhyme and meter (he doesn't like the word "prosody," either, because it "sounds so stuffy"). Still, I'm always eager to learn how to write poems, so I opened the *Home Repair Manual* at random and got some important advice: "Say a poet writes, 'She had eyes like a chicken.' Presto! A chicken pops into your mind." And, presto, a chicken *did* pop into my mind! Why, it was simple as that! But things soon got a bit more complicated, and I began to wonder if this metaphor and simile business wasn't harder than it was cracked up to be. A couple of paragraphs later, the poet complained, "You know what I'm talking about. We've already got a lot of chickens and a couple of washing machines on the table." And, presto! there *were* a lot of chickens and a couple of washing machines on the table, clucking and sloshing away, so I turned to another page. There I found Kooser—I imagined him whittling away at a stick all the while—comparing the words of a poem to a bunch of ham cubes on a styrofoam tray, covered in shrink-wrap. And, presto! . . .

The odd thing is, on rare occasions Kooser writes as if he knows more about poems than he lets on. A widow speaks:

> How his feet stunk in the bed sheets!
> I could have told him to wash,
> but I wanted to hold that stink against him.
> The day he dropped dead in the field,
> I was watching.
> I was hanging up sheets in the yard,
> and I finished.

Though the poem is unambitious in the virtuous, Calvinist way Kooser admires, there's a darkness here that Frost would have recognized.

The prairies were once so lonesome and dreary and treeless that men called them the Great American Desert. A hundred and fifty years later, they're growing lonesome once more, and the unspoken subject of Kooser's poetry is the gradual depopulation of the Great Plains. There has always been emptiness and madness in those small towns (Kooser was a life insurance executive—the one thing such an executive knows about is death), and also the silent desperation that leads to Kooser's whimsies about, say, mice abandoning a newly ploughed field, dragging tiny carts and carrying miniature lanterns. It's a pity that these strange, unsettling poems were all written more than twenty years ago. There are a couple of disturbing narrative poems in his new volume (Kooser's real gift may be for narrative), but everything else is straight as a rail fence and just as wooden, too. Before he let plain speech become its own tyranny, before he started worrying about "poetry cops" intent on enforcing the "rules," he showed signs of becoming a poet who knew something about cruelty and had a retrospective melancholy eye. Then he decided he'd be better off chewing plug tobacco and selling straw hats to tourists.

Richard Wilbur

In the past, I have written with such pleasure on Richard Wilbur's elegant and well-mannered verse that perhaps I may be forgiven for not cracking a full bottle of champagne across the bow of his latest *Collected Poems*. Wilbur has added a dozen new poems, as well as the contents of *Mayflies* (2000), to the *New and Collected Poems* of eighteen years ago (he has also provided, like sweepings, a few show lyrics and his verse for children). About the best that can be said of the new poems is that they are reminiscent of Wilbur's late Frostian style and impressive poems for any octogenarian to write. Here are houses seen at night in Key West:

> *Yet each façade is raked by the strange glare*
> *Of halogen, in which fantastic day*
> *Veranda, turret, balustraded stair*
> *Glow like the settings of some noble play.*
> . . . .
> *A dog-tired watchman in that mirador*
> *Waits for the flare that tells of Troy's defeat,*
> *And other lofty ghosts are heard, before*
> *You turn into a narrow, darker street.*
>
> *There, where no glow or glare outshines the sky,*
> *The pitch-black houses loom on either hand*
> *Like hulks adrift in fog, as you go by.*
> *It comes to mind that they are built on sand,*
>
> *And that there may be drama here as well,*
> *Where so much murk looks up at star on star:*
> *Though, to be sure, you cannot always tell*
> *Whether those lights are high or merely far.*

This is the sort of thing Wilbur does well on a good day and on a bad one does so half-heartedly it calls the whole enterprise into question. The quiet intelligence of these lines—the calm unfolding of their perceptions—looks so easy anyone should be able to do it; and almost no one can. I love the reference to the watch fires that begin *Agamemnon*, love those houses drifting along in the fog like mysterious ships, love the reminder that the houses are built on sand; but the end, however quietly it invokes Frost's "Desert Places," seems muddled and listless. It's curious that John Ashbery, who is only a few years younger, still seems our contemporary, while Wilbur sounds like an old fussbudget sorry he threw out his last pair of spats.

A year ago American poetry, very briefly, possessed two centenarians, Richard Eberhart and Carl Rakosi. Rakosi has since died, but this year there will be another, Stanley Kunitz. As far as I know, no country has ever been able to boast of so many centenarians among its poets; and I suspect we will see many more (I'm not sure whether this trend is scary or not—what Keats was able to accomplish in four or five years is quite beyond what most poets can do in eighty). I trust that Richard Wilbur will be writing poems for a long while to come, and that some will be better than the new poems here. His *Collected Poems*, which includes poems so ornate Fabergé would have wept, deserves to be on the bookshelf of any serious reader.

The State with the Prettiest Name

The names of the American states—those pioneer hopes, homage stained with arrogance or contempt—have long since lost the furtive tang of accident. They have become what they never could be at first, inevitable. Think how many pay dubious respect to the natives slaughtered, driven off, forced onto agencies (as reservations once were called), or who, having no immunity against smallpox or measles, did not survive the encounter with trapper or trader: Arkansas, Illinois, Indiana, Kansas, Massachusetts, Missouri, North and South Dakota, Oklahoma, Utah, with perhaps fifteen more taken from Indian words. Think of the names that courted the favor of kings or queens (Maryland, Virginia, North and South Carolina, Georgia, Louisiana) or acknowledged a founder's father (Pennsylvania) or a founding father (Washington). As soon as a thing is named, it begins to acquire associations that divide it from what it was named for. Who thinks now of Hampshire, Jersey, or York?

Of all these, can "Florida" really be the prettiest? If so, it will always be so, no matter how overrun with shopping malls and pasteboard houses it becomes. Elizabeth Bishop's was the Florida of the late thirties, though—undeveloped, larval, not yet emerging from the 1925 crash of the land boom that ruined John Berryman's father. This was the South beyond the South, a land with an atmosphere no less seductive than the gauzy, hand-colored views of Egypt, or Samarkand, or Japan, all sites once of Western reverie and bemusement. Depression Florida was still in touch with the days when Henry Flagler, one of the founders of Standard Oil, reorganized and extended the state's East Coast rail lines, having already started to build his giant mirage-like hotels, the Disney Worlds of their day.

During his American tour in 1904–1905, Henry James felt he had to see that peninsula of the "velvet air, the extravagant plants, the palms, the oranges, the cacti, the architectural fountain, the florid local monument, the cheap and easy exoticism." He stayed, almost as a matter of course, at Flagler's Ponce de León in St. Augustine. This grandiose example of "Moorish" architecture was otherwise as up-to-date as the Tiffany glass with which it was filled or the poured concrete from which it was made. Rockefellers and Vanderbilts trained south in private railway cars, when Florida was the winter destination of those who summered in Newport or beside Long Island Sound (*The Age of Innocence* has its St. Augustine scenes). Henry Plant, another railroad baron, built a verandah onto his Tampa Bay Hotel more majestic than the Grand Union's more famous one in Saratoga. Plant's Moorish extravaganza saw, in its heyday, performances by Sarah Bernhardt, Nellie Melba, and Anna Pavlova. Surrounding everything was that air of strangeness, of otherness, of things newly seen and yet always known, a place slightly hostile to human presence. Normally the most buttoned up of writers, James comically grasped after images adequate to what he had seen: "I found myself loving, quite fraternally, the palms, which had struck me at first, for all their human-headed gravity, as merely dry and taciturn, but which became finally as sympathetic as so many rows of puzzled philosophers, dishevelled, shock-pated, with the riddle of the universe." The flora's oddity, its vacant and humid sulkiness, its erotic silkiness, had fascinated and appalled the first explorers. Elizabeth Bishop might have understood:

> *The state with the prettiest name,*
> *the state that floats in brackish water,*
> *held together by mangrove roots*
> *that bear while living oysters in clusters,*
> *and when dead strew white swamps with skeletons,*
> *dotted as if bombarded, with green hummocks*
> *like ancient cannon-balls sprouting grass.*
>
> ("Florida")

Portraits of Florida, its beauty almost too beautiful, often risk a shallow, shoreline prettiness, the preciousness of the postcard, whose penny purpose is always to incite a twinge of jealousy. Bishop's poem instead recalls the "brackish water," the skeletons of dead mangroves, swamps pummeled as if by cannon. Her poem contains people only at its edges: those "ancient cannon-balls," though merely a simile, have the memory of conquest behind them (her "green hummocks" mark her as a tourist—the locals call them *hammocks*); the turtle skulls have "round eye-sockets/twice the size of a man's";

the lists of shells and alligator calls are those of a naturalist; in the "gray rag of rotted calico," in the very mention of "obbligatos" or a "post-card," there is evidence of an absence. This is Bishop's characteristic strategy, to push the center to the margins (making more intense what cannot be seen, merely implied). Civilization, already encroaching acre by acre on a prehistoric Florida, here just nibbles at the borders.

In Bishop's day (she lived in Key West off and on from 1936 to 1949), primeval nature had already been half destroyed. Today you have to go farther to see it; yet, even in my sprawling north Florida town, cattle graze beside shopping malls, sandhill cranes stalk the university feed lot, flocks of ibises and wood storks browse the mall retention-ponds, and every body of water bigger than a bathtub seems to boast its alligator—glowering, patient, inhuman. When an alligator has seen enough of you, has decided you are larger than its appetite, it sinks back into its watery home with an air of condescension.

William Bartram, tramping through Florida in the 1770s, mentioned that the "noise of the crocodiles kept me awake the greater part of the night" (he used "crocodile" and "alligator" indiscriminately). Bishop's alligator, with its bold calls of war and warning, is reduced to a whimper after dark, when it "speaks in the throat/of the Indian Princess" (what some critics have called a buried or mythic figure is more likely the flowering shrub). One of the alligator's calls is a throaty growl, a "speaking in the throat." Does Bishop mean the gator tells of the land's lavish beauty, of which the flower is a convenient symbol— with a sidelong glance, perhaps, at real Indian princesses, who might once have provided objects of longing for a lovesick reptile? Or is that gator whimpering *into* the throat of the flower or skeletal girl—out of fear, desire, or merely sudden shyness, to make common cause or merely to seduce it, trying to speak to what cannot reply?

If the last, the alligator mimics the poet's condition and burden—here, where people have been swept aside (Bishop is never all that comfortable with people), this touching and hopeless encounter reminds us that the natural world can never answer the poet. The impasse is reminiscent of the more complicated exchange in "Cirque d'Hiver" (the poem printed just before "Florida" in *North and South*), where the speaker watches a toy ballerina ignoring the mechanical circus horse she rides. In the end, speaker and horse stare at each other, saying together with a certain dry fatalism, "Well, we have come this far." This gloomy admission contains a resistant and battered pride.

Bishop's Linnaean habits hint at the scientific curiosity that did not drive early exploration so much as hitch a ride with it. Joseph Banks in his long journey on Cook's *Endeavour* and Darwin in his prowl aboard the *Beagle* had the smallest roles in a general land rush, partly to discover and record new plants and animals, mainly to claim them as property and ship them around like baggage—tea bushes were hauled from China to India, breadfruit trees from Tahiti to the Caribbean plantations, where the slaves loathed the taste. Pure science does not like to recall its impure beginnings—the very observations that secured our knowledge often condemned, or began the ruin of, what they observed. In every discovery lies the seed of destruction: we are grateful that Audubon saw Cuvier's kinglet, the carbonated warbler, Townsend's bunting, and the blue mountain warbler. Perhaps he mistook what he saw, or perhaps to paint them he killed some of the last survivors. In any case, no naturalist has ever seen them again.

Gold miners used to believe their occupation more noble than any conducted in cities, because metal had been left in the ground by God—by mining it, every man partook of the divine. The conquistadors were little different: their rape of the land (think of the old meaning, *seizure*) was of the very image of Paradise—Bishop's tropical poems contain some of the explorers' astonishment at boundless fertility (now we know better the fragility of such flora). Even James caught the whisper of Paradise rediscovered: "Was not the train itself rumbling straight into *that* fantastic Florida, with its rank vegetation and its warm, heroic, amorous air?"

The casual, florid, uncontrollable growth, unlike anything in the Old World, fostered myths of eternal youth, though perhaps explorers were misled when they encountered tribes where few lived to great age. Behind such tales shimmers the branching river of Eden, where Adam and Eve might have lived into a monstrous dotage. The Fountain of Youth, like the city of El Dorado, proved a frustrating, ever-receding will-o'-the-wisp (the fountain was almost certainly the invention of later writers, a miracle of which Ponce de León had never heard). Much of Florida's later imagery and iconography pays homage to eternal youth and eternal riches, to the romantic idea that amid such plenty no one has to work, because there are always fish to jump into your net and fruit to be plucked—no penalty for fruitfulness but more fruitfulness.

It was once said of an English cricket star, late in his career, that the "legend has become a myth." A reader may feel, reading poems about Florida, that the myths have been rubbed into ghostliness, referring, not to living tradition, but to tradition's tradition, the ghost of a ghost—even myths grow old, in a world forever new. What have they been replaced by? Walt Disney, perhaps:

And even at the moment one resolved
Not to come back, the scent of fruit and flowers
Brought on a sadness as the past dissolved:
Arcades, courts, arches, fountains, lordly towers. . . .

The shore of sunset and the palms, meanwhile—
Late shade giving over to greater shade—
What were they? With what did they have to do?
It was like a myriad pictures of the Nile,
But with a History yet to be made,
A world already lost that was still new.
                    (Joe Bolton, "Florida Twilight, 1905")

Here the buildings vanish at sunset, architecture laid down tentatively on pristine Nature. The odor of those flowers brings on the sadness of a present unable to make terms with the past: that world always new, but now always lost, too.

This alien and exotic world had to be found before it was lost. Though Florida appeared in many poems before the twentieth century, few poets had actually seen the place. The earliest poetic references are to a land encountered in books and therefore already part historical fiction, however begemmed and begummed with fact. One hears the distant echo of those early tales in James's lament that, even in his day, the "novelists improvise, with the aid of the historians, a romantic local past of costume and compliment and sword-play and gallantry and passion." So Thomas Greepe, perhaps the first in a long line of fantasists, in 1587:

Then homeward as their course did lie,
At sundry Iles they put a shore:
Their former wantes for to supply,
With victuales and fresh water store.
At Florida they did ariue:
Saint Augustine for to atchiue;

or Anne Dowriche, in 1589: "'Great matters moue our minde against the King of Spaine,/For he hath taken Florida, and late our sister slaine.'" Nathaniel Baxter, in 1606, absorbed this pastoral state within a convenient pastoral mythology:

> *These foure followed blessed Cynthia,*
> *To view the gardens of Hesperida.*
> *With many another honourable Dame,*
> *Blessed Phileta, Clara, Candida;*
> *These lodge within the house of Cynthia,*
> *Within the Lande of Terra Florida.*

Such were the purposes of polemical statecraft or enchanted allegory for which the shores of Florida could be enlisted. Only gradually did it become, in poems, a land lush to the point of surfeit. Laurence Eusden, in 1722: "But let th'Italian Canvass vital glow, / And FLORIDA her woven Plumage show" ("woven Plumage" is a delicious touch). Ebenezer Elliott, in 1818, knew how, in search of the sublime, to employ the Keatsian strain:

> *There is a lovely vision in her soul,*
> *Delicious as the gale of Florida*
> *Which, over fragrance, bears the tiny bird,*
> *The feather'd bee, dipp'd in the morning—Aye,*
> *But she is human! and Reality*
> *Shall wake her from that dream, to agonize.*

So, more haplessly, in out-of-date Augustan couplets, did the American poet John Pierpont, in 1829:

> *Hear yon poetic pilgrim of the west,*
> *Chant Music's praise, and to her power attest.*
> *Who now, in Florida's untrodden woods,*
> *Bedecks, with vines of jessamine, her floods,*
> *And flowery bridges o'er them loosely throws.*

Such observation, which may not have been firsthand, reveals the familiarity with local flora and fauna necessary for backdrops to a modern mythos. (James asked, about Florida, "what the play would have been without the scenery.") Distance did not prevent poets, especially those lounging comfortably across an ocean, from continuing to apply that scenery to romantic venture. Here in 1838 is Robert Southey, the poet laureate, who when young wanted to emigrate with Coleridge to the banks of the Susquehanna:

But he to Florida's disastrous shores
In evil hour his gallant comrades led,
Through savage woods and swamps, and hostile tribes,
The Apalachian arrows, and the snares
Of wilier foes, hunger, and thirst, and toil.

Even the young Tennyson provided lines keen on the invasion of the frigid north by the lushness of a passive south: "Ev'n as the warm gulf-stream of Florida / Floats far away into the Northern seas / The lavish growths of southern Mexico."

Amid so much of serious purpose, however ill favored or ill formed, I cannot bear to omit a Byronic satire that pours cold water on such romantic effusions. The American poet John Townsend Trowbridge, in 1878:

He had come down at first as far as Florida,
*   And seen the alligator and flamingo;*
Then, passing on to regions somewhat torrider,
*   Reached the French-negro side of San Domingo,*
*   And learned a little of the curious lingo*
The people speak there, but conceived no mighty
Love for those Black Republicans of Hayti.

The politics are suspect now, but *torrider* and *Florida* makes you want to read the rhyme royal of the whole epic, called *Guy Vernon*. Not until relatively late did poems about the Sunshine State, as it now styles itself, save themselves from embarrassment; and even then there was ample scope for disaster. Paul Laurence Dunbar plumbed the depths of humiliation in racial dialect: "Florida is lovely, she 's de fines' lan' / Evah seed de sunlight f'om de Mastah's han', / 'Ceptin' fu' de varmints an' huh fleas an' san'." Langston Hughes's "Florida Road Workers" and a number of brief poems by William Carlos Williams are, if possible, even worse.

For the better part of three centuries, then, Florida existed almost entirely outside firsthand knowledge, a *tabula rasa* on which the poetic imagination might inscribe itself. Like all lands imagined, it was Narcissus's pool: if you looked too deeply, at last you saw yourself. Eventually poets who had seen this absurd, sandy peninsula began to describe it, at times blinded by the beauty of subtropics ever more tropical, using it as so many Jamesian backdrops:

Here has my salient faith annealed me.
Out of the valley, past the ample crib
To skies impartial, that do not disown me
Nor claim me, either, by Adam's spine—nor rib.

The oar plash, and the meteorite's white arch
Concur with wrist and bicep. In the moon
That now has sunk I strike a single march
To heaven or hades—to an equally frugal noon.
                              (Hart Crane, "Key West")

This might as well be Finland as Florida. Most of Crane's "Key West: An
Island Sheaf" shows little interest in the place, except as it can be turned into
archly mythic fantasy (he was not an abstraction blooded, as R. P. Blackmur
said of Stevens, but an abstraction that bled to death). His gift was never one
for observation and detail; but here he seems like a steam shovel, clearing the
swamps for a gimcrack strip-mall of his own design.

   Sometimes it is hard to see beyond such florid surrounds; in views so
lushly baroque, the language may be infected—infested!—by what it would
describe:

A mile-long vertebrate picked clean
To lofty-plumed seableached incurving ribs

Poor white the soil like talcum mixed with grit
But up came polymorphous green

No sooner fertilized than clipped
Where glimmerings from buried nozzles rose

And honey gravel driveways led
To the perpetual readiness of tombs
                              (James Merrill, "Palm Beach with
                                    Portuguese Man-of-War")

You want to say, *How lovely!* And then you think, *How sad!* Merrill's eye is
always being caught by something, his very language an act of flaunting pos-
session; yet Nature's tangled bank and Palm Beach's clipped lawns threaten

to become mere show, playing endless matinées to manatees. If the reader is suspicious of splendor so indulged, so indulged in, that is what Florida offers: excess without guilt, sin without price. When the exotic is your address, it's difficult not to recognize the there there; but the words may become immersed in the vacuous sensuality on ready display—then there's no *more* than there there. The sensuality of language necessarily holds life at a distance—the artist cannot embrace the model while he paints.

Gaze is a fraught term in criticism now, one perhaps impossible to restore to innocence; yet consider Elizabeth Bishop's coolly calculating appraisal of her surroundings:

> *White, crumbling ribs of marl protrude and glare*
> *and the boats are dry, the pilings dry as matches.*
> *Absorbing, rather than being absorbed,*
> *the water in the bight doesn't wet anything,*
> *the color of the gas flame turned as low as possible.*
> *One can smell it turning to gas; if one were Baudelaire*
> *one could probably hear it turning to marimba music.*
>
> ("The Bight")

The ribs *protrude* and *glare*, seemingly the bones of some great prehistoric creature—is that sunlit reflection or a hostile stare? If the latter, the observer cannot escape being seen (how easily Bishop turns the view back upon herself while fending it off—she has it both ways, a hard-boiled reporter with a heart of Spanish moss). The pilings seem about to go up in flame; the poor water cannot wet anything. And then the scent of gas—how adroitly the poet lets that faint whiff of danger (or suicide) linger, only to turn it into a joke. The mortal thoughts shadow the comic antics that follow:

> *The birds are outsize. Pelicans crash*
> *into this peculiar gas unnecessarily hard,*
> *it seems to me, like pickaxes,*
> *rarely coming up with anything to show for it,*
> *and going off with humorous elbowings.*

For all Bishop's lightness, these lines are haunted by fatality, as if she could not help trying to ease life's tragedy with a few humorous asides (or dampen its comedy by reminding us of the tragic). Her clownish pelicans crash about

like the Marx Brothers and in the end get little for their labors. Her obser-
vations, more standoffish than Merrill's or Crane's, suggest how much of a
poem's inner life is created entirely by imagery. Bishop does not fail to see
through the exotic to a deeper discontent—or, in that vulnerable way of hers,
to be seen despite the exotic for what she is.

Other poets have applied the wry view of the solitary to more voyeuristic,
Lowellesque scenes:

> Six girls round the pool in Stranglers' weather,
> tanning; then three; then one (my favourite!),
> every so often misting herself
> or taking a drink of ice water from a plastic beaker.
>
> Only the pool shark ever swam,
> humming, vacuuming debris, cleverly avoiding its tail.
> The white undersides of the mockingbirds
> flashed green when they flew over.
>   (Michael Hofmann, "Freebird")

The Stranglers are a British punk band, though the poet may be thinking
of the murders of female undergraduates about that time. This would be an
innocent appreciation of youth and beauty, if the observer did not linger so
long. The girl misting herself is damp with the promise of eros. On a beach
such scenes might be different; but the speaker is probably unseen, perhaps
peeping through his blinds.

> The frat boy overhead gave it to his sorority girl steamhammer-style.
> Someone turned up the Lynyrd Skynyrd,
> the number with the seven-minute instrumental coda.
> Her little screams petered out, inachevée.

Those unapproachable sirens, that sorority girl taken "steamhammer-style,"
her modest yelps of pleasure not quite reaching climax, make the surround-
ing loneliness all the lonelier. The speaker's detachment becomes a kind of
longing. Though his sardonic and amused judgments embrace the soul with
Terentian generosity ("Homo sum, humani nihil a me alienum puto"), this is
life lived almost without hope (the darkness is in the form of observation), not
despite the surrounding narcissism and sexual congress but because of them.

One who lives in a state of nature, which is rarely a state of grace, may be tempted to discover there the hidden layers of the self (I once heard a poet say that walking on a swampy Florida prairie was like walking in the Unconscious), to read into landscape his own tortured predicament.

> When I poked the wet, mahogany mud,
> it felt like something human I had my hand on,
> as if the earth were a girl's black-haired head
> being lifted up in a great clatter that ebbed
> and flowed, like sea foam or a red sky or pain
> obscuring pleasure in a flesh tunnel.
>   (Henri Cole, "Medusa")

Here the creation myth has been spliced into a myth more troubling. (Wasn't Freud an adept of the sailor's splice?) At first that seems to be Eve rising from the mortal mud, created from virgin earth as Adam was; but the title shoulders the meaning aside. The black hair must be snakes, the great clatter that of the wood storks the poem has already mentioned. This is a woman part animal (how appropriate for a state gone feral), one you cannot look upon without dying—an inversion of birth, where you cannot look upon your mother without being born. The poem ends on that vulgar and unromantic "flesh tunnel," sexual pleasure set at one with the nature surrounding it, but made *merely* flesh, mortal and a little disgusting. The line that precedes this passage now makes sense: "as if freedom meant proximity to danger" (all sorts of dangers tremble within sex, from Medusa's stare to AIDS). Cole's poems are often about a love once called unnatural: here lies the secret, the turn— perhaps the flesh tunnel is not a woman's after all. Flora and fauna have been pressed into service (*pressurized*, as the British say, where we would say *pressured*), the poem set deep into its own humorless pain, darkly wounded, finding no solace in revelation.

What unites these uses (or abuses) of local mythos is how they have been determined by outsiders, those who have only visited, those who have come and found an uneasy home amid the otherness. Florida lay beyond the reach of the original thirteen colonies—it was foreign ground until 1821. For decades after, much of it remained terra incognita. The original inhabitants had been almost entirely killed off by disease, and the lower Creeks (later called Seminoles) who moved there in the early eighteenth century found a primeval emptiness. The noxious, mosquito-infested swamps kept settlement slow (disease was a problem throughout the Caribbean—during the Spanish-American War, yellow fever and malaria killed more soldiers than enemy guns).

Whitman felt the lure of this strange, exotic place, part of and yet somehow separate from that great poem, America:

> *A lesser proof than old Voltaire's, yet greater,*
> *Proof of this present time, and thee, thy broad expanse, America,*
> *To my plain Northern hut, in outside clouds and snow,*
> *Brought safely for a thousand miles o'er land and tide,*
> *Some three days since on their own soil live-sprouting,*
> *Now here their sweetness through my room unfolding,*
> *A bunch of orange buds by mail from Florida.*
>
> ("Orange Buds by Mail from Florida")

Here we have a Whitman surprised, tender, curious, content to know strange places from afar, not the blowhard who pretended, however compellingly, to have been places where he'd never set foot. (The "hut" has been humbly reduced for his audience, but how fast the mails were in those days!) In the Calamus poems, he wrote, "Here, out of my pocket, some moss which I pull'd off a live-oak in Florida as it hung trailing down." This might seem a fraud genial enough, as he'd never been closer to Florida than New Orleans; yet consider this longer fantasy:

> *O magnet-South! O glistening perfumed South! my South!*
> *O quick mettle, rich blood, impulse and love! good and evil! O all dear*
> *to me!*
> *O dear to me my birth-things—all moving things and the trees where I was*
> *born—the grains, plants, rivers,*
> *Dear to me my own slow sluggish rivers where they flow, distant, over flats*
> *of silvery sands or through swamps,*
> *Dear to me the Roanoke, the Savannah, the Altamahaw, the Pedee, the*
> *Tombigbee, the Santee, the Coosa and the Sabine,*
> *O pensive, far away wandering, I return with my soul to haunt their banks*
> *again,*
> *Again in Florida I float on transparent lakes, I float on the Okeechobee, I*
> *cross the hummock-land or through pleasant openings or dense forests.*
>
> ("O Magnet-South")

This is "Walt Whitman," not Walt Whitman. Though it is tempting to dismiss the pious old fraud's wish to embrace multitudes, these fictions pay homage to the depths of that most wishful of intelligences, idealizing and credulous at once. In such lines some essence of Florida has been seen and acknowledged, not allowed to exist merely as exotic (or erotic) detail but absorbed within a private philosophy that allows it new form. If Florida has been read through the poet's imagination, the poet has been read through Florida's.

This is the key to three poets who, having borrowed Florida's myths, have transformed them into purloined goods, as if Circe's pigs had been given Circe's power: Stevens, Rimbaud, and Coleridge. In them Florida is purified but altered, until what emerges is the mutability of art, what it could not be without the superaddition of such myth.

> *She sang beyond the genius of the sea.*
> *The water never formed to mind or voice,*
> *Like a body wholly body, fluttering*
> *Its empty sleeves; and yet its mimic motion*
> *Made constant cry, caused constantly a cry,*
> *That was not ours although we understood,*
> *Inhuman, of the veritable ocean.*
>
> *The sea was not a mask. No more was she.*
> *The song and water were not medleyed sound*
> *Even if what she sang was what she heard,*
> *Since what she sang was uttered word by word.*
> *It may be that in all her phrases stirred*
> *The grinding water and the gasping wind;*
> *But it was she and not the sea we heard.*
>
> (Wallace Stevens,
"The Idea of Order at Key West")

As late as 1890, Key West was the largest city in Florida—Stevens made annual winter "jaunts" there through the twenties and thirties. The singer *may* be singing only what she hears in the ocean and the wind. Her song is not the same as theirs, and—a canny observation, this—the singer may even drown out the sea. Here we have Stevens's version of the complex relation between the artist and his material. The sea is "merely a place by which she walked to sing," yet her song recreates it ("the sea,/Whatever self it had, became the self/That was her song"). This suggests, not just the artist's dependence on the world, but his ability to make it seem that the world has been created by him. If the poem accomplished only so much, it might be enough; yet, as in much of his major work, Stevens considers the subject afresh:

> Ramon Fernandez, tell me, if you know,
> Why, when the singing ended and we turned
> Toward the town, tell why the glassy lights,
> The lights in the fishing boats at anchor there,
> As the night descended, tilting in the air,
> Mastered the night and portioned out the sea,
> Fixing emblazoned zones and fiery poles,
> Arranging, deepening, enchanting night.
>
> Oh! Blessed rage for order, pale Ramon,
> The maker's rage to order words of the sea,
> Words of the fragrant portals, dimly-starred,
> And of ourselves and of our origins,
> In ghostlier demarcations, keener sounds.

Stevens could make a metaphysical poem out of a pig and a whistle, it sometimes seems; but the world beyond intrudes upon this poem more deeply than usual in his work. His vistas often seem those of the smoke-filled study, though apparently written down in a smoke-filled insurance office. (How curious the metaphor when he writes from Long Key, "The whole place: it is an island, is no larger than the grounds on which the Hartford Fire has its building"). Stevens, a man who almost never left the borders of his country, found in Key West the symbol of that world the artist worked to control. In such isolated, out-of-the-way habitations (trains did not reach Key West until 1912, and the tracks were blown down in 1935), art makes order, the order that is the world, from the disorder of the world.

Such fantasy could be pressed further. It's common to pine for distant places, ones impossible to reach, the blood stirring with desire that can never be satisfied, common to feel some magnetic affinity with a place you've never visited (more frequently, I suspect, when travel was expensive). Few states in our country, other than California, have borne such a share of unfulfilled desire as Florida.

I have struck, do you realize, incredible Floridas,
where mingle with flowers the eyes of panthers
in human skins! and rainbows stretched like bridles
under the seas' horizon with glaucous herds!

I have seen the enormous swamps seething,
traps where a whole Leviathan rots in the reeds!
Downfalls of waters in the midst of the calm,
and distances cataracting down into abysses!

Glaciers, suns of silver, waves of pearl, skies of red-hot coals!
Hideous wrecks at the bottom of brown gulfs
where the giant snakes, devoured by vermin,
fall from the twisted trees with black odours!
　　　　　　　　　(Rimbaud, "The Drunken Boat,"
　　　　　　　　　　　trans. Oliver Bernard)

I have arranged the translator's prose gloss as poetry. It is as if Rimbaud, only sixteen when he wrote this, had bought a whole rack of postcards, so well does he reproduce Florida's penny-ante images. The sea voyages of "Narrative of A. Gordon Pym" and further back of "The Rime of the Ancient Mariner" lie behind the romantic longing here. Those who cannot escape their home often dream of such journeys; but the maturity of Rimbaud's immature imagination (how Stevens would have loved a poem spoken by a boat) has, again, that added turn of the turnbuckle, not taking for granted the original impulse—in the end the boat wants to sail back to Europe. Florida becomes, not just the longed-for destination, but the exotic from which one must at last come home.

James saw what was at the heart of this retreat, why one might flee what had been desired: "Even round about me the vagueness was still an appeal. The vagueness was warm, the vagueness was bright, the vagueness was sweet, being scented and flowered and fruited; above all, the vagueness was somehow consciously and confessedly weak." If you stay too long among the lotus-eaters, at last you have to eat the lotus, too:

All the succulence of the admirable pale-skinned orange and the huge sun-
warmed grape-fruit, plucked from the low bough, where it fairly bumps your
cheek for solicitation, and partaken of, on the spot, as the immortal ladies
of Cranford partook of dessert.

This surfeiting banquet, this pliant vagueness, of which Florida has more than its share, prove ever tractable to the poet's design.

What separates the strongest poems that have used this giant semicolon lying under the East Coast, this ornate bracket, this sandy stump of old ocean bottom, from the mere stuff of journals or journalists, from the self-regarding or self-inflamed? The ability, not just to succumb to seductive myth, but to transform it. Coleridge, who once dreamt of living in America as part of a society of Pantisocrats, used Bartram's *Travels* to feed his vision of a place wholly other (as Shakespeare used reports of the Bermudas as background for *The Tempest*). His dream vision, famously incomplete, its transcription interrupted by the mysterious visitor from Porlock, suggests in its interior bafflings the ways by which the poet, both insatiable and a perfectionist, managed his failures by not taking himself to account for them.

Coleridge's compressive imagination drew from many sources simultaneously, if one trusts the patient detective work in John Livingston Lowes's classic, *The Road to Xanadu*. Amid the quieter passages of Bartram's journals (those in which he was not fending off alligators trying to overturn his canoe), the poet found descriptions of the fountains and disappearing rivers common in northern Florida. From these scanty sources he made his Xanadu.

> And from this chasm, with ceaseless turmoil seething,
> As if this earth in fast thick pants were breathing,
> A mighty fountain momently was forced:
> Amid whose swift half-intermitted burst
> Huge fragments vaulted like rebounding hail,
> Or chaffy grain beneath the thresher's flail:
> And mid these dancing rocks at once and ever
> It flung up momently the sacred river.
> Five miles meandering with a mazy motion
> Through wood and dale the sacred river ran,
> Then reached the caverns measureless to man,
> And sank in tumult to a lifeless ocean.
>
> ("Kubla Khan")

These are neither the most memorable nor most carefully written lines in Coleridge's vision, showing every sign of half-hearted (or half-heated) composition—the repetition of *momently*, the clumsy wording at line end (often to secure the rhyme), the wounded syntax and half-comic phrasing (those *fast thick pants*, those *dancing rocks*). Only in the passage's last lines does the writing have the confidence of sources absorbed and converted— there we have Florida no longer, but something, if not measureless, then very difficult to measure.

Florida has gone from a vague report, used like a mirror, to the scientific account (Bartram was Florida's Joseph Banks) altered and distorted and re-arranged, emerging almost as a dream of itself: one paradise has begotten another. The state's characteristic vagueness here disappears into the mists of someplace ever more distant. What has been lost in the reaches of Xanadu is the Florida that is only itself:

> *Smoke from woods-fires filters fine blue solvents.*
> *On stumps and dead trees the charring is like black velvet.*
> *The mosquitoes*
> *go hunting to the tune of their ferocious obbligatos.*
> *After dark, the fireflies map the heavens in the marsh*
> *until the moon rises.*
> *Cold white, not bright, the moonlight is coarse-meshed,*
> *and the careless, corrupt state is all black specks*
> *too far apart, and ugly whites; the poorest*
> *post-card of itself.*
>
> (Bishop, "Florida")

How different Coleridge's dreams from what Bishop saw—her cooler eye, which celebrates the darker character of this somewhat absurd place, has all the virtues that lie beneath ambition. Sometimes the still waters of modesty may be deepest, after all.

Not many miles north of Lake George, where Bartram saw that geyserlike fountain, was the Alachua savannah, which he visited some days later. On the shores of that swampy expanse, two years before the poet died, the Treaty of Payne's Landing was signed, a document riddled with bad faith and outright lies. There followed the Second Seminole War, the death of the great chief Osceola, and the forced removal of most Seminoles to the Indian Territory. The swamps allowed a remnant band a place of concealment. Coleridge's poem is devoid of real history, and that is the danger of using sources without taking them beyond their word.

Yet poetry, too, is a kind of bad faith. In our own visions, our own dreamed privacies, there is much a place cannot take into account or render us responsible for. How else would a name bequeathed merely because Ponce de León first spied the land on or about Easter Sunday (in Spanish, *Pascua Florida*, the Feast of the Flowers) still seem so beautifully appropriate? Florida did not have to grow into its name, because it was already all that its name could ask it to become.

Elizabeth Bishop Unfinished

Readers admire Robert Lowell; entertain a fondness for Marianne Moore; respect Wallace Stevens and T. S. Eliot; become fanatics, a few of them, about Ezra Pound; even compete to join the cult of Sylvia Plath; but they fall helplessly in love, over and over, with Elizabeth Bishop. In the markets of reputation, the past quarter century has seen the rise of a poet considered by some of her peers to be frivolous, whimsical, even trivial. Why has our age become so enamored of a poet who almost to the end of her life required a special taste?

Though she was praised by Lowell and Randall Jarrell, Bishop's early reviews were less lavish than those lavished on others ("bizarre fantasies," said one critic of her poems). She later won the Pulitzer Prize and the National Book Award but never campaigned for literary recognition and spent almost half her adult life in Brazil. (Those who hate the hoopla of the literary world find that absence makes the hearts of other writers grow fonder—if they don't forget you entirely.) For a long while, she lived in the shadow of Marianne Moore, who had befriended the young poet and commented on her work; Bishop adapted, in her own shy, cross-purposed way, Moore's quirky gift for description yet for a long while was seen as a minor disciple of a poet odder and more original.

The future may appreciate our age for poetry we despise rather than poetry we love. Having better taste than we do, the future usually has the good sense to judge an age by its one or two poets of genius (if you have four or six, you're living in 1600 or 1820—that is, a golden age) while cheerfully and cruelly ignoring the hundreds who gratified the taste of the day. What would American poets of 1875 have thought could they have peered into a glass and seen that, before a few decades had passed, their age would be known only for that great American poseur, Walt Whitman, and some unknown spinster from Amherst?

Readers adore Bishop and adore themselves for adoring her. She never found writing easy, one reason nonwriters like her—an artist who must plod toward genius bears the mark of humanity (Beethoven is human, Mozart only divine). After her midthirties, she finished fewer than two poems each year; and her papers contain notebook after notebook and file after file of poems in fragmentary or unfinished form—some just dust heaps of phrases, others roughly glued into shape, some dragged through numerous frustrating drafts, and a few that seem to lack nothing but the poet's approval. Since Bishop scholars have mined this trove haphazardly, readers will be grateful that Alice Quinn, poetry editor of the *New Yorker*, has gathered the best of this raw material in *Edgar Allan Poe & the Juke-Box: Uncollected Poems, Drafts, and Fragments*.

The deceptive ease of Bishop's poems conceals her trouble in finishing them—she worked hard to make them fresh and offhanded, as if they hadn't been written at all. (She's hardly the first artist to use great labor to make labor look easy.) When she was stuck, she would pin a poem to her bulletin board and wait for the right word to come along. Sometimes this was a very long wait. "The Moose" took more than two decades to finish; and "12 O'Clock News," finally published in the seventies, was started at Vassar forty years before. Her letters are littered with references to poems just begun or half done, poems she wanted to include in her next book or dispatch to a dedicatee; but months and years piled up while such poems were abandoned, revisited, abandoned once more.

City Stars

Perishable, adorable friends,
each sometimes ends.
No rhyme to it at all
and not less of reason.
The miles of dirty air—
it's dim, but one is there,
and there's another, fairly bright
white, or is it a jet?
They're there, they're there.

From a distance, it's hard to imagine what she found wrong with such lines. The editor has printed the poems partly in draft form, with the messiness a copy editor would have tidied up. The good argument for this (it reminds us the poems never received the poet's imprimatur) goes only so far, since the defects (punctuation gone astray, lines hovering between two or three phrases) make it hard to see the poem plain. (I have added clarifying punctuation and capitals, here and elsewhere, and made minor adjustments.) For a lonely child, the stars might invite the same longing for intimacy as the mute toy horse in "Cirque d'Hiver." ("City Stars" seems related to various big-city poems, like "The Man-Moth," that Bishop began in the thirties while living in New York just after college.) The stars are one more example in Bishop of the beautiful concealed by dross, her version of the ugly-duckling theme. That final line insists the stars are there, after all; but beneath it lies a mother's soothing *there there, there there*—Bishop was good at reassurance cut with desperation.

Often bedridden as a child, wheezing with asthma or coughing from bronchitis, Bishop was shuffled from house to house and relative to relative after her father died and her mother went insane. The warring sides of her family treated the child, all but orphaned, like a shuttlecock—she felt, looking back, that she was "always a sort of a guest." In the end, she was dispatched to the stark and forlorn apartment of an aunt and uncle in a poverty not at all genteel.

The poems in her first book, stuffed with allegories and fables, betray too close a reading of George Herbert—sometimes she seems a Metaphysical, Third Class. (The juvenilia included here show how long it took her to trust her instincts—worse, she didn't know she *had* instincts.) Yet a poem like "Sestina," with its mournful old woman and trusting granddaughter, today appears painfully autobiographical; we know so much more now about Bishop's life, it's easier to see, as in Eliot, where the personal wormed into the poetic. Even in Worcester, the child found small, obscure delights—the pansies on the back porch every spring; the two canaries, Sister and Dickie; even the quarreling neighbors (you can tell she was deprived because the pleasures were so small). She turned the ordinary into an Aladdin's cave of wonders because she had to.

Bishop's poems, as aesthetic organizations, often look ruefully toward the past or reinvent the present in fabulous terms. There are sorrows available in both. This was written in her twenties:

> *The past*
> *at least*
> *is polite:*
> *it keeps out of sight.*

The present
is more recent.
It makes a fuss
but is unselfconscious.

The future
sinks through water
fast as a stone,
alone alone.

After she had rejected a boyfriend who had twice proposed, he shot and killed himself, having first sent her a postcard that read, "Elizabeth, Go to hell." Her lovers thereafter were not always women, though in her late thirties, as far as her biographer can tell, Bishop accepted what was probably always her inclination (she had fallen in love with her Vassar roommate). The small legacy her father left could never support her in New York; through her thirties she moved around restlessly, looking further and further away for a home. In 1951, during a stop in Brazil on a cruise around South America (she arrived on the pleasantly named S. S. *Bowplate*), she suffered an allergic reaction to cashew fruit. While recovering, she fell in love with Lota de Macedo Soares, the aristocratic Brazilian with whom she shared a long domestic contentment but who in the end also committed suicide.

A reader searches the poems in vain for this romantic life—there are gestures or countergestures of affection, but rarely do you feel the disruptions of passion. (Bishop wasn't careful or even faithful in love—the beautiful villanelle "One Art" is almost an apology for all the unwritten love poems.) A few poems in the archives live on the remembered edge of sex; but they seem oddly uncomfortable with physical desire, the poems suppressed, not perhaps because of what they revealed (homosexual poets of Bishop's generation sometimes still couched love for one sex in terms of the other), but because of the sentiment lurking there. Bishop's reticence had little room for sentiment, and less for immodesty.

Poets with a perfectionist streak are often depressives. (This is not to say that misery loves poetry, though it does.) When you read Bishop's letters, you wonder how—alcoholic, asthmatic, living in clouds of unhappiness—she finished anything at all. The poems are a triumph over what the false starts and dead ends succumbed to. The perceiving squint that attracted Bishop in Marianne Moore's descriptions, where its origins lay in an eccentricity

squeezed into whalebone-bodiced propriety, alters the ordinariness that sur-
rounds and imposes upon depression, the commonplace touched with Ovid-
ian metamorphosis.

> *Off to the left, those islands, named and renamed*
> *so many times now everyone's forgotten*
> *their names, are sleeping.*
>
> *Pale rods of light, the morning's implements,*
> *lie in among them tarnishing already,*
> *just like our knives and forks.*
>
> *Because we live at your open mouth, O Sea,*
> *with your cold breath blowing warm, your warm breath cold,*
> *like in the fairy tale.*
>
> *Not only do you tarnish our knives and forks*
> *—regularly the silver coffee-pot goes into*
> *dark, rainbow-edged eclipse;*
>
> *the windows blur and mirrors are wet to touch.*
>
> ("Apartment in Leme")

How often Bishop liked to observe sleepers—you cannot quarrel with a
sleeper. These islands off Rio become part of a domestic scene estranged
from its usual identities—the islands renamed into erasure, the coffeepot
eclipsed by its own tarnish. In her poems, no identity is safe.

Her childhoods, imagined or real, are flecked with sadness, sometimes even
besieged by it. (She once said that families were like "concentration camps.")
There's a childlike naïveté to her poems—Bishop is the best American poet
on childhood and the least sentimental about it; yet the comforts taken there,
comforts she enjoyed too rarely, can be touched with the morbid:

> *For M.B.S., Buried in Nova Scotia*
>
> *Yes, you are dead now and live*
> *only there, in a little, slightly tip-tilted graveyard*
> *where all of your childhood's Christmas trees are forgathered*

> *with the presents they meant to give,*
> *and your childhood's river quietly curls at your side*
> *and breathes deep with each tide.*

The matter-of-fact opening, the comical "tip-tilted graveyard," like one a child might draw, lure us into a poem where death is childhood lived over, more happily; the poem might be callous without the last lines, which make death, too, a consolation—the river curls against the dead woman like a dog at the feet of a knight on a medieval tomb. (I have changed "present" to "presents" on the authority of another draft.)

These poems brought so near perfection (a dozen are as good as all but her best) make us lament Bishop's too critical eye; but others exist only as fragments or pipe dreams, without the will to become poems. The failures explain more about Bishop's talents than the successes—she worked by accretion, stumbling through early drafts by phrase or fancy (often you see her characteristic gestures without their magic), trying to get at the resistant matter of the poem. Sometimes it's important that a writer find out what she can't do, as well as what she can. She must have asked herself if these really *were* poems (she worried about her "cuteness" and her "exotic or picturesque" details)—we love them now because they're like no one else's. It was that irregularity, that off-balance tilt, that made her poems poems. Jarrell and Lowell, among others, saw how much moral brooding and unsettling vision lay beneath their glittering surfaces. No wonder she found it impossible to write criticism—the critical restrictions of period taste were what she was trying to escape. Self-doubt is not the least attractive of her vulnerabilities.

Certain memories haunted her, cast and recast over the years as she tried to find the form nascent there. When most subservient to memory, she fell into the rambling narrative of poems like "The Moose" and "In the Waiting Room." The crucial moment of self-awareness in the latter ("you are an *I*, / you are an *Elizabeth*"), an epiphany on its way to becoming a joint-stock company, has given critics a field day, though it's one of her few false moments. Her troubled memories are less affecting than ones where despair, as in "Sestina," is half suppressed beneath her playful manner. A poet, over time, discovers different ways to write a poem, ways, once discovered, often hard to change—most poets never learn more than three or four. What we see in her drafts is how often Bishop tested her routines; if there were failures, they were the price of her successes.

Reading through her collected poems, you marvel at how often she suc-
ceeded (great poets commit their share of mediocre sins; but some with a pe-
culiar limitation of means—like Eliot and Auden—write, at least for a while,
almost nothing but masterpieces). If she knew intuitively what made her po-
ems work, should these drafts and fragments have been left unpublished? At
their deaths, Shelley, Housman, and many another left lovely poems in rough
draft. (The entire works of Wyatt, Traherne, and Dickinson, which remained
in manuscript, might have vanished into a kitchen fire.) It would be criminal,
by whatever statutes apply, to leave in dusty archives poems so touched with
mournful knowledge, with the sense of a life sometimes wrongly spent.

> *A great and early sunset,*
> *a classic of its kind, went unobserved,*
> *although today the sun himself swerved*
> *as far out of his course as he could get,*
>
> *taking the opportunity*
> *to see things that he might not see again;*
> *letting the shadows poke their fingers in*
> *and satisfy their curiosity.*
>
> *Now, down below,*
> *the darkness-level rises in the valley.*
> *In the small tip-tilted town already*
> *those gold cats' whiskers show*
>
> *where six streets lie.*
>   ("St. John's Day")

Bishop's calm powers conspire here toward a majesty of observation (think of
Wordsworth on Westminster Bridge, but with her nervous comic touches)—
and then, as if she didn't know how to go on, the poem staggers forward a cou-
ple of stanzas and loses its way. The volume has many gorgeous beginnings
that come to nothing in the end. (That shyly absurd adjective "tip-tilted" tries
again, and in vain, to sneak into a poem she could publish.)

Alice Quinn's thoughtful editing has returned these poems to the density
of their histories. Full of quotations from Bishop's memoirs, notebooks, and

letters, the notes set the poems into the life surrounding these interrupted and abandoned works. The fragmentary memoirs included in the appendix form a major autobiographical supplement to Bishop's childhood, which they treat with more depth and less critical posturing than Brett Millier's workmanlike biography *Elizabeth Bishop: Life and the Memory of It* (1993). Unfortunately, it takes only Bishop's stray mention of stars or lime trees or graveyards for the editor to throw in everything the poet said on the subject—some notes are so long you feel you're being punished for bothering to look them up.

Despite long immersion in Bishop's work, the editor has found it difficult to order or date these drafts (the fonts of the poet's apostolic succession of typewriters have proved of some help); but Quinn's editorial decisions are never doctrinaire—her affectionate tone is among the pleasures of this edition. Like most editors, she misses a trick or two—she doesn't mention, for example, the relation between some draft lines and Bishop's lovely "Cirque d'Hiver" or between others and "Sleeping Standing Up" and "Filling Station" (and surely it's odd to say that a poem is "terribly prescient" about the death, twenty years later, of a lover Bishop hadn't even met yet). Some of the editor's judgments bewilder me—I don't see why the prose and poetry in the appendix lack notes (or why the villanelle "Verdigris" is placed there rather than in the body of the book). Some drafts have been printed in photographic facsimile, which lets us see how the pages looked to the poet; yet these often lack transcriptions. These are minor flaws in a book that will be indispensable to readers of Bishop.

Readers who bother to read acknowledgments may notice my name. In 1992, while spending an afternoon in the archives at Vassar, I first saw many of these poems. I approached Bishop's publisher with the idea of an edition of unfinished poems. Though initially encouraging, after seeing a draft manuscript he decided not to pursue the idea, which by then conflicted with other plans. Some years later, the project was revived. Alice Quinn started from scratch, though she saw the draft of my labors, and pursued a very different and far more inclusive idea for the collection.

Having scoured the archives, Quinn has perhaps included too many drafts that barely escape their fragmentary phrases—that's the risk when a poet's editor loves the poet's work (lovers want to see every scrap, even the laundry lists). If it is a flaw, it's better than the vices to which editing is sometimes prey. Is there anything left after so thorough a trawl? At least two poems, perhaps.

Newsreel

Pompeii and Herculaneum,
smuts floating from an unsnuffed lamp,
two cinders; we got used to them.
We rubbed them in our eyes to weep
for man drawn up in igneous cramp,
the posture of those burnt asleep,
a man burnt up alive asleep.

In the country movie hall
many of the hard seats go
down too far or not at all.
An unremarking hierarch
steers us to a middle row.
In draughty interrupted dark
we sit and wish for darker dark.

The oddly emphasized opening is similar to the italicized close of "The Armadillo," which has often puzzled readers. (Is there a change in emphasis or a change in speaker?) The horrors of Pompeii, the igneous cramp of the dead, are those of the photographs of bodies piled at Dachau. The wistfulness in the last line contains something like hope, but something like horror, too—as if the only moral response were not to see at all. Oedipus reacted to horror in that way.

Bishop's poems were so modestly disposed, so full of delightful and startling images, like a tray of weird candies, it's hard to say just where their fragility, so similar to Dickinson's, sinks into something darker, more frantic, less in control:

Bicycles

The bicycle riders
work like insects,
each bicycle
a pair of spiders,

each wheel filled
solid silver,

buckets of water
swing unspilled.

Each gray wing
held by webs
slips to and fro,
kept from flying

by the wheels:
a pair of spiders;
they've caught the wings,
they've caught the riders,

bent on tiny seats,
spinning two webs
at the same time spinning
long threads in the streets.

Something about Bishop makes readers feel proprietary—Shakespeare and Milton are everyone's property, but Hardy and Larkin and Bishop each reader's alone. Her vulnerability, her charming chaos (even when complete, the poems feel fragmentary, like her personality) were not overcome but succumbed to—she lacks that seriousness, that pretentiousness in the poet's lingua franca, that in Lowell, Jarrell, and Berryman now seems leaden, done by union rule for union wages. Bishop emerges from this book a more personal poet, the made surfaces of her poems concealing the disorder from which they were made. In "'The past . . . ,'" "City Stars," "'From the shallow, night-long graves . . . ,'" "The Street by the Cemetery," "The Salesman's Evening," "Key West," "'Don't you call me that word, honey . . . ,'" "For M.B.S., Buried in Nova Scotia," "Suicide of a Moderate Dictator," "St. John's Day," "Foreign-Domestic," "All Afternoon the Freighters—Rio," "Mimosas in Bloom," "Apartment in Leme," "Salem Willows," "Just North of Boston," "Mr. and Mrs. Carlyle," and in dozens of fragments, there is a Bishop we recognize and a Bishop we do not quite know. Readers will remember some of these poems as long as they read her.

Bishop's life was a series of frustrations, tragedies, accidents—the extraordinary was her only means of disabling the terrors of the ordinary. This makes more affecting the transfigurations in "A Miracle for Breakfast" and "Filling

Station," the metamorphosis of her desk in "12 O'Clock News" and of the view out her window in "The Bight." That our age remains in love with a poet of such reticence and tact, one often frustrated by her gifts, is as much a mark of the age's intelligence as of its mawkishness. (*There there, there there,* readers seem to say over her wounds.) Her make-believe world, so like Joseph Cornell's boxes, can be too perfectly self-contained; perhaps the childlike awe was put on, after a while—yet Bishop was so afflicted by self-doubt, it's hard to believe the awe became merely a mannerism. And, if it did, there are worse forms of insincerity.

Elizabeth Bishop's Sullen Art

Michelangelo was the last poet to show much talent as a painter. In our narrow century poets have with few exceptions confined themselves to the art of words: Pound plunked away at opera (with dismal results), Cummings was a rough-and-ready dabbler in oils; but we have been spared the sculpture of Robert Lowell and the ballets of T. S. Eliot. It is charming to find that a poet secretly practices another art and consoling to know he's no good at it. This is partly *Schadenfreude* and partly relief that talent is not a gift completely selfish in its distribution.

After her death, Elizabeth Bishop's cheery watercolors appeared on her *Complete Poems*, her *Collected Prose*, and her selected letters, *One Art*. Modest, sweetly colorful, and full of quiet exuberance, the paintings transposed to the visual world the deceptive innocence of her poems. Indeed, they seemed to have been drawn by children—no set of parallel lines ever parallel, no circle ever circular, perspective lost in some twelfth-century muddle of vanishing points, everything thumbed onto the page with the spirit not of art but of need. "Her method," writes her editor William Benton, "for the most part consisted of making a simple drawing and, unceremoniously, coloring it in." *Exchanging Hats* gathers the surviving three dozen or so fragile watercolors and drawings (as well as two box constructions indebted to Joseph Cornell), some of them now mysteriously missing and available only as reproductions from slides.

Poetry and painting are not antagonistic arts: artists can live without writing a coherent word, and poets can be color-blind. Proudly diffident though she was about her verse, Bishop knew the difference between primitive poetry and primitive painting. Of her own paintings she said, "They are Not Art—NOT AT ALL"; yet some of what we admire in her verse lies in just its amateurish, old maidish, slightly fussy and unexpected graces—hers is the verse of an amateur who believes in the professional (Hardy's verse was the other way around). It is the primitive in her poems to which we respond.

Bishop lived at leisure until late in life, when she was forced into teaching (she didn't think she was much good at it, and by most accounts neither did her students). As a young woman she had a little money, a very little, and spent months in France and nearly a decade in Key West. Earlier she had tried a job or two in New York, but in the early fifties she escaped on a cruise and ended up in Brazil, more or less by accident. She lived there for nearly two decades. When you don't work, there's a great deal of life to be gotten through. Despite various projects (a book on Brazil, an anthology of Brazilian poetry, a translation of *The Diary of "Helena Morley"*), despite squabbles with her lover and visits with her friends, despite depression and alcohol and the two poems or so she managed to finish each year, there must have been long vacant hours. We can never get close enough to some writers—their love letters and even their laundry lists promise the human side of what is the mystery of art, but it is failure (in love or laundry) that finally makes the artist human again.

Bishop made a few botanical illustrations, one or two landscapes, and a couple of portraits, but mostly she painted buildings and interiors. Buildings offered the least resistance to her lack of skill. The earliest watercolor is of a small brick townhouse in Greenwich Village, its windows festooned with long vines of ivy, like wreaths of mildew. She tended to paint what was in front of her and often positioned herself so a building stood four-square opposite, eliminating any need for the confusions of perspective. The battlements of a school in Key West make it a castle, or a prison. A deformed bicycle has been abandoned outside, near a pair of trees whose whitewashed trunks look like tight skirts. Her other buildings can be slightly terrifying. The one painting of Paris is touchingly labeled, in her clumsy printing, "PALAIS DU SENAT PARIS FRANCE," the monumental stonework and balustrades outlined in Chinese white, as if it were a Ferris wheel. Two statues on the parapet appear to be hailing a cab.

It is not much use talking of possible influences on her work. As the editor recognizes, there's a little Klee, and a lot of Vuillard (she loved the floral); but they have been filtered through an unyielding artistic sinlessness. Her wavering line resembles that of *New Yorker* cartoonists like Steig and Thurber, where the visual is the pathos of its own incompetence.

Bishop was attracted to the painterly, as an appendix of her remarks makes plain; but her watercolors, often helped along with gouache and ink, never got any better in three decades of practice, and there's no sign she thought to take lessons. (Hitler's watercolors are far more accomplished.) Her empty yellow ship's-cabin resembles the inside of a steamer trunk, and out the curtained porthole is the sea; you can tell it's the sea because the waves are the little jagged v's amateur painters use. Those waves recall "Large Bad Picture," its bay "masked by perfect waves" above which are "scribbled hundreds of fine black birds/hanging in n's in banks." Her poems depended on the loneliness or unhappiness that drove her to words (often cheerful, but just as often rueful); painting was an escape from the pressure of the artistic.

Bishop must have recognized she had no gift for drawing people—the streets and buildings here are eerily empty. Still, in the one carefully rendered portrait, her friend Sha-Sha (Charlotte Russell) leans (or floats?) jauntily against a grade-school blackboard. She's dressed for summer, the little smear of lipstick, the plucked black eyebrows beneath blonde hair, the darkly handsome eyes, and the knowing posture a kind of Rorschach. The self-possession of the figure exceeds the crudity of expression. It doesn't quite matter that her head meets her neck in an alarming way.

There's something tender in the one other portrait, of a cartoonish sleeper who looks like a misshapen doll. In her poem "Sleeping Standing Up," Bishop wittily remade the world from the sleeper's ninety-degree-tilted point of view (some of these paintings are similarly vertiginous, and many almost dreamlike). Bishop was drawn to sleep, as many depressed people are; people who spend a lot of time in bed are intimates of the ceiling. In one of the best of the still lifes, a hydra-like chandelier casts gooseneck shadows on a large patch of ceiling. The editor calls it "untypically arty" and attempts to explain away the cropping; but Bishop wrote "Sleeping on the Ceiling" about another chandelier:

> It is so peaceful on the ceiling!
> It is the Place de la Concorde.
> The little crystal chandelier
> is off, the fountain is in the dark.

There's also a large branched chandelier (and a stain on the ceiling) in one of Bishop's remarkable unpublished poems. There have been many paintings of landscapes, but how many just of ceilings? Michelangelo painted ceilings, but not paintings of ceilings.

The difference between poetry and painting lies in their resolution of the visual. In "Over 2,000 Illustrations and a Complete Concordance," Bishop wrote, "The branches of the date-palms look like files"; but they don't, not really, and not in her paintings (the branches aren't even branches—they're fronds). That is the advantage of poetry—poetry, in the act of naming, is the action of metaphor. Metaphor is the improvement of the visual; the pictorial truth is another, homelier matter. The one painting where the visual approaches the shock of metaphor is a Nova Scotia landscape: there are grassy, overgrown fields, some white houses, a gray spireless church, and in the foreground a low field of blue flowers. Field? No, a pond that looks like a field. But it's not the least like a pond, more a field of flowers in which two rowboats are tossing.

A few allegorical paintings lie even deeper within the poetic, allegories in the way her poems "The Weed" and "The Monument" are—dream visions all too nakedly cozy with the psychological life. The most curious, a design for "E. Bishop's Patented Slot-Machine," shows a box with a handle labeled "The 'Dream'" and, inside, numbered gears and a crystal ball. Where do you put the money? What is the prize? Is it the record of a dream, or only a "dream" slot machine? Does it produce dreams for a penny, or perhaps fulfill them? This, alas, is an unwritten poem.

In their wobbling lines, their clumsy childlike intensities, these watercolors reveal a little of the world her timid, homely poetry concealed, a world of lopsided buildings, nightmarish night scenes, and interiors where nothing meets at right angles. For a moment, their defenseless lack of skill lets us view that world through Elizabeth Bishop's not-so-innocent eyes.

Verse Chronicle

Jumping the Shark

Kim Addonizio

Kim Addonizio is that New Formalist wet dream, a hot babe who can bang out a sonnet on demand. If your vice runs to forms a little more obscure, you could hardly resist her. Her come-on seems to be, "Wouldn't you like to peek at my sexy little sonnezhino?" or "Baby, baby, you gotta lick my paradelle all over." The question isn't why sexual intercourse didn't begin for Larkin until 1963; it's why—after Chaucer and Rochester and Burns, after all the ways they found to load every rift with sex—modern poetry is as erotic as a meat locker. The anesthesia and impotence of Eliot (when there's sex in Eliot, it's grimy and repulsive) seem to have become, not just the model for English verse, but the ideal.

Addonizio's poems are always looking for love, and in *What Is This Thing Called Love* they take their desperate pleasures where they can. The hot sex takes place with a Baedeker in hand—against a chain-link fence in one poem, against a fridge in another. (If you're going to be one of her lovers, I suspect you have to sign a legal release first.) Since the men who straggle through these poems are never named, it's hard to tell them apart—there's Vulnerable Kiss Guy and Orange Wedge Guy and Guy Who Drinks the Rain from the Hollow in My Throat Guy, and after a while they all seem the same. When you look at the world through her glasses, sex is everywhere; and even the muse is just a hottie on the make: "They fall in love with me after one night,/ even if we never touch. // I tell you I've got this shit down to a science." (It's not clear if this is a bimbo acting like the muse or the muse acting like a bimbo— but, hey, does it matter?) We know sex is war, all strategy and tactics and lost battalions (and mostly Pyrrhic victories), but it's refreshing to hear it said with such panache.

Sharon Olds is one of the few contemporary poets to treat sex with animal pleasure; and for her it's an Olympic event, pursued with an athletic single-mindedness that, in one poem, is not distracted even by a recent rape elsewhere in her building. (My favorite, however, is her paean to her early mastery of the arts of oral sex.) Addonizio is wittier about the physical acts that occupy so large a mental part of our waking (and, as Freud reminds us, sleeping) lives. She records some of the ambivalent appetites that seethe within the body politic and is not beneath ranting about her secret desires, like strangling people who miss her literary allusions.

Such facetiousness is part of the latest contemporary manner—ha! ha! poetry can be just as dumb as television, too! When you stoop so low to conquer, however, it's hard to stand up again. On occasion, Addonizio tries a subject more serious. (Bathing her elderly mother, she tries "to be more merciful/than God, who after creating her//licked her clean with a rough tongue"—so God is a cat?) Alas, she's so used to primping and posing and smirking, she can't recall what it's like to be reflective.

It would be pleasant to blame Billy Collins for the dumbing down of American verse, but there's so much dumbing down I fear he's more a symptom than the cause. The trouble with being a crowd pleaser is that, after you have the crowd, you have to please it—too many of Addonizio's poems are made in Betty Crocker style, all helpful hints and ingredients whipped up in a jiffy for a dish tasteless as a stuffed pillow. When Addonizio uses some arcane form, you never feel the form is happy to be there—it's used just as carelessly as her lovers, discarded when she's had her way with it. She finds charmingly weird subjects for poems—dead girls in movies, serial killers, why the chicken crossed the road, liver-transplant surgeons—but often the idea is all there is.

After so many poems about partying and drinking (there's a whole section devoted to them), the poet turns just as woozy and sentimental as that loser down the bar surrounded by shot glasses. Awful things may be happening elsewhere, things the poet can't stop, but

> *I separate*
> *the two halves of another cookie and lick*
> *the cream filling, and pour myself one more*
> *and drink to you, dear reader, amazed*
> *that you are somewhere in the world without me,*
> *listening, trying to hold me in your hands.*

I like Addonizio's poems best when she's vulnerable, when the bravado is just for show, as in her poem to a younger lover—"When he takes off his clothes / I think of a stick of butter being unwrapped." (The calculating fuck bunny part of her is fun, too.) It's all very well trying to make poetry relevant, to portray ruthlessly the way we live now; but in the end the poor poet is still stuck with having to say something, and to do that he has to make sure he has something to say.

Billy Collins

Speak of the devil. The proofs of Billy Collins's *The Trouble with Poetry and Other Poems* came prefaced by a letter from his publisher, addressed "Dear Reader." Why, I thought, this might be addressed to me! "The *real* trouble with most contemporary poetry," the letter said, "is that it is piled high, mostly unread and gathering dust, in the attic of its own obscurity." I was confused by the real dust in that metaphorical attic—but then I thought, contemporary poetry, obscure? Isn't the trouble with contemporary poetry that you read book after book of it without an obscurity in sight? (Next year the government plans to put Poetic Obscurities on the endangered species list.)

"Everyone can connect with his humor and his humanity," the letter continued. "Reading his poetry is no diagramless chore with recondite clues." So, it's all the fault of those other damned poets—you know who you are, leaving your recondite clues lying about, where anyone might trip over them. Go back to the hellhole you sprang from, John Keats. Get thee gone, John Milton and Alexander Pope, you diagramless whoremongers. And don't get me started on you, William Shakespeare!

Billy Collins is apparently the antidote to all this. He's an entertainer who gently thinks about gentle things (even when he has a harsh thought, it's whimsically harsh), with a half-baked goofy curiosity about the world and a penchant for odd bits of information. He'll write a poem about the code behind equestrian statues (if the horse is rearing, the rider died in battle— neat, huh?). He'll write about a dream where he lost his nose in a sword fight (Freud knew exactly what that means), or about how he wants to be buried (fetal position, clean pair of pajamas), or about magic sunglasses that filter out an ex-lover. And what about that dog you once put to sleep? Well, he's come back,

come back to tell you this simple thing:
I never liked you—not one bit.

When I licked your face,
I thought of biting off your nose.
When I watched you toweling yourself dry,
I wanted to leap and unman you with a snap.

Don't worry about the dog, though—he's in heaven, where all the animals "can read and write,/the dogs in poetry, the cats and all the others in prose." I suspect the dogs compose poems just like Billy Collins (the cats, they're writing poetry criticism).

Collins has the offbeat angle down pat. His images often reduce things to the size of childhood (a building with its façade torn off by a bomb is "like a dollhouse view"). On occasion—I'll admit it—he can be hilarious. One poem mimics the patter poets use at readings, trying to be as helpful as the footnotes in the *Norton Anthology*:

And you're all familiar with helminthology?
It's the science of worms.

Oh, and you will recall that Phoebe Mozee
is the real name of Annie Oakley.
Other than that, everything should be obvious.
Wagga Wagga is in New South Wales.
Rhyolite is that soft volcanic rock.
What else?
Yes, meranti is a type of timber, in tropical Asia I think,
and Rahway is just Rahway, New Jersey.

Anyone who has suffered through a poetry reading will sympathize; but, as a poem, it's like the rat so hungry he ate his own tail and didn't stop until he'd gobbled himself up. Many of Collins's poems are about poetry, though his references to poets past are often condescending. The pretensions of poetry need desperately to be mocked, but perhaps not by someone who doesn't like it all that much.

Collins suffers from mortal thoughts (there's a dry poem about what happens when a man sees the Grim Reaper coming for him) and would like to add a few words to the ancient themes of "longing for immortality/despite the roaring juggernaut of time." But he can't, or he won't, because his nervous jokes are just a way of staving off despair—his humor has only an empty pit beneath. The trouble with poetry, it turns out—and it's a bit of an anticlimax—is that poetry "encourages the writing of more poetry." And the trouble with *The Trouble with Poetry*, it turns out—and it's a bit of an anticlimax—is that, once you know the premise of a Billy Collins poem, the poem seems to write itself (he's almost a metaphysical poet, his poems are so entirely exhausted by working out the idea—but his two-a-penny ideas would have driven Donne to drink).

What Collins does, he does very well. There are many poets who, seeing his example, seeing that poetry can reach the masses and make them laugh (this begins to sound like the plot of *Sullivan's Travels*), want to stuff feathers in their heads just to be like him. The world can stand one Billy Collins, but what happens when everyone writes poems that humiliate the art they practice? I feel like a grouch to ask, but what then?

Kay Ryan

Kay Ryan's shy, skittish poems are so small they scarcely seem to *be* poems. Her lines are very short (even William Carlos Williams might have found them pinched), usually three words, or four, or five, as if she hardly had anything to say—once I counted eight words in a line and fell off my chair. When a poem in *The Niagara River* threatens to go beyond half a page, as a few do, it makes her jumpy, because there's hardly anything holding them together except spit and chewing gum. Yet, though she shrinks like a hermit crab (nothing tries to hide that hard except an animal wary of predators), her delicate modesty cannot conceal a poetry of winning oddity, with an off-kilter view of a world that always seems too big.

> *Everything contains some*
> *silence. Noise gets*
> *its zest from the*
> *small shark's-tooth-*

shaped fragments
of rest angled
in it. An hour
of city holds maybe
a minute of these
remnants of a time
when silence reigned,
compact and dangerous
as a shark. Sometimes
a bit of a tail
or fin can still
be sensed in parks.

Here each small notion leans against the next, aided (rather than, as in so many poems, frustrated) by line breaks brutal as a modernist collage. In Ryan, the enjambment sharpens her quirky prose into a series of deft pauses and releases, with the occasional ring of buried rhyme or rhyme left to linger at line end. The whole is never so economical it seems starved; but the poems are reduced to minimal gestures, like those of a Noh play.

I have nothing against William Carlos Williams; but poets who love his mastery of American speech are rarely masters themselves, and he has been a terrible influence on those for whom imitation is the sincerest form of bad poetry. His poems were wonderful when they were the exception, but prose has so infiltrated and terrorized American poetry it's now the rule—poets who prefer a subtler form of grace are criticized for being too difficult. Ryan, nevertheless, convinces me that prose can still have a sting to it. Her cunning twists and turns (like a creek meandering through a scrap yard), her way of conjuring a poem out of nothing (sometimes the poems are over before you realize they've begun), show how a poet overcomes the cruelty of style.

There are poets whose work is memorable because they have a quirky, slant-sided way of looking at the world; and often such poets are women. Emily Dickinson, Marianne Moore, Elizabeth Bishop, and contemporaries like Anne Carson, Marie Ponsot, and Kay Ryan are poets devoted to the small, oblique idea, and of all things they love Blake's grain of sand—or, in Bishop's lovely phrase, "my crumb/my mansion." (There are men of such ideas, too, like Clare and Carroll—a study of the sociology of such poetry would be of interest.) These garden ontologists are all shrinking violets (think how housebound Dickinson and Moore were, and even Bishop); but a poet doesn't have to be in the world to be of it, and there are advantages to watching intently and keeping mum—they are the virtues of predator as well as prey.

These poets often seem to have suffered some terrible wound; a hidden pain shadows their stickery poems, sometimes so imperceptibly that if you read quickly you miss it.

> *Today her things are quiet*
> *and do not reproach,*
> *each in its place,*
> *washed in the light*
> *that encouraged the Dutch*
> *to paint objects as though*
> *they were grace—*
> *the bowl, the*
> *goblet, the vase*
> *from Delft—each*
> *the reliquary*
> *of itself.*

I've quoted these poems whole, because Ryan is not a good poet of parts. You have to read her slowly, if you're to read her at all—the line breaks and rhymes remind you that patience is a virtue (not that most readers are virtuous these days). Some of her poems, I admit, are tiresome, washed with prim sentiment, plummily self-satisfied—Ryan can seem a one-trick pony. I don't want to make large claims for her, because she's a minor poet of a rare and agreeable sort. Her best work sits there meekly, tender but askew (practicing the "oiled motions/of avoidance"), hardly daring to ask the reader's attention. In a time of immodesty, when overgrown monsters stalk the earth, perhaps modesty should have its day.

Mark Doty

Late in the life of a television show, there comes the hour when the writers, having flat run out of ideas, invent some desperate turn of plot or bizarre coincidence, after which the show is never the same. This is called "jumping the shark," after a gruesomely unlikely episode of the sit-com *Happy Days;*

and for some critics it registers the moment when the willing suspension of disbelief loses its will. I hadn't thought about its bearing on poetry until, reading Mark Doty's *School of the Arts*, I found myself in the middle of a poem about an ultrasound exam of his dog, a poem whose style would have been over-the-top describing the Passion:

> *No chartable harmony,*
>> *less anatomy than a storm*
>>> *of pinpoints subtler than stars.*

> *Where does a bark upspool*
>> *from the quick,*
>>> *a baritone swell*

>> *past the sounding chambers?*

If the phrase "jumping the shark" weren't so good, I'd propose that in poetry such a moment be christened "ultrasounding the dog."

As they age, poets are more willing to smuggle into their work the humdrum events of their lives—in high art, you get *The Pisan Cantos*; in low, the ultrasound of a dog. Mark Doty has never been shy about the tragedies of his life; but his recent books have forgotten that poetry needs to be shaped, that the mere mortal record of life's ups and downs is not art. The poems in his new book sometimes sound like one side of a cell-phone conversation about people you don't know, will never meet, and don't give a hoot about. Or they're about dogs.

I've never met a dog I didn't like, but Doty makes me reconsider. There are half a dozen poems here about his dogs (which he calls, unbearably, "Time's children"), and I began to cringe every time one of the poor mutts appeared. Doty has always been a sucker for sentiment, and there's no crime in going all gooey over your pets—I just wish he wouldn't write poems about them. There's a poem about a dog so old it can't climb stairs and sits at the bottom whimpering. There's a fable about dogs writing a letter to God to protest the way they're treated. (I'm not inventing this.) It's an origin myth to explain why dogs sniff each other's asses—guess where the dog messenger has hidden the letter.

Doty invokes high art on occasion; but, if he mentions *Mrs. Dalloway*, he takes us to a movie set where a crew is filming Michael Cunningham's homage *The Hours*, not Woolf's novel. Doty is no slouch at the symbolic possibilities of pinchbeck; but a poem about a movie of a book that adopts the characters of another book leaves us very distant from life (like a footnote to a footnote to Walter Benjamin's "The Work of Art in the Age of Mechanical Reproduction"). This cozy world, everything a shadow or reflection of something else ("beautiful versions . . . no more false than they are true"), is all the cozier for being set in Doty's neighborhood, cozier still when he makes sure we know the novelist is a close friend. And, of course, the dogs come trotting out, too.

There ought to be a certain resistance in the subjects a poet chooses; but Doty now grabs his subjects right off the shelf and his attitudes from the bargain bin. (A laggardly ten pages are required to memorialize two friends in a lot of scatty philosophizing and stray quotations from Lucien Freud's notebooks.) Some poets suffer the delusion, later in their careers, that they can make a poem out of anything (it takes a Kurt Schwitters to make art from the gutter). When they think they are using their materials, the materials are just using them.

Few poems in this volume trouble the surface of this courtly, complacent life; but a sequence about masochistic sex, in which submission is sought and vulnerability gained, turns uneasy and even unpleasant. Parts of it rise toward the cheesy transcendence that makes Doty seem a pitchman for the human potential movement (one poem describes a boy being massaged as the "corpus of our Lord / still nailed to his cross"); yet the poems recognize, here and there, the seeming heartlessness of that sexual subculture, the invited pain, the loveless need of release. Then it's back to an epiphany every thirty seconds and transcendence by the hour, as if all you needed for revelation were to trot down to the Jiffy Lube.

> *If I were a sunflower I would be*
> *the branching kind,*
>
> *my many faces held out*
> *in all directions, all attention,*
>
> *awake to any golden*
> *incident descending;*
>
> *drinking in the world*

> *with my myriads of heads,*
> *I'd be my looking.*

This isn't just embarrassing. This is the new theme for *Sesame Street*.

Doty can still be a sweet and gorgeous writer, one who sees the Poundian glamour of things: "All smolder and oxblood, / these flowerheads, / flames of August: // fierce bronze, / or murky rose, / petals concluded in gold." As the silly and inane poems pile up, however—on a photo shoot (of him), on mnemonic devices for remembering gym-lock combinations—self-indulgence seems its own passion, affirmation its own disease.

Jack Gilbert

There are poets reluctant to write and poets reluctant to publish, and Jack Gilbert is a little of both. His first book, *Views of Jeopardy* (1962), won the Yale Younger Poets award; but in the following decades he published only two others. If you can trust the articles that accompanied publication of his new book, *Refusing Heaven*, the manuscript had to be pried from his fingers. Many poets publish far too much; but, in the long run, the longest of runs, the niggardly turtle probably has the advantage over the profligate hare—he leaves less junk for the future's derision. (If you think this doesn't matter, consider how high Kipling's standing might be if he'd been more circumspect.)

Gilbert's prosy, cheerless sentences pile up in patient suffering, suffering that prides itself on being without pity or delusion (which means it's riven with self-pity and self-delusion). One of the pleasures of his work is that the pathos is cut with masochism—you feel he couldn't write so much about misery without a taste for it, and like many miserable people he writes about laughter in ways that make you want to weep:

> *There is laughter*
> *every day in the terrible streets of Calcutta,*
> *and the women laugh in the cages of Bombay.*
> *If we deny our happiness, resist our satisfaction,*
> *we lessen the importance of their deprivation.*
> *We must risk delight. We can do without pleasure,*
> *but not delight. Not enjoyment. We must have*

> *the stubbornness to accept our gladness in the ruthless*
> *furnace of this world.*

I had to check the cover of the book to be sure this hadn't come from a self-help handbook or an old Jonathan Edwards sermon. Gilbert's sorrows require more than a little preaching, though even the desert fathers entered into more-miserable-than-thou competitions.

Gilbert, who came of age among the Beats in San Francisco, fled the poetry world for a reclusive, peripatetic life, one interrupted by long romances. Most poets are either a man's man or a woman's man (though Byron was perhaps both), and for Gilbert the world is a world of women. (The poems make him seem the last man standing. If you subtract the Greek gods and various poets and novelists, there's hardly another man in sight—Hannibal isn't exactly competition.) Gilbert has had three great loves. One of his wives died young of cancer, two decades ago; his poems indulge in the consoling passions of memory—and the consoling negations of grief. Yet the memories too often seem thumbed over, his love a kind of knight-errant narcissism: "We are allowed/women so we can get into bed with the Lord,/however partial and momentary that is."

Gilbert is a curiously parsimonious poet, loving abstraction the way some misers prefer bonds to cold cash—parsimony is often meanness of spirit, whatever the dividends. With age he has grown crafty and codgerlike, scorning, not just the siren songs of the poetry world (which make most good poets pour wax into their ears, if not molten lead), but the siren songs of words themselves. He sets them down grudgingly but obsessively, so even longer poems tend to be flavorless and bureaucratic (he's a clam-tongued parson with a Richardson novel somewhere inside him). If you drop a hat, he'll launch into a lecture:

> *Poetry registers*
> *feelings, delights and passion, but the best searches*
> *out what is beyond pleasure, is outside process.*
> *Not the passion so much as what the fervor can be*
> *an ingress to. Poetry fishes us to find a world*
> *part by part, as the photograph interrupts the flux*
> *to give us time to see each thing separate and enough.*
> *The poem chooses part of our endless flowing forward*
> *to know its merit with attention.*

This is duller than a freshman aesthetics textbook, with a metaphor so clumsy ("Poetry fishes us") you wonder if it wasn't ghost-written by an ad copywriter.

The poems in *Refusing Heaven* spill out, full of their own rectitude but often haggard and marooned—they're gloomy, tarnished fragments of some lost silvery life. Beyond the pissing and moaning, the endless refresher courses in self-pity, lies an old man facing death, clawing over his past and, despite the lip service to stoic resignation, absolutely terrified. His poems are interesting, not for the honesties they intend, but for the ones they conceal.

Geoffrey Hill

On Michaelmas night of 1634, the Earl of Bridgewater's children and their music teacher presented a candlelit masque at Ludlow Castle. It was probably the composer Henry Lawes, that teacher, who asked a young poet of their acquaintance to provide the verse. Only a couple of years removed from Cambridge, not yet twenty-five, entirely unknown as a poet except among close friends, the young man was John Milton. Geoffrey Hill's *Scenes from Comus* is a typically complex, crabbed, benighted, and frequently bewildering meditation on this strange allegorical entertainment.

In his late age, Hill's work has too often become a frustrating cacophony of fabulous and tedious monologues—a welter of howls, of the pained protestations of the damned. It used to be that, if you worked away patiently at a Hill poem, it would yield its beauties. Some lay temptingly on the surface, where they lie still; but the matter of the poem was often hidden in allusion or obscure fact (and obscurer wit). In his recent poems, the spillage of bile and mechanic observation by a lamely joking observer has left a reader bankrupted by the labor required to understand them. (Not surprisingly, Hill now lacks an American publisher.)

In *Scenes from Comus* (dedicated to his friend the composer Hugh Wood, whose symphonic cantata of that title was written forty years ago), an anguished calm has settled upon this frequently unsettled poet. The coarse asides and annoying mannerisms have been chastened if not subdued, the language has become less resistant, the bullying marks of punctuation less frequently indulged (in his Hopkins phase, Hill wants to sit at the reader's shoulder and rap time with a ruler, which is foolish but not criminal).

Hill is meditating here on character, on license and chastity, on the "covenants with language" that have inspired him to imperturbable obscurity, since public speech so often caters to emollient lies. Milton's Comus is a magician, a goatish enchanter who can turn men half into beasts (his mother was Circe)—he might easily be seen, like Prospero, as the poet's alter ego. The thematic strain of Milton's closet drama is chastity threatened and preserved: a lady is captured by the enchanter, who binds her with a spell. Hill's meditation is scouring but tangential—the poem touches most tellingly on the alchemy of sexual love and, perhaps, on the chastity required when two lovers live at a distance. (It is no secret that Hill lives in Boston, while his wife, a librettist, serves as curate in an English church.)

One of many clues to this dark poem comes from Hill's quotation of a phrase ("not in these noises") from Milton's description of his early reading, which included

> the divine volumes of Plato, and his equal Xenophon: where, if I should tell
> ye what I learnt of chastity and love, . . . whose charming cup is only virtue,
> which she bears in her hand to those who are worthy (the rest are cheated
> with a thick intoxicating potion, which a certain sorceress, the abuser of
> love's name, carries about) . . . , it might be worth your listening, Readers.

Hill ranges widely around "licence and exorbitance, of scheme/and fidelity; of custom and want of custom;/of dissimulation; of envy//and detraction." A good part of the poem takes place in Reykjavik, for reasons that remain mysterious. Hill expects his readers to be familiar with Hallgrímur Pétursson (a priest whose Passion hymns are among the beauties of Icelandic poetry), and brennivin (Iceland's favorite alcohol, made from scorched potatoes), and *gutta serena* (the form of blindness from which Milton suffered), and *Comus* itself, or at least to spend the time looking them up. (If he tries to look up "titagrams," however, he'll be plumb out of luck—could these be the same as strip-o-grams?)

A woman asked Browning, so goes the anecdote, probably apocryphal, what he meant by a certain knotted passage in *Sordello*. "Madame," he replied, "when I wrote that only God and I knew what it meant. Now only God knows." (Carlyle said that after reading the poem his wife didn't know "whether 'Sordello' was a man, or a city, or a book.") Some of poetry's obscurities may be recondite clue-mongering, perhaps; but most are a lively demand upon the reader's intelligence and an entrance to those dark realms where literature does its work. I don't say Hill always knows the difference; but he is an old-style modernist, whose style is didactic when it isn't simply hectoring, who still believes that poetry might be a machine for making the reader think. And he is capable of passages of stirring beauty:

> While the height-challenged sun fades, clouds become
> as black-barren as lava, wholly motionless,
> not an ashen wisp out of place, while the sun fades.
> While the sun fades its fields glow with dark poppies.
> Some plenary hand spreads out, to flaunt an end,
> old gold imperial colours.

The English landscape haunted by the past is an exemplary check to Hill's splenetic pride. It will take long critical reflection for readers to come to terms with this obdurate poem, but *Scenes from Comus* shows the valedictory temper and devious revelry of the most brilliant and irritating poet we have. Besides, how often will you read a book with a blurb by the archbishop of Canterbury?

Verse Chronicle

Victoria's Secret

Seamus Heaney

Last year a Dublin literary magazine sponsored an open competition for the best Seamus Heaney imitation. The winning poem began,

> *Niall FitzDuff brought a jar*
> *of crab apple jelly*
> *made from crabs off the tree*
> *that grew at Duff's Corner—*
> *still grows at Duff's Corner —*
> *a tree I never once saw*
> *with crab apples on it.*

This would be hilarious, if Heaney hadn't written it himself (I was kidding about the competition, though surely he would win). At sixty-seven, his Nobel dusty on the shelf, Heaney is old enough and honored enough not to have to impress anyone. He's so full of genial sanity and sly little tricks with syntax (no one since Shakespeare has been shiftier at manipulating the sequence of tenses), it's easy to be gulled by his calloused facility.

The poems in *District and Circle* (the names of overlapping London Underground lines) sometimes take up the subjects of poems from twenty or thirty years ago. You go through the book thinking, *Oh, there's the Tollund Man again, and there's Glanmore, and there's the Underground*—you'd be forgiven for thinking this a Seamus Heaney greatest hits collection. He's still a poet of wood smoke and heather, imbued with the Irish past, a sucker for every hand tool and stove lid that comes his way—he goes into a swoon over farm machinery the way Auden did over coal mines. Heaney will make a poem, as Frost and Hardy could, from something seen out of the corner of his eye; he gives you an Ireland where the ancient flows beneath the leaf litter of the modern. When critics say he's the best Irish poet since Yeats (I've said it, too), they mean there hasn't been an Irish poet as full of blarney and yet so honestly brilliant at being himself.

And yet. And yet! The verse in this new book is sloppy and casual, the poet running through his routines with great skill—but they *are* routines, without the routine magic he once brought (whatever's at stake in these poems, it's much less than two decades ago). It's a good day when he drags out the poetry engine and cranks it up; but I'm not sure the old Heaney would have settled for lines as fumbling as "Like a scorch of flame, his quid-spurt fulgent" or "But if kale meant admonition, a harrow-pin/Was correction's veriest unit." (*Veriest unit!*) Heaney has done a lot to smuggle Irish dialect into the emollient diplomacies of British English; but the new poems sometimes sound as if he were still translating *Beowulf.*

> *And for me a chance to test the edge*
> *of* seggans, *dialect blade*
> *hoar and harder and more hand-to-hand*
> *than what is common usage nowadays:*
> *sedge—marshmallow, rubber-dagger stuff.*

These lines have wrestled with Grendel, and lost.

Nobody does a better Heaney imitation than Heaney, but you can get a little tired of the tweedy offhand wisdom and sentimental touches (of a gift of ferns: "So here they are, Toraiwa, frilled, infolded, tenderized, in a little steaming basket, just for you"). The language is over-earnest, over-egged, the poems collapsing on occasion into lathers of guff. Heaney is an old master, but mastery must be refreshed and deepened if it's not to congeal into mannerism:

> *If self is a location, so is love:*
> *Bearings taken, markings, cardinal points,*
> *Options, obstinacies, dug heels, and distance,*
> *Here and there and now and then, a stance.*

This plummy set of abstractions ought to make you laugh as hard as at hearing that *Seamus Heaney* is now Cockney rhyming slang for *bikini.* (I'm not kidding about that.)

When Heaney relaxes a little, when he simply observes nature and mus-
cles it into poetry ("Panicked snipe offshooting into twilight,/Then going
awry, larks quietened in the sun"), he seems again the voice of the age on the
history of the age:

> "We were killing pigs when the Americans arrived.
> A Tuesday morning, sunlight and gutter-blood
> Outside the slaughterhouse. From the main road
> They would have heard the squealing,
> Then heard it stop and had a view of us
> In our gloves and aprons coming down the hill."

The Americans are training for the Normandy invasion; and this small in-
vasion of the killing fields, the slaughterhouse, is a quiet reminder of all the
killing to come.

Readers are by now familiar with Heaney's fascination with bog bodies,
his laments over the Industrial Revolution and the Troubles. He knows a lot
about writing poems, knows it in a craftsman's split-nailed, horn-handed way.
The things he does well he can still do brilliantly (he's the rare contemporary
poet unabashed about being a man, and not creepy or depressing about it),
but they were trademarked by a younger poet also named Seamus Heaney.
His poems carry a whiff of the ould sod, but they've been dug from peat bogs
and packaged for garden centers. If he's not careful, he'll become the equiv-
alent of a faux Irish pub, plastic shamrocks on the bar, Styrofoam shillelaghs
on the wall, and green ale on tap.

Louise Glück

The tense, overwrought poems in *Averno*, nervous in their very syllables,
are striking additions to one strain of the American psyche—if there were a
Goddess of Anxiety, Louise Glück would be the temple priestess. Her recent
books have drawn their mysteries from the Greek gods to a degree even Freud
might not have anticipated. For a woman who bears the "horrible mantle/of
daughterliness," there's no more desirable origin myth than Persephone's—
should the psychiatrists of the future need a Persephone complex, they'll
have to pay Glück royalties.

Glück revisits the scenes of childhood as if bad memories held some masochistic allure. Though Greek myths thrived on punishment repeated—the temptations of Tantalus, the labor of Sisyphus, the torture of Prometheus—they were never masochistic (to invent the sadistic torments of the *Inferno*, however, Dante must have studied Roman law and Greek myth). The troubled daughter looks over her shoulder at her parents, seeking a scapegoat or feeling like one.

> *"You girls," my mother said, "should marry*
> *someone like your father."*
>
> *That was one remark. Another was,*
> *"There is no one like your father."*

Who wouldn't trade a mother like that for a goddess, one who would rescue you from hell? The Christian Passion, with its mother of sorrows, its barren cave, its descent into and resurrection from hell, seems a distant echo of the myth.

Glück's poems inch forward, phrase by weary phrase, line by doomed line, as if it killed her to write every word. These monologues of distress have no time for chitchat—her mortal longings find their subjects in death, or dying, or the soul.

> *What will the soul do for solace then?*
> *I tell myself maybe it won't need*
> *these pleasures anymore;*
> *maybe just not being is simply enough,*
> *hard as that is to imagine.*

A little of this goes a long way. Glück's neurotic intensity lies plain on the page, bleached of descriptive pleasure, because any image of the world is taboo ("when the sun sets in winter it is/incomparably beautiful and the memory of it/lasts a long time"—*Gee, thanks,* you want to say).

The claustrophobic form of Glück's verse—the nervous, shivery lines; the agitated sentences—whispers what the poems sometimes shout, that we are lonely, atomized beings with little to offer each other, or nothing at all. Glück lives for extremes. Indeed, her nature is drawn *only* to extremes—every beautiful moment makes her think of death, as thought of her terrible return to

the marriage bed no doubt tormented Persephone, the months she was al-
lowed to walk the earth. (The Romans believed she emerged every spring
from the crater lake of Avernus, the doorway to the underworld; the Greeks,
that she appeared in fall, after the long drought of the Greek summer). The
unnerving quality of these poems lies less in what the myth offers the poet
than in what she offers the myth.

The purity of death may be glamorous; but as a subject it's exhausting, and
monotonous, too. (Emily Dickinson had visions of death some days, but she
had other days.) Glück can't provide the gratifications of a poet more will-
ing to come to terms with the rhetorical possibilities of the art—every line is
stripped bare, naked to the knife edge of hysteria, the poetry of denial some-
times laced with a quiet paranoia: "I know what they say when I'm out of the
room. / Should I be seeing someone, should I be taking / one of the new drugs
for depression."

Glück is so easily caught up in fortune-cookie wisdom, capable of hokum
like "You exist as the stars exist, / participating in their stillness, their immen-
sity," I appreciate her more the further away I get. This doesn't mean her
poetry works best when half forgotten, only that it disturbs me more deeply
when I can ignore the straitened language, the tight-lipped grimaces, the
brittle and petulant temper. In fading recollection, the brittleness becomes
all too human fragility, the stifled speech a guarded honesty, the airy thin-
ness a rueful taciturnity. Glück has made her own an abandoned back al-
ley of the Plath estate, her poems like chamber music for bandsaw and ra-
zor blades. Had Plath survived, grinding on decade after decade, would she,
too, have become a minimalist, enamored of the pregnant pause, the pious
hush?

Not all Glück's previous encounters with myth have evaded blind comedy,
but the success of *Averno* is that the reader isn't tempted to laugh too often.
Limited in range and tone and figure, limited to a degree you're surprised
they work at all, these eighteen poems repeat themselves until her repetitions
have a mythic squalor. You're glad to shut this airless book and look at the
dumb world outside, a blackbird taking up tufts from an old doormat, two
roofers squatting on broken slates—all that life excluded from a book like this.
But a book like this can unsettle a life like that. If you want to avert your eyes
from the pain recorded, the fretful worrying, the bloodless anxiety, you must
remember that the torment Glück suffers is to be stuck eternally writing Lou-
ise Glück poems.

Don Paterson

The Scottish poet Don Paterson has a distinctive voice, at once confident and rhetorical (not an easy combination, though one sometimes found in haggis), and his poems are fond of abstractions unexpected as a view of the ocean after rounding a bend on a dingy lane. He can write largely of large things, but also largely of small ones—Seamus Heaney was like that at the start.

> *Here, beside the fordable Atlantic,*
> *reborn into a secret candidacy,*
> *the fontanelles reopen one by one*
> *in the palms, then the breastbone and the brow,*
>
> *aching at the shearwater's wail, the rowan*
> *that falls beyond all seasons. One morning*
> *you hover on the threshold, knowing for certain*
> *the first touch of the light will finish you.*

Landing Light is a convenient introduction to a poet with a deceptive touch. The poems seem written from necessity, not simply to satisfy the small itches many poets feel; yet Paterson is oddly ill at ease at the center of his poems. Indeed, the persona he creates, everywhere given the lie by the subtleties of his language, is slightly doltish and cowardly, rather surprised to be writing at all. In British poetry, there's a long strain of gawky hayseeds like Clare and Burns, and Paterson takes every advantage of it.

English verse has had a torrid love affair with Ireland but remains standoffish toward Scotland, as if Hadrian's Wall had never been dismantled. There were the Scottish Chaucerians, of course, and later Burns and Stevenson, but otherwise almost no one until Hugh MacDiarmid. The Scottish are all too fond of their own poetry, which to the English is part of the comedy—and there is the further problem of verse in Scots or Lallans, once an honest dialect but now reduced almost entirely to a literary language. There have been loving translations into Scots of the New Testament and *Macbeth*, translations so good you think the gospel writers and Shakespeare must have worn kilts. In the late stages of a dialect, poets turn into stuffy antiquarians, guarding themselves against influence, or end up sounding like the dominant fashion in the dominating tongue—the dialect is no longer powerful enough to influence itself. Paterson includes two or three halfhearted poems in Scots, dragging their glosses; but, like the best Irish poets, he writes in English because it happens to be his language.

Paterson often steers his poems toward small epiphanies, approached with wary patience.

> They caught him by the thread of his one breath
> and pulled him up. They don't know how it held.
> And so today I thank what higher will
> brought us to here, to you and me and Russ,
> the great twin-engined swaying wingspan of us
> roaring down the back of Kirrie Hill
>
> and your two-year-old lungs somehow out-revving
> every engine in the universe.

This is for his younger son, who almost died at birth. Other poems defeat me—I end up feeling that their mysteries lie just beneath the surface, lacking only one small fact to make them plain. Paterson loves turning the dailiness of life into something mock heroic; the rhetoric comes within a breath of being blowsy, but his homely honesty keeps the lines genuine as lead pipe.

Paterson is willing to turn his hand to any sort of verse—there's even a concrete poem shaped like a guitar (he's a professional musician on the side). A master of the short lyric, he rarely suffers from Muldoonitis, that general affliction of British poetry these days (Paterson's earlier books did show a touch of the fever)—there's so much he does with ease and flair, it's interesting to note the little he can't do. His translation of Canto XIII of the *Inferno* is cast into quatrains, a daring choice; but the stanzas reach for their rhymes, padded out in a way his other poems are not. Whenever he tries to be entertaining, Paterson becomes gauche and uncertain (his gifts are entertainment enough); and his long-winded long poems tend to beetle off into a fabulistic realm from which there is no return.

Paterson is never afraid to ask the reader's attention, just unwilling to bow or scrape for it. There are a score of ambitious, intricately spoken, devious poems here, self-mocking in their mythologies, quietly waving the cross of St. Andrew, their local humilities somehow the more spacious for that. Paterson has been the best thing to happen to British poetry since Glyn Maxwell and Michael Hofmann. For a small book, *Landing Light* covers a large stony ground.

Tess Gallagher

Tess Gallagher's wide-eyed, well-meaning poems were the embodiment of seventies narcissism—conversational and intimate, chatty at times, they burnished old hurts into the sentimental routines of confession. *Dear Ghosts,* (the comma, part of that title, is one her many affectations) is recognizably the work of that younger poet, now more than sixty, long widowed, suffering the aftermath of operations for breast cancer—her new poems are roughened by a mortality that has brought not serenity but doubt.

Gallagher's virtues have gradually slipped into vices—the poems are now dusted with New Age spirituality (often Buddhism lite), the once-easy phrases kinked, the imagery tortured or simply malformed:

> *Our inner plea: not to be absent*
> *from pain through the tourniquet*
> *of irony, denial's tepid bath water*
> *that poisons the soul's aquifer.*

Everywhere you turn you find the nest of self-regard fouled by the bandage of metaphor in the forest of piety: "I apologize falsely/for my counterfeit amalgam" or

> *the rain-telegraph keeps getting through—its urgency*
> *so like the midnight flag*
> *of a chewing gum I bought in Tokyo.*

Drama queens can be charming at thirty; at sixty, they're insufferable. Gallagher's new poems don't think the unthinkable so much as unthink the thinkable: they turn honorable reservations about war into op-ed pieces. During a week of R & R with her first husband, a Vietnam War pilot, the poet kisses a young sailor in a sugarcane field. It's a small moment of grace and absolution; but you're still reeling from her Billy Sunday sermon about the soldiers' wives, "their suitcases/crammed with department-store negligees for conjugal trysts/that seem pornographic now in their psycho-erotic/rejuvenation of the killing." *Psycho-erotic rejuvenation!* And how snobbish that *department-store.* (Where else could you buy lingerie then? Victoria's Secret hadn't been invented yet.) Later, her head shaved after chemotherapy, the poet compares herself to the Jews whose heads were shaved at Auschwitz.

Gallagher assumes that the reader will find her life endlessly fascinating while she kneads her tidy domestic moments into parables (and ties them with the ribbon of homily in the boudoir of second thoughts on the avenue of regret). She's become so garrulous and windy, however, that what's intended sincerely often seems grotesquely funny. When she rescues a lamb from the slaughterhouse (you may not care how much she paid, but she'll tell you), it's a mawkish gesture; and she knows it. That ought to be enough; but she has to make the grand statement, too: "While / my country makes war, one lamb / is saved in the West of Ireland, / a sign to what oppresses." Warmongers, take note.

The best poems here stay subdued in their moments: during World War II, her father rises before dawn to light the fires in his neighbors' stoves, a job he's taken to help his family get by. Such a poem might be modest and affecting if the poet didn't feel it necessary to drag in the atomic bombs about to fall on Hiroshima and Nagasaki. (The connection? The "use of people, their homes, as incidental / combustibles.") An uncle meets his dead brother in a field, and no one believes him; yet the poem can't stop there—the poet must have her say, and she always has her say. You feel helpless as a crowd being worked by a snake-oil salesman.

A poet has to think pretty well of herself to begin her book with an epigraph from one of her own poems (and, better still, to misquote it). Poets often use the acknowledgments page to pay off debts to their nearest and dearest, but it's remarkable how many nearest and dearest there now seem to be. I've been wondering where this self-congratulatory gesture would end; but Gallagher has set the all-time record, unlikely ever to be broken—she thanks 101 people, including her hairdresser. The credits of many Hollywood movies have been shorter. She even apologizes for leaving anyone out—"Maybe I can add you into the next edition!" she says winsomely.

The language of gratitude needn't be so overwrought ("their gifts are contributions at a level where even thanks is a kind of ragged attempt to express the blessings of right companioning") or sloppy with self-regard (of her mother: "she has been a great and overweening cherishing"—does Gallagher know what *overweening* means?). No one would begrudge the poet her appreciations, but when flaunted they seem boastful—gratitude may be the eighth deadly sin. Like her prose, her poetry is now studied in artifice, oddly informal and tarted up at once, as if plastered with Kabuki makeup. Perhaps the reader won't notice, still in shock after learning that one of these poems "will appear on coffee mugs at Starbucks across the country." Gallagher's new poems are so manufactured you wouldn't be surprised to turn them over and find MADE IN CHINA on the bottom.

Anne Carson

There are no sins in literature except unsuccessful ones. Successful sins are called virtues. Anne Carson, who moonlights as a classics professor (unless she's a classics professor who moonlights as a poet), has for the past decade been the acceptable face of the avant-garde. In *Autobiography of Red* (1998) and *The Beauty of the Husband* (2001), her poems promised that postmodernism might be a new dispensation, that if you stole, borrowed, and begged enough, something interesting might come. Her love of the classics gave a *gravitas* to poetic experiments that otherwise would have been trivial.

I was never sure how far Carson could take such experiments, which despite their deadpan charms used up all the oxygen in the room. The poems began to seem less original and more a slightly frenzied burlesque. Being an iconoclast is a good thing until you start trying to live up to your reputation; before you know it, you're swallowing a flaming sword while balancing a copy of Heraclitus on your nose. *Decreation* is a ragbag of strange ambition— there are four essays (on sleep, Longinus, eclipses, and "decreation"), three sequences of poems sometimes in brute or ironic relation to them, a choral response to a painting, the shot list for a documentary, a note on a pair of Beckett's television plays, as well as a screenplay, an oratorio, and an opera.

Carson delights in dizzy leaps of thought—the essay on Longinus also tangos with Antonioni, and soon she's writing poems with titles like "Longinus' Dream of Antonioni," "Ode to the Sublime by Monica Vitti," and "Kant's Question about Monica Vitti." The poet can make the intellectual seem jolly while puncturing its pretensions; but the only good things about these poems are their titles, the lines often rambling along in the opium dream of café philosophers: "blondes/being/always/fatally/reinscribed/on an old cloth/faintly,/interminably/undone, why/does Plato/call Necessity/a 'wandering clause' isn't it because/you can/'t/tell/where/she got in?" Plato seems thrown in only to anchor this mess of academic jargon and lapsed punctuation.

Carson is intent here on the relation between fact and documentary, on jealousy, on the feeling of wrongness, and on "decreation," a notion (about effacing the self) borrowed from Simone Weil. The poet stalks her subjects from oblique angles, but her critical readings are often bullying and contrived. Elizabeth Bishop's Man-Moth becomes, courtesy the temple of Askle-pios and Jacques Lacan, not a strange unworldly creature but "sleep itself." There's not much in the poem to support this reading, but Carson's slippery use of symbol (she has the love of symbolic readings found in those with a taste for psychoanalysis) is like the philosopher's stone—with it, you can turn every scrap of metal in the junkyard into gold.

Many of Carson's ideas are first pitched as essays; by the time they've been worked into poems, they seem pawed over and secondhand. She knows she has an odd view of things; when she trusts her inspiration too much, she seems to believe every idea brilliant *because* it is odd. Her oratorio "Lots of Guns," a self-conscious tribute to Gertrude Stein, uses five performers, each "equipped with a triangular white paper flag on a long stick, . . . snapped smartly up and down," and has choruses even kindness can't help giggling over:

> *The mythic past.*
> *The curious past.*
> *Lots of guns expressing restlessness.*
> *Lots of guns with cherry cobbler.*
> *The man is tremendously.*
> *The woman almost.*

For pompous silliness, this is hard to beat, but her opera manages to beat it. A single stage direction may give the flavor: "Sung by Simone and Madame Weil waltzing in an empty factory while the Chorus of the Void do calisthen-ics in slow motion." The Chorus of the Void consists of ten transparent tap-dancers. What are the lyrics like? Here are Madam and Mademoiselle Weil:

> *Please translate the word* thankyou.
> *Ontologically not new!*
> *Theoretically blue!*
> *Naked as the dew!*
> *I'm lime green who are you!*
> *No idea what to do!*
> *Just be glad this song is through!*

No comment.

I linger over Carson's striking insights into classical texts (a beautiful pas-sage is devoted to sleep in the *Odyssey*) and the psychosocial dialogue in her poems, recording the fraught moments of couples at odds. Even her offhand remarks can be provoking—who else would have noticed the "poached-in-eternity look Beckett has in his last photos"? Yet far too much of this book has the burnt-toast reek of academic air—her poems have become parlor games of extraordinary tedium. When you're told that the opera requires "7 female robots built by Hephaistos," you're not sure whether Carson has spent too long reading *R.U.R.* or watching *Star Wars*.

Geoffrey Hill

No sooner do I finish reviewing one book by Geoffrey Hill than another thumps onto my desk. In late age, Hill has found a devil-may-care giddiness, a taste for diatribe and invective that seems unstoppable this side of the grave. This famously taciturn and thin-skinned poet, so constipated in his early years, can be forgiven for carousing now—it took him a quarter century to publish his first five books, but in the last decade he's published half a dozen more. His new style may well be the result of antidepressants, as he confessed in an interview; but who will complain if the muse can be found in a pill bottle?

Hill's recent books have been at times unreadable, even by those who want to read them (taking pills against depression has done nothing for his cussedness). *Without Title* is clearer and less frustrated than his ranting monologues, but its short poems and one long sequence are no less stringent in their demands. Hill has often given the impression of wanting to communicate, if only he didn't find it humiliating (communication being an act of love)—he has dressed up this aversion in thunderous essays, but I don't believe that clarity inevitably soils meaning with the unctuous language of public consumption. Besides, there are moments when no living English poet has written more gorgeously:

> *the singing iron footbridges, tight weirs*
> *pebble-dashed with bright water, a shivey blackthorn's*
> *clouded white glass that's darker veined or seamed,*
>
> *crack willow foliage, pale as a new fern,*
> *silver-plated ivy in the sun's angle.*

Hill's redolent landscapes have excited suspicion among critics, though it's possible to see them as indulging in the aesthetic, like a warm mineral bath, while calling such beauty to account—his snarled complications allow him to have things both ways. ("Shivey" is wool cloth full, like Hill's poems, of dark burrs or splinters.)

The new poems live gloomily under sentence of death—"Death fancies us but finally/leaves us alone," he says mordantly; and it takes a second to register what that leaving alone means. Hill believes in syntax's autocracy, and a reader must sound the sentences before the drama of meaning comes plain (the violent riddles beneath syntax are more darkly defended). When the mood takes him, he'll coat every phrase with tar and dare the reader to grasp it:

> *Vorónezh: Ovid thrusts abruptly wide*
> *the ice-locked shutters, discommodes his lyre*
> *to Caesar's harbingers. Interrogation,*
> *whatever is most feared. Truth's fatal vogue,*
> *sad carnifex, self-styled of blood and wax.*

Even these brutish lines can be winched to the surface, given patience and a stout cable. Mandelstam was exiled to Vorónezh, cast like Ovid far from the warm society of the capital. The interrogation remembers 1984, where men were broken using their worst phobias (rats, in Winston Smith's case). A carnifex is an executioner.

There are poems here of the most defiant opacity, others that descend into an old man's muttering, especially the fraught meditations of a series of "pindarics" (a form Congreve called a "bundle of rambling incoherent thoughts"), each inspired by a scrap from Cesare Pavese's journals. It's easy to grouse about Hill—the phrases piled up like rear-end collisions, the "savage rudeness" (to use a phrase quoted from Emerson), the knee-jerk wordplay, the odd marks of punctuation, the Colonel Blimpish apophthegms ("Women are a contagious abstinence," "Small hotels are to die in"). "I tell myself," he boasts, "don't wreck a good phrase simply to boost sense." Don't murder your darlings, then—simply embalm them.

Hill desperately needs a group of acolytes to tease out his meanings. It's not that his verse is austere and forbidding, not that the price of admission is so high—the truth is that Hill just doesn't like the reader all that much. Readers are a tax on his purity, but few can bear to be loathed by the books they read. (Reading, after all, is a *voluntary* labor.) Pound, however difficult, has a far more welcoming intelligence; but Pound longed to be a teacher—hence his lectures, and *The ABC of Reading*, and his plans for an Ezuversity. If Hill wants to transform the reader, it's a prophet's task; the only reader worthy enough may be Hill himself, though poets are forever deprived of the salvations of their work.

> *One solstice has swung past, the immeasurably*
> *varied, unvarying, profusion of hedge-burgeon*
> *stays richly dulled, immoveable for a while.*
> *Over by Studley the close air is dove-grey,*
> *a hollow without sun*
> *though heat had filled it; shadow-reservoir,*
>
> *more than a mirage, however you chance to look.*

More than any poet alive, Hill has the pulse of English inside him, knowing like a lawyer all its loopholes and vagrancies. The stopped energy of his landscapes has become a valediction, the epitaph of a poet who cannot give up his rages, even as age grinds him down. In a few months this book will be available in the United States. That this brilliant, maimed, and cantankerous poet lost his American press and was for a time published only in Britain did not flatter our publishers, much less our poetry.

Attack of the Anthologists

The Oxford Book of American Poetry, ed. David Lehman

American poetry began with a governor's daughter, a Puritan minister on the Massachusetts frontier, a ship captain who edited an anti-Federalist newspaper, and a slave. Often the best thing about these poets is their biographies. All but the captain were born outside the colonies; but, even before there was a United States, they wrote in the democratic helter-skelter of the New World. To paraphrase Samuel Johnson, the verse written during the century and a half before the Revolution was "like a dog's walking on his hinder legs. It is not done well; but you are surprized to find it done at all."

Anne Bradstreet leads off anthologies of American poetry because she's the first American poet who wasn't perfectly awful. Daughter of one governor and wife of another, she wrote with the high-minded clumsiness of the imperfectly educated.

> Art can doe much, but this maxime's most sure,
> A weake or wounded braine admits no cure.

The early American poets were naïfs with the memory of sophistication, like carpenters working with primitive tools under primitive conditions. There's a quaintness to the work of the preacher Edward Taylor and the ship captain Philip Freneau and the slave Phillis Wheatley, but sometimes a queer rightness, too. When Taylor writes, about infinity, "Who in this Bowling Alley bowld the Sun?" you think how much Donne would have liked the metaphor; but you only have to compare the work of these poets to what was being written across the water by Dryden and Pope to see how bad the home team was.

The glimmers are the more disheartening for being only glimmers. Joel Barlow, the most technically accomplished poet of the Revolutionary period, wrote heroic couplets with the droll intelligence to bring them off. "The Hasty-Pudding" embodies the American drive to meet the British on their own terms and go them one better, even if he is competing with Pope's "The Rape of the Lock," a poem most of a century old, its style long out of date.

Poets born after the Revolution grew up in a different world, where Americans developed the self-consciousness necessary for a literary tradition not so intransigently innocent. This was the age of literary men who made their living as editors and lecturers and even poets, an age where the economies of leisure meant that a man could earn his bread by his words. Yet with that self-consciousness came a certain conservatism. William Cullen Bryant and Ralph Waldo Emerson and Henry Wadsworth Longfellow were poets of more power than originality, still looking over their shoulders to check what the British were doing; and with every backward glance they failed to behold the America lying before them.

We should wonder, not how an American at the age of seventeen could compose a poem as death-hunted as "Thanatopsis," but why Bryant produced such porridge afterward. He's not the only might-have-been in American poetry, just one of the saddest—his poetic powers were soon lost in "rosy depths" and "plashy brinks." Edgar Allan Poe, on the other hand, is a reminder that our poetry has often depended on wounded oddballs more than literary men but that not all wounded oddballs make good poets—he wrote in a fanciful poetic diction coated in tar and set alight.

Emerson, though only a mediocre poet himself, was the first to see that there was an American poetry to be written. Imagine his excitement as he read a thin vanity-press quarto published by an anonymous author, a quarto titled *Leaves of Grass*. Walt Whitman, that American self-invention, was not the rough in a slouch hat he pretended to be but a Brooklyn printer and newspaper editor with an overactive imagination. He had seen the West only from the deck of a Mississippi sidewheeler; yet his longings held a mirror to the American soul, its taste for guilt and reinvention, its wanderlust, its love of its own raw language. Whitman gave Emerson exactly what he'd asked for, a poet of our "ample geography" who could make use of "our logrolling, our stumps and their politics, . . . our boasts, and our repudiations." More than he ever realized, Emerson was responsible for Whitman's imposture and masquerade.

We must not forget that secret sharer who influenced American verse in more subterranean ways. Emily Dickinson's self-mutilating psychology and silvery unhappiness give a differential specimen of the American character. A bloodless recluse in Amherst, indrawn as a clam, she developed her own shorthand language, one so powerful the rhythms borrowed from hymns seem resolutely her own. Dickinson wrote almost half her poems during the Civil War, scratching out a poem a day during the hard year of Shiloh. Perhaps something of the horrors far to the south touched the death fantasies within her. From these two damaged psyches, American poetry has borrowed more than it cares to admit; yet our poetry was just as tormented and even more deeply molded by the King James Bible, Shakespeare, Milton, Coleridge, Wordsworth, Keats, and many another Briton. It was our language and our landscape that we were a long time accepting.

The dirty secret of American poetry is that until Whitman and Dickinson it was no damned good, and until the modernists it was not good again. It takes only ten pages for the new *Oxford Anthology of American Poetry*, edited by David Lehman, to get through the seventeenth century, and ten more for the eighteenth. The whole nineteenth century takes fewer than two hundred, half of these devoted to Whitman and Dickinson. After that, for nine hundred pages, it is one long diet of the twentieth century.

Lehman, though a poet himself, is better known as editor of the annual series *The Best American Poetry* and author of *Signs of the Times*, an attack on deconstructive literary theory. *The Oxford Book of American Verse*, as it was first known, was edited by the distinguished scholar F. O. Matthiessen in 1950 and, as *The New Oxford Book of American Verse*, revised by the equally distinguished Richard Ellmann in 1976. Lehman's introduction, a good deal of it a defense against his predecessors, lives in a prose world where assumptions are *governing*, essays *seminal*, and stock always goes *sky-high*. He's proud of what he calls the "widening of focus" here, though it's hard to see why this isn't just "out of focus" by another name. Matthiessen, as Lehman notes, included 51 poets, and Ellmann 77; Lehman has 210, a quarter of them born between 1940 and 1950. This grotesquely overrates the wartime and baby-boom generation, still an amorphous crowd of genial talent through which Lehman offers no path.

A good anthologist must have a few bizarre quirks, though preferably not too many. Lehman's catholic taste and appreciation of minor voices make him ill at ease with major ones. Take his treatment of the moderns, the most radically complex generation American poetry has produced. Robert Frost, whose dark American pastoral is heir to Dickinson's private shadows, produced such a crop of famous poems it's difficult to leave any out; but Lehman offers too many of the chalk-board set pieces beloved by generations of high-school teachers. Marianne Moore's most disturbing animal poems and the later meditative poems of William Carlos Williams are ignored. Wallace Stevens finds himself naked without even a stanza from his long poems, while T. S. Eliot is begrudged the roustabout humor of the Sweeney poems or "The Hippopotamus." And Ezra Pound, poor Ezra Pound, hardly sets foot here, receiving fewer pages than any of the others despite his influence on a century once called the "Pound Era." After the moderns, the next major American poet is . . . W. H. Auden! Auden lived in New York for some thirty years and wrote poems about his adopted country; but it's odd to include a poet of such English intonation and character, especially with poems written, a few of them, before he'd ever set foot in America.

Lehman is such a democrat, he can hardly bear to leave anyone out (sixteen of the eighteen editors of *The Best American Poetry* are included, and the missing pair were born after 1950, the cutoff). It's one thing to leaven the majors with wits like Dorothy Parker or kooky originals like H. Phelps Putnam (who wrote, among other things, a pair of sonnets about genitals), quite another to try to revive the long dead reputations of Emma Lazarus, Adelaide Crapsey, Angelina Weld Grimké, Samuel Greenberg, Leonie Adams, Mark Van Doren, John Wheelwright, and dozens of other trivial worthies (even on a bad day, a battered stanza by Eliot makes these poets look like a dish of mealworms). In a lengthy anthology, this means there are vast desert spaces between the poets worth reading.

The editor has wisely not welcomed song lyrics, though he has wavered enough to include one hymn, two blues, and a song by Bob Dylan; yet I miss a section of American folk songs and ballads. We're given little more than "Casey at the Bat," that great American paean to failure. None of the poets, Lehman claims, has been favored for race or gender (too many anthologies balance the great white males of the past by ignoring the lesser white males of the present); but it's no improvement to offer, as representative of contemporary poetry, a swarm of mediocre white men and almost as many mediocre white women.

Lehman's introduction is not much help in coming to terms with his taste. He's suspicious of overanalyzing poems and would prefer that readers experience a poem's "uncanny mysteriousness," which sounds like the credo of the Know-Nothing Party. (This may explain the book's frustrating lack of notes.

It can't explain why the poems are littered with errors.) "I prize, as do many readers," he declares, "eloquence, passion, intelligence, conviction, wit, originality, pride of craft, an eye for the genuine, an ear for speech, an instinct for the truth"—this must be more gaseous blather than any anthologist has fit into one sentence for a long time.

As Lehman nears the present, his choices grow off balance and whimsical. John Ashbery receives twice as many pages as Pound and almost three times as many as Robert Lowell, who might just as well never have written his extraordinary early poems. (You can get the idea of Ashbery in two pages—almost everything after that is sludge.) It's simply madness to reduce John Berryman to half a dozen pages and Randall Jarrell to five (scanting his great war poems), while lavishing eight on Charles Bukowski and ten on James Schuyler. Lehman's fondness for the Beats and the New York School (their glamour largely faded now) means that Allen Ginsberg and Kenneth Koch and Frank O'Hara are given acres of elbow room, though Ginsberg is weirdly denied *Howl*, the most famous poem of the postwar period. The strangest inclusion is the Canadian Anne Carson, here because she "has taught in the United States and has a wide following among younger poets"—with standards like that, you could include any poet who ever came here for a long weekend.

Reading through the poets even younger, I'm drawn to some I've frequently criticized—to the strangled psychology of Louise Glück and C. K. Williams's voyeuristic confessions, to the smudged Turneresque landscapes of Charles Wright and Jorie Graham's MRI cross-sections of consciousness. Yet far more pages are wasted on giddy, crowd-pleasing poets like Billy Collins and James Tate. Worse, the younger poets are getting older—the youngest in Matthiessen was thirty-three; the youngest in Ellmann, forty-two. The youngest in Lehman is fifty-five, and at this rate the baby in the next edition will be over seventy.

Anthologies age as badly as fashion, and the pillbox hats and pearls of one generation must give way to the tattoos and tongue studs of another. It took a long while for the most distinguished press in the mother country to notice that Americans wrote poetry at all; but where Oxford's first anthology of American verse could have been carried around in a small handbag, the new one has to be wheeled around in a shopping cart. This bloated, earnest, largely mediocre new *Oxford* takes up a lot of space on the shelf without providing a clear view of our moment. That chance won't come again for another generation.

100 *Great Poems of the Twentieth Century,* ed. Mark Strand

In Greek, an anthology meant a bouquet. The existence of such bouquets tells us two things—that the ancients liked cut flowers and that they found them-selves short of time. Mark Strand's 100 *Great Poems of the Twentieth Century* has trouble figuring out what it wants to be, and his introduction is hedged with excuses for what it is. You might make all sorts of assumptions after read-ing the title, and the introduction is in a hurry to tell you how wrong you are. The editor announces, in a somewhat embarrassed fashion, that the poets come only from the Americas and Europe (one manages to straggle in from Australia), that no poet was born after 1927 (or, if foreign, somewhat later—there's a Danish poet as young as seventy), that each poet is permitted the star turn of only one poem (though due to an editorial mishap one poet had to be given two), and that an attempt was made to balance the usual suspects with others scarcely guilty of anything.

After the editor's nervous apologetics, you're grateful he does not invoke, as anthologists almost ritually do, poetry's Luminous Richness, or Humanizing Power, or any of the broad claims that make reading poetry irritating and be-ing a poet a torment. You are not spared, however, the reassuring knowledge that the poems chosen "require no special knowledge for their appreciation" and that in the editor's opinion they "can be read more than once without diminishing their power to persuade, amuse, or entrance," statements that come with a whiff of condescension.

A reader might be forgiven for wondering who needs such an anthology, since anyone who loves poetry will be depressed to see Eliot's "Prufrock" or Auden's elegy for Yeats, poems any tenth grader should know, yet taken aback to find Elizabeth Bishop represented by a diffuse and overly earnest poem like "In the Waiting Room" (much beloved by scholars of "identity") or Yeats by the laggard "In Memory of Eva Gore-Booth and Con Markievicz." The editor might answer that he means to be provocative; but surely readers unfa-miliar with poetry ought to be given the best poems at hand, while familiar readers ought to be jostled and stirred by every page—it is difficult to serve both masters. A good poetry anthology requires taste combined with irratio-nal prejudice. There are poems here by Marianne Moore, Robert Lowell, Theodore Roethke, and Dylan Thomas already collected to death, and po-ems good enough by poets who have written much better (it's hard to choose a weak poem by Frost, but Strand has succeeded). Any anthologist who includes Alan Ansen instead of Randall Jarrell or Edwin Muir instead of A. E. Housman comes from a region where the bears are princes.

Poetry has never been entirely the preserve of men, though until the present generation you had to look very hard to find women, so it is perhaps understandable that the editor has looked a little too hard and included mediocre work by mediocre poets like Louise Bogan, Ruth Stone, May Swenson, and Edna St. Vincent Millay (responsible for the anthology's worst line, "White against a ruddy cliff you stand, chalcedony on sard"). Readers who already adore Elizabeth Bishop and Marianne Moore, however, will be grateful, if they don't know her work, for a typically charming and idiosyncratic poem by Amy Clampitt.

Half the anthology consists of poets born in the United States or Great Britain, which leaves the other half for the rest of the world; and as a result the quality there is somewhat higher, or would be in that utopia where translations are better than the originals. Alas, the reader limited to English may wonder why anyone would bother reading Neruda, Hikmet, Akhmatova, or Alberti. A reader must usually take poets in translation at a deep discount (it's odd that wit translates better than humor, since you'd think it would be the other way around)—it's a miracle that the reader sees a glimmer of the gifts of Rilke and Cavafy, Pavese and Tsvetaeva. Translation may be a bad business, but it's the only business for the monoglots Americans have become.

100 Great Poems of the Twentieth Century, its title reminiscent of the marquees that used to line Broadway ("100 Dancing Girls 100"), is unlikely to convince new readers to throw down their tabloids and pick up a book of poetry. What might do so would be an anthology much more personal and crotchety, full of poems the anthologist simply and helplessly loved—whatever the promises of the introduction here, too many poems seem like timeservers or pensioners, included out of a desire to please (or, worse, a desire not to offend). It may seem ungrateful to complain about an anthology so catholic in its tastes; but the former poet laureate is one of the few poets who could produce an anthology worth the reading, and he has wasted an opportunity. Anthologies like this are published for occasions on which a present is traditional but diamonds too expensive. Never meant to be read, the guilt book ends up on a thrift-store shelf, with forlorn inscriptions like "Happy Birthday" and "To the young graduate with love from Cousin Jake."

The Lost World of Lawrence Durrell

C zech has one word for *Schadenfreude*, I'm told, but another for taking delight in the misfortunes others have caused themselves. Though most poets are neglected, few have been the source of their own neglect. Lawrence Durrell is so well known for the steam-heated sex and casual betrayals of *The Alexandria Quartet* and for travel journals like *Prospero's Cell*, it's difficult to remember that he was once considered a poet of great promise.

Though he wrote mediocre novels in the thirties, including one under a pseudonym, Durrell's literary imagination was from the first devoted to poetry (he must have tired of hearing that his prose was "poetic"). Like Faulkner and Joyce, he found his way to fiction through poetry and, once there, discovered it hard to make his way back. His first book of poems, published in 1943 when he was thirty-one, had a touch of Auden, a dab of Eliot, and the amalgam of period manners young poets fool themselves into thinking original, when it is just theft in parts.

> *Curse Orion who pins my man like moth,*
> *Who sleeps in the monotony of his zone,*
> *Who is a daft ankle-bone among stars,*
> *O shame on the beggar by silent lands*
> *Who has nothing but carbon for his own.*
> *Uncouple the flutes! Strike with the black rod!*

Reading Durrell's apprentice verse is like strolling through a regional museum whose exhibits have never been updated—a dinosaur wanders through the foyer, missing its tail; glass cases imprison a moth-eaten panda and seven tigers shot in a single afternoon; and off in a corner a woman in an eighty-year-old apron pours eighty-year-old tea.

The lines quoted above come from the most ambitious and protracted of Durrell's early poems, "The Death of General Uncebunke: A Biography in Little," which proclaims itself "not satire but an exercise in ironic compassion," meaning satire by another name. This jaunty, overextended joke, a portrait of a fictional explorer and Tory M.P., "must be read like a novel," the author declared, "to be really appreciated." It's hard to know how poker-faced he was, since he also advised that the poem "should be read with the inner voice, preferably in some dialect."

Indebted more to Eliot's Sweeney and Auden's James Honeyman than to the surrealists mentioned by Peter Porter, the editor of this *Selected Poems*, such a poem shows Durrell straining, not so much at what poetry could do, but at what he could do in poetry. Like many minor poets, he might have made a greater mark had he written nothing but light verse:

> *Now the blacker the berry, the thicker comes the juice.*
> *Think of Good Lord Nelson and avoid self-abuse,*
> *For the empty sleeve was no mere excuse*
>   *Aboard the Victory, Victory O.*

> *"England Expects" was the motto he gave*
> *When he thought of little Emma out on Biscay's wave,*
> *And remembered working on her like a galley-slave*
>   *Aboard the Victory, Victory O.*

Heroic verse is one thing, but antiheroic verse is almost better.

When a poet writes a novel, especially one that attracts a devoted following, it's common to look to the poetry for signs of the fiction struggling to escape. Durrell's taste for characters as peculiar as General Uncebunke makes the poems read like trial pieces; but, if you view his poetry as a false start or dead end, as the fiction's forethought afterthought, you can't see what the poems were before they Whiggishly turned into something else. (The General makes you think that had Eliot really been interested in Madame Sosostris or Phlebas, he might have become a minor novelist instead of a superb poet.)

Lyric sensibility of a Keatsian sort has for a century been tolerable only in prose—Faulkner and Joyce would never have been great poets, not just because they were not talented enough, but because they loved the lushness of language too well. There's a book to be written about the novel's appetites of style—Durrell needed the form's capaciousness, because the pressures and tensions of verse brought out only his vices, and the poetic manner could not contain the worlds he beheld.

Porter's introduction to this compact selection reads like a brief for the defense, beginning with an apology for suggesting, in an old encyclopedia entry, that Durrell's "poetry did not mature and produce the masterpieces his readers had every reason to expect" and that the poet was "more a Mendelssohn than a Mozart." I'm not sure what Porter has to apologize for, except that calling Durrell a Mendelssohn grossly exaggerates his talent. Such an introduction (which, to add injury to insult, suffers from various typos and misquotations) does the poet little good—the reader ends up having to translate the editor's enthusiasm: "important but somewhat neglected" means "almost entirely forgotten," and the "appropriateness with which he builds lyrical afflatus into aspects of reality" means the poet was a bit of a blowhard. The editor himself falls victim to the style when he writes that certain poems "shine as brightly as the Ionian Sea or the chips of unfading mosaic in the temples and palaces of the Ancient World."

In order to extract any pleasure from Durrell's poetry, the reader must cross acres of humorless blather:

> The sumptuary pleasure-givers living on
> In qualities as sure as taste of hair and mouth,
> White partings of the hair like highways,
> Permutations of a rose, buried beneath us now,
> Under the skin of thinking like a gland
> Discharging its obligations in something trivial:
> Say a kiss, a handclasp: say a stone tear.

It's not that a little of this goes a long way but that a lot goes such a little way. Occasionally some descriptive phrase ("riding through the soft lithograph/ Of Paris in the rain") or emotive expression ("The sense of his complete unworthiness/Pressed each year slowly tighter than a tourniquet") catches the reader's dimming eye; but the main impression is of a man unsuited to this line of work. In the end, whatever Durrell considered himself, being a failed poet was the making of him. The vices of his poetry were not exactly the virtues of his prose, but they didn't get in the way of its virtues—they were diluted until they became only an irritant of style.

After the early poems, Durrell abandoned his lyrics for a style closer to journal writing. The poems became warmer and more rueful, not straining for effects so much as waiting for them to occur; despite continuing trouble with tone, the poems were closely and attractively observed, when there was something close and attractive:

> The mauve street is swallowed
> And the bats have begun to stitch slowly.
> At the stable-door the carpenter's three sons
> Bend over a bucket of burning shavings.

Such lines show the same denial of spectacle that divides Edward Lear's watercolor sketches from his labored oil paintings.

Durrell never stopped writing poems, though after the forties he rarely managed more than a few pages a year. The poems became annotations on the loss of youth and the deteriorations of age, but with the authority of plain feeling:

> I shall die one day I suppose
> In this old Turkish house I inhabit:
> A ragged banana-leaf outside and here
> On the sill in a jam-jar a rock-rose.

(He outwitted himself by dying in France, not Cyprus.) Here, for a moment, he was capable of abandoning that "lyrical afflatus" and becoming the latest in a long line of warm-blooded Mediterranean poets from Horace to Cavafy. Then a "single pining mandolin" strikes up a tune, and none of the good habits can make the bad ones go away. Except in a very few poems, Durrell never captured the watchful melancholy or local habitation of the poets he most admired. He saw that poetry was the "perfect form of public reticence," though he could rarely be reticent in any form—the rare moments of restraint, like the ending of his elegy for George Seferis, are therefore the more poignant:

> You show us all the way the great ones went,
> In silences becalmed, so well they knew
> That even to die is somehow to invent.

Bad poetry is a foreign country—we have a steady series of readings of the good poetry of the past but broken relations with the mediocre, and we must learn to read like innocents.

Whether you think it a Proustian masterpiece or overheated tosh, *The Alexandria Quartet* is an affair of style, a poet's novel full of sentences that outstay their welcome, jewelry trays of adjectives, and more overpolished prose than in a year of Anglican sermons; yet you would trade most of these poems for the clarity of a sentence like "At the time when I met Justine I was almost a happy man." Few besides the editor will believe Durrell, as a poet, "one of the best of the past hundred years," a period in which the "three most remarkable first collections of poetry" in English were, he claims, by Stevens, Auden, and . . . and Durrell. Lawrence Durrell was never a poet's poet but something slightly sadder, a minor poet's minor poet.

Hart Crane Overboard

Before Hart Crane leapt into the Atlantic that fatal April noon in 1932, he folded his topcoat over the ship's rail with impeccable manners. (He was, however, clad in pajamas.) Disappearing into the violent wake, he was seen no more, dying younger than Byron but older than Shelley. Not being a seagoing breed, poets rarely die by water—Shelley drowned in a sudden squall; but he had written fifteen hundred pages of poetry, while Crane left only two very short books and the scraps of a third. The hope for a homegrown American epic that died with him has never entirely revived.

The precocious son of a wealthy Cleveland candy manufacturer (Crane's father created the Life Saver mint but sold the rights cheap), Crane dropped out of high school and convinced his parents to send him to New York, where he hoped to make his way as a writer. Wearing the scarlet A of Ambition, at seventeen he confidently predicted that he would "really without doubt be one of the foremost poets in America." Somewhat surprisingly, Crane was soon published in some of the best little magazines. He impressed his friends, not just with his bulb-eyed and brutish good looks (there's always room in New York for a handsome boy with manners and a wild streak), but with his canny critical judgment. He was a fan of Pound before *The Cantos* and Joyce before *Ulysses* and was terrified by Eliot before *The Waste Land*. As early as 1920, he was recommending, before either had published a book, Wallace Stevens and Marianne Moore, whom he referred to as "Marion"—Crane's deranged spelling offers one of the quiet comedies in the new Library of America edition of his *Complete Poems and Selected Letters*.

Most of Crane's short life was spent scuffling for money. His tight-fisted father kept him on an allowance at first but expected Crane to get a job. The poet tried various fits and shifts, finding employment most frequently in advertising (writing copy for, among other things, a new synthetic leather called

Naugahyde), though at times he was forced back to Ohio, where he spent an unhappy Christmas selling candy from an Akron drugstore counter. No doubt his father saw this as his son's first step toward inheriting the family business, but the experiment was not a success.

Crane's early poems showed more style than talent, and from the start he was attracted to a brute opacity that left some readers cold:

> And yet these fine collapses are not lies
> More than the pirouettes of any pliant cane;
> Our obsequies are, in a way, no enterprise.
> We can evade you, and all else but the heart:
> What blame to us if the heart live on.

It helps only a little to know that this dreadful, pretentious mess was called "Chaplinesque." One of Crane's friends later knocked on his door with Charlie Chaplin in tow, and the three went out on the town until dawn. Having learned this, a hundred American poets will begin odes to Angelina Jolie.

Crane was mystified, as most murky poets are, when people found his poems difficult—after all, they were perfectly clear to him. His obscurity was not that of Eliot or Pound, not a layered and allusive language whose intrigues deepened the more one examined it. Crane's language, when not a matter of tangled metaphors (he mixed metaphors almost more often than he mixed drinks), was a schoolboy code for which an English-Fustian, Fustian-English dictionary would have proved helpful. He came by his obscurity honestly—he didn't read Gerard Manley Hopkins, whose style might have influenced him, until much too late. When you clear away the clutter from Crane's verse, often you find only banalities—he flinched from Eliot's dour observations and pince-nez disillusion, wanting to embody a rhapsodic vision of poetry it was difficult not to glaze with sentiment.

Crane tried on various identities as a young man and failed at most of them. He was frank about his homosexuality only with close friends—his sexual appetites were voracious and involved far too many sailors. (The definitive work on the U.S. Navy's contributions to cruising has yet to be written.) Crane dreamed of being a poet a lot more often than he sat at his desk and wrote poems; and he was forever complaining in letters that he had no time to write, though he found plenty of time to drink. He conceived his major poem *The Bridge* as early as 1923 but made only desultory progress toward it. (Remaining drunk all through Prohibition proved surprisingly easy.) It was hard work avoiding real work; but Crane became an expert at writing cadging letters to his divorced parents and playing one against the other.

Forever broke, dramatically threatening to slave away on the docks or drive a truck, Crane took to writing begging letters to millionaires, or at least one millionaire, and got lucky. The financier Otto Kahn, the major shareholder in the Metropolitan Opera, offered to loan him two thousand dollars to write *The Bridge* (Kahn also backed Gershwin and Eisenstein). The poet was soon ensconced in a shabby house in upstate New York, spending his benefactor's initial installment as if it would last forever (on snowshoes, as well as wood carvings from the Congo, among other things) and asking for advances on the remainder. Kahn hardly lacked the wherewithal—his fireproof castle on Long Island grew to one hundred thousand square feet in size and his eighty-room Fifth Avenue mansion was stuffed with old masters.

Crane usually bit the hand that fed him, but you have to like a poet whose revelation of his own genius occurred in a dentist's chair ("an objective voice kept saying to me—'You have the higher consciousness. . . . This is what is called genius'"). He told his father that critics believed his first book, *White Buildings* (1926), would be the most important debut in American poetry since *Leaves of Grass*. These critics, who happened to be his friends, often loyally judged him by the poems he had yet to write.

Chronically out of sorts, creatively ill (his life would have been far happier after the introduction of decongestants), prone to "enthusiasms" we might now call mania, argumentative, often spectacularly drunk, Crane would have gotten on anyone's nerves. He had spent most of the millionaire's thousands when he departed abruptly for his mother's ramshackle plantation off Cuba (his family owned houses all over the place). There, after much grouching and complaint, he completed half of *The Bridge*, which he saw not as an epic but as a "long lyric poem, with interrelated sections."

It would take Crane three more years to finish the poem, spending months in California as companion to a neurasthenic stockbroker, squandering an inheritance from his grandmother on a trip to Paris, his drunkenness meanwhile growing wilder and more uncontrollable. When *The Bridge* was finally published in 1930, Crane felt betrayed by the mixed reviews it received from his old friends Allen Tate and Yvor Winters, who had begun to have second thoughts, not about Crane's gifts, but about his ability to profit from them.

Much of *The Bridge* seems inert now—overlong, overbearing, overwrought, a myth of America conceived by Tiffany and executed by Disney.

Crane imagined the Brooklyn Bridge as a mystical symbol for art, for history, for America, for any old thing; in this spiritual version of Manifest Destiny, he threw his poem backward to Columbus and worked forward to the invention of the airplane. The canvas was broad, but its success would have required a language less Alexandrian than Crane possessed. At his best, he stayed just this side of wild-eyed prophesying, though his grandeurs might easily be mistaken for grandiosity:

> How many dawns, chill from his rippling rest
> The seagull's wings shall dip and pivot him,
> Shedding white rings of tumult, building high
> Over the chained bay waters Liberty—
>
> Then, with inviolate curve, forsake our eyes
> As apparitional as sails that cross
> Some page of figures to be filed away;
> —Till elevators drop us from our day.

This is a beautifully managed passage; but even Crane's most thrilling lines can be cloying, always an adjective too rich or a noun too boisterous, the most beautiful stanzas naive as history or infused with a crude faith in progress almost embarrassing now. He was drawn to a high-amp schmaltziness he must have taken as the proper emotional tone for a visionary.

Crane wanted to drag the language of Marlowe and Webster into the Jazz Age. Beneath his jewel-encrusted lines, however, the poem seems trivial, its ideas torn from the daily paper or the pages of a high-school history textbook:

> *While Cetus-like, O thou Dirigible, enormous Lounger*
> *Of pendulous auroral beaches,—satellited wide*
> *By convoy planes, moonferrets that rejoin thee*
> *On fleeing balconies as thou dost glide,*
> *—Hast splintered space!*

We have no long poems this close to being great that are greater failures. (Why do American poets so often lose their bearings, and their taste, when writing about America?) The poem's creaky swiveling through time, its brassy versifying, and its phony slang seem dated now, not because Crane was heavily indebted to *The Waste Land* (despite frequently disparaging Eliot), but because he learned so little from it. Reading *The Bridge* is like being stuck in a mawkish medley from *Show Boat* and *Oklahoma*—you'd *buy* the Brooklyn Bridge to make it stop. Critics have often tried to make a case for the poem, for the coherence of its incoherent parts (criticism, like poetry, is often wishful thinking); but *The Bridge* remains a fabulous architectural blueprint that wanted a discipline Crane could never provide.

The poet's last year was spent on a Guggenheim fellowship in Mexico (we are lucky he left nothing of his projected epic on the Aztecs). He behaved so badly that his friend Katherine Anne Porter ratted him out to the foundation, which almost terminated the fellowship. In his final months, exhausted and miserable, he began an affair with Malcolm Cowley's estranged wife, an older woman Crane called "Twidget," and wrote a homosexual friend that he had "broken ranks" with the "brotherhood." Perhaps the romance was merely a sign of his boredom and mental exhaustion—it did nothing to slow down his secret pickups and Jack Tar chasing.

The Library of America edition, edited by Langdon Hammer, contains more of Crane than most readers will ever need. The poems take up so little space, this well-edited volume has been pieced out with five hundred pages of letters (Crane was an energetic correspondent though rarely one memorable or even bearable—great correspondents usually don't whine so much). E. E. Cummings once remarked that Crane's mind was "no bigger than a pin"; but Crane had a sharp critical temperament that appears to best advantage in his letters: "God DAMN this constant nostalgia for something always 'new,'" he wrote, and "I detest a certain narcissism in the voluptuous melancholics of Eliot." The edition's scattershot notes are helpful, but the chronology of Crane's life averts its gaze from his athletic philandering and the exact events leading to his suicide—he had been badly beaten during the night by a sailor he had propositioned.

Crane still makes young men want to write poetry—his best lines are extraordinary, even if there are few major poems, or even very good ones. It's almost un-American not to love some of Crane; but it's interesting that, when Crane lovers gather, they almost always love the same lines—a few passages from *The Bridge* and the sequence "Voyages" (and usually only II, III, and VI). These are among the few places where Crane's rhetoric overcame the leaden gravity of his sentimentality, where his superb ear triumphed over his loopy vocabulary.

And so, admitted through black swollen gates
That must arrest all distance otherwise,—
Past whirling pillars and lithe pediments,
Light wrestling there incessantly with light,
Star kissing star through wave on wave unto
Your body rocking!
                    and where death, if shed,
Presumes no carnage, but this single change,—
Upon the steep floor flung from dawn to dawn
The silken skilled transmemberment of song;

Permit me voyage, love, into your hands . . .

Passages like this make people love Crane beyond reason—though even such passages have their share of clumsy phrases ("transmemberment of song"!). I love such passages, but reason reminds me that however brilliant they are they're not enough. If I may speak like the Red Queen, Crane was so much greater than poets who were lesser, and so much less than poets who were greater.

Crane failed to write the poetry of the American continent Emerson was calling for before the Civil War; if the ideal seems naively nativistic now, the country was once younger and less cynical. Crane was no innovative genius like Whitman; he was perhaps closer to a peasant poet like John Clare, an outsider too susceptible to praise and other vices of the city. Defensive about his lack of education, a Midwestern striver out of a Sinclair Lewis novel, Crane tried to make it among the big-city literary men, a rum in one hand and a copy of *The Waste Land* in the other. Had beauty been enough, he might even have succeeded.

On Reviewing Hart Crane

I f you happen to be a critic, it may come as a shock that not all readers share your opinions. Worse, they write letters to the editor demanding that you be punished for the sins of your reviews. Some magazines and newspapers allow the critic to reply; others feel that, having had his say, he has undoubtedly said more than enough. Why give the critic the last word?

In the case of Hart Crane, there can be no last word. His star has been up and down so often in the three-quarters of a century since his death, it seems unlikely that critic or reader will settle the matter soon. Crane was the great might-have-been of American verse—superbly talented, ambitious as a hammer blow, full of plans and postures and persuasions galore. Most poets have their admirers by the time they arrive at that final mausoleum, the poetry anthology; Crane is one of the few who has votaries and devotees (Sylvia Plath is another). Whatever his flaws, personal or poetic, they pale before what some see as his genius. If you don't see the genius, all you have left are the flaws.

I've always loved Hart Crane; but I love him in fractions, delighting in half a dozen of those rhapsodic poems long on style and short on sense but finding the rest mystifying as a Masonic ritual. In some of his best poems, I merely admire lines, and in some of those lines I merely admire phrases—and yet what phrases and lines and, more rarely, what poems he wrote! When I reviewed Crane's *Complete Poems and Selected Letters* for the *New York Times Book Review*, I was not surprised that some readers objected, since many value Crane even more than Crane valued himself; and he valued himself quite a lot.

Reviewing Crane, if you don't review him fondly, is like poking a pencil into a hornet's nest. The *Times* had room to publish no more than half a dozen letters, which with one exception were furious. You discover a lot about readers from their letters, and most of what you discover leaves you dumbfounded—sometimes, however, you learn a thing or two. The most substantial letter came from Paul Mariani, one of Crane's biographers. I'm so used to correcting others, I'm delighted when someone corrects me—it's humbling to be caught in a boneheaded mistake, and critics generally need to eat crow every few months to keep them sane. Mariani noted first that, when Crane walked to the railing of the steamship *Orizaba*, preparing for his suicidal leap, he was wearing a light topcoat, not, as I had written, a jacket. Second, the sea he leapt into was not the Caribbean but the Atlantic. Last, the sea was not glassy, as I had proposed, but had "sizable waves."

No error is trivial, but how are such errors made? Out of sheer doltishness, in my case. I can tell a man's jacket from a topcoat at a hundred yards; but I failed to check my memory against the four biographies I consulted (Peggy Cowley, who was in her cabin below deck, said it was a light topcoat used as a robe and that Crane was wearing pajamas underneath). No doubt I'd fail a final exam in marine geography, but the notion that Crane leapt into the Caribbean came not from me but from his biographer Clive Fisher. He was wrong. I had forgotten the two rules on which all sound criticism is based: (1) take no fact or quotation on trust, and (2) buy a map. Both errors have been corrected.

The biographers disagree, however, about the condition of the Atlantic when Crane jumped. Mariani fails in *The Broken Tower* to describe the roughness of the ocean (he mentions the "impenetrable waters off which the noon sun gleamed," which doesn't sound choppy or rugged); Philip Horton in *Hart Crane* claims the "sea was mild"; and Clive Fisher, quoting Cowley in *Hart Crane: A Life*, says the sea was "like a mirror that could be walked on." I changed my "glassy sea" to a "violent wake" (the wake, some think, dragged Crane under). On balance, however, the "glassy sea" seems likely.

In his description of Crane's death, Mariani was attracted to the captain's notion that the poet might have been eaten by a shark—"Did he feel something brush his leg, the file-sharp streaking side of concentrated muscle, before the silver flash and teeth pulled him under?" This is sheer moonshine, but a biographer's fantasies—and gruesome fantasies they are—don't mitigate the critic's error of fact. (The biographer then throws some of Crane's purple prose—or rather purple poetry—back at him: "But this time the calyx of death's bounty gave back neither scattered chapter nor livid hieroglyph." The allusion is to "At Melville's Tomb," but as prose it sounds like a canceled passage by Sir Thomas Browne.) The aggrieved reader's fondest delusion is that a critic's sidelong errors undermine a disagreement about taste; yet don't we prefer Eliot's opinions, despite his habitual misquotation, to the arguments of some bozo supported by quotes correct to the last nicety? That doesn't make the errors less embarrassing.

I had written that, after the failure of *The Bridge*, the "hope for a home-grown American epic . . . has never entirely revived." Mariani took exception to this, citing the long poems written since Crane's death by Williams, Olson, Berryman, and Lowell. I hadn't meant the idea to be contentious—the ruin of *The Bridge* cast a long shadow over long poems for a long while. In a way, it casts that shadow still. Will we ever have a truly American epic, a poem of American history? (I mean one that's any good.) I love passages in *The Cantos* and think *Leaves of Grass* the foundation of modern American verse, but *The Cantos* is hardly homegrown (the poem remembers America from London and Paris and Rapallo), and *Leaves of Grass* is not an epic but a collection of lyrics. Shakespeare's sonnets are not an epic, either.

The idea of the Great American Poem no longer seduces young poets the way the Great American Novel, that will-o'-the-wisp, still haunts American novelists. (The Great American Novel has already been written, and it is called *Moby-Dick*.) Because they have usually failed so badly, we forget how *many* long poems have been written in this country—who except at gunpoint would reread Delmore Schwartz's autobiographical epic *Genesis, Book One* (Book One!) or the leaden historical poems of Archibald MacLeish or Selden Rodman? For Lowell, for Berryman, for many another, the long poem became a scatter of disconnected lyrics. That was Crane's legacy.

A second letter to the *Times*, from the poet and editor Daniel Halpern, grumbled that "in this era of conflict, when America can use all the good poetry it can find, it's dispiriting to encounter a reviewer who uses one of our most important reviewing venues to exercise an organ of bile." How poets like Crane are going to make readers feel better about a dirty and unpopular war is beyond me; but the unstated premise is even odder—criticizing poets is all right in peacetime; but, when the artillery begins to boom, critics should shut up. Halpern believes that "poetry is what people turn to during times of duress and celebration—marriage, death, 9/11—that is, our rites of passage." I'm not sure how the destruction of the World Trade Center qualifies as a *rite de passage*. As for such high-flown hopes for poetry, well, wouldn't it be pretty to think so?

Halpern groused that "when the Library of America takes on as part of its mandate the showcasing of essential American poets like Hart Crane, we look to our reviewers to address the importance of the poet's writing, not his lifestyle." A publisher would be gratified if reviewers assumed that every book under its imprint were beyond criticism. Halpern also reproached me for "disingenuously ignoring the memorable ending" of Crane's hapless little poem "Chaplinesque":

> *but we have seen*
> *The moon in lonely alleys make*
> *A grail of laughter of an empty ash can,*
> *And through all sound of gaiety and quest*
> *Have heard a kitten in the wilderness.*

A grail of laughter? A *kitten in the wilderness?* I failed to quote these lines because they're embarrassing—I don't see why they don't seem embarrassing to Halpern. Crane sent the poem to Chaplin, who kindly acknowledged it. Late one night, a couple of years later, a friend dragged Chaplin to the poet's apartment. "Having learned this," I wrote, "a hundred American poets will begin odes to Angelina Jolie." Halpern claimed that this was "delusional," a sign of the critic's "self-importance." A critic learns that no joke is so obvious someone will fail to get it, but I have it on good authority that seventy-seven American poets have now written such odes and anxiously await the results. Even so, Halpern was right that I hadn't quoted enough Crane, nor enough of the best of Crane—sometimes a critic sees everything but the obvious, and in revising the review I have included lines from one of the most beautiful of Crane's poems, "Voyages III."

One reader accused me of slighting young women when I wrote that Crane made young men want to write poetry—yet I didn't want to ignore the fact that, in my experience, his audience remains largely male. (I take this as a sign that women have less taste for gassy romantic rhetoric.) Many readers tasked me for writing too much about Crane's life and too little about his art. Some assumed that I disapproved of his fondness for sailors. During the war, my own father was a sailor on the New York docks; had Crane survived and picked him up for some rough trade, I'd have been flattered. "How many sailors is too many?" asked one reader privately, apropos my remarks on Crane's love life. The answer is, it's too many when they start to beat you up.

The book under review consisted of a hundred and fifty pages of Crane's poetry and more than five hundred pages of his letters. Unlike many poets, Crane stands revealed in biography. It's difficult to ignore the life when you read the letters, because the messiness of daily living so often interfered with the art. Crane's wheedling, his inflated self-opinion (wildly in advance of any real achievement), his self-pity, his difficult relations with his mother and father, his plagiarism of Samuel Greenberg—surely these lie at an interesting angle to the art, even if, in the end, we have nothing but the art by which to judge the achievement. Letters should never be taken as gospel. I have my doubts that writing poetry was quite as painful or time-consuming as Crane made it out to be—the complaints to his parents sound like the exaggerations of a young man short of cash and the complaints to his friends like the excuses of an alcoholic. Crane always knew how to play on his reader's sympathy, at least until he got what he wanted. If the letters are unmemorable as literature, compared to those of Byron, or Coleridge, or Keats, or many another, they are riveting as the record of a striking and fame-hungry young man trying to make his way in New York.

Happy readers are all alike; every unhappy reader is unhappy in his own way. Yet I could not help but feel, knowing how infuriated I had made these lovers of Crane, that I had misunderstood the passions he still excites. There's something in this poet (in the life as much as the art) that calls forth the protective instinct in his readers, as well as an exaggerated sense of his loss, which Mariani called "unbearably tragic." Crane's death was sad, but not tragic—he was the author of his fate in a way few men are, but he was no Oedipus or Hamlet. It's not just that Crane was young, though poets who die prematurely, especially by suicide, often find readers who believe the world has done them wrong. (Though why not think that in all sorts of ways Crane and Plath did the world wrong?) If he had lived a lot longer and written a lot more, we might think much less of him.

Many readers want vision rather than poetry; cold analysis of Crane's vague rhetoric, his naive sentiment, and his semireligious adolescent yearning is not to their taste. A reader upset by a review often invokes higher authorities, roughly in this order: his own good taste, the taste of the mob, the taste of other critics, the taste of God—and all except the taste of God were invoked by these letter writers. Crane's prophetic zeal, his sense of his own destiny as well as that of his country (sometimes he mistook one destiny for the other), seems to give his words numinous meaning:

I feel persuaded that here are destined to be discovered certain as yet unde-
fined spiritual quantities, perhaps a new hierarchy of faith not to be devel-

oped so completely elsewhere. And in this process I like to feel myself as a potential factor.

The poem he wanted to write was the *Aeneid,* to which he compared *The Bridge.* Some ambitions are disastrous.

The problem with taste is, yours is right and everyone else's is ridiculous. (I once knew a poet who, no matter how kind the reviews of his work, said that every specific complaint was "wrong.") Criticism is the exercise of taste under the guise of objective argument—the psychology of taste is such that few readers are perturbed when some mediocrity is praised, but mobs begin lighting torches when their favorites are ignored or damned. Yet criticism is surely most valuable when it argues against the grain—at least, the reader is likely to learn more from it, even if he disagrees down to his horny soles. We are forever grateful to a critic able to put into words something we have only vaguely felt. Barring that, a critic makes himself necessary to the extent that when reading him we whisper, "No! No! No!"

Critics are the sum of their biases—they begin as arbitraries and end as certainties (the course of my own criticism has sometimes been the other way round). You can't stand that ditherer Coleridge, she can't stand that whiner Keats, I can't stand that dry fussbudget Wordsworth, and we all hate Shelley— poets are Rorschach tests. If there's a negative case for Crane, it lies in all that waxy rhetoric, glossy on the outside and rotten within. Criticism, however put, can never harm Crane in the eyes of the devoted, because what such a critic despises is exactly what those readers adore.

Why make the case at all, then? Doesn't it harm that uplifting, ennobling, transcendent thing, poetry—the poetry people need and want and *deserve,* the poetry that in time of war raises the downtrodden spirit, the poetry that comforts the helpless in their distress and in their trial of spirit steels the weak? I once heard an undergraduate, a stack or two over in a faceless library, say plaintively, "What are you going to do about the Jesus in my heart?" What are you going to do about the poetry in my heart? If the critic were meant to offer solace, he would have taken up a different line of work. All he can do is record his feelings for the one or two readers willing to look again at Crane— the critic's job is not to pat the reader on the head and whisper sweet nothings in his ear.

However captious or confident a critic may be, even the lightest reading of the critical past shows that the mountains of one day may be molehills to another. Critic A and Critic B may disagree so strongly they threaten to cut each other's windpipes. A year may pass, or a hundred; and another critic will come along and say that A was right about such and such, and B about so and so, but that taken as a whole there was not much difference between them. When I look over the early reviews of Whitman, I agree with almost every obstreperous howl and every quiet reservation, yet mostly the critics missed the point. Such recognitions keep a critic awake at night.

Postscript

This piece almost inevitably called forth letters further letters of protest, which I responded to at some length. Letters from Neil Hampton and Marjorie Perloff were published in the December 2008 issue of Poetry. *The arguments of these writers will be implicit in my reply, but Perloff asked specifically what I found "hit-and-miss" in Langdon Hammer's edition. She also claimed, in reference to my mixed feelings about Crane, that "this reviewer doesn't care that every important American poet from Robert Lowell to the present or every major critic of the past few decades, beginning with Harold Bloom, has felt otherwise."*

I'm not sure why Neil Hampton would think that I'd waste time "tackling" the "manifest prejudice" of my original review. I still believe every word of it. Since he offers the usual apologetics for Crane's wearying and often impenetrable obscurity, I assure him that I understand the poet's argument, or excuses, in his letter to Harriet Monroe on the "logic of metaphor." I simply disagree with it. (Would anyone, reading Crane's explication, have pieced out his meaning the same way?) If we took poets at their own valuation and judged them by their own methods, every scribbler would be a genius. As for the connection between Crane and Clare, they were both from the hustings, insecure about their education, and efficient autodidacts. The main difference is that Crane was mollycoddled by wealthy parents. I would be the last to condescend to John Clare, who deserved far better than he got.

If Hampton really believes the lines on Chaplin are genius, there's no helping him:

> And yet these fine collapses are not lies
> More than the pirouettes of any pliant cane;

Our obsequies are, in a way, no enterprise.
We can evade you, and all else but the heart:
What blame to us if the heart live on.

For me, they are as hapless and tone deaf as the schmaltz about the "kitten in the wilderness" and the "moon in lonely alleys" that makes the "grail of laughter of an empty ash can." In 1921, when Crane wrote them, Chaplin was every bit the celebrity Angelina Jolie is now. We have no equal of Chaplin; but, though Crane was awed by the Little Tramp's art, let's not deny it-the poet was starstruck. After Waldo Frank had dragged the actor to Crane's apartment, the young man from Ohio reported to his mother, "I was smiling into one of the most beautiful faces I ever expect to see."

As my critics have every reason to know, a reviewer has only a limited amount of space in which to shift-in the case of the *New York Times Book Review*, no more than two thousand words. If I were reviewing Eliot's poems and letters, I'd be obliged to talk about his life as well as his art-I doubt there would be room for a complete account of the structure of *The Waste Land* or for close readings of its lines. You wouldn't know from Marjorie Perloff's characterization that almost half my original review was spent on *The Bridge*, both the poem and its composition.

No essay of mine on the subject of Hart Crane would please Perloff; but let me answer some of her questions and, no doubt, confirm many of her suspicions. She seems to understand that many critics, once upon a time, found Crane's rhetoric hard to bear; but then she asks questions that seem disingenuously naïve. Since she asks, I find the Proem of *The Bridge* stuffed with the excesses of detail, some slight and some more egregious, for which Crane's style is notorious-among the adjectives, I dislike the religious hint in the bridge's "inviolate" curve (I like the "chained" bay waters better, as long as I think of them visually and not, as I suspect Crane preferred, "shackled"), the empty rhetoric of the movie house's "flashing" scene, the over-richness of the "silver-paced" bridge, the melodrama of the "shrill" shirt of the suicide and the "cloud-flown" derricks, and the false piety of "speechless" in the slightly nonsensical line "A jest falls from the speechless caravan." Among the nouns, Crane is overegging the pudding with his subway "scuttle"; his seagull's "white rings of tumult"; the exaggeration of the "rip-tooth" of noon light and the sky's "acetylene"; and, worst of all, his wretched "bedlamite"-is this a real madman, escaped from his "cell or loft," or just a hapless, fed-up, crazed commuter? I'm not sure what the speechless "caravan" might be; it could be so many things (likely he means just the passing crowd)-but I'm sure Crane would have had some ingenious explanation for it.

Why go on with such dispiriting detail, or try to tease out every banality Crane tortured into verse? I'd start with the lines I once quoted, in which the dirigible, his ungainly symbol of progress (he put his money on the wrong symbol), was ludicrously addressed, "Cetus-like, O thou Dirigible, enormous Lounger / Of pendulous auroral beaches,-satellited wide / By convoy planes, moonferrets that rejoin thee / On fleeing balconies as thou dost glide." *Cetus-like? Pendulous auroral beaches? Moonferrets?* It's not that these are obscure, not exactly (the whale-like dirigible lounges on the beach-like, pendulous clouds, surrounded by its convoy of planes that look like, well, moonferrets)-it's that the rhetoric is so childish and extravagant. With Crane, you either accept such romantic goofiness, along with a host of O *thou's* and *thou dost's*, or you don't. Alas, I'm not even keen about the symbol at the heart of the poem, the bridge itself-epic poems have been built from unlikely things, but the Brooklyn Bridge is one of the least likely.

I admire Langdon Hammer's edition, but his notes are hit and miss-there are all sorts of references in the letters left unexplained (the "famous Stevens-35," anyone?), though similar things are given delicate attention. Shouldn't we be told that "Menchen" was presumably H. L. Mencken? Younger readers, at least, might need to know who Billy Sunday was. Who is Mr. Charles Brooks, whose book, *There's Pippins and Cheese to Come*, Crane recommends? Or Jean Catel? Or Mr. Ely and Miss Bohn? To call Walter Camp merely a "sportswriter" rather stints on his achievements. Why not note that, when Crane pretended to write from the ship *Rumrunia*, he was joking? And so on. More culpably, Hammer is factually parsimonious about Crane's borrowings from the manuscripts of Samuel Greenberg for "Emblems of Conduct" (almost entirely composed of lines and phrases from the dead young poet), and in much lesser ways for "Voyages" and other poems. Greenberg is mentioned only twice in the notes, where Hammer leaves a misleading impression about the extent of Crane's indebtedness. Further, the editor omits the letter Crane wrote to Gorham Munson on December 20, 1923, detailing Crane's close reading and copying from Greenberg's notebooks.

I'm sorry if Perloff mistakes my tone as world-weary or condescending, but there's no helping that-she manages to make even "reasonable" sound like a dirty word. I won't apologize for mocking, a little, a poet whom so many readers blindly adore. (Had Crane's taste run to chorus girls instead of sailors, I'd have been no less sardonic-it was the constant self-destructive indulgence that's worth recording.) Crane was the architect of his own grand disaster. The disaster of the life didn't ennoble the art-it was responsible for the failure of the art.

I wish Perloff had provided me with a wall chart of "every important American poet from Robert Lowell to the present" and "every major critic of the past few decades, beginning with Harold Bloom." This is a carefully delimited list-she knows that Crane's poems have excited hostility among critics, even very great critics, since the books were published. Perhaps I'm out of step with the critics of our day-but is there anything more deadening than a consensus? I'm bemused by a critic who thinks like a commissar, as if something must be true because at the moment everyone believes it. In a stray scan of my shelves, I could not find that two critics I admire, Christopher Ricks and Geoffrey Hill, had written much or anything about Crane (though Hill in some "improvisations" on Crane wrote, "All in all / you screwed us, Hart, you and your zany epic"-his feelings seem mixed). I must assume that Perloff is the victim of her own exaggerations.

As for American poets, Lowell adored Crane, it's true-though the younger man was a better poet when he had purged his verse of Crane's influence. But look at Lowell's own generation. Randall Jarrell was supposed to write a book on Crane yet never managed to get very far. In a review of Dylan Thomas, he wrote; "[Thomas's poems] mean much less than Crane's-but when you consider Crane's meanings, this is not altogether a disadvantage." John Berryman, though influenced by Crane, said in a letter, "Crane had probably the most useless mind any poet worth mentioning has had." In a review, he referred to the "successive logical disintegration" of Crane's poetry. Elizabeth Bishop wrote, after finishing books of letters by Crane and Edna St. Vincent Millay, "I don't know which is more depressing. I suppose his is, it was all over quicker-but she isn't quite so narcissistic and has some sense of humor, at least." Of Crane's most ambitious poem, "I went through *The Bridge* all very carefully again, and like it less."

Nothing I say will convince these critics that Crane was a flawed genius, if a genius at all. I say that he wrote barrels of lovely lines and two or three poems of sustained attention and achievement, but also that he squandered his gifts, falling prey to preposterously silly phrases, heavy-handed rhetoric, sewer-pipe obscurity, and the worst kinds of sentiment-all of which a reader could forgive, if Crane had written more great poetry. What little he wrote will have to be enough, but I think it far littler than these critics who have had the kindness to write. I feel about Crane as the curate did about the rotten egg he had been served, that it was excellent in parts.

The Endless Ocean of Derek Walcott

Poets behave like conquistadors wherever they roam, picking up a new verse form, a lover, some inventive cursing, a disease. Would Byron have been Byron without Italy and Greece? What would Eliot and Pound have become without the hostility of London? Can we imagine Hart Crane without the Caribbean or Elizabeth Bishop without Rio? Derek Walcott has crossed so many borders, his poems read like a much-thumbed Baedeker. To a boy born on St. Lucia, the rhythms and intonations of English verse were a passport to the elsewhere; but they came with a burden—the language of the colonial masters was not the one caught in his ear at home. "How choose," he wrote, "Between this Africa and the English tongue I love?/Betray them both, or give them back what they give?"

Walcott's new *Selected Poems* begins with poems of disturbing self-confidence—amused, self-mocking, mildly self-hating, his youthful work is filled with language that eases itself off the tongue (if some tongues are silver, his must be platinum). A powerful maker of phrases from the start, he adopted the English of an empire that, having once painted the map red, was slowly being dismantled: the ruins of a great house, "Whose moth-like girls are mixed with candledust,/Remain to file the lizard's dragonish claws./The mouths of those gate cherubs shriek with stain."

Walcott had barely been noticed before he became noted. By his midthirties, he was composing a verse autobiography (an act of hubris akin to a pop star writing his life at nineteen). *Another Life* (1973) is a pretentious, pressure-cooker affair, a tour de force fatally uneasy with itself. (Surely you give a hostage to describe yourself as a prodigy, even if a "prodigy of the wrong age and colour.") At times it reads like *The Prelude* by a writer far more elegant than Wordsworth, though almost every line about the poet himself sounds false:

> *Afternoon light ripened the valley,*
> *rifling smoke climbed from small labourers' houses,*
> *and I dissolved into a trance.*
> *I was seized by a pity more profound*
> *than my young body could bear, I climbed*
> *with the labouring smoke,*
> *I drowned in labouring breakers of bright cloud,*
> *then uncontrollably I began to weep,*
> *inwardly, without tears, with a serene extinction*
> *of all sense; I felt compelled to kneel,*
> *I wept for nothing and for everything.*

This idea of compassion requires a lot of scenery chewing. (I hope the houses were small, not the laborers.)

Most poets compromise between the diction of the poems they love, often centuries old, and the language they hear in the streets (the tin-eared poems in island patois have been among Walcott's least successful); but, for the exile, language is a daily form of betrayal. Walcott has remained a figure of divided loyalties and a double tongue—though his grandmothers were descended from slaves, his grandfathers were white. As a child, he "prayed/nightly for his flesh to change,/his dun flesh peeled white"; but, like any young man of parts, he was enamored of himself. Even the late verse can seem shallow and narcissistic, beauty seized in his own beautiful eye—he treats women ("O Beauty, you are the light of the world!") in a manner closer to lechery than to old-style courtesy. Caught between two races and two worlds, he has sometimes succumbed to pride or self-pity, or to that pride indistinguishable from self-pity.

Although his taste for the sententious remark has never quite abated ("To change your language you must change your life," "There is no harder prison than writing verse"), Walcott grew able to tame the rhetoric that, like a forest fire, occasionally roared out of control. He became the most striking poet of seascapes since Coleridge (between them lie only a few lines in *The Waste Land*), rivaling the older poet's sense of the uncanny.

> *I saw men with rusty eyeholes like cannons,*
> *and whenever their half-naked crews cross the sun,*
> *right through their tissue, you traced their bones*
> *like leaves against the sunlight; frigates, barquentines,*

> *the backward-moving current swept them on,*
> *and high on their decks I saw great admirals,*
> *Rodney, Nelson, de Grasse.*

This is no mere practiced and prettified version of "The Rime of the Ancient Mariner"—later poets learn their craft from earlier; but they must provide the originality themselves, in resistance to what they learn.

Walcott's most fluid and achieved work lies in the books from *Sea Grapes* (1976) through *The Arkansas Testament* (1987), where a mature intelligence no longer wrestles with language like an Antaeus but subdues it by being subdued. *Midsummer* (1984) long seemed to me the exception, a laggard book of hours by an author too often at his desk. Reading the selection here, I realized I missed something. Without the shape of the lyric subject, Walcott's poetry becomes the registration of sensibility—and in texture and sensibility he has been a master, even if the redolently patterned verse has sometimes been laid down like linoleum. Overstuffed with images, his languid, occasionally lackadaisical style is more in love with words than with what they represent. He's a better poet when just mulling things over, in a louche beachcomberish way—when he talks politics, the taste seems bitter in his mouth.

The colonized, decolonized islands, victims of what Walcott calls the "leprosy of empire," have been taken up by scholars in subaltern studies, postcolonial studies, and studies whose very names are subject to rancorous argument. The poet too often borrows the academic's vaporous editorials (the "politicians plod/without imagination") and self-service sentiments ("poetry is still treason/because it is truth"). If he had not invented himself, academia would have had to invent him. In condensed form, Walcott believes that the British Empire was bad, except where it was good, and English literature good, except where it was bad. His islands are ravishing but painterly, observed with a detachment that leaves him more a tourist than a fortunate traveler, not a man who got away but one who was never quite there.

Many critics see Walcott's major achievement as *Omeros* (1990), a version of the Homeric epics translated to the Caribbean, the Trojan War reimagined as a struggle between two fishermen, Achille and Hector, over a woman named Helen. Despite imperious passages of broken terza rima, this epic of nearly eight thousand lines is spoiled by its clumsy narration (Walcott can never tell a story without losing his way in lovely detail), the black characters bloated with the poet's ambition, the white no more than ludicrous caricatures. Whether describing a man's scar "puckered like the corolla/of a sea-urchin" or an egret that "stabs and stabs the mud with one lifting foot," Walcott never met a metaphor he didn't like—or, indeed, that a reader wouldn't love. But a tale can't eat only rubies.

Walcott's most frequently announced emotion is joy, a joy that rarely seems joyous—his eye lacks nothing but a touch of sympathy (he could turn a cancer into a bauble from Fabergé). He has become a man for whom introspection never seems natural, though perhaps we've had too many poets confessing every sin under the sun (Walcott has none of Lowell's ravaging candor or unsettling mildness). He started as a painter, his failure likely the making of him as a poet; but the words sometimes seem mere daubs, skillfully pushed around the canvas while the pictures remain dead at the center.

In the years since his Nobel Prize, Walcott's work has been haunted by the dissolutions of mortality—*The Prodigal* (2004), his most recent book, sounds exhausted in its exits. He seems almost unmoved when taking the roll call of the dead, even when writing of the death of his twin brother; but when that reserve almost breaks down, as in a poem for Joseph Brodsky in exile, it produces some of his finest work:

> *The last leaves fell like notes from a piano*
> *and left their ovals echoing in the ear;*
> *with gawky music stands, the winter forest*
> *looks like an empty orchestra, its lines*
> *ruled on these scattered manuscripts of snow.*

The elegiac tone is embedded in Walcott's meditation on the belated life exiles inhabit—an exile is like a death. Usually uneasy with strong emotion, here he mourned Brodsky's life as he did his own (a man without a country is also a country without a man). The self-devouring figures, turning the tool kit of poetry into metaphor (his cane fields are "set in stanzas," his "ocean kept turning blank pages"), speak to something almost unsaid—writing was Walcott's escape from the islands. The metaphors whisper their quiet acknowledgment of guilt.

Edward Baugh, the Jamaican poet who has edited this modest selection, has slapped on a slightly embarrassing fan's introduction, gushing about poems that are a "distillation from the harvest" and claiming that "reading Walcott is also an adventure in poetic form and style." These are the metaphors of a vodka salesman and an army recruiter. Few poets have been lavished with greater gifts than Walcott; but much of his later work has been unadventurous (and undistilled), full of stock passages and stale opinions. He arrived at a few views when young and has trotted them out ever since. There are always marvelous passages, passages most poets would sell their souls for; but there are too many pages whose marvels have become all too routine.

The poetry of exile begins in sorrow. No matter how awful Rome, the Black Sea will never seem like home (when you have to go home, the landscape is what has to take you in). Walcott has captured his islands with a lushness and richness rare in our poetry—the outposts of empire once seemed as strange as Kipling's India or Bishop's Brazil. If air travel has brought them closer, it has brought their tragedies closer as well. No living poet has written verse more delicately rendered or distinguished than Walcott, though few individual poems seem destined to be remembered. For more than half a century he has served as our poet of exile—a man almost without a country, unless the country lies wherever he has landed, in flight from himself.

The Civil Power of Geoffrey Hill

G loomy poets are rarely very good, and good poets rarely very gloomy. There was Edgar Allan Poe, of course, and Thomas Lovell Beddoes, denizens of that funereal, willow-shadowed decade of the 1840s, a decade half in love with Keats and half in love with easeful death. Thomas Hardy had his black moods, but was not without his moments of sour levity. For more than fifty years, however, Geoffrey Hill has written a pinch-mouthed, grave-digger's poetry so rich and allusive his books are normally greeted by gouts of praise from critics and the bewilderment of readers who might have been happier with a tract on the mating rituals of the earwig.

Hill has made brutally plain that the common reader is of no interest to him. Indeed, he feels that sinking to common ground betrays the high purpose of verse; with a withering pride he has refused, time and again, to stoop to such betrayals. This has made him a poet more despised than admired, and more admired than loved. His poetry has been composed of harsh musics, the alarums of battle and the death struggles under the reading lamp—his poetry takes to contemplation the way some men take to religion (Hill's relation to Christianity has been famously cryptic). Such poetry lies deep in the long wars of English kingship and a long shelf of books on the Reformation and Counter-Reformation.

> The other Cromwell, that strange muse of Wyatt
> and master of last things: it makes a fine
> edge—wisdom so near miswielding power.
> I think of the headsman balancing that
> extraordinary axe for a long instant
> without breaking the skin; then the engine
> cuts its ascending outline on the air,

wharrs its velocity, dreadful, perhaps
merciful. And that moment of spreading
wide the arms as a signal. In fact it's all
signals. Pray, sirs, remember Cromwell's trim
wit on the scaffold, that saved Wyatt's neck;
the one blubbing—talk of the quiet mind!—
the other a scoundrel, yet this redeems him.

The lines have all the strength of Miltonic enjambment (the *fine* that hesitates before *edge*; the engine balancing before it cuts; and the resistant, ambivalent *perhaps* before *merciful* stands revealed)—but it also has a clotted and defensive mystery.

To penetrate this arras of history, the reader must recall some of the obscure political maneuvering in the court of Henry VIII. Thomas Cromwell, the king's vicar-general, oversaw the dissolution of the monasteries. He may have been overhasty in promoting the king's marriage to Anne of Cleves; when the marriage failed, Cromwell was arrested and eventually executed. The clumsy teenaged headsman, perhaps chosen by the king himself, needed three strokes to sever Cromwell's head. Before the blows fell, the condemned man asked his friend Wyatt to pray for him. There is more, a good deal more; but the poem makes no sense without the tapestry of background. Perhaps a reader should know that Wyatt helped reinvent iambic pentameter in English verse (a tuned ear might detect something of his jammed, chockablock meter in Hill's choppy lines). And Wyatt, of course, translated Plutarch's *Quyete of Mynde.*

Modernism asked just how far the poet could expect the reader to mole about in old books to make sense of a poem. Eliot provided the notes to *The Waste Land* as a casual afterthought, to fill out a slim volume; and Pound buried so many moldy allusions through *The Cantos* that scholars have been hunting the truffles ever since. Both poets felt that poems could survive obscurity without help from the slush of footnotes we expect in the *Norton Anthology;* yet, without explication, a poem like Hill's is hardly a poem, just language at war with itself.

Hill taxes the reader to buy a good library or—in these fallen days—sail the traitorous Internet between the lies of Scylla and the damned lies of Charybdis. A reader must want to thumb through dusty pages, or dustier Web pages, to learn more of Burford's Levellers (New Model Army mutineers), Clock House (in Bromsgrove, Hill's birthplace), Randolph Ash (a character in A. S. Byatt's *Possession*), Quid, Obtuse Angle, and Inflammable Gass (all from a manuscript by Blake), and much else. Good luck finding "Mrs. Nani-cantipot," whose name Hill misspells (she's from the same Blake manuscript). Such stray facts are the price of admission to Hill's poetry; and the reader might reasonably ask if these devious, dissuasive poems are worth the penalties of sense.

Over the past decade, Hill has made this quarrel more strenuous (his poems are full of antique quarrels, which is fine if you like quarrels). Once a poet of archly mannered speech, for whom every stanza was a quiet martyrdom, he found himself during a course of antidepressants suddenly keen to talk a leg of mutton off a lamb—books began to tumble forth every year or two, rambling monologues full of jokes at his own expense, dumb raillery, heavy-handed argument. The caterwauling of *The Triumph of Love* (1998), *Speech! Speech!* (2000), *The Orchards of Syon* (2002), and *Scenes from Comus* (2005), despite their peculiar gifts, has diluted a career of painstakingly crafted, close-managed poems. There's no telling now what Hill might say, just embarrassment at some of the things he does say.

A *Treatise of Civil Power*, like its predecessor *Without Title* (published belatedly in America last spring), returns to the fertile densities that characterized Hill's earlier verse. English has rarely possessed a poet who listens so closely to its whispers or is as willing to expose its secret etiquettes. Hill lies at the end of a long line of Romantic poets with classical reserve—Coleridge and Eliot stagger through the background here. It's no coincidence that they are the most distinguished poet-critics of the past two centuries. Hill lives with ghosts; and the new volume is haunted by that poet-critic who never was, John Milton. Had he lived in less interesting times, Milton might have rivaled Johnson or Coleridge; but he deployed his prose gifts elsewhere—among other places, in his pamphlet *A Treatise of Civil Power in Ecclesiastical Causes*, which argued the case for religious tolerance (Papists, of course, excepted). Hill's own criticism, aware of its burdens and its brilliance, is too guarded, too miserably grave, to yield to casual reading (his dislike of readers has been a disease in the poetry but a pathology of the prose), though he understands that his inability to bend a knee, to seduce where he cannot bully, is a weakness, not a strength.

Hill is the most glorious poet of the English countryside since the first Romantic started gushing about flowers, his verse so radioactive in its sensitivities that his landscapes have been accused of cheap nostalgia. There is, perhaps, the taint of doomed self-love in the way Hill adores the "autumn crocus with its saffron fuse" or the "stark storm-severed head/of a sunflower blazing in mire of hail"; but, whatever the progress of psychology, few readers would trade the drenched phrasings of Hill's backlit scenery for his brooding on obscure theologians. Hang the cost in moral uplift.

> Not to skip detail, such as finches brisking
> on stripped haw-bush;
> the watered gold that February drains
> out of the overcast; nomadic aconites
> that in their trek recover beautifully
> our sense of place,
> the snowdrop fettled on its hinge, waxwings
> becoming sportif in the grimy air.

Hill may hedge his love with the thorns of attitude ("Not to skip detail"), the dour grievance of notice ("stripped," "drains," "overcast," "grimy"), or the fillip of the foreign (the waxwings can be *sportif* only by migrating through France); yet his poetry is burnished by the late lights of observation. Philosophy is not enough to turn the gold entirely to gloom.

The oddity of Hill's recent verse lies less in its gabbiness, its anxiousness to speak the unspoken, than in the occasional bowing and scraping to popular culture. Wittgenstein loved his cowboy movies, and Hill admits that he listens to Jimi Hendrix—even so, the revelation seems disingenuous. In the diorama battles between high and low, cooked and raw, there's no doubt of Hill's loyalties—you don't write on Holbein, on Blake, on Burke, on Handel without staking your claim in cold didactic ground. What to make, then, of his offhanded exclamation that "Things are not that bad./H. Mirren's super"? So, Hill watches *Prime Suspect*. Is he secretly boogieing to Eminem and Puff Daddy? Not quite yet—but he talks about "lyric mojo." Who'd have thought?

These solemn, po-faced allusions (the only thing more frightening than Hill's grimaces are his attempts at humor) suggest how peculiar his late tone can be—Francis Bacon sits ill at ease with Princess Diana, Elias Canetti with the Scorpion King. Are these his meager concessions to the masses? Yet Hill thinks his readers so thick that, after writing that Blake "could/contradict and contain multitudes," he feels forced to confess the theft from *Leaves of Grass* ("I've/cribbed Whitman, you stickler").

A *Treatise of Civil Power* is a measured, brilliant book; but its measurements are at times disfigured by Hill's peculiar sidling, forelock-tugging commentary, full of nervous gestures and mock afflictions ("This I can live with," "I know that sounds / a damn-fool thing to say"), as well as subtle misreadings or corrections of things just said, as if every page required an errata sheet. At least the book suffers from few of the irritating accent marks with which Hill has lately tried to muscle the metrics of his verse. There's one peculiarity that should be mentioned: Hill published an earlier version of A *Treatise of Civil Power* two years ago with a small English press. The long title poem is missing from this new edition, though scattered stanzas show up as individual poems, tossed in helter-skelter like the limbs of Osiris. Of this austere revision, the poet says not a word.

There are passages of stunning beauty, however, like views through the lens of a Leica, for which a reader will forgive many a sin.

> *I see Inigo Jones's great arches*
> *in my mind's eye, his water-inky clouds,*
> *the paraphernalia of a royal masque;*
> *dung and detritus in the crazy streets,*
> *the big coaches bellying in their skirts*
> *pothole to pothole, and the men of fire,*
> *the link-boys slouching and the rainy wind.*

It's dangerous for a poet to believe that gloom is the precondition for seriousness. If poetry for Hill is a *"mode of moral life"* ("charred prayers / spiralling godwards on intense thermals"), the evidence here lies more in design than in example—the morals are in lieu of, not on behalf. Poetry provides a moral life the way that standing on a pillar in the desert provides salvation—fine if you have a pillar, and a desert, and a terrific sense of balance, and, if not, not.

Verse Chronicle

God's Chatter

Natasha Trethewey

Natasha Trethewey's well-mannered, well-meaning poems are as confused about race as the rest of us. The daughter of a black mother and a white father, she was raised in the Deep South of the sixties, when the civil rights acts had still not penetrated the backwaters of her state. (Some would say that in large swatches of the South they haven't penetrated yet.) Under the miscegenation laws, her parents' marriage was illegal. In *Native Guard*, she has wrapped a memoir of her childhood around Civil War history—across the waters from her hometown, miles off the coast, former slaves and free men-of-color mustered into the Union army stood guard over Confederate POWs at a ramshackle island fort. A soldier notes in his diary:

> *Truth be told, I do not want to forget*
> *anything of my former life: the landscape's*
> *song of bondage—dirge in the river's throat*
> *where it churns into the Gulf, wind in trees*
> *choked with vines.*

Soldiers don't write this way, but poets do. The *landscape's song of bondage*, the *dirge in the river's throat*—this ex-slave's fancy phrasemaking makes a lie of that "Truth be told," because every scrap of art here falsifies the past. There *were* literate slaves, all too few, and perhaps none among the lowly soldiers serving at the sandy, fly-ridden prison near Fort Massachusetts. (The major of the regiment, however, a slave-owning Creole, spoke five languages and was the highest-ranking black officer in the Union army.) To recreate a voice rendered mute by history, Trethewey has sometimes borrowed from a white colonel's memoir to make do. Putting the words of an educated white into the mouth of a freed slave isn't so bad; but, when Trethewey is forced to choose between the pretty and the profane, the pretty wins every time. She's an aesthete in wolf's clothing.

Trethewey's last book, *Bellocq's Ophelia* (2002), was a portrait of a prostitute in Storyville, the red-light district of turn-of-the-century New Orleans where E. J. Bellocq took his spectral glass-plates of local whores, who looked at times surprisingly genteel. The poems invent a past reimagined through the wishful thinking of the present, in that theme park of the oppressed designed by modern academics. Forty-five years ago, an amateur historian who took the trouble to record Storyville's surviving denizens and habitués found many prostitutes still alive—a couple of the transcripts are as brilliantly foul-mouthed as any episode of *Deadwood*: "I been fucking f'om befo' I kin remembuh! Shit, yes! Wit' my ol' man, wit' my brothas, wit d' kids in da street. I done it fo' pennies, I done it fo' nothin' . . . An' you know whut, mistuh? I got a quatah fo' sucking off a ol' niggah yes*tiddy!*" It's a long way from there to Trethewey's prim, rose-colored-glasses whore, who however borne down seems sad in the pluckiest possible way.

As soon as you know the premises of Trethewey's poems, you know everything—they're the architecture of their own prejudices. Though fond of form, she fudges any restrictions that prove inconvenient, so we get faux villanelles, quasi-sonnets, and lots of lines half-ripened into pentameter—most poems end up in professional but uninspired free verse. Trethewey wears the past like a diamond brooch. She writes of her parents with no fury or sympathy or even regret, just the blank courtesy of a barista at Starbucks. You read the tales of prostitution and slavery without feeling a thing—the slaves might just as well be dressed by Edith Head, with a score by Max Steiner swelling gloriously over a Technicolor sunset. Trethewey's moral sunniness has all the conviction of Scarlett O'Hara gushing, "As Gawd is mah witness, I'll nevah be hungry agai-yun."

Since the poems know where they're going long before they get there, it's a shock when one takes a wrong turn: as a girl, bringing daffodils to her mother, Trethewey sees in them something of herself ("each blossom a head lifted up // toward praise"):

> *I knew nothing*
> *of Narcissus or the daffodils' short spring—*
>
> *how they'd dry like graveside flowers, rustling*

> *when the wind blew—a whisper, treacherous,*
> *from the sill.* Be taken with yourself,
>
> *they said to me;* Die early, *to my mother.*

Such lines face the guilt other poems resist, though there are secrets they can't confess (they're cagiest about a stepfather's violence). Soon it's back to a tone-deaf blues ("When the preacher called out I held up my hand;/When he called for a witness I raised my hand—/*Death stops the body's work; the soul's a journeyman*") or four photographs of the South tortured into poems, each duller than the last. The poems move excruciatingly slowly, their symbols marked like road signs—a landscape is never just a landscape, it's the "buried/terrain of the past"; and, as for history, the "ghost of history lies down beside me,//rolls over, pins me beneath a heavy arm." You're surprised *Native Guard* doesn't contain a tourist's guide to the symbols, to make sure the reader doesn't miss a thing. The book does come with notes, as if mounting every epigraph like a dead bug and pointing out each historical source made the poems any the livelier. Trethewey so wants to be praised, she has injected these poems with the formaldehyde of style.

Mark Strand

Mark Strand's louche charm and languid good manners (he's as debonaire as Cary Grant in a tux) let him treat weighty matters as if they were light as feathers and feathery matters as if they weighed out as lead. His teasing, self-mocking parables, so even-tempered a flamethrower couldn't ruffle their composure, have made many readers wonder if he can take anything seriously. The new poems in *Man and Camel* don't try very hard to be exceptions.

> *I am not thinking of Death, but Death is thinking of me.*
> *He leans back in his chair, rubs his hands, strokes*
> *his beard, and says, "I'm thinking of Strand, I'm thinking*
> *that one of these days I'll be out back, swinging my scythe*
> *or holding my hourglass up to the moon, and Strand will appear*
> *in a jacket and tie, and together under the boulevards'*
> *leafless trees we'll stroll into the city of souls."*

There's much to be said for treating even Death with devil-may-care careless-ness; but critics have long had trouble dividing the absurdist Strand, the one who could sell Dada to Eskimos, from the moody, philosophical poet who has occasionally made an appearance through this long and desultory career. Even Strand has trouble telling them apart.

The eerie fables and quirky anecdotes in *Reasons for Moving* (1968) and *Darker* (1970) were told with a minimum of detail and all the affect of a dry martini. They were much imitated in their day (sometimes they even imitated themselves), but the longer and more pretentious poems that followed in *The Story of Our Lives* (1973) were more tedious to read than they must have been to write. Strand's reputation never quite recovered, though he was very quickly promoted to that Grand Old Man status in which poets win awards for books not half as good as ones ignored when they were Sweet Young Things.

Had Sylvia Plath never written a line, Strand would have been the most gifted American poet born in the thirties; and his darkly cynical poems some-times sound like a posthumous version of hers, what she might have written after laying waste to everything in sight. Shorn of metaphors and similes, pro-saic as a paper bag, Strand's poems come long after an apocalypse no one can quite remember.

Man and Camel seems at first by the Strand whose every poem is a varia-tion of a joke about a man walking into a bar with a parrot on his shoulder. A man begins to act like a horse, but he can't fool real horses ("they might have known me/in another life—the one in which I was a poet./They might have even read my poems"). A man finds he can walk into fires and emerge unscathed. A man on a porch sees a man and a camel stroll by. The man and animal wander up the street and out of town, singing a haunting song, then stop and return to the man on the porch. "You ruined it," they say. "You ru-ined it forever." It's amusing, a little, this thinly disguised revenge on people who want something from art. Strand is often most heavy-handed when he's writing about nothing at all.

It's a surprise, then, after so many poems half thought and half baked, to find a group written in the same style but violently sad and unappeasable.

> *I still recall that moment of looking up*
> *and seeing the woman stare past me*
> *into a place I could only imagine,*
> *and each time it is with a pang,*
> *as if just then I were stepping*

from the depths of the mirror
into that white room, breathless and eager,
only to discover too late
that she is not there.

The poet seems to have woken to some arctic world of Schopenhauerian suffering. These poems rely too heavily on props left over from the seventies—*night* and *moon* and *stars*, all available by mail order—and you're never sure this more solemn poet isn't going to tie your shoelaces together when you're distracted. Worse, the book closes with an overwrought sequence, "Poem after the Seven Last Words" (the last words of Christ), commissioned to be read between movements of a Haydn string quartet (or, as the proofs had it, "Hayden"). Religious poetry is not the ironist's métier, because it removes his chief weapon: "you / shall be with me in paradise, in the single season of being, / in the place of forever, you shall find yourself"—who knew that Christ had mastered, not just the pop-psych jargon of "finding yourself," but the run-on sentence? Still, it's good to be reminded that sometimes, when this poet balances doubt against absurdity, doubt still triumphs.

A. R. Ammons

In 1955 a sales executive for a medical glassware firm paid a notorious vanity press to publish his first book of poems. The book sold sixteen copies (royalties amounted to "four four-cent stamps," the poet joked), other copies being palmed off on business cronies by the poet's father-in-law. Exactly a century before, Walt Whitman had paid the printer's bill for *Leaves of Grass* out of his own pocket. The young glassware man, A. R. Ammons, went on to win two National Book Awards and the Bollingen Prize. The reissue of his rare first book, *Ommateum, with Doxology,* completes the barrel scraping that followed his death five years ago.

Ammons was always an oddball in American poetry, producing lyric reflections and rambling meditations on nature, philosophy, science, the verse stumbling along as if it couldn't quite catch up. He wrote in inspired fits, good and bad indifferently jumbled together, and is perhaps most famous for *Tape for the Turn of the Year* (1965), composed on an adding-machine tape, which made the lines short and the poem nearly endless (you wonder if he took the tape on his way out the door of the glassware business). A new preface by Roger Gilbert proposes that, after *Leaves of Grass*, *Ommateum* may be the "most important self-published book of American poetry"; but it must compete with first books by, among others, Edwin Arlington Robinson and Ezra Pound.

If *Ommateum* was the "first expression of a mature, startlingly original artist," as Gilbert believes, it would have taken a crystal ball to tell. The poems are fervent and indistinct, not at all like the house style of the fifties, but not very original, either—the best are faded washes of Pound in high Romantic mode, and indeed many use as their protagonist a heroic figure named Ezra, half prophet and half wandering Ishmael: poems have been set in Sumer, as well as at a crucifixion, in a crusade, and during a medieval plague. For all his heroic fortitude and heroic claptrap, the hero seems less Gilgamesh than Gumby.

The worst poems are impossibly dotty, so awful you wonder what the author ever saw in them:

> *Silent as light in dismal transit*
> *through the void, I, evanescent,*
> *sibilant among my parts,*
> *fearing the eclipse of a possible glance*
> *and not glancing, shut-eyed,*
> *crouch froglike upon my brain.*

Even if you paid through the nose to get a vanity press to publish this, you'd have to bribe the typesetter not to cut his own throat.

One scholar has suggested that *Ommateum* is an example of "outsider art"—the folk art, often touching and strange, sometimes quite mad, of uneducated naïfs and mental patients. Ammons was a thoroughly educated navy veteran (he studied for an M.A. in English at Berkeley), not some hick with a charred twig and a slab of bark; yet the implicit comparison to Whitman, another outsider, has curious merit. Ammons and Whitman both pretended to be more naive than they were (Whitman was self-educated and a newspaper editor, not the slouch-hatted bumpkin of *Leaves of Grass*), and each violated the poetic constraints of his day. We look back at Whitman and see his peers writing third-rate Keats; we look at Ammons and see his peers writing third-rate Eliot and Pound—yet *Leaves of Grass* is a work of genius, and *Ommateum* a collection of thoughtless witterings:

My dice are crystal inlaid with gold
and possess
> *spatial symmetry*
about their centers and
mechanical symmetry and
> *are of uniform density*
and all surfaces have equal
coefficients of friction for

my dice are not loaded
> *Thy will be done*
whether dog or Aphrodite.

The young poet eventually learned how to make the short line bear more weight (here the lines stutter with ecstatic nonsense: "Come word / I said / azalea word / gel precipitate / while I / the primitive spindle . . ."). Ammons the woodsman and natural philosopher is occasionally on display ("The grasses heading barbed tufts / airy panicles and purple spikes"), but the poems celebrating the cornucopia of the earth's business lie a good distance in the future.

Ammons took the long way around to become a poet. *Ommateum* disappeared without notice, apart from one dismal review in *Poetry*; and it was eight years before he published another book. He was lucky this volume became so rare (God help him, he thought it might have been his best), because for a long while the poems lay hidden from sight. This reissue commemorates the ambitions of that young ampoule and urine-bottle salesman. The only way Ammons could have improved *Ommateum* would have been to burn it.

Louise Glück

Many poets never live down their first books (a few find they cannot live up to them); but sometimes later books take such a radical turn, the first is forgotten or dismissed as youthful folly (Frost's agreeable and slight *A Boy's Will* was soon overwhelmed by the genius of *North of Boston*). Sometimes in this chronicle I want to look back at neglected books, even books that might have to be rescued from the author's distaste. Think of Louise Glück's *Firstborn*, published in 1968. The original dust jacket referred to her as "Miss Glück," a form of address that sounds almost Victorian now—you're surprised she wasn't called a poetess. When reprinted in the eighties, this debut was practically orphaned by its author, who felt only "embarrassed tenderness" toward it.

The disconcerting, morbid psychology of *Firstborn* seems heavily marked by the influence of Sylvia Plath (*Ariel* had appeared only three years before). The younger poet's lines are seductive as a tango as she tries to shake off all the older poet knew (the debts accrued as inspiration were paid in resistance). Where Plath was a poet of melodrama and rude outburst, Glück is all pinched reserve (she speaks like Atropos, every sentence cut short), the poems reduced to slivers of glass. She watches a family on a train:

> *the kid*
> *Got his head between his mama's legs and slept. The poison*
> *That replaces air took over.*
> *And they sat—as though paralysis preceding death*
> *Had nailed them there. The track bent south.*
> *I saw her pulsing crotch . . . the lice rooted in that baby's hair.*

How Freud would have loved the violence of her seeing! Brute but matter-of-fact, the lines have the rhythm of complaint but not concession; they're almost sorry for the world they have to record. The pleasure the poet takes in the senses lies partly in the gratification of disgust—Sharon Olds and C. K. Williams might have learned at her feet.

In *Firstborn*, everything happens for the observer's eye (urgent as tabloid headlines, the poems are cast all too frequently in the present tense). Though later books reconvened Glück's life as myth, here she lives in the world of cars and soup cans, the world of the everyday. The world of boys.

> *Requiring something lovely on his arm*
> *Took me to Stamford, Connecticut, a quasi-farm,*
> *His family's; later picking up the mammoth*
> *Girlfriend of Charlie, meanwhile trying to pawn me off*
> *On some third guy also up for the weekend.*
> *But Saturday we still were paired; spent*
> *It sprawled across that sprawling acreage*

> *Until the grass grew limp*
> *With damp. Like me. Johnston-baby, I can still see*
> *The pelted clover, burrs' prickle fur and gorged*
> *Pastures spewing infinite tiny bells. You pimp.*

This is a Glück you recognize and a Glück you don't, not quite. The rhymes that button up these poems—rhymes she soon abandoned—have been lost in the avalanche of enjambment. The economy becomes a declaration of pain, with nothing left beneath terseness except despair. Glück's later poems in *The House on Marshland* (1975) and *Descending Figure* (1980) turn woozy and narcotic, living in the bedclothes of dreams and myths, drawn to female sufferers like Joan of Arc and Abishag. The rough edges have been planed off, the anxieties battened into place—self-consciousness has set in.

There are lines in *Firstborn* like shavings from Plath's workshop floor (the "click,/Click of his brain's whirling empty spindle," the "moon as round as aspirin"), but Glück has a dour comedy of her own: "I watch the lone onion/ Floating like Ophelia, caked with grease." Like Dickinson, she's a flawed solitaire sometimes grimly amused by herself. The poems are not the practiced, French-polished productions of a professional—there's raw nerve in their claustrophobic interiors. Only one or two of these apprentice pieces have the shimmer of lasting work, but all are triumphant—even gloating—in their losses.

> *Fish bones walked the waves off Hatteras.*
> *And there were other signs*
> *That Death wooed us, by water, wooed us*
> *By land: among the pines*
> *An uncurled cottonmouth that rolled on moss*
> *Reared in the polluted air.*
> *Birth, not death, is the hard loss.*
> *I know. I also left a skin there.*

She must be one of the few poets to imitate "The Quaker Graveyard in Nantucket" and live to tell about it.

Though Glück never formally entered college, she attended a few courses at Columbia and Sarah Lawrence (Hart Crane's father invented Life Saver mints, Glück's the X-Acto knife)—her career is that of an outsider looking in, while the poems reveal someone trapped in a body looking out. Why return to this book almost forty years later? Not just to examine how much the poet left behind, but to note how much still seems fresh and unexhausted. In her first book, Glück had already reached the limits of her skin. The poet she became had to be different—a metamorphosis few poets have managed with as much grace, or success. Quarrelsome though I have often been about her later work, she has earned my admiration for the way she has wrestled with what might be called the music of a career—with being a poet over time.

Franz Wright

The potential market for poetry action-figures must be enormous, so why not start with that holy terror Franz Wright? Every figure must come with accessories: in Wright's case, one set for before rehab (bottle of whiskey, hypodermic, glassine envelopes), one for after (twelve-step pamphlet, Good News Bible). Wright has never had to choose between perfection of the work and of the life, the life is already so imperfect; but, like many ex-drunks and ex-junkies, he can't let you forget his glory days. He never lets himself forget, either—he revels in old sins while begging praise for new virtues. (Some sinners end up holier than thou, some druggier than thou, though a few want desperately to be both.)

God's Silence lives in the suffering of forgiveness (Wright seems stuck on step five of the famous twelve: he can't forgive himself and sometimes can't forgive God), but it's hard to tell when the suffering stops and the wallowing begins. The poetry is romantic in all the wrong ways—it's the work of Peck's Bad Boy gone straight, of Byron in a dog collar, the pages stained with self-loathing piety. Wright's relation to his God is that of whining schoolboy to distant headmaster, a headmaster who refuses to speak to him.

> I am very afraid but still know You
> are taking care of me, and even live in hope
> You will one day see fit to put into my mouth
> words that will explain it all, floating before me in letters
>
> of fire.

The religious poems here—delivered in spews of cringing self-abasement—are the more moving for being so unconvincing. Like many solipsists, Wright can't relate to others without sentimentalizing them; and that includes God, the most forbidding of father figures. Few poets since Plath have dissected themselves so publicly for their art (I'm not even going to suggest the accessories required by the Plath action figure), and Wright is the last and most frustrated of confessionals. He has few poetic gifts beyond displaying his wounds in public; but the breast-beating apologias are cast in language so clumsy and affected, they seem a lie. Has any poet ever wanted so badly to be sincere, or failed so miserably?

> One of the few pleasures of writing
> is the thought of one's book in the hands of a kindhearted
> intelligent person somewhere. I can't remember what the others are right
> now.
> I just noticed that it is my own private
>
> National I Hate Myself and Want to Die Day.

I hope I'm not the only reader who finds this both hilarious and insufferable. If I were a "kindhearted/intelligent person," I'd put my head down and run like blazes.

Wright's father, the much loved and much honored poet James Wright (they are the first father and son to win Pulitzer Prizes in poetry), was a hard act to follow—and I say that despite never having been a fan. He comes in for abuse here, but he was a poet of more dignity and modest seriousness than his son; indeed, the son's poetry contains the negative virtues of the father's: brutish where his father's affected a plain elegance, sniveling where his father's remained sensitive, ordinary where his father's could be unsettling.

Franz Wright longs for the annihilations of faith (he has so many poems here about a blinding light, I tried to buy stock in Sylvania; then I realized he meant the light of God); but he doesn't have a vocabulary sophisticated enough to render them. Most poets want to write about sinners, few about saints, because sinners are better box office—they make everyone else feel virtuous. Wright drops into quasi-religious blather at the drop of a hat ("I cling to the Before/The spirit face/behind the face/yearning for light/the water and the light/And I am flowing back to the Before")—you'd think he was angling for an appearance on *The 700 Club*. His faith barely conceals the rage beneath: "Poem is not composed in states of exaltation: most that are, in fact, result in total doggerel and, frankly, insufferable puke."

The peculiar mixture of pride and self-loathing makes these poems rude, unlovely things, like papier-mâché sculptures by a roomful of fifth graders. Wright's readers seem fascinated by a man obviously held together, like his poems, with spit and glue. Beyond the gruesome sentiment, the ranting and raving, the hunger for praise no Pulitzer could satisfy (it would take nine yards of cement to ruin the appetite of someone who feels so unloved) lies a damaged soul with wry self-knowledge: "Nobody has called for some time. / (I was always the death of the party.)" I wish Wright could laugh at himself more often, because when his morose, tortured poems stop asking for sympathy they start demanding pity; and then they want all the money in your wallet.

Paul Muldoon

Say the muses want to lay a terrible curse upon a child. They give him a bat's ears, a code breaker's eye, the ability to juggle words like flaming torches; then they say, "You will have all the gifts a poet desires, but nothing whatever to write about." Paul Muldoon's early poems were quirky and modest, and it's hard to tell exactly when he went beyond baroque. What was manner became mannerism—he turned into one of those Las Vegas interior decorators whose motto is "If it doesn't move, gild it!" A poet, as he ages, can become so secure in his tendencies he can't remember when he didn't have tendencies at all. The Muldoon of thirty years ago might shake his head in bewilderment at the poems in *Horse Latitudes*:

> *Not the day-old cheep of a smoke detector on the blink*
> *in what used to be the root cellar,*
> *or the hush-hush of all those drowsy syrups*
> *against their stoppers*
>
> *in the apothecary chest*
> *at the far end of your grandmother's attic,*
> *not the "my sweet, my sweet"*
> *of ice branch frigging ice branch,*
>
> *nor the jinkle-jink*
> *of your great-grandfather, the bank teller*

who kept six shots of medicinal (he called it "therap-
utraquist") *whiskey like six stacks of coppers . . .*

Here are the cheerfully swollen vocabulary, the onomatopoeia ("jinkle-jink"),
the queerly fabricated words ("therap-/*utraquist*") of late Muldoon. Should
you wonder why the little soufflé of "therap*utraquist*" has been divided like
East and West Berlin, you only have to look at the end words—alternate stan-
zas rhyme with each other. (Muldoon's so addicted to rhymes, for a good one
he'd sacrifice three goats and a dozen lambs.)

This is the sort of tour de force Muldoon lives for; but after you read nine-
teen sonnets, each named for a battle beginning with the letter *B* (including
Basra, where the armored cavalry of Gulf War II forms a counterpoint to the
horses of earlier wars), or the villanelle, or the double villanelle, or the ses-
tina, or the pantoum, or the ninety haiku—most of these forms with his own
madcap stamp upon them—you wonder if there was a point. He never runs
out of things to say, only things worth saying. There were other poets like this
once, and they wrote in Latin two thousand years ago and were ridiculed as
Alexandrians.

There's nothing natural about Muldoon's poems now—they're full of arti-
ficial sweeteners, artificial colors, and probably regulated by the FDA. Poem
after poem fires off words with such abandon, they're noisier than Phil Spec-
tor's Wall of Sound (if at fifty-five you title a book *Horse Latitudes*, write a ter-
rible set of couplets about Bob Dylan, and start your own rock band, people
will wonder if you're having a midlife crisis). Muldoon's a Wittgenstein dis-
ciple who believes the world is everything that is the case, and he can't bear
to leave anything out: you can find Gene Chandler, stilettos, spivs with shivs,
tweenie girls, and anti-Castro Cubans, all within half a dozen lines. He has
a riddle about *griddle* that takes thirty lines (if you haven't gotten the hint,
Muldoon's favorite rhea is logorrhea—or is that his favorite logo?). Like God,
he loves all things equally and not wisely but too well; in the democracy of
such love lies tedium.

What happens if you patiently untangle the spells of this sorcerer? (It helps
to have some hepcat up on the latest lingo as well as a fat dictionary.) "The
Old Country" seems composed of nothing but frothy contrivance:

Every flash was a flash in the pan
and every border a herbaceous border

> *unless it happened to be an*
> *herbaceous border as observed by the* Recorder
>
> *or recorded by the* Observer.
> *Every widdie stemmed from a willow bole.*
> *Every fervor was a religious fervor.*

This rings its changes all the way through a crown of sonnets; yet, if you examine every line, you see the terrible small-mindedness of a town where everyone watches everyone else, noting his pronunciation and the newspaper he takes—and all the local conventions are clichés. When you penetrate the asphalt of these poems, you may find a nugget of gold; but sometimes you need a jackhammer to do so.

Becalmed in the horse latitudes that afflict most writers, Muldoon will pitch logic, truth, beauty, and meaning overboard, just to save the cheep-cheep of that smoke detector. A very few poems, like "The Treaty" and "Eggs," though dressed in the bling-bling of his later work, return him to the Ireland before and during the Troubles (he's now an American citizen and a professor at Princeton). Something has been gained, a lot of it twenty-four carat; but much has been lost as well.

Verse Chronicle

Let's Do It, Let's Fall in Luff

John Ashbery

John Ashbery has long threatened to become a public monument, visited mainly by schoolchildren and pigeons. For half a century, he has pressed the limits of the expected and at last become an expectation itself—if the avant-garde has to die somewhere, become rear guard at last, it will be in poems like those in *A Worldly Country,* where promises remain unkept, meaning is never surrendered or redeemed (as worthless as a Confederate bond), and gestures are frozen in medias res. Ashbery has become too self-parodic not to be his own joke ("So why not, indeed, try something new? / Actually, I can think of a number of reasons. / Wait—suddenly I can't think of any!"), yet that joke lays waste to a lot of the poetry of the past half century. If such a curate's egg loves to be bad, God help us should he ever try to be good.

> *Not the smoothness, not the insane clocks on the square,*
> *the scent of manure in the municipal parterre,*
> *not the fabrics, the sullen mockery of Tweety Bird,*
> *not the fresh troops that needed freshening up. If it occurred*
> *in real time, it was OK, and if it was time in a novel*
> *that was OK too. From palace and hovel*
> *the great parade flooded avenue and byway*
> *and turnip fields became just another highway.*
> *Leftover bonbons were thrown to the chickens*
> *and geese, who squawked like the very dickens.*

This is tosh, but Ashbery's patented, vitamin-enriched tosh. The lines begin with Augustan composure, like Auden fingering his favorite props and imagining himself John Dryden. Ashbery can't pretend to be a philosophe very long; his inner child soon drags in Tweety Bird and then all hell breaks loose—the syntax remains formal and proprietary; but the age slips between the eighteenth and the twenty-first, the diction between *palace and hovel* and *real time.*

There's so much froth and frippery here, the reader might not even notice the rhymed couplets. Many of Ashbery's poems recall, with ironic fondness (or sullen mockery), the age of the age of reason; in our own muddled, maddened century, apparently all we can expect from a philosopher prince is the notion that the fissure between fact and fiction is of little consequence. Postmodernism's fond delusions give comfort to many a religion; but, if real life doesn't matter, why should we care about the dying or the dead? In the aesthetic fiction Ashbery inhabits, Death never calls—perhaps the Grim Reaper hasn't thought of a punch line yet.

Ashbery's new poems are wearyingly discursive (Helen Vendler suggests that his short poems are diary entries, but I prefer to think that Ashbery writes every morning and never has a thing to say). The poet's continual low mutter about art and perception is often brilliant in a secondhand way. He can make sense when he wants to ("Self-Portrait in a Convex Mirror" is one of his few poems of sustained invention that doesn't lack sustained sense), but he's a lot more fun when he's goofing off.

> *Cannily you looked on from the wings,*
> *finger raised to lips, as the old actor*
> *slogged through the lines he's reeled off*
> *so many times, not even thinking*
> *if they are tangential to the way we*
> *slouch now.*

The way we slouch now! The stray lines offer social commentary as keen as anything Trollope wrote about Victorian England.

Perhaps I'm not the only reader who thinks that, while scribbling down far too much poetry in the past fifteen years, Ashbery has lost the cunning of his sentences, which sometimes dodder about as if they've forgotten their subject. Were he unfortunate enough to develop Alzheimer's, the poems wouldn't change a bit. Besides, he long ago created a world nonsense surplus—with a nonsense mountain somewhere in Belgium, like the EU butter mountains of old. Ashbery has written some of the worst lines in contemporary poetry, just to show he can:

> So often it happens that the time we turn around in
> soon becomes the shoal our pathetic skiff will run aground in.
> And just as the waves are anchored to the bottom of the sea
> we must reach the shallows before God cuts us free.

The ghost of William McGonagall must be jealous.

Critics have often compared Ashbery to the abstract expressionists (I've probably done so myself); but his hectic, Scotch-taped compositions are much closer in spirit to Roy Lichtenstein—campy, cartoonish, with no pretension but a lack of pretension. Pop art never wanted to be taken seriously, which means it's treated far more seriously than necessary. Though nearly eighty, Ashbery still loves to shatter the small vases of lyric, even if he doesn't know what to do afterward. (He stares at the reader, as if to say, "I *told* you they were glass!") If the old lyric was fragile, the new one offers little beyond glib puckishness. As soon as you think Ashbery has a serious idea, he makes you regret it; yet we return to him, those of us who return, because we don't always mind regretting it.

Frieda Hughes

Happy families are all alike, but unhappy families . . . look out! Your mother will leave journals, Hollywood will option them, and Gwyneth Paltrow star in the movie (lucky you, it will bomb at the box office). Frieda Hughes is the daughter of Sylvia Plath and Ted Hughes, a fact suppressed in her first book but known to anyone not on long-term duty in the Antarctic. Her original idea in *Forty-Five*, her fourth, is to devote a poem to each year of her life— and then make a painting about it, too.

Hughes was too young to remember her mother's suicide, which remained a secret kept from her until a newspaper published the story. This may explain the lack of emotion in the daughter's memory:

> My mother, head in oven, died,
> And me, already dead inside,

> *I was an empty tin*
> *Where nothing rattled in.*

Had the poems continued in this Hansel-and-Gretel vein, the book might have become a remarkable document of a child's growth to consciousness, something Wordsworth attempted in *The Prelude*, not entirely successfully. (The believable children in literature are rarely interesting, and the interesting rarely believable.) Hughes thought her aunt was her mother; when her father remarried, her new stepmother stepped from the pages of "Snow White"—"She thought me too familiar/She said, smiling over spaghetti sauce/In the frying pan." (Her father's seven-year affair with Assia Wevill, who also committed suicide by gas oven, is dismissed in a single obscure phrase.)

The princess in this fairy tale grows up fat, insecure, bulimic, and soon develops a thing for bikers. Later, she marries any guy with a smooth line of patter, specializing in men who will slap her around or rob her blind. (The poems read like a captivity narrative.) She takes a naive pleasure in being married, in becoming a "Mrs.," the *same* naive pleasure her mother recorded in her journals. It's eerie—you wonder if all young children who lose a parent feel so unloved. Where's Father in this? Brooding, remote, apologetic, he's a faraway mountain seen across an armed border.

Few confessional poets have possessed a life with so many built-in headlines; it's a shame Frieda Hughes doesn't have the literary skill to take advantage of them. She excels in wide-eyed, slightly crazed run-on sentences that sound like excuses and read like indictments—they're so near to being illiterate, you weep for English syntax:

> *My new lover was as rotten as bad meat*
> *At the bin's bottom. His truth*
> *Rang hollow in the separation*
> *That now divided me from his daily anger*
> *At my head full of independence.*
> *But my business plan became a funnel*
> *Straight into the new man's business arms,*
> *His blacklisted insurance sales history*
> *Making a proxy of me,*
> *And I'd no idea he'd fuck a friend*
> *And make her my enemy.*

About the time the *plan* becomes a *funnel*, I no longer know what's fact and what's figure—and I'm not sure Hughes can tell the difference.

There's nothing wrong with going into the family business, but literature offers no capital accrued by previous generations (even Dumas *fils* had to bribe Dumas *père* with a steaming chop for help in finishing some play or other). It pays to be talented; but, if your parents are *very* famous poets, you're forever going to work in their shadows (at twenty-four, Hughes "gave up writing poetry;/The parental comparisons/Would be too painful for me"— unfortunately her resolve didn't last). It makes things no better if you have trouble keeping your thoughts in order:

> *Excitement at my first Sydney exhibition*
> *Launched me straight into the gallery owner's*
> *Locked doors, behind which*
> *He drank my sales, and endometriosis*
> *Bled me inwards, until a hysterectomy.*

Even before the litany of Hughes's illnesses (endometriosis, chronic fatigue, M.E., Crohn's disease, a twisted colon, an allergy to fleas, and some mysterious problem with her feet), her roller-coaster ride of elation and depression provokes the reader's sympathy. The poems are hypnotic as a train wreck; but it's hard to pity someone so good at pitying herself, someone who loves playing the victim and manages to be humorless about it.

Hughes has the bad luck she inherited and bad luck all her own—the long-awaited London show of her paintings was hung the day of Princess Diana's death (the poet bitterly refers to the "vast scow of national grief," a witty phrase). Her dead mother half-possesses her; but, when Hughes writes a line that begins "Daddy, Daddy," the effect isn't accidental—it's creepy. There's so much melodrama in these poems, the reader is numb by the time she gets around to September 11:

> *The Twin Towers fell,*
> *And all the people in them, I had never seen*
> *Such carnage on a TV screen,*
> *The images remain with me.*

The images remain with me. All you can say is "Huh?" Hughes is a perfect example of what happens when a poet, though possessing none of the art necessary to turn a plain old messed-up life into literature, is the sun in her own Copernican system (she puts the Sol back in solipsism). We remember Plath, not because her life was worse than anybody else's, but because she was able to set it down in blood. Every poem here comes with its very own five-foot-long abstract painting, displayed on a handy Web site (if you want to save yourself the trouble, the lurid, blobby images resemble a dissection of diseased kidneys). The poems don't make you like Frieda Hughes. They make you afraid Robert Lowell's children will take up poetry, too.

Cathy Park Hong

When Alice fell down the rabbit hole, the Mad Hatter and the Queen of Hearts at least spoke the King's English; but novelists who invent a new country sometimes like to make up a language to go with it. The Lilliputian and Houyhnhnm of *Gulliver's Travels*, the Elvish of *The Lord of the Rings*, and the Nadsat of *A Clockwork Orange* are highbrow equivalents of *Star Trek's* Klingon and the fertile babble of countless science-fiction tales. In *Dance Dance Revolution*, Cathy Park Hong has created a future resort called the Desert, whose hotels are modeled on famous cities and whose people speak Desert Creole, a weird mish-mash of languages very hard on the ear. The place sounds like Las Vegas.

The speaker of these headlong, take-no-prisoners poems is a tour guide who chatters away cheerfully to an unnamed historian.

> . . . *Opal o opus,*
> *behole, neon hibiscus bloom beacons!*
> *"Tan Lotion Tanya" billboard . . . she*
> *your lucent Virgil, den I's taka ova*
> *as talky Virgil . . . want some tea? Some pelehuu?*

The advanced publicity copy called this a "fluid fabricated language." I'd go as far as fabricated (it sounds too much like the ludicrous speech of Jar Jar Binks in *Star Wars*). Hong is droll enough to make the guide our Virgil, though the inspiration of the *Inferno* goes no deeper. However tiresome the sci-fi premise, she sees the advantage, as Swift and Tolkein and Burgess did, of making things new by making them partly incomprehensible. When the guide refers to each hotel as a McCosm, the microcosm has just met McDonald's.

A little Desert Creole goes a long way; after a few pages of this contorted pidgin, though it's sometimes mellifluous as Caribbean patois, the reader might well demand a Berlitz course, or subtitles.

> *See radish turrets stuck wit tumor lights around hotel*
> *lika glassblown Russki castle sans Pinko plight,*
> *only Ebsolute voodka fountains. Gaggle fo drink?*
>
> *Hundred ruble, cold kesh only. Step up y molest*
> *hammer y chicklets studded en ruby y seppire almost*
> *bling badda bling. Question? No question! Prick ear.*

Not many poets can go from *bling bling* to Shakespeare's *prick-ear'd* in a line; but the joke begins to wither even before you realize the author has a not-so-subtle agenda. Born in Korea, the guide was one of the dissidents behind the Kwangju Uprising of 1980, in which hundreds were killed or imprisoned. Beyond the Desert lies a heavily guarded ghetto for exiles and malcontents, off limits to visitors. It's no shock that Adrienne Rich, who chose this book for the Barnard Women Poets Prize, is delighted by the heavy-handed politics ("The Guide . . . plays whatever role she must in the world of the global economy, using language as subversion and disguise"—this isn't an introduction; it's a manifesto).

For the poems, however, the political gloss is like a bad coat of varnish. Armchair lessons in modern Korean history gradually take over, and the reader might reasonably feel that the ticket he bought for Club Med turned out to be for a visit to the Black Hole of Calcutta. The narrative stalls badly, while the nosy historian (whose father was once the guide's lover—what are the odds?) provides her own tiresome memoirs and pages of workshop poetry— what the author herself might write without the trappings of Desert Creole. The guide's demented gabble is far more poetic, if far less intelligible:

> *Odes scuppa off lika fat wingless birds*
> *from hum-a-day coralim streets.*
>
> *Hurdy-gurdy sounds: cricket shrieks*
> *o mahikit, abraded music slum scent.*
>
> *How-kapow pops, a lime streak starled*
> *lika Gerty's bloomas fire crack de dusky violet sky.*

This has its own cracked genius and nutty integrity—Gertrude Stein would have lapped it up.

In the end, Hong has built an elaborate superstructure just to set out some shopworn academic notions about the dispossessed, whose plight here is transparently allegorical (sci-fi has always suffered problems of affect). Still, it's good to know that in her strange future world, where words are patented and auctioned off, where the patois apparently changes minute to minute, a guy can still go down to a karaoke bar and pop a Viagra to forget his troubles.

Frederick Seidel

The rich are different from you and me. They write better poetry, or did when poetry was an art of leisure. It sometimes seems that, in the centuries after scops stopped singing for gold rings in the meadhall, few men except Sir This or Lord That had the free time to bother with verse—if you weren't nobility, or landed gentry, or clergy, you were plumb out of luck. Later, poetry made some great poets rich, like Shakespeare and Pope, and some rich poets great, like Byron and Shelley. Wordsworth and Coleridge were able to scrape by without much by way of day jobs; and neither Tennyson nor Browning ever had to shovel coal. There are exceptions, but many well-known poets never earned a paycheck. Only in the twentieth century did poetry become an art not just read but written by the middle class.

Frederick Seidel is a throwback, a *bon vivant* who rubs shoulders with politicians and film directors, fashion designers and heads of state, at least when he isn't roaring around on a handbuilt motorcycle or getting measured for a pair of bespoke shoes. You have to admire a poet who finds time to worry about the rag trade:

> Huntsman indeed is gone from Savile Row,
> And Mr. Hall, the head cutter.
> The red hunt coat Hall cut for me was utter
> Red melton cloth thick as a carpet, cut just so.
> One time I wore it riding my red Ducati racer—what a show!—
> Matched exotics like a pair of lovely red egrets.

The jaunty meter underlies a lament for vanished graces—Seidel is a man who believes that "Civilized life is actually about too much."

Seidel dares you to dislike *Ooga-Booga* for who he is. (He dares you to dislike the title *Ooga-Booga*. Perhaps it's not surprising that he's so rarely anthologized, while so many right-thinking sapheads are.) He won't kowtow to the mob; yet there's a great deal of tastelessness in his good taste, not just in the designer goods and dropped names ("Diane von Furstenberg in those sweet bygone days / Got it in her head I had to meet her friend"), but in the masochism, the Balthus-style Lolita watching, and the priapic sexuality that absorb his waking imagination. When I wrote that American poetry had too little sex in it, I wasn't hoping for lines like "My dynamite penis / Is totally into Venus" or "I love it when you make me get down on all fours and crawl."

The mystery of Seidel is whether his abasement is a vulnerability indulged or an act of power disguised as submission. His early poems, in *Final Solutions* (1963) and *Sunrise* (1980), were so much under the thumb of Lowell they bore the older poet's inky fingerprint; but the later poems, produced with ever greater rapidity in late maturity and old age, are full of brute misanthropy and lavish disgust—Seidel revels in the savagery of the underclass and the decadence of the obscenely wealthy:

> *White linen summer clouds squatted over Điên Biên Phu.*
> *It must be 1954 because you soil yourself and give up hope but don't.*
> *The boys are reading L'Étranger as summer reading.*
> *My country, 'tis of thee, Albert Camus!*
>
> *The host sprinted upstairs to grab his fellow Existentialist—*
> *To drag him downstairs to the Embassy's July Fourth garden party.*
> *The Ambassador's son died horribly the following year*
> *In a ski lodge fire.*

That world of linen suits and embassy parties seems as distant as Edwardian England, but then so do existentialists. Seidel is a connoisseur of experience, and expensive handmade goods are one of the last preserves of the artisan—it's not the price Seidel admires, but the authenticity. (It's curious that he's such an unreflective soul—he's one of those existentialists who uses Nietzsche as an excuse not to think.) Beneath his contradictions there must lie some simple slogan like MASS MARKET = FASCISM. As for Fascists, he turns them into a joke: "Mussolini in riding boots stood at his desk to stuff / Himself into the new secretary who was spread out on the desk. He goes *uff.* / He goes *uff wuff, uff wuff,* and even—briefly—falls in luff." *In luff!*

It's hard to get the radical sympathy and aristo loathing in focus—Seidel's an original, but you're glad there aren't more like him. At best, this Cassandra offers a peek from behind the arras at the "useless royals," beautiful people, and oligarchs who run the world. These new poems are clumsy, hideously uneven, smug in their misanthropy, sometimes more agitprop than poetry, jingly, and often comically vulgar ("I'm in such a state of Haut-Brion I can't resist./A fist-fucking anus swallowing a fist"). The fretted, distressed lines itch to be something else and end up like nothing but themselves.

Is it possible Seidel knows no more senators than he does sultans? I've always thought there was half a chance he was a Walter Mitty figure holed up in some East Village garret, doomed to press his nose against shop windows like most of the rest of us. It worries me that such a high-hatter doesn't know that H. Huntsman and Sons still sits proudly at 11 Savile Row, as it has for almost a century. What sort of snob wouldn't know that?

Robert Lowell

The year before his death in 1977, Robert Lowell published the most peculiar of his many books, a *Selected Poems* that featured maimed and crippled versions of some of his most famous poems. Lowell suffered from revision mania, never content unless tinkering with his lines; his poems endured so many home improvements, he sometimes seemed to forget why he'd written them in the first place. His friends indulged him in this practice, when they did not encourage it.

Having belatedly published Lowell's *Collected Poems* (2003), his publishers have done an about-face and dragged the ruins of *Selected Poems* back into print, now in an expanded edition, as if enlarging a bad idea somehow improved it. What were they thinking? The unwary reader will find some poems in versions no reader could love—once a poet contracts revision mania, there's no stopping him until he has revised his poems down to a line, then a word, and finally just a punctuation mark. (Yet, in Lowell's case, what a punctuation mark!)

Lowell's bouts of revision may not have been wholly separate from his manic depression. Confined to a mental hospital, he once started to rewrite *Paradise Lost*, convinced he was John Milton. The poems in *Selected Poems* were revised as if Lowell were under the impression he was Robert Lowell. He reduced "In Memory of Arthur Winslow," "The Death of the Sheriff," and "Her Dead Brother" to their first sections, "Thanksgiving's Over" to its opening and close, and his longest poem, "The Mills of the Kavanaughs," to its last five stanzas. You open *Selected Poems* to discover corpses with only the head or feet remaining, or in one case the head *and* the feet. (Perhaps stung by his reviewers, in a revised edition Lowell restored the cuts he made to some poems, but not to those above.) *Selected Poems* is the most famous example of poetic butchery since Marianne Moore took a hatchet to her *Collected Poems*. The notes to this expanded edition make almost no mention of Lowell's roughshod alterations and say nothing of the controversy they engendered.

Frank Bidart, the coeditor of Lowell's *Collected Poems*, has provided a peculiar, woolgathering foreword to this edition; but he nowhere takes credit for editing it. He argues that Lowell was what is now called a "transgressive" artist—"his art again and again broke taboos, both thematic and formal." It's true that Lowell changed American poetry at least twice, first in the high-octane meter of *Lord Weary's Castle* (1946), which won the Pulitzer Prize, and later in the guilty family gossip of *Life Studies* (1959). The hurricane of the first book passed away quickly, but we have lived in the climate of the second for half a century.

Lowell's formal poetry, however, shattered no taboo, merely reviving and elaborating, with a strong dose of Milton, the style of Fugitives like Allen Tate. The verse of *Life Studies* was a sea change in subject more than theme or form—Lowell, to use a theatrical metaphor, broke down the fourth wall of the stage, speaking *in propria persona* of the private life once off-limits to poetry. (It hardly broke a taboo when the poet at the same time, partly influenced by the Beats, changed his style to a metrically haunted free verse.) Lowell saw the advantage of being Lowell—or seeming to be. He considered the poems a fictive autobiography, changing details like a Flaubert, not a Rousseau. Still, having long been a cousin of the novel, poetry after Lowell became the stepdaughter of autobiography. This change was as radical as modernism's shift to free verse.

Like Picasso, Lowell was a restless artist who believed that originality required constant change (unfortunately, as with urban development, if you tear down too much, you have no *urbs* any more). Bidart calls him the "poet of the irremediable." Though Lowell often considered the past with a rueful despair, a poem like "Skunk Hour" isn't beyond hope, having found, in the lowliest places, the will to go on.

The anonymous editor has restored Lowell's prose memoir "91 Revere Street" to *Life Studies*, now printed in its entirety, adding a couple of poems to *For the Union Dead* (1964) and a dozen or more sonnets to one of Lowell's beautiful follies, the sonnet-mad volume of *History* (1973). Poems from *Day by Day*, published weeks after Lowell's death, have now been included. Many of these new choices show a sensitive and informed taste. Less happily, seven sonnets have been dropped in Lowell's revised selection from *The Dolphin* (1973)—why keep his deformed versions of some poems only to banish poems he wanted to include? (Indeed, why not call this the *Expanded and Contracted Edition?*) No justification is made for such eclectic pantry-raiding masquerading as sober editing. Worse, the informative notes, borrowed from *Collected Poems*, remain uncorrected, though reviewers took pains to point out many errors of fact and fancy.

Lowell was the most brilliant poet of the postwar period. If he remains out of fashion, our postmodern day loathes poetry that refuses to be easy or clever. (I feel like a reviewer with a taste for Bergman when most everyone wants to watch *Pirates of the Caribbean* 3). An editor with a fresh and severe eye must produce the selected edition of Lowell's work now desperately needed. There were no reasons other than perversity and laziness to bring this bedraggled *Selected* back into print, where it will confuse Lowell's readers for years to come.

Henri Cole

Henri Cole's spare new book is a meditation serving as memoir—scenes come and go; parents fade away; the poet takes sidelong glances at his aging, graying face in the mirror. *Blackbird and Wolf* shows the confidence of a poet no longer struggling toward expression (Cole's early books were rococo wedding-cakes of expression). These quiet, unsettling poems often seem fractured from within, distracted in the intensity of their observation.

> *My lilacs died today, floating in a bowl.*
> *All week I watched them pushing away,*
> *their pruned heads swollen together into something*
> *like anger, making a brief comeback*
> *toward the end, as if secretly embalmed.*

The psychological nuance of these images shows the botanical eye of Plath, not the naive curiosity of Roethke. Few recent poets have been this Freudian, Viennese to their fingertips—it's as if Cole had read *The Interpretation of Dreams* and then memorized it. (For the past century, the chicken-and-egg problem has been whether dreams are Freudian because they're dreams or because the dreamers of dreams read Freud.)

The speaker here—cautious, anxiety-ridden, homosexual, devastated by the air he breathes—is trapped in the self, which would seem self-centered if self were not the very thing he was trying to escape. Cole's recent books, *The Visible Man* (1998) and *Middle Earth* (2003), gave astringent analysis to a temperament tormented and miserable. The new poems wrestle with an inarticulate anguish. As with Bishop, as with Moore, the poet has found, among animals and in the "effortless existence" of the plant world, surrogates for all he cannot say. (The things a writer most wishes to say may be what he has no words for—and the love that dare not speak its name is sometimes, like all love, the love of which nothing can be said.) Of a dead wren:

> When I open your little gothic wings
> on my whitewashed chest of drawers,
> I almost fear you, as if today were my funeral.
> Moment by moment, enzymes digest
> your life into a kind of coffin liqueur.
> Two flies, like coroners, investigate your feathers.

Those hilarious fly-coroners give almost scientific detachment to death (the "coffin liqueur" might have come from an episode of *C.S.I.*); but *gothic* takes us back to the incense-laden air of medieval churches, to the old religion that no longer consoles or absolves. The poet has mixed relations with his God, wrestling, not just with faith, but with the faith in faith.

Blackbird and Wolf is fascinated by nature's violence—in the human world, there is only a mediated loneliness. These poems are more obscure than Cole's recent work, more uneasily and sometimes clumsily phrased. All the guff about animals can make him seem a poor man's Galway Kinnell, going on about bears, or a slightly dotty Dr. Doolittle (the poet talks to crow and hornet and weed, but the poems are no wiser for it). Worse, there are poems about the war in Iraq that try to turn the poet's gifts for troubled reflection into a medium of public outrage.

When Lowell wrote his version of family history, he did not omit the comedy; and Cole is most indebted to the older poet when seeing his father plain:

> *My father lived in a dirty-dish mausoleum,*
> *watching a portable black-and-white television,*
> *reading the Encyclopaedia Britannica,*
> *which he preferred to Modern Fiction.*
> *One by one, his schnauzers died of liver disease,*
> *except the one that guarded his corpse*
> *found holding a tumbler of Bushmills.*

The schnauzers, the tumbler of Bushmills—these are the inheritance of *Life Studies*, the Flaubertian details that secure the habitation of the eye. The precision of observation has its dry philosophical flourish—to the voyeur comes loneliness, but also the spoils of beauty.

> *Poured through the bees, the sunlight, like flesh*
> *and spirit, emits a brightness pushing everything*
> *else away except the bees' vibrating bronze bodies*
> *riding the air as if on strings that flex*
> *and kick back as they circle the hive.*

The moody grandeurs of this short book are those of a poet who keeps company with himself and can offer no more, not the social torsions of Lowell or the vengeful hostilities of Plath. Misery doesn't love company—misery *is* company.

Pynchon in the Poetic

The monastic saints . . . familiarly accosted, or imperiously commanded, the lions and serpents of the desert; infused vegetation into a sapless trunk; suspended iron on the surface of the water; passed the Nile on the back of a crocodile; and refreshed themselves in a fiery furnace. These extravagant tales . . . display the fiction, without the genius, of poetry.
—Edward Gibbon, *The Decline and Fall of the Roman Empire*

Poetry was the mother of fiction, and its reduction to a minor species of memoir has not been without cost. That poetry and fiction share more than they divide (fiction at times bearing the private burden of memory, poetry failing memoir in pure fictions) is often concealed by the hermit-crab isolation of contemporary novels, for which realism is old-time religion.

What makes Thomas Pynchon's *Mason & Dixon* a poetic act is, not just its fanatic ignorance of current fashion (this historical novel almost makes a reader forget that beneath his cocky demeanor and hipster's cant Pynchon has always been a throwback), but its use of means, in its languors as well as its language, more properly poetic. There have always been fiction writers of poetic temperament: Joyce and Faulkner not surprisingly began as poets— minor poets, perhaps, but ones who took their early understandings of language through a form very different in its pretense, its rhythm, its design. (Melville was a much better poet as a novelist than he ever was writing verse.) Though Pynchon has learned from the modernists by coming after them, he is a novelist of old-fashioned sentiments, not just in historical curiosity (his novels of contemporary life, *Vineland* and the thinly mannered *The Crying of Lot 49*, have been his weakest), but in his adoption of Dickensian comedy, beginning with his absurd and fantastic names.

The narrator of *Mason & Dixon* is Reverend Wicks Cherrycoke. One difference between Dickens and Pynchon is that Dickens usually gets away with his names—Dickens invents characters so true to their names they are false to their unreality; Pynchon loathes the idea of character, and his names wither into whimsy at the expense of character. The philosophy of names is too divisive to have bearing here; but there are few words more Falstaffian, considering the worlds they include, than *poem* or *novel*. Our unwillingness to deny anything with the ambition of being a poem the honor of the name may make discretion impossible, yet most readers have a Platonic sense of what a poem is and is not (that sense may be merely typographical). Though it may be modified by experience or experiment, this sense is unlikely ever to admit a doughnut, a desk lamp, or any literary act wearing the clothes of other conventions (whether diary, play, or novel, though there may be novels in verse, verse plays, and perhaps rhymed diaries—they may use poetry without being poems). What calls itself a poem may, within limits, be taken as poem; but those limits are less enclosing boundaries than liberated tyrannies.

Mason & Dixon is a novel, and yet the experience of reading it is at times purely poetic. Pynchon has embraced in his arguments and actions the crowded ambiguity and frothy imagery of poetry; and to examine them is not to suggest these means lie outside the novel, but to recall how long they have been estranged, not just from recent fiction, but from recent poetry as well.

> *Snow-Balls have flown their Arcs, starr'd the Sides of Outbuildings, as of Cousins, carried Hats away into the brisk Wind off Delaware,— the Sleds are brought in and their Runners carefully dried and greased, shoes deposited in the back Hall, a stocking'd-foot Descent made upon the great Kitchen, in a purposeful Dither since Morning, punctuated by the ringing Lids of various Boilers and Stewing-Pots, fragrant with Pie-Spices, peel'd Fruits, Suet, heated Sugar,— the Children, having all upon the Fly, among rhythmic slaps of Batter and Spoon, coax'd and stolen what they might, proceed, as upon each afternoon all this snowy Advent, to a comfortable Room at the rear of the House, years since given over to their carefree Assaults.*

This clamorous opening sentence, dense with the chaotic rush of new sensation (every novel plunges into the cold river of a New World), is rife with the novel's animating themes—the ascents and descents of lives beneath those of the stars. Jeremiah Dixon is a journeyman surveyor, Charles Mason an assistant to the Astronomer Royal at Greenwich. The arcs and stars of those hurled snowballs are the heraldic signs of their professions: in the comedy of their lives, cutting arcs across oceans, siting stars, these characters make order from the anarchic motions suggested by the children in their frolic. The heated sugar is the earliest intimation of the trade that drove colonial expansion (its sweetness cost the lives of slaves): the lively microcosm (the whole novel might be said to be *upon the fly*, the characters ever in *purposeful dither*) serves a macrocosm yet unknown, a universe whose existence, whose author, is adumbrated by fond jokes—of punctuation called up by *punctuated*, of beginnings (and religious awakenings) summoned by *Advent*.

The microscope of the sentence reveals the universe of a novel. Pynchon is everywhere sensitive to what a sentence bears, eighteenth-century punctuation not taxing his inventions with the firmer syntax and fixed stops of a later era (the characters meet in 1761). The comic irritation of the capitals (no Bar to Readers of the Period, accustomed to such Emphases) removes the novel to the bewildering thicket of the past, as old spelling does to *Hamlet*; but apart from its manipulation of reader psychology (we must become the readers of the past), the distancing of such capitals makes pastiche the comedy of form the way a sonnet is a comedy of emotion, the compression and entanglements of love finding their spirit in the spirit of form.

This intensity of imagery, this continual and immodest word-by-word invention, ruptures the plain understandings most fiction now requires. Novels must in part be linear and straightforward—they have somewhere to get to. Pynchon's have coiled upon themselves, devouring their bodies, as if distrustful of the long vista, cut straight through Appalachian forest and over mountains, that is the narrow goal of his novel's characters: the settlement of an eighty-year-old boundary dispute between Pennsylvania and Maryland by drawing an imaginary line, the line that would soon become the worried demarcation between states slave and free.

When a word quibbles, the reader's attention turns minute and cautious. Mason's chat with Martha Washington (one of many clumsily imposed encounters with historical figures) defends astronomy in terms shivering with ambiguity, jokes that darken his speech with the pressure of the unsaid.

> "All Lens-fellows, I mean, recognize that our first Duty is to be of pub-
> lick Use. . . . Even with the Pelhams currently in Eclipse, we all must pro-
> ceed by way of th' establish'd Routes, with ev'ry farthing we spend charg'd
> finickingly against the Royal Purse. We are too visible, up on our Hilltop, to

spend much time among unworldly Speculations, or indeed aught but the
details of our Work,— focus'd in particular these days upon the Problem of
the Longitude."

"Oh. And what happen'd to those Transits of Venus?"

"There we have acted more as philosophical Frigates, Ma'am, each
detach'd upon his Commission,— whilst the ev'ryday work of the Observa-
tories goes on as always, for the task at Greenwich, as at Paris, is to know
every celestial motion so perfectly, that Sailors at last may trust their lives
to this Knowledge."

Here his professional vocabulary summons his metaphors, his private world
mirrored in the limits of his language (the author's conscious authority al-
ways concealing from his characters their unconscious—the author *is* their
unconscious). The Pelhams (a powerful pair of English brothers who served
in succession as prime minister) are not out of favor; they are in *eclipse.* The
astronomer is *focus'd.* The hilltop the stargazers stand on is at once literal
and figurative, but their own "speculations" (their stargazings) shade uneasily
into speculations philosophical and financial (talk of money is close by—it
isn't just time that is spent). Mason claims he has no time for unworldly
speculations, and yet he does and doesn't—a stargazer's "speculations" are all
unworldly. Even the financial gambles of astronomers are not likely to have
much worldly in them—Mason means his God is in the details, but he means
so much more than he means.

A speech later, these speculations transform into "philosophical" frigates,
a metaphor compacted of the wars raging on the Atlantic (Mason and Dixon
have already been hapless participants in one skirmish), the individualism of
the period's philosophy (each man well armored in his belief, as well as stoic in
it), the isolation of the astronomer's work (as well as the diaspora of astronomers
to far-flung outposts to observe the transit of Venus), and the self-observant
comedy necessary to such a metaphor. To be "detached" is to have profes-
sional standing, professional disinterest, and professional disengagement,
without forgetting the literal meaning: to be sent on a military mission. That
a commission is a document of work in hand does not ignore the commis-
sions necessary to officer any vessel. (In this novel, all commissions hint at the
secret world of decision making of which Pynchon makes such delightfully
paranoid use.) Those metaphorical frigates steer toward real sailors for whom
lack of an accurate way of determining longitude at sea cost their lives. The
search occupied much astronomic and horological research for a century and

saw the creation of the Board of Longitude (the naturalist Joseph Banks was a member) to adjudicate the scientific disputes and judge the winning method.

The pleasures of such a nervous, finicky style (each farthing of meaning charged against the reader's attention) are densely repeated at many levels of discourse and disputation. At times, one image awakens a world of vertiginous richness. Here a cook, in company, admires a fop's recently brandished sword:

> "*Damascus steel, 's it not? Fascinating. How is that Moiré effect done?*
>
> "*By twisting together two different sorts of Steel, or so I am told,— then welding the Whole.*"
>
> "*A time-honor'd Technique in Pastry as well. The Armorers of the Japanese Islands are said to have a way of working carbon-dust into the steel of their Swords, not much different from how one must work the Butter into the Croissant Dough. Spread, fold, beat flat, spread, again and again, eh? till one has created hundreds of these prodigiously thin layers.*"
>
> "*Gold-beating as well, now you come to it,*" *puts in Mr. Knockwood,* "*—'tis flatten and fold, isn't it, and flatten again, among the thicknesses of Hide, till presently you've these very thin Sheets of Gold-Leaf.*"
>
> "*Lamination,*" *Mason observes.*
>
> "*Lo, Lamination abounding,*" *contributes Squire Haligast, momentarily visible,* "*its purposes how dark, yet have we ever sought to produce these thin Sheets innumerable, to spread a given Volume as close to pure Surface as possible, whilst on route discovering various new forms, the Leyden Pile, decks of Playing-Cards, Contrivances which, like the Lever or Pulley, quite multiply the apparent forces, often unto disproportionate results. . . .*"
>
> "*The printed Book,*" *suggests the Rev^d,* "*— thin layers of pattern'd Ink, alternating with other thin layers of compress'd Paper, stack'd often by the Hundreds.*"

From this single object, families of reference flood, each lowly example claiming an ever-more-distant cousin, the layered patterns of Damascus steel (its secret still hidden from the modern world) metamorphosing into samurai swords, croissants (the fop is known as a Macaroni),* gold beaters, the Leyden

---

* According to my old *Brewer's*, the Macaroni in their outlandish dandy's costumes were the "curse of Vauxhall Gardens" in the years before the American Revolution, responsible for introducing macaroni to English cuisine as well as the word "bore," applied to their critics.

pile, each image itself beaten and folded into another, the layers of imagery creating just that concentration of power, that multiplication of forces, to which Squire Haligast refers. This tour de force is a miniature of Enlightenment knowledge—knowledge by association, advancing insight by applying the stray evidence of one field to the general principle of another. This ability to draw theory from the mass of particulars is scientific method in small.

Such an unruly mob of images might have been mere caprice, if the Leyden pile were not elsewhere the controlling metaphor of the novel's own preoccupation with the advance of science (each repetition making the Leyden pile its own Leyden pile). The image that follows the passage above is of a heap of broadsides, "dispers'd one by one, and multiplying their effect as they go," dispersed like the astronomers scattered to their transits, gathering knowledge while also broadcasting it. That the harvest of examples may itself form an ars poetica gives the passage its bookish purpose: to end with the power of printing first to focus and compress information (words by themselves each performing nothing) and then to scatter it. Images that might have radiated into ornament become instead the novel's enterprise, to make the free market of reference part of the nascent laissez-faire economy slowly emerging from monopolies of commerce, the chartered companies that held the reins of empire (the novel's failure is its failure to find a plot beyond such local communities of power).

These intoxicating leaps (one of the novel's larkish inventions has students taught to fly along ley lines) are Pynchon's signature, perhaps his scrawl, here secured within an age where such fresh infusions of knowledge were actively sought in common room and coffeehouse, the Renaissance cabinet becoming the experimental laboratory and the radical pamphlet, knowledge precipitated into the typographical boundaries of Johnson's dictionary and Diderot's *Encyclopédie*. Here Dixon's teacher (the master of flight) lectures on the possibly druidic or Mithraic origins of ley lines:

> "The Argument for a Mithraic Origin is encourag'd by the Cult's known preference for underground Temples, either natural or manmade. They would have found a home in Durham, here among Pit-men and young Plutonians like yourselves,— indeed, let us suppose the earliest Coal-Pits were discover'd by Mithraist Sappers . . . ? from the Camp up at Vinovia, poking about for a suitable Grotto,— who, seeking Ormazd, God of Light, found rather a condens'd Blackness which hides Light within, till set aflame . . . mystickal Stuff, Coal. Don't imagine any of you notice that, too busy get-

ting it all over yerselves, or resenting it for being so heavy, or counting Chal-
drons. Pretending it solid, when like light and Heat, it indeed flows. Eppur'
si muove, *if yese like."*

The pressure of history compounds the force of allusion, from the Roman
army's religious cults (Mithraism once rivaling Christianity for the empire's
soul) to Iron Age mining operations, from the obscure English measure for
coal (a chaldron being from thirty-two to thirty-six bushels, depending on
shire) to Galileo's bitter, if apocryphal, aside after his forced recantation of
belief in the Copernican system. Coal is another (unacknowledged) exem-
plar of the power of lamination: those densely compressed layers of decaying
leaves, like gilt-edged leaves of a black book, were the source of the Industrial
Revolution, the blackened miners slaves below to the temples of industry ris-
ing above. Dixon is from this hard-pressed country and only through educa-
tion escapes a life in the pits or indebted to them (his father is a local baker):
only knowledge of coal lets him flee the coal. The turn back to the themes
of the novel, the private history of a character, anchors Pynchon's whimsy in
something more than whimsy, the random motions of imagination (their deft
Brownian dance) serving laws otherwise invisible.

This improvement from detail to design is poetry's conscious method—a
poem's metaphorical invention may confound logic or sense, moving crab-
wise across knowledge, but always returning to source (if poetry had a cal-
culus, it would be integral). At such moments Pynchon's imagination would
otherwise seem out of control, firing off examples and suggestive metaphors
without taking them to account, but with an élan almost comically Shake-
spearean. Most novelists invent their worlds by minute cross-reference to this
one, meant to mirror our humdrum life with subdural shocks of recognition
(genre writing, including science fiction, is the crudest form of such represen-
tation). Consider this quicksilver remark on politics (as well as fictions): "'Yet
Representation must extend beyond simple Agentry,' protests Patsy, '— unto
at least Mr. Garrick, who in "representing" a rôle, becomes the character, as
by some transfer of Soul.'" This is followed by wit about "Actor-Envoys" and
"Stroller-Plenipotentiaries."

Pynchon never intensifies the familiar except to disrupt or destroy it; in
his novels the realistic convention is merely convention, the fabric on which
it is projected, like a movie screen, torn apart and patched together. It is not
the denial of conventions that distinguishes his fiction so much as the layer-
ing of them: at any moment Howellsian realism underlies Dickensian farce,

magic realism overlays Loony Tunes. What should be a conflict or comedy of manners becomes a Leyden pile of them: in this Pynchon is indebted to Joyce, though he has a curious way of disabling the anxiety of influence—by placing his own style so deep in history, he seems Joyce's ancestor, not his descendent.

Pynchon's most poker-faced inventions test this freedom from the shackles of genre (conventions operating like universal axioms). Hardly have Mason and Dixon been introduced in Portsmouth, to the reader and each other, than they meet a talking dog—not just any talking dog, but one that styles himself the Learnèd English Dog, one of great prepossession ("I am a British Dog, Sir. No one owns me") and perhaps prophetic insight. In a few pages Pynchon uses him to comment obliquely on traveling animal acts, music-hall songs (the dog sings), Mesmerism, metempsychosis, the vices of sailors, the cooking of dogs on savage isles, the difference between preternatural and supernatural, the souls of animals, Zen koan, the Age of Reason, and pets as Scheherazades. At times the prose takes a Dickensian turn (the dog is exhibited by a married couple, the Fabulous Jellows, and Mr. Jellow warns of his Mrs.'s temper: "'Do not oppose her,' Jellow advises, 'for she is a first-rate of an hundred Guns, and her Broadside is Annihilation'"). There is reeking description of the sailors' dockside haunts before the dog vanishes for most of the rest of the novel (with only a small doggy encore many years later).

The deadpan description ("Out of the Murk, a dozen mirror'd Lanthorns have leapt alight together, as into their Glare now strolls a somewhat dishevel'd Norfolk Terrier, with a raffish Gleam in its eye") goes a long way toward establishing the dog in the fabric of the fiction, and the reader's belief wars with disbelief in proportions equal to those reported by Mason and Dixon. Pynchon's ability to unite the expectations of his reader with his characters while constantly exceeding expectation lets him introduce talking clocks, a knife plucked from a dream, a severed ear (Jenkins's infamous Ear) still capable of listening, an oaf who under the full moon turns into not werewolf but dandy, a perpetual-motion watch, a worldwide conspiracy of Jesuits, a mechanical duck with artificial intelligence and a taste for vengeance, and the Devil in need of a lawyer.

The astronomers inevitably confront the solar workings of the calendar and the upsetting moment, only a decade before the action of the novel, when England lost eleven days (September 3–13, 1752) in switching from the Julian to the Gregorian calendar. Already in use in Europe, the Gregorian adjustment of leap years prevented the slow advance of seasons century by century (an advance that after millennia would have brought winter to July). Workers were not paid for those missing days, and banners of protest read "Give Us Our Eleven Days," or so historians once believed—the calendar riots turn out to be one of history's many myths. Pynchon suddenly proposes, in his offhand way, that Mason lived through those eleven days; and the premise raises matters from the difference between names and things to the remarkable books Mason discovers on secret shelves in the Bodleian: Aristotle on comedy (a nod to Umberto Eco as well as Richard Janko), the Infancy Gospel of Thomas, and a lost Shakespeare tragedy. The consequences, for astronomy as well as the missing population (Mason is the sole inhabitant of those days), take only a few deft pages to work out; but they create, as so much of the novel does, a world behind our world—the world invented with each discovery by novelists as well as scientists.

At times it doesn't seem to matter in which direction the novel advances. This indulgence in Keats's negative capability operates within the text as a suspension of alternatives, as if there were no correct or deterministic way in which the fiction was destined to proceed. That Pynchon for so long staves off the suspicion that his novel doesn't *have* anywhere to get to (years advance, the line will be completed, but the actions of the characters remain empty and purposeless—the *purposeful dither* is finally just dither) is a tribute to his ingenuity in the subatomic realm of the word, the phrase, the sentence. These are usually the proper concentrations of poetry, language for many novelists being merely the medium to advance character and plot. In Pynchon, character and plot have been mediums of an imagination elsewhere occupied and have therefore been treated farcically—but a farcical plot is still a plot.

Pynchon uses ideas—cultural counters, memes—the way a poet uses words, as objects of contemplation and gratification, whatever their meaning. The overstocked repository of his imagination is full of the cultural junk, as well as the minutiae of science and technology, of sadly little use to most fiction and poetry. To an extraordinary degree, one more common to poetry, his ideas come dense with symbolic opportunity—no wonder his metaphysical notions are Enigmas of hermeneutic coding, his main structures coincidence and conspiracy. The novel's obsessive schemes swallow each unexpected invention, no matter how absurd, with insatiable and interpretive appetite.

In small, such ideas may be no more than imaginative sleight of hand. The country between York and Baltimore may be high in iron content. This ought to be just the trivia of encyclopedic reading, and yet:

The earth hereabouts is red, the tone of a new Brick Wall in the Shadow,
due to a high ratio of iron,— and if till'd in exactly the right way, it be-
comes magnetized, too, so that at Harvest-time, 'tis necessary only to pass
along the Rows any large Container of Iron, and the Vegetables will fly up
out of the ground, and stick to it.

Only a passing fancy, of no importance to the novel, even this reveals old pat-
terns afresh: nature's secrets illuminated by science, the Age of Reason com-
manding the motion of progress, and the ingenious application of old force
to new invention, with tacit reference to other sites of earth's magnetic power
(the mysterious ley lines, for instance). Pynchon's reckless ingenuity is a sci-
ence in opposition to the science we know. That poetic touch of the shadowed
brick wall (few poets show such delicate skill or darkening eye—not a brick
wall in shadow but a *new* brick wall in *the* shadow) is passed over as swiftly
as a reference to iron deposits by Squire Haligast some forty pages before:
"For without Iron, Armies are but identically costum'd men holding Bows,
and Navies but comely gatherings of wrought Vegetation." The beauty of this
epigrammatic idea, tossed off without comment, is how much Pynchon sees,
not just in presences, but in absences: war becoming with the disappearance
of guns a kind of parish cotillion, the men "identically costum'd," the navies
"comely gatherings." Are the embroidered dresses of women not "wrought
Vegetation"? Are those men, in a vicious pun, holding weapons or ribbons?

This exhaustive digestion of ideas, this poetic invention of the previously
unimaginable (that is the fiction of poetry), culminates in the remarkable vi-
sion that, the Mason-Dixon line completed, closes the climactic section of
the novel. What will Mason and Dixon do next, they are asked.

"Devise a way," Dixon replies, "to inscribe a Visto upon the Atlantick
Sea."
    "Archie, Lad, Look ye here," Mason producing a Sheaf of Papers, flap-
ping thro' them,— "A thoughtful enough Arrangement of Anchors and
Buoys, Lenses and Lanthorns, forming a perfect Line across the Ocean,
all the way from the Delaware Bay to the Spanish Extremadura,"— with
the Solution to the Question of the Longitude thrown in as a sort of
Bonus,— as, exactly at ev'ry Degree, might the Sea-Line, as upon a Fidu-
ciary Scale for Navigators, be prominently mark'd, by a taller Beacon, or
a differently color'd Lamp. In time, most Ships preferring to sail within
sight of these Beacons, the Line shall have widen'd to a Sea-Road of a

thousand Leagues, as up and down its Longitude blossom Wharves, Chandleries, Inns, Tobacco-shops, Greengrocers' Stalls, Printers of News, Dens of Vice, Chapels for Repentance, Shops full of Souvenirs and Sweets,— all a Sailor could wish,— indeed, many such will decide to settle here, "Along the Beacons," for good, as a way of coming to rest whilst remaining out at Sea. A good, clean, salt-scour'd old age. Too soon, word will reach the Land-Speculation Industry, and its Bureaus seek Purchase, like some horrible Seaweed, the length of the Beacon Line."

The vision continues toward the depredations of land speculators at sea, the founding of a "Coral-dy'd cubickal Efflorescence"—St. Brendan's Isle, pleasure ground and pensioners' home—to which Mason and Dixon will retire, holders in the scheme, under the watchful eye of the "Atlantick Company." Each stage of this vision begets a new stage more outlandish and yet more plausible, part of Pynchon's wry commentary (notice how masterfully, almost without detection, he modulates out of Mason's speech into authorial narration) on the age's chartered companies, the solution to the problem of longitude finally neither astronomical or horological but mechanical, the sea colonized like the land. The end returns to the provision for sailors' vices with which the voyages of Mason and Dixon began.

If Pynchon's invention in language mimics the inventions of science, where one explosion is always fuse of the next, it is no more than the way science mimics poetry. The problem of this overstuffed work, what makes it finally a spoil heap of a novel, is just the poetic method that works so well in the microcosm. It is easy to take the petty irritations of Pynchon's mind as exuberance and recklessness—the bad jokes and worse puns, the cheap anachronistic references to contemporary phenomena. The pages are intercalated with songs and poems, but when Pynchon tries to write poetry, as opposed to embodying the methods of poetry, he shows a wooden and unschooled ear (even Jenkins's ear could write better verse). His heroic couplets could not have been written by even a bad poet of the period, having little acquaintance with the age's metrical practice, which would have been natural as breathing (even provincial poets could imitate Pope with success); but they're masterful compared to his music-hall frolics, like this Jesuit recruiting song:

So,—
Have,—
A,—

> 'Nother look,— at the Army that
> Wrote the Book,— take the Path that you
> Should've took— and you'll be
> On your way!
> Get, up, and, wipe-off-that-chin,
> You can begin, to have a
> Whole new oth-er life,—
> Soldj'ring for Christ,
> Reas'nably priced,—
> And nobody's missing
> The Kids or th' Wife!

There is not a page of *Mason & Dixon* without its droll or disturbing invention, satires on colloquial speech (a milkmaid who uses "as" the way Valley girls use "like"), Jesuit coaches larger inside than out (a subtle slur on sophistry), a musical on the Black Hole of Calcutta, even a visit to the hollow Earth. Such lavish imagination (including his inventories—he's a lover of lists) has not been so magnificently sustained since Joyce. The novel's refusal to muster invention toward anything resembling plot, rather than just the spillage of events over time, seems finally a cowardice: by abusing the privileges of fiction (even picaresque's frivolous motions and meetings are a moral commentary on emptiness), Pynchon loses control of the advantages. His inability to exploit the contrived meetings with Franklin, Jefferson, or Washington, for example—he might have deepened his designs by ignoring their didactic promises—is everywhere repeated in encounters with minor characters. It seems not realism but carelessness (a carelessness so winning in the details). He exhausts so many small opportunities with a master's skill, it's a pity he has no interest in larger ones.

The novel's infinite deferrals, its postponed consummations (sex is on both Mason's and Dixon's minds, but every seduction is soured) finally become an aversion to any conflict or resolution. No one comes to grief; episodes both lethal and erotic collapse without consequence (a long-awaited confrontation between Captain Zhang, master of dark Chinese arts, and his Jesuit nemesis, Father Zarpazo, vanishes in thin air)—it's as if Pynchon loses interest. A novel may need neither plot nor character alone—Joyce and Proust offered character in lieu of plot, and many novelists substitute plot in lieu of character. It's difficult for a novel, even a novel everywhere touched by brilliance, to offer so little of either. Pynchon may have conceived *Mason & Dixon* as a supreme fiction, a poetic act freed of the slavery of plot and character; but conventions are cruel to those who betray them. As his stand-up comedy becomes merely a seven-hundred-page improvisation, the jokes grow hollow as the Earth itself. Here Pynchon's poetics have seduced him: it hardly matters if most poems mean what they say. Poetry is the saying, but fiction (the drama, the action, the consequence, the regret) is the having said.

Back to the Future (Thomas Pynchon)

Thomas Pynchon's sprawling, untidy new novel, *Against the Day*, is only as frustrating as most of his fiction. It starts in the air, high-minded as a kite, and gradually flutters groundward, dragged down by subplots galore and characters thrown in willy-nilly, as if a novel's only virtue were how many characters it could stuff into a phone booth (no doubt Pynchon, who has loaded the book with more Victorian mathematics than Carter had pills, has an algorithm up his sleeve).

The Chums of Chance

Against the Day opens aboard the hydrogen skyship *Inconvenience*, sailing in stately fashion toward the Columbian Exposition in Chicago. The year is 1893. The crew belong to a "celebrated aeronautics club" called the Chums of Chance, which dispatches its fleet of dirigibles on heroic exploits. The narrator quietly identifies himself as the author of the dime novels that record these deeds of daring. This sidling revelation complicates the authorial voice; but, as so often in Pynchon, revelation has no relevance. It's only an arpeggio from an author who specializes in red herrings and dead ends.

Behind the Chums, whose wanderings form the first thread of the tangled plot, lies a droll homage to boys' fiction—to the technology of Verne, the allegorical futures of Wells (though Pynchon loves allegorical pasts even more), the manic improvisations of the *Uncle Scrooge* comics, and the hackwork of Tom Swift tales and Hardy Boys mysteries (Tom Swift and the Boys often referred to their friends as "chums"). Titles like *Tom Swift and His Aerial Warship* and *Tom Swift and His Big Dirigible* suggest that Pynchon is not alone in his fascination with giant gasbags, while *Tom Swift and His Big Tunnel; or, The Hidden City of the Andes* and *Tom Swift in the Land of Wonders; or, The Underground Search for the Idol of Gold* prefigure, or rather postfigure, those in the Chums of Chance series. The Chums are the Tom Swift books rewritten by James Clerk Maxwell and Buster Keaton.

Deviant History

Because Pynchon writes neither counterfactual history nor historical fiction, perhaps the term should be deviated, like a septum—or, as his advance statement warned, "what the world might be with a minor adjustment or two" (if there are alternative universes, there are alternative Pynchons in them). Counterfactual history begins with a striking premise—Caesar surviving the knives on the Ides of March, Lincoln dying of pneumonia after his first inaugural, the Nazis winning World War II. Historical fiction, on the other hand, devotes itself to recreating the small details of dress and dinner, reproducing the archaeological to speculate upon the biographical (historical fiction often aspires to be history plus dialogue). Though he introduces elements of fantasy, like airships far in advance of their day, Pynchon bends his narratives around historical events (the Exposition, the collapse of the Campanile in Venice, the Galveston hurricane), which provide the backdrop for his comic-book characters, esoteric conspiracies, and zany inventions. These absurdist romps, ensnaring common men in the machinations of government and shadow government, show a fidelity to the past even historians might admire. In his almost seamless integration of history into the fictional world (which, to the reader, gives the illusion of the reverse), the story gets pried this way and that to accommodate whatever lumps of fact the past requires; but the leverage is so obvious it contributes to the maniac comedy. The verisimilitude that licenses Pynchon's flights of fancy may corrupt (may even intend to corrupt) a reader's faith in any chronicle, whether of antiquity or the day before yesterday.

Pynchon is fanatical about trivia; and you'd be wise not to engage him in a bar bet on Edwardian insurance trends, Russian crew nomenclature, the use of pneumatic tubes in London, or the international language of Idiom Neutral. The novel is a drunk man's walk through the Americana of scorcher caps, Nernst lamps, Saratoga chips, Floradora girls, Little Nemo, and Arbuckle's coffee. (Anyone who revels in the pastness of the past will find pleasure on every page.) The pains taken over insignificant matters, however, don't mean Pynchon can be trusted with significant ones. (He wrote in *Slow Learner*, with slightly tipsy syntax, that "it may not be wrong absolutely to make up, as I still do, what I don't know or am too lazy to find out.") Indeed, his watchmaker's care may lull the reader into a trust undeserved—in *Against the Day*, crossword puzzles appear a dozen years before their introduction in 1914, and Joe Hill was hardly urging American workers to organize before he had arrived in the country, much less joined the Wobblies.

Questions to Which a Reader Would Like an Answer

What is the evidence for the motorcycle act called the Wall of Death prior to the twenties? Was there a twelve-shot Confederate Colt, or has Pynchon confused it with the ten-shot LeMat? How can a character recite "The Shooting of Dan McGrew" years before Robert Service wrote it? Did Yale have a drama department in 1905? Were novelty X-Ray Spex available before the forties?

Language as a Yoohoo

The verbal texture of his novels derives partly from Pynchon's delight in slang and cant, meticulously corrected to the period. The appearance of the words below, however, predates their first use in the *OED* or the existing volumes of the *Random House Historical Dictionary of American Slang*.

gumshoe (1899)
jake [adj.] (1914)
jass [jazz] (1916)
dazzle painting (1917)
highhat [vb.] (1922)
gunny [gunman] (1926)
paradiddle (1927)
wingding (1927)
nooky (1928)

snoot [to snub socially] (1928)

sports page (1930)

keester (1931)

boilermaker [whiskey with a beer chaser] (1934)

rat [to inform] (1934)

cupcake [attractive young woman] (1939)

hootenanny [social event] (1940)

double-dome (1943)

yoohooing (1948)

chip shop (1953)

cannonball [vb.] (not in *OED* or *RH*)

pre-owned (not in *OED*)

twofer (usage not in *OED*)

Slang is not always trapped in print until years or decades after its first use. The locker loop on the back of a man's shirt, for instance, though called a "fag tag" in Long Island high schools as early as 1967 (and often torn off to comic and destructive effect), does not receive its first citation in *Random House* until 1980.

Words Surprisingly in Use Long Before the Novel

dittoes [clothing] (1755)

nautch girl (1809)

skylarking (1809)

lettuce opium (1816)

solenoid (1827)

on spec (1832)

discombobulated (1834)

bell-buoy (1838)

picnic (1838)

splendiferous (1843)

Vulcanized rubber (1845)

pixielated (1848)

empowerment (1849)

skeezicks (1850)

Mafia (1866)
running mate (1868)
bucket shop (1872)
fox trot (1872)

Does Pynchon use the *OED*? See his introduction to *Slow Learner*.

Naming Names

Even in the novel's final pages, new characters come trooping in, as if the author suffered some strange compulsion to expand the cast (novelists don't have to budget as playwrights do). Yet who would want to be deprived of the "old-school spagyrist name of Doddling," the "star, Solange St.-Emilion," "Octave the barman," a "U-boat captain named Max Valentiner," the "baby Plebecula," a "strangely possessed algebraist named E. Percy Movay," or half a dozen others left to the bitter end? Pynchon (a man with an odd name himself) cooks up names the way some novelists slop in adjectives—he invents characters to swell the crowd, as a bad painter uses landscape to fill the canvas to the frame. This perhaps explains why so many of Pynchon's characters (more than seven hundred in *Against the Day*, almost twice as many as in *Gravity's Rainbow*) are hilariously named but inanimate as rocks.

Dickens established through character the realism his naming threatened to subvert (you wonder if he feared being sued for libel, his christenings grew so outlandish). His names offer a public-spirited advertisement of moral virtue, measured by pun if not mellifluousness (there is morality to music, so musicians believe, with every sour note a sin)—Dedlock and Skimpole and Vholes, to get no bleaker than *Bleak House*, prove more flawed or vice ridden than Summerson or Woodcourt, who enjoy the pastoral virtue of their surnames; but even a Guppy, trivialized in the very saying of him, has his saving graces.

Pynchon, by contrast, rejects the novel's realist longings whenever names are named, though last names like Suckling and Grace may be found in the telephone directory. However extravagant, even preposterous, his *dramatis personae*, they are different in bearing from Sheridan's Lady Sneerwell or Mrs. Candour, Dickens's Thomas Gradgrind or Uriah Heep, where the character's character precedes him by his calling. Pynchon's names, more often than not, seem the gift of an evil fairy-godmother or a god with a malign sense of humor. They form part of the aesthetics of doubt fate introduces right at the start.

Characters disappear, dropped after some considerable space and attention, for no better reason than that the author has galloped off after some will-o'-the-wisp, or no worse than that the plot found no further place to accommodate them—though it could be argued that after prolonged effort Pynchon has not really constructed a plot at all. The ingenuity with which he ushers characters into the book and then gives them the bum's rush secures him large reinforcements, should coincidence require a familiar face or, rather, a familiar name.

A Few Names from a Stroll through a Hundred Pages or So

Reverend Moss Gatlin
Mayva Dash
Alden Vormance
Chick Counterfly
Constance Penhallow
Templeton Blope
Hastings Throyle
Otto Ghloix
Dodge Flannelette
Burke Ponghill
Clovis Yutts
Dr. Oyswharf
Rica Treemorn
Deuce Kindred
Sloat Fresno
Jimmy Drop
Linnet Dawes
Nicholas Nookshaft

Pynchon also has a taste for the oddball names history itself supplies: the almost forgotten actress Olga Nethersole, for example, or the mathematician Ernst Zermelo, formulator of the Axiom of Choice.

The Construction of Character, Lesson I: Introduction by Epithet

"Chinchito, a jumped-up circus midget"

"East Coast nerve case Thrapston Cheesely III"

"a certain Madame Aubergine"

"the provocative and voracious Ruperta Chirpingdon-Groin"

"Wolfë Tone O'Rooney, a traveling insurrectionist"

"the messenger, one 'Plug' Loafsley"

"Mr. Gideon Candlebrow . . . , who had made his bundle back during
    the great Lard Scandal of the '80s"

"Captain Q. Zane Toadflax, Commander"

"a civilian passenger, Stilton Gaspereaux"

"an American stoker named O. I. C. Bodine"

"a wealthy coffee scion named Günther von Quassel"

"the noted Uyghur troublemaker Al Mar-Fuad"

"a telepathic waiter named Pityu"

"a fandango girl named Chiquita"

The Novel as Juggernaut

A long novel is as difficult to shift from its course as an ocean liner; and Pynchon is no novice captain of the stout tug *Coincidence*, the favorite of every clumsy novelist since Thomas Hardy, if not long before. (The line of coincidence starts with *Oedipus Rex*—Shakespeare, Defoe, Charlotte Brontë, and many another have kept it alive.) Novels are famously more conservative in their social physics than in their propriety; random acts offend the reader's expectation of a moral fate and undermine the Whig view of history on which much modern fiction is based. Novels that embrace the Mode of Perennial Accident—sometimes generated, like the productions of OuLiPo, by chance method—often comment upon fiction in a meta-novelistic way. These are gestures of an art fatally uneasy with its means.

Pynchon does everything possible to prevent the reader from taking his novels seriously. Realism, however (like the sincerity and authenticity so beloved in contemporary poetry), is itself full of secret inauthenticities—fiction's handling of dialogue, for instance, rarely echoes the way people actually talk. As a young writer in the fifties, Pynchon was drawn to the new diction promised by the civic poetics of Roth and Bellow (which, however rowdy once, now seem merely an updating of Edith Wharton), as well as the howls howled by the Beats, the jazzy riffs of Norman Mailer, and the lofty-headed formalism of Vladimir Nabokov, whose oracular, idiosyncratic, and apparently nearly inaudible lectures Pynchon attended at Cornell. There are seeds of Nabokov in Pynchon's giddy use of coincidence to poke fun at novels plotted out like a housing development. (Given names in *Lolita* like Clare Quilty, Dolores Quine, and Humbert Humbert, Pynchon was perhaps more influenced by Nabokov than at first appears.) Half a century later, the younger author's struggles for style seem out of date, less a Masonic high sign than a habit that has outgrown its virtue—the coincidences in *V.* took a shortcut to meaning, but the ones in *Against the Day* seem a lame excuse for failing to provide one.

Pynchon knows that the reader's tolerance for accident is limited and therefore uses chance to begin a scene, not to end one. His coincidences are usually meetings of the "As destiny would have it, whom did she run into out on the town that very evening but . . ." or the "In a train depot up in Montana . . . , who'd they happen to run into but . . ." or the "whom should he run into but his father, . . . whom he hadn't seen since 1892 or thereabouts" variety. Amusing alternatives are the "Who had come blowing in to town" dodge as well as the "Cyprian came unexpectedly face-to-face with . . ." ploy, the "Who should appear but . . ." maneuver, and the "Only to find out that . . ." gambit. Pynchon is not a Dickens who could master plot by being mastered by it. The later author's story lines are coercive to an unusual degree—though coercion multiplied doesn't always equal comedy, even 1984 can seem a species of farce.

Against the Day is not immune to other methods of muscling the plot, developing as it does by fits and starts, unlikely detours through the center of the Earth and visitations by trespassers from the future. Occasionally, all else failing, in the space of a sentence one character will develop a marked and unlikely crush on another, which proves that Eros can be as effective a *deus ex machina* as any god. Many of these *divertissements* prove *culs-de-sac*, making the reader wonder whether Pynchon's novels are planned in any conventional sense or mere constructions of whim plus steroids. He has long depended on charm to escort him past logic.

The universe of chance, Pynchon's novels long ago discovered, is one in which almost anything can happen, but only certain things do. Physics receives a partial exemption. Pynchon allows himself extraordinary leeway in the world he creates, introducing sentient ball-lightning, a dog that can read

Henry James, and even time travel, which, apart from a horrifying premonitory vision of World War I, promises more than it delivers. Fiction is like radio—it can get away with more impossibilities than movies or television, and for just the price of a pen and a sheet of paper.

It isn't clear whether Pynchon plots by the seat of his pants or has his own secret and impenetrable designs—the hither-thither meanderings of character, the appalling songs, the Rube Goldberg contraptions (some not yet invented, some perhaps never to be invented in our time stream) might all be constituents of some larger, rational order. Such wishful thinking it is criticism's usual duty to propose. "Yeah, yeah," the author might reply.

In Tin Pan Alley

The dust jacket warns that "characters stop what they're doing to sing what are for the most part stupid songs." Pynchon's characters at first did this with clunky parody lyrics (sung to tunes like "Aura Lee" or Cornell's "Alma Mater") but, from *Gravity's Rainbow* onward, with goofy humor, methedrine rhymes, and little discernible talent. The results sound like W. S. Gilbert on a very bad day or Noel Coward on LSD. An allegedly "melancholy yet catchy tango" floats out of a Montparnasse nightclub:

> *Vege-tariano . . .*
> *No ifs ands or buts—*
> *Eggs and dairy? ah no,*
> *More like roots, and nuts—*
>
> *Pot roast prohibido,*
> *Tenderloin taboo,*
> *why should my heart bleed o-*
> *ver the likes of you?*

The songs rarely function as the comic relief the porter scene in *Macbeth* is said to provide, because they're funny only in a strained and sniggering way. There's little more embarrassing than to see a writer of genius fail at something trivial (it's difficult to prevent the shiver of *Schadenfreude* that follows). Pynchon obviously delights in writing dreadful lyrics; otherwise he would stop. He's hardly unaware of how bad they are—the jacket copy was written by Pynchon himself.

Bad Jokes

"It is comforting to imagine this as an outward and visible manifestation of something else," chuckled one of the Austrians, puffing on a cigar stub. "But sometimes a Tatzelwurm is only a Tatzelwurm."

"Ich bin ein Berliner!"
"Excuse me?" The patient seemed anxious to speak with Kit.
"He will not harm you," Dr. Dingkopf assured him as attendants adroitly steered the patient away. "He has come to believe that he is a certain well-known pastry of Berlin—similar to your own American, as you would say, Jelly-doughnut."

"There is now an entire branch of spy-craft known as Applied Idiotics— yes, including my own school, a sort of training facility run by the Secret Service, near Chipping Sodbury actually, the Modern Imperial Institute for Intensive Instruction In Idiotics—or M6.I., as it's commonly known."

Pynchon's attorneys might mutter that such jokes are never "bad" in an absolute or moral sense but merely the projection in our "time-stream" of a humor (call it a "variant stimulus to laughter") in common use in the future but not yet available to us. They are therefore not prochronistic, rotting away any slim foundation of realism that remains, but always already anticlimactic.

Pynchonian Acronyms

F.I.C.O.T.T. (First International Conference on Time Travel)
I.G.L.O.O. (Inter-Group Laboratory for Opticomagnetic Observation)
L.I.S.P. (Lieutenants of Industry Scholarship Program)
M.6I. (Modern Imperial Institute for Intensive Instruction in Idiotics)
R.U.S.H. (Rapid Unit for Shadowing and Harassment)
T.W.I.T. (True Worshippers of the Ineffable Tetractys)

Lists

The nightly talent included Professor Bogoslaw Borowicz, who put on what he called "Floor Shows," which, due to his faulty grasp of the American idiom, turned out to be literal displays of floors— . . . as well as "trainers" of stuffed animals whose repertoire of "tricks" inclined to the rudimentary, narcoleptics who had mastered the difficult but narrowly appreciated knack of going to sleep while standing up, three minutes or less of which had audiences, even heavily opiated themselves, fighting to get out the exits, and crazy inventors with their inventions, levitating shoes, greenback duplicators, perpetual-motion machines which even the most distracted of audiences understood could never be demonstrated in any time frame short of eternity, and, strangely often, hats—notably The Phenomenal Dr. Ictibus and His Safe-Deflector Hat.

The rooms seemed to run on for blocks, stuffed with automata human and animal assembled and in pieces, disappearing-cabinets, tables that would float in midair and other trick furniture, Davenport figures with dark-rimmed eyes in sinister faces, lengths of perfect black velvet and multicolored silk brocade a-riot with Oriental scenes, mirrors, crystals, pneumatic pumps and valves, electromagnets, speaking-trumpets, bottles that never ran empty and candles that lighted themselves, player pianos, Zoetropic projectors . . .

The list may be the manifest sign of research the novelist can't bear to throw away—anyone with a little dangerous knowledge knows how deep Pynchon's reading runs. He is rarely as poetic as when indulging himself in lists, arias to the material probity of the world, to the existence whose dissolution the novel makes its stuttering stand against—a dissolution toward that greater entropy predicted by Newton's second law of thermodynamics, the law Pynchon would have loved to discover. That doesn't mean the author hasn't realized the humorous dimension to this, like a fourth hovering above the material three—the matter of matter is almost always farcical in accumulation, from Dickens's dust heaps in *Our Mutual Friend* to Imelda Marcos's shoes.

The list, taken to such extremes, is a provision beyond the reader's appetite, a local surfeit that imitates, if it does not divine, the overindulgence intimate to the long novel itself. The meaning of the title, should *Against the Day* mean anything, lies in shoring up the present against those ruins of the future—and, to that end, the list stockpiles odds and ends, like boxes of Civil

Defense crackers, as a specific against destruction. The question is not why Pynchon's one short novel and his stories seem trivial; it's why most of his epic novels do not.

Webb Traverse & Sons & Daughter

Dynamite, the anarchist Webb Traverse believes, is the "medium of truth." Patriarch of the clan that makes *Against the Day* far more a family saga than previous novels, Traverse makes his journeys through western mining camps where ten-dayers and nippers and swampers fight it out with mine bosses. His sons emerge into a world where the antagonists are less clearly identified and the moral choices less easy. Shortly after being introduced, Webb blows up a railroad bridge, allowing Pynchon to digress, as he is all too delighted to do, on the methods in favor among dynamiters of the day—gelatin vs. sticks, oak magneto box and spool of wire vs. two-dollar Ingersoll watch and time delay. The use of modern explosive (one character snacks on a variety of it) warns of that terrible future the novel cannot avert, where warfare employs more and more monstrous ways of blowing men up. Dynamite, introduced after the Civil War, was once called Nobel's Safety Powder, one of the few facts Pynchon doesn't mention.

The novel uncovers anarchists wherever it goes—even Pugnax, the canine mascot of the *Inconvenience*, is seen reading *The Princess Casamassima*. Pynchon's absorption in anarchist thought might suggest a curiosity born in aesthetic prejudice, given that his novels, should they require a justification of form, might find it more easily in Bakunin or Kropotkin than in the divine right of the author or the democracy of plot. (If science were wanted, the equations describing Brownian motion were scribbled down by the young Einstein during the *annus mirabilis* of 1905.) Pynchon's novels begin in confusion and end in mystery, with so many diversions, divagations, and dead ends a reader would at times like to blow up a few railroad bridges himself.

Webb, who may moonlight as a dynamiting outlaw named the Kielselguhr Kid, is assassinated by agents of the plutocrat R. Scarsdale Vibe, whose own family saga shadows the Traverses. The knop on Vibe's walking stick is a miniature gold-and-silver globe (the stick houses a gun with which he wounds anyone who crosses him), a nicely judged symbol for a man who dominates the world by buying and selling it. Though Webb's sons diverge in their occupations, scattering across the planet of which Vibe controls so much, they are haunted by their father's death and vow to avenge it. The eldest, Reef, becomes a wandering gambler mixed up in various bunco schemes, rejecting yet almost helplessly drawn to his father's legacy. After an avalanche in which he is presumed killed, he takes a new identity as a neurasthenic easterner before hightailing it to dig tunnels in the Alps. The next son, Frank, a metallurgist for hire in a Mexico on the edge of revolution, is jailed in a fantastical underground prison complete with cantina, fandango girls, a nickelodeon theater, and gambling tables. Shortly after his escape, he kills one of his father's murderers. (A daughter, Lake, eventually marries the other. Pynchon's women are dishrags when they fall in love—they don't just stand by their men; they sit, kneel, and flatten themselves.) The youngest boy, Kit, a math whiz and the most important character in the novel, has even before his father's assassination been lured into unholy alliance with the Vibe Corporation, which pays his tuition at Yale.

The labyrinthine journeys of the Traverses through North America and Eurasia form the most dramatic feature of the novel, which might be called a revenge comedy—the narrative, against a background of great-power maneuvers, consists largely of liaisons between the boys and such mutable and seductive women as Estrella "Stray" Briggs, who marries Reef but ends up with Frank; Dahlia Rideout, who marries Kit long after meeting him on an ocean liner that turns into a battleship and then back again; and Yashmeen Halfcourt, a woman with mysterious and perhaps extratemporal powers who eventually becomes Reef's lover. The sexual reticulations are Byzantine, unrepentantly sleazy, and cheerfully absurd.

Plot is the most irrelevant portion of a Pynchon novel, as character sometimes seems superfluous in James, whose great character is the prose itself (Aristotle no doubt said that, with access to one of Pynchon's time machines). As it includes as many unidentifiable and miscellaneous ingredients as a fruitcake, however, the telling is itself the form of genius. Even an admiring reader might admit that Pynchon has an aversion to design or just doesn't show much talent for it. He trusts that, if he marshals a battalion of characters and hurls a cannonade of ideas at them (improvising madly the while), when the smoke clears some kind of incoherent coherence will result. This worked fairly well in *V.* and *Gravity's Rainbow,* fairly ill in *Mason & Dixon* (the most dazzlingly written of the novels), and not at all in *Vineland.* Even to begin to compass the historical mechanisms of *Against the Day,* a reader would have to go beyond anarchism to the turn-of-the-century battle between the Vectorists and the Quaternionists, played out in universities across North America and Europe; to the aftermath of the "War of Currents" between Tesla and Edison, Tesla's AC power illuminating the Columbian Exposition; to theories about the ether (Pynchon is largely a bore about ether); to the Tunguska incident in Siberia (which conspiracy theorists blame on Tesla instead of a meteor); and to various sideshows in the Great Game (*V.* was Pynchon's earlier novel on the subject), including some vicious skirmishes in the Balkans. Pynchon is not a polymath but an omnivore, so far as arcane learning is concerned.

Infiltrating these real-world events are the imaginary shenanigans at the imaginary Candlebrow University, periodically assaulted by a peculiarly long-lived tornado dubbed Thorvald and infiltrated by visitors from the future; the roguery of a mad inventor operating a secondhand time-machine deep in Greenwich Village (which lets Pynchon drag in notes from Herbert Asbury's *The Gangs of New York*—much of the bloated farce takes place in the demimonde of cities); the search for Shambhala, which may or may not exist; the hunt for a Quaternion weapon, which may be the A-bomb (or just another MacGuffin); and various ideas about double worlds and lateral realities, islands both present and absent, Earth and Counter-Earth, Venice and contra-Venezia, phantom railways, ghosts, and more bilocation than a Christian saint could manage. If someone mentions that he owns a certain map, off the characters go on another Pynchonian wild-goose chase—but the novels are all wild-goose chases, whether the characters are in search of V. (*V.*), or a V-2 rocket (*Gravity's Rainbow*), or some ancient conspiracy involving the mail (*The Crying of Lot 49*). In *Mason & Dixon*, the novel seems to be in search of the story itself.

Sex

Pynchon's sex scenes are unconvincing at best, and he finds it hard to keep them in register between slapstick and blouse-tearing Harlequin romances (sometimes he seems to be trying both at once, with hazardous result). Most people believe they're good in bed, so it's no surprise that most novelists think their characters are good in bed, too.

> *"Quickly now. Into his mouth Reef in one stroke, no more, and then you must be perfectly still and allow this wicked little fellatrice to do all the work. And you, Cyprian, when he spends you must not swallow any of*

it, you must keep it all in your mouth, is that understood?" By now she could barely maintain the tone of command, having aroused herself with kid-gloved fingers busy at clitoral bud and parted labia now sleekly framed among the foam of lace around her hips. "You are both my . . . my . . ." She could not quite pursue her thought, as Reef, having lost all control, came bursting in a great pungent flood, which Cyprian did his best to accommodate as he had been ordered to.

It isn't clear whether this parodies popular fiction or merely succumbs to it. *Gravity's Rainbow,* after being selected by the judges, was turned down for the Pulitzer Prize in part because the Pulitzer board found it obscene. The current novel has more pneumatic coupling than Updike in his heyday. That board might have expired of apoplexy could it have read the already infamous passage of doggy sex:

He stroked the diminutive spaniel for a while until, with no warning, she jumped off the couch and slowly went into the bedroom, looking back now and then over her shoulder. Reef followed, taking out his penis, breathing heavily through his mouth. "Here, Mouffie, nice big dog bone for you right here, lookit this, yeah, seen many of these lately? come on, smells good don't it, mmm, yum!" and so forth, Mouffette meantime angling her head, edging closer, sniffing with curiosity. "That's right, now o-o-open up . . . good girl, good Mouffette now let's just put this—yaahhgghh!"
Reader, she bit him.

Pynchon in Style

Pynchon is more a mechanic of sentences than a stylist, even when the prose doesn't drop into Late Hipster, which may be his default tongue. As he says in the most complete aesthetic statement he has made, the introduction to *Slow Learner,* "But as we all know, rock 'n' roll will never die, and education too, as Henry Adams always sez, keeps going on forever." The line was written in 1984, a little late to be a hepcat. Apparently Pynchon never grew up, or the world grew up, leaving him behind. His famous Garbo act has had obvious advantages— but what if it has kept his diction isolated, even mummified his syntax, too?

In his novels, Pynchon tends to stutter out phrases in workmanlike fashion, pushing the boulder of narrative uphill like a Sisyphus. (Compared to that of a master like Melville, Pynchon's dialogue is disastrous—he has charmingly blamed this on an affliction known as "Bad Ear.") There are, however, passages of consummated beauty, often a vision of capital where the phrases pile up like consumer goods.

> *Against the greased writhings of these dark iron structures, a brightwork of brass fittings and bindings, kept a-shine through the nights by a special corps of unseen chars, flashed like halos of industrious saints in complex periodic motion everywhere. Hundreds of telegraphers, ranked about the great floor attending each his set, scarcely looked up from their universe of clicks and rests—uniformed messenger boys came and went among the varnished hardwood labyrinth of desks and sorting-bureaux, and customers leaned or paced or puzzled over messages they had just received, or must send, as cheerless London daylight descended through the windows and rising steam produced an all-but-tropical humidity in this Northern Temple of Connexion.*

These are almost the rhythms of Dickens, whose freakish surplus of characters, juddering episodic plots, and teary sentiment Pynchon half imitates, though in each case with a nearly lethal dose of irony (no one has ever wept over the death of a Pynchon character the way thousands wept over Little Nell). Something in the long sentence draws out his craft, just as the hammering together of obscure ideas sparks something remarkable in his intelligence:

> *"The sauce was invented as a new sensation for jaded palates at court by the duc de Richelieu, at first known as* mahonnaise *after Mahon, the chief port of Majorca, the scene of the duc's dubious 'victory' in 1756 over the ill-fated Admiral Byng. Basically Louis's drug dealer and pimp, Richelieu, known for opium recipes to fit all occasions, is also credited with the introduction into France of the cantharides, or Spanish fly. . . . What might this aphrodisiac have in common with the mayonnaise? That the beetles must be gathered and killed by exposing them to vinegar fumes suggests an emphasis on living or recently living creatures—the egg yolk perhaps regarded as a conscious entity—cooks will speak of whipping, beating, binding, penetration, submission, surrender. There is an undoubtedly Sadean aspect to the mayonnaise. No getting past that."*

Undoubtedly is a touch bullying, but a paragraph like this—improbable, brilliant, ragged with learning—is what keeps his cult in fresh recruits. (The

Thomas Pynchon wiki is likely to prove a permanent resource on the Web—authors who traffic in obscurity are perfect subjects for the slow accumulation and manic trivia of the wiki.)

There are some things Pynchon does superbly well as a novelist, and others he does intolerably ill, though his fans can be counted on to call his sins saintliness. He writes like a savant missing significant parts—a piston here, a gearbox there—of the necessary machinery. If I say Pynchon is ungraceful, I don't mean beyond grace, because he can whip up a landscape of which any Dutch painter of the seventeenth century would have been proud:

> *For the sunlight had to it the same interior darkness as the watery dusk last night—it was like passing through an all-surrounding photographic negative—the lowland nearly silent except for water-thrushes, the harvested fields, the smell of hops being dried in kilns, flax pulled up and piled in sheaves, in local practice not to be retted till the spring, shining canals, sluices, dikes and cart roads, dairy cattle under the trees, the edged and peaceful clouds. Tarnished silver.*

That last touch of color returns to photography's silver-nitrate solutions, quietly surrendering to the metaphor that binds these lines like the sheaves themselves. "Grace" is the last word in the novel.

Pynchon the Pub Bore

On the other hand, Pynchon launches himself into numerous lectures on great-power politics of the day, lectures that would suffocate an audience at a hundred paces. Let a character say, "But you're itching to be filled in, I can see that," and the author scurries to the library table to pot some history (he's suspected of relying on the famous eleventh edition of the *Encyclopedia Britannica* for his facts, but his reading is far richer and more mutinous). The more he writes, the more stiff-necked the movements of armies and politicians, though these are Astaire waltzes compared to the global wars in mathematics:

> *"And that's what has kept driving Cantor back into the* Nervenklinik," *added Humfried, "and he was only worrying about line-segments. But out here in the four-dimensional space-and-time of Dr. Minkowski, inside the*

*tiniest 'interval,' as small as you care to make it, within each tiny hyper-
volume of* Kontinuum—*there likewise must be always hidden an infinite
number of other points—and if we define a 'world' as a very large and finite
set of points, then there must be worlds. Universes!"*

If this sort of thing gives you goose bumps, there are more than enough pas-
sages in *Against the Day* about zeta functions and the Riemann hypothesis
to gratify you, as well as any of your relatives who happen by (like a gas, the
math expands to fill the space available). Pynchon is perhaps the only novelist
who could have written that "all mathematics leads . . . to some kind of hu-
man suffering." After the publication of *V.*, he was supposedly turned down
for graduate work in math at Berkeley. He avenges that humiliation here.

Whimsies

Pynchon is so full of intrigue, so full of intriguing idea, each chapter casts off
a premise whose particulars a lesser novelist might have taken a novel to tease
out. The Chums of Chance are ordered south to Antarctica to go north to the
Arctic, their route mapped straight through the Earth, where a vast civiliza-
tion is secretly lodged. They stop, merely for a page, to render the denizens
of the hollow Earth assistance against an army of gnomes. The author—in as
much of a hurry as the Chums, it seems—apologizes for not giving the details,
referring the reader to *The Chums of Chance in the Bowels of the Earth.* The
unwritten novel has been written, only to join the Borgesian library of books
whose spines have titles but whose insides are blank, at least to us—the library
of all fictional books mentioned in fiction. (This incident seems curiously to
be the only place in the novel the Chums prove of much help—mostly they
lumber along above, well-meaning but feckless, accomplishing little except
perhaps the accidental destruction of the Campanile.)

When Dr. Watson alluded to the case of the giant rat of Sumatra, he
piqued the reader with a world beyond his grasp, a world composed of the
lost passages of fiction, availing but unavailable (how different this is from
knowing the titles of Sophocles' lost plays, yet in the end how frustratingly
similar). Apart from the deft and childish joke of it, this reminds the reader
of all an author imagines but has chosen not to explore. The titles of other
Chums novels are tauntingly scattered through the text, naming adventures
left undetailed. Perhaps Pynchon has all these years been writing a series of

boys' adventure novels (the sort he himself read as a boy)—in this guise, some aspects of his fiction make more sense.

Pynchon's indulgence in Borgesian whimsies, though they barely skirt outright doltishness (the sophistication of the author's humor has always been in doubt—you get the feeling that he cracks himself up a little too often), is often where his most appealing contrivances occur. In *Against the Day*, these include:

- *The Book of Iceland Spar* (spar is a form of calcite used as a polarizing filter), which contains an up-to-date record of an Arctic expedition, "even of *days not yet transpired*," presumably due to the double refraction of which the crystal is capable;
- Pugnax, the sky dog who reads Henry James and can talk in primitive fashion (in *Mason & Dixon*, set more than a century before, the Learnèd English Dog spoke English impeccably and was even a singer of some talent);
- Snazzbury's Silent Frock, a dress that works on the principle of noise-canceling headphones, the "act of walking being basically a *periodic phenomenon*, and the characteristic 'rustling' of an ordinary frock an easily computed complication of the underlying *ambulatory frequency*";
- a philo-Semitic version of "*Gaudeamus igitur*";
- the game of Anarchists' Golf, which possesses no defined sequence or number of holes;
- an intelligent example of ball lightning, named Skip;
- the previously mentioned character who nibbles on a form of explosive called Cyclomite, just as the British eat Marmite and Vegemite (it's a toss-up which of the three might taste the worst);
- an annual conference on time travel where the dead are resurrected (those who have visited the MLA know that this is closer to truth than satire).

These concoctions might be more amusing if they didn't come with a note of giddy self-congratulation. Though he often sounds like a mad scientist, Pynchon has trouble harnessing his clever ideas—when he drags them into the story, he can't always make them sound credible or, worse, make the reader care which end of the ill-delivered crate is up. In his alternative worlds, the whimsies have a strange logic (the novel at least doesn't break down bearing such a cheerful wastage of material); but he is less successful in employing such devices for any purpose but decoration. You think he's about to pull a rabbit out of a hat, but there are always three hundred rabbits and twelve dozen hats. Perhaps readers ought to be grateful, as his comedy is successful only in gestures—too much of Snazzbury's Silent Frock would not be a good thing. (Science fiction is full of such bright ideas while being empty of most everything else.)

Novels in the Chums of Chance Series

The Chums of Chance and the Evil Halfwit
The Chums of Chance at Krakatoa
The Chums of Chance Search for Atlantis
The Chums of Chance in Old Mexico
The Chums of Chance and the Curse of the Great Kahuna
The Chums of Chance in the Bowels of the Earth
The Chums of Chance and the Ice Pirates
The Chums of Chance Nearly Crash into the Kremlin
The Chums of Chance at the Ends of the Earth
The Chums of Chance and the Caged Women of Yokohama
The Chums of Chance and the Wrath of the Yellow Fang

Three Corny Pop-Cult Allusions
Pynchon Couldn't Resist Making

This person greeted the Cohen by raising his left hand, then spreading the fingers two and two away from the thumb so as to form the Hebrew letter shin, signifying the initial letter of one of the pre-Mosaic (that is, plural) names of God, which may never be spoken.

"Basically wishing long life and prosperity," explained the Cohen, answering with the same gesture.

Reindeer [after the Tunguska event] discovered again their ancient powers of flight, which had lapsed over the centuries. . . . Some were stimulated by the accompanying radiation into an epidermal luminescence at the red end of the spectrum, particularly around the nasal area.

"The operetta, all the rage in Vienna at the moment, was called The Burgher King."

The Chums of Chance (Slight Return)

Over the three decades of the novel, the *Inconvenience* is outfitted with new technology, grotesquely increasing in size. By the end, it has grown "as large as a small city," resembling those utopias, suspended in the air, so beloved of science fiction.

> *There are neighborhoods, there are parks. There are slum conditions. It is so big that when people on the ground see it in the sky, they are struck with selective hysterical blindness and end up not seeing it at all.*

The crew has not changed in decades; and the Chums of Chance organization has almost collapsed, individual chapters now negotiating their own contracts and profiting accordingly. Though they show little sign of it, the boys must by this time be in high middle-age. The *Inconvenience*, "transformed into its own destination," has become a metaphor for the long novel itself, one at least not inaccurately named.

The Critic Invents Fourteen Characters Who Do Not Appear in the Novel

Leavisite Snack
Duodecimo Gazebo
Tanya Polyglot Moonlight
Wang Cheyenne
Judge Portobello Grim
Clive Polonaise-Boxer
Chauncey Hiccups
Warrant Dolomite
Chili Condominium, Jr.
Jeremiah "Dell" Delaware
Brightware T. Polonian
Sir Chloral Fundamentum
Typhus Smythe
Chad Ravine

Subplots the Critic Will Not Have Time to Mention

- The intrigues of a neo-Pythagorean cult called the True Worshippers of the Ineffable Tetractys, devoted to identifying the living avatars of the twenty-two cards in the major arcana of the tarot deck;
- The appearance of the Archduke Ferdinand at the Columbian Exposition—a roisterer knowledgeable about the "pastry-depravity" of American detectives, he is discovered trying to engage angry patrons of the Boll Weevil Lounge in a primitive version of the "dozens";
- The casebook of the detective Lew Basnight, once known as the Upstate-Downstate Beast, guilty of some horrible crime he cannot remember;
- The Sodality of Ætheronauts, a society of women "dressed like religious novices," bearing names like Heartsease and Primula, who fly winged-and-feathered machines and in short order marry the crew of the *Inconvenience*;
- The travels of the subdesertine frigate *Saksaul* beneath sands inhabited by schools of iridescent beetles—as well as giant sand-fleas able to converse in ancient Uyghur;
- An offer of eternal youth (perhaps the promise of fiction itself) that drives the crew of the *Inconvenience* to the "brief aberration in their history known as the Marching Academy Harmonica Band";
- Ukeleles.

Still Reading Pynchon/Reading Pynchon Still

Pynchon's novels seemed crucial to the late sixties and early seventies. If there is a *Zeitgeist* (perhaps there are always incomplete, overlapping, competing *Zeitgeister*), there must be—should anything like a certainty principle operate in culture—music, and art, and literature to complement it, if they do not create it. In America, this has probably long been an adolescent or post-adolescent phenomenon. In that dead world of 1969, that world of Vietnam and Cambodia, post–Civil Rights and pre–Ronald Reagan, post-Woodstock and pre-Altamont, public life ratcheted along full of secrets; and government had a thousand closets with a skeleton in every one (no doubt we open-minded many had many secrets of our own). The signs of resistance and disorder were a code well understood: Jimi Hendrix's version of "The Star-Spangled Banner," psychotropic drugs, the Firesign Theatre, Barthelme's semi-surrealist tales,

Transcendental Meditation, Pynchon's novels, and much else represented a deviant metaphysics, one perfect if irrational, like the square root of –1. Watergate, a few years later, proved that the government lived on lies; but we were too young to realize that lies were the meat of democracy.

The residual fondness of older readers for Pynchon's work is an eternal return to their own dumb innocence, before that innocence guaranteed they deserved what they got. Indeed, Pynchon's later fiction, tacking between modern California and the Enlightenment, has been, not merely an acknowledgment of the betrayal of values, but a recognition that the young were betrayed by themselves. If Pynchon seemed on the wavelength of some unreality that looked more promising, no doubt the hallucinogens played a part. A friend of mine, who once bombed a building or two for Weatherman, went underground and became a waitress in California named Roxy. She met Pynchon while there, but decades later she sounds like a character he made up.

When I look at my friends from college—now Fortune 500 execs, Rand Corp. think-tankers, museum presidents, tech wizards, sad-sack pols, sawboneses and mouthpieces, even a few casualties—I think the sixties were over before they properly began. Pynchon seems to have boarded the bus with the Merry Pranksters and never gotten off. He's a throwback, a hipster, a true dreamer, and a truer cynic. All the bad methods of writing he confesses to at the beginning of *Slow Learner* he's using still, and just as blithely when pushing seventy as when he was wet-eared in college. Some of the flair is gone, used up or burned off since he started writing nearly half a century ago, like a chemical process that on repetition grows less efficient and the resulting solution less potent, until it doesn't work at all. Yet he has matured in many ways, grown rueful and ramshackle. This gives *Against the Day* its bittersweet sadness for a fin de siècle world that had only begun to adore science and invention, a world that had not yet learned to distrust them. Those states and bodies politic knew the horrors of the Crimean and Civil Wars but not yet those of the Great War. After that heroic disaster—fought, so everyone was told, to end war—the common man might have thought things were looking up. Pynchon's task has been to remind us that worse was to come.

Finis

The mulligan stew of *Against the Day* includes a boys' dirigible novel, a spy novel (Pynchon is all too enamored of spies), a mathematician's novel (half a sentence about the Zermelo axioms may send the reader straight to sleep), a Wild West anarchist novel, a European anarchist novel, a search-for-Shambhala novel, and probably four or five novels the reader would rather forget. Pynchon makes a halfhearted attempt to tie up a few loose ends; yet vast stretches of *Against the Day* point toward something but finally have nowhere to get to. The true Pynchon fanatic would never be worried by this—as people say about their lives these days, it's all about the journey. This gives Pynchon a license for picaresque most authors would kill for—his vices have been transmuted into virtues, a better bargain than that offered by the philosopher's stone.

Intelligence makes *Against the Day* bearable, though everywhere it creates its own rules, undermines its own *gravitas*; in this it already satisfies the first condition of a classic: a novel we appreciate because of its flaws (the second condition is longevity). As an artist of paranoia, that American state of mind occupying the space between New York and California, Pynchon is the comic opposite of Kafka, whose *Weltanschauung* he otherwise embraces—a world of conspiracy and liminal terror, of shadow worlds that lie beneath real ones. Paranoia is the limiting climate in fiction, as depression is the limiting climate in depressives—if everything is a conspiracy, there's no getting to the bottom of it, because fiction is a conspiracy of conspiracies, where a wizard, or a bunco man, always stands behind the curtain. And there's a wizard behind him.

At the heart of *Against the Day* lies a terrible longing to redeem and amend—the theme is taken up as vengeance but played out as nostalgia. Order is never restored in Pynchon's universe, though things change: an old enemy dies ignominiously at the hands of his bodyguard, an assassin is taken unawares, third parties do away with a traitorous spy. No one takes much pleasure in these messy ends—death comes too quickly to afford the living any satisfaction. The final pages of the novel offer a frazzled sentimental tale of coupling and growing old, where antique outlaws are domesticated and matters come more or less right only in the way they go more or less wrong. The idea of time travel, though lugged in for laughs, suggests a hankering to go back and fix things (in science fiction, the theme usually turns into tragic farce—tragedy if you like science fiction, farce if you don't). Yet when men arrive from some indefinite future, fleeing some unimaginable global catastrophe, they seem only to want to be left alone, the most pitiable of refugees.

Verse Chronicle

The World Is Too Much with Us

Les Murray

Les Murray is an outsized poet, big as a barge—no, broad as the outback itself. The poems in *The Biplane Houses* are earthy, strange, almost unclassifiable at times, delivered as if he thought real poetry too hoity-toity for a bloke with 4X in the esky (I mean, beer in the fridge). In many ways, the poet's playfulness comes from acting like a cartoon Aussie, the Crocodile Dundee of the poetry circuit. (In a world of glossy-magazine morality, you admire a man who takes epicurean pleasure in being fat.) Back home Murray is called a diehard reactionary, one who loves too well the country that was, the country that has changed around him; but he loves the country of information more, the odd facts and snippets he works up into verse. You never know, as you turn the pages, what you'll come across: a poem about the placement of verbs in different languages, the fate of the descendants of the *Bounty* mutineers, or the exhibition of ancient skeletons:

> crusty little roundheads of sleep,
> stick-bundles half burned to clay by water.
>
> Their personhoods had gone, into the body
> of that promise preached to them. What had stayed
> in their bones were their diseases, the marks
> of labour in a rope-furrowed shoulder blade,
>
> their ages when they died, and what they'd eaten:
> bread, bacon, beer, cheese, apples, greens,

> *no tomato atoms in them, no potatoeines,*
> *no coffee yet, or tea, or aspirin.*

This is typical Murray: overbaked metaphors, the occasional oafishness in tone or diction (perhaps that should be *dictionhood*), the list that becomes a longing, the long view across centuries, the deep intimacy with the past—his history has a dark physicality reminiscent of Heaney's. Murray often seems the Diderot of contemporary verse: the world is everything that is the case, and all of it ripe for poetry. His gargantuan appetite can give a poem the look of a python that has swallowed a Volkswagen or two (for better or worse, he doesn't possess the censoring demon that rejects outlandish ideas out of hand). Murray has never been a natural poet—he has trouble relaxing into his lines, or making them seem more inspiration than perspiration. He loves roughneck rhymes or a slapdash prose that doesn't even pretend to be poetry. Just when your guard is down, when you think he's matured, he'll give a whoop and write something like "Pork hock and jellyfish. Poor cock. / King Henry had a marital block. / A dog in the manager? Don't mock! / Denial flows past Cairo." Get it?

Though you have to forgive Murray for a lot, if you bear with him he can transform the way you see, if what you see is a stallion's "progeny drop in the grass / like little loose bagpipes" or a display of Japanese swords, "Merciless whitewater craft / keel-upwards in long curve. . . . // Why, I said to Yojimbo, this / is an exhibition of lightnings!" When the vehicle so overwhelms the tenor, you enter a world where metaphor acts less like Midas and more like the neighborhood bully; but in poetry sometimes you learn to love the bullies.

Murray's poetry is unafraid of being local, as if truth were by nature parochial. He's the ultimate outsider—the metaphors transform his country like a spell in Ovid, leaving it unrecognizable. I like the homebound, staggered, guilt-ridden Murray quite a bit and the gallivanting, cantankerous, pun-loving Murray little at all; but unfortunately it's the latter self the poet seems to prefer. He's weakest as a moralist, hammering his points home like a small-town editor on a manual typewriter:

> *Gentrifical force turned Prunty to Brontë*
> *and shipped myriads more to colonial bounty*
> *where some, abashed to be safe on the fringe,*
> *still feed wars and guilts to their cultural cringe.*

"Gentrifical" is Murray's play on "centrifugal," but the pun doesn't make his hatred of immigrants any more appealing. He's a genuine oddity, a man of the people who doesn't much like people, not even his own people. I've been wary, not of his oddity, but of the bumptiousness that comes with it—I'm so busy resisting his vices, there's no time to appreciate his virtues.

Some critics have applauded Murray's clumsiness as an endearing quirk or a necessity of character; but it's clumsiness by any other name. The new poems are warmer and more personable, as if the poet, though not filled with self-love, were no longer so disfigured by self-loathing. (Perhaps Murray's near death a decade ago has softened his character.) In *The Biplane Houses*, Murray has done what all good poets do, remade the world in his image—like Falstaff and Henry VIII, those other outsized figures, he is magnificent despite the monsters within.

Robert Pinsky

Robert Pinsky's poems are so professional, you feel he dresses in a suit and tie before sitting down at his desk. Even when he goes a bit wild, as he does at times in *Gulf Music*, merrily discarding verbs, yodeling when he feels like it ("Mallah walla tella bella. Trah mah trah-la, la-la-la"), or simply *making things up*, his rashness is the soul of caution—he has all the reckless daring of Walter Mitty. Pinsky's new poems are often political, politically political in that contemporary way, kowtowing to the golden idols of the moment, casting dung upon the correctly incorrect villains, all without a breath of cross-grained opinion.

> *At Robben Island the political prisoners studied.*
> *They coined the motto* Each one Teach one.
>
> *In Argentina the torturers demanded the prisoners*
> *Address them always as* "Profesor."
>
> *Many of my friends are moved by guilt, but I*
> *Am a creature of shame, I am ashamed to say.*

It's hard to know exactly what the poet is fessing up to here, unless he's ashamed of being a professor. E. R. Dodds made the distinction between shame culture and guilt culture more than half a century ago, but isn't it time to look more closely at the idea and not simply make flippant remarks? Shame cultures, in these days of honor killings, have a lot to answer for. And doesn't invoking the imprisonment of Nelson Mandela and the tragedy of the *desaparecidos* seem all too convenient, done this callow way?

Pinsky is an old-fashioned poet of a recognizable sort, a gentleman buffer who takes up verse the way others take up gardening. Well-meaning, often charming, sincere as a traffic sign, he has all the gifts that education and rationality can provide; but you never feel he's actually *moved* to write. His early poems were composed as carefully as chess problems—the grace of calculation rarely possessed the scent of inspiration. Though his lines are still prosy and narcotic as Department of Transportation reports, *Gulf Music* represents a departure, an attempt to unchain his inner pit-bull and let slip the dogs of war.

Pinsky's howl, when he howls, has the manic, improvisatory, catch-as-catch-can quality of Allen Ginsberg; but the style sits on this more buttoned-up poet like a hat three sizes too small.

> *Joan of Arc tortured to death by clergymen*
> *And failure incidental as for Jackie Robinson engaging*
> *At one and the same time two worthy difficulties.*

> *Other athletes succeed and get rich and in attained*
> *Leisure even in Eden or Gomorrah they seek the green*
> *Fields of the idiocy Golf because it is reliably difficult.*

> *Old joke It has to be hard to be good. Manipulable*
> *Light of the Xbox for all its eviscerations or hoops*
> *Like chess a grid of exploits adequately difficult.*

This sounds like some old hipster dumping his verbs and commas in order to feel young again. (A lot of commas go missing in this book—charitable gifts of punctuation should be sent directly to the publisher.)

Many of Pinsky's new poems read like notes for a set of position papers. I love Auden's didactic mode, but didacticism can be leaden and antiseptic if you're not as clever as Auden. The précis for one particularly clotted poem might read:

Recollects singing Christmas carols—Jewish boy tells him he won't go to heaven—boy later dies in LSD accident—ancient Jewish community included non-Jews—Maimonides temporized on Jewish resurrection—thoughts concerning the nature of heaven—thoughts concerning Milton's shampoo—older generation named children Milton, Sidney, Herbert.

This pinball path to meaning looks just as crooked when written up as verse. Too often, Pinsky has thrown out the idea of organization without supplying in its absence anything as cheerful as coherence. A long, stolid section on "things" (book, photograph, jar of pens) reminds us how delicately subversive Elizabeth Bishop and Seamus Heaney are when writing about objects, or how Auden turns a tour of his house into a tour de force about living. Pinsky may be trying to see things again from the atoms up; but the results are studious, blind to the magic of objects, and reductive about the horrors of the world.

When Pinsky forgets about the poet he would like to be, when he stops posing and finds a way to tell an old story afresh, the results can be devastating in the detail. It happens only once in this book, but perhaps once is enough. Eurydice meets Stalin in the underworld:

> *She crossed a bridge, and looking down she saw*
> *The little Georgian boiling in a trench of blood.*
> *He hailed her, and holding up his one good arm*
>
> *He opened his palm to show her two pulpy seeds*
> *Like droplets—one for each time she lost her life.*
> *Then in a taunting voice he chanted some verses.*
>
> *Poetry was popular in Hell, the shades*
> *Recited lines they had memorized—forgetful*
> *Even of who they were, but famished for life.*

Here the poet bureaucrat has heard the voices of hell.

Sandra McPherson

Sandra McPherson began as a delicate, dilettantish observer of nature, her eye a direct descendant of Moore's and Bishop's. There was a meticulousness, an otherworldly clarity, in the way her early poems refused the mundane for metaphor (Bishop called the poems "clean," which suggested both their freshness and their starched, virginal quality). Intensity of description can transform the world but also displace it; in some fifteen books, McPherson has struggled to balance the pure pleasures of the eye with the soiled, rueful life that exists when pleasure is past—this is not merely the slow Hogarthian progress of innocence to experience, but the rise to vision of all the experience the innocent eye fails to see.

The new poems in *Expectation Days* are sometimes an embarrassment of riches, so clotted with detail and crowded with metaphor, they're like beautiful lakes overrun with hydrilla—yet every nuance of the visual world has been refreshed by observation:

> *This water flows dark red*
> *from alder tannin:*
> *boot-stain river*

> *between white rocks.*
> *An ouzel, flannel-feathered,*
> *sips the current up.*

There's nothing McPherson can't compare to something else (she sees the world through rose-colored metaphors); yet, however acute or transforming the eye, a poem can't be simply a static roster of observations, checked off like a "To Do" list.

McPherson's recent poems have become meditative, roughened with grief after the death of her husband, a younger man who died young. The darkness that has entered her work presents the beauties in a more fragile light—it's not merely that in nature the gorgeous dies, only heartbreakingly to be reborn, but that to the bereft every beauty can seem criminal. The husband, during his illness, apparently suffered from drug-induced hallucinations, which the poet records with wry fondness:

> *And so when he whispered*
> *I should buy medallions for dressing up dogs*
>   *Or revealed the "I'm a little grandpa" secret*
> *Or pointed to five men he noticed*
>   *"Counting a green fish"*

> Or introduced me to the Concertina Brothers
>   Or asked how many people I saw
> Put on feather suits in our living room,
>   Coaxed me with
> "Let's go shopping for mirrors in the dark,"
>   That was his newfledged
> Lucidity.

At such moments, McPherson redeems the horrors by having witnessed them. Too many of these new poems, however, are private and elusive, rising into quasi-religious vacancy—the world is cast down in fragments, thought cast down in fragments, too. Though meaning may be the more valued for being won bitterly, the cloudy and broken phrases emphasize the difficulty McPherson has in rendering whole a talent for discrete glances. Her poems are so often about happenstance, it seems odd when she has in mind a particular subject—the illustrations on an old book of needles, say, or the death of a bat from the bat's point of view. You might think her exotic vision would be just the thing for a creature so strange, but the results are tear-stained and precious—"A kind neighbor / drowns me. Phoenix sloshing in a pail. / He drops me on a glacier."

McPherson has gone from a poet whose gifts seemed natural to her, as easy and involuntary as breathing, to one who has to win her successes by hard graft, when she can win them at all. Sometimes a poet seems to improve his work with every small change, only to end with a style worse than when he began. And yet, in half a dozen of the poems here—when McPherson sees in a sand road the "Broken armor of a crustacean age" or, scattered about her, "Miner's lettuce, / Its sake cups // Moored to leaf's center by ruddled, bronzed umbilicals"—nature presses so close we want to be in thrall to it. If there is a world that is too much with us, this is that world.

Charles Wright

Americans wander about like nomads, their true home the interstate highway or the airport hub; but they never lose their loyalty to place. American poets are no different. Allen Tate taught in Minnesota for decades, a Southern poet to the end. Lowell's poems, no matter where he lived, never seemed more at home than when taking place on Boston Common or in the "brackish reach of shoal off Madaket."

Charles Wright was born in Pickwick Dam, Tennessee, which sounds like a good place to be from. After early poems of a lickpenny, scraped-knuckle kind, the words rare as dropped silver dollars, he remade himself as a poet of lush Southern landscapes and genial woolgathering. Often, early and late, his thoughts turned to Italy (just as his rhythms turned to Pound)—if he invoked some literary forebear, it wasn't Faulkner or Sidney Lanier but someone Pound had approved, like Wang Wei or Dante. Wright became the émigré poet who mostly stayed home, a poet whose local hills were his Harvard and his Yale. Still, it seems odd for any poet to write

> It may not be written in any book, but it is written—
> You can't go back,
> you can't repeat the unrepeatable.

Didn't Thomas Wolfe write a novel on the subject? Didn't Heraclitus once say something about a river?

Charles Wright has been doing what he does for a long while, and it shows—it shows in the ease and confidence of his line, in the way he warms to his material, and in the lackadaisical manner of his delivery. Set around the poet's seventieth birthday, *Littlefoot* is a meditation on age (like Wright's recent books), a meditation on nature (ditto), a meditation on memory (ditto once more), with more valedictory gestures than could be stuffed into a fishing creel. (If Wright lives to be a hundred, we'll have thirty more years of valedictory gestures to look forward to.) The book is broken into numbered sections broken into smaller sections, a daybook or night journal rather than a series of poems, catching whatever orphan thoughts strayed into his mind and got trapped there.

The graces of Wright's mature poems have been in landscape, where he displays, not the *phanopoeia* of Pound's crisp, sculptural images, but a broader-stroked, more richly hued impasto. Wright has a religious awe of the world around him, which he sees with luminous intensity.

> The cardinal in his fiery caul,
> The year's first dandelion globe,
> ash-grey on the ash-green lawn,

> *Dear tulip leaves, color of carp bellies, wisteria drools*
> *Withered and drained dry—*
> *All light in the gathering darkness,*
>   *a brilliance itself which is set to come.*

One can love these moments, can cherish their invocation of the American sublime (though Wright's notion of the sublime seems closer to the lurid paintings of Bierstadt than to Whitman), and yet dislike the cracker-barrel philosophizing in which they're embedded. If you're going to stand around a cracker barrel very long, you'd better have a sense of humor—Wright will allow himself the occasional dry remark (he describes herons lifting their legs "silently, and very slow," which is funny if you recognize the allusion to Auden), but mostly he likes the sort of *sententiae* a Roman orator kept a warehouse of: "The language of landscape is language," "Love of the lack of love is still love," "A word to the wise is a word to the wise," "Life is a long walk on a short pier." A little of this goes a long way; a little more, and you start thinking fondly of the fate of Cicero.

Wright isn't writing poems any longer—he's laying down a coat of sensibility, as if sensibility were somehow enough; but sensibility isn't like house paint. You have to have a house to paint. America is a forgiving country, and old geezers can write old-geezer poetry for decades without suffering any punishment worse than having a sack of awards dumped on their heads. Wright's late poetry has fallen into a kind of dumb rumination—like the beasts of the field, he has to be prodded not to chew the same damn thing over and over. It might be amusing to see an index to this long, lazy, undemanding book, with entries like:

memory, a lonely observer, 25
memory, deep blank of, 55
memory, immeasurable, like the heart, 25
memory of fur coats, erotic and pungent, 32
memory, slide show of, 3
memory, thick staircase of, 17

Wright was more ambitious once. I wish he'd drop the immanences and immensities, the references to angels and the moony vacancies ("We're not here a lot longer than we are here, for sure. / Unlike coal, for instance, or star clots." *Star clots?*). He's gone over this ground so often, it has begun to look like an open-pit mine.

Kathleen Jamie

We have lost so much American dialect in the past fifty years, it's difficult to remember how strongly regional American English used to be—you can scour Flatbush now and rarely hear English murdered the Brooklyn way, or walk halfway across Boston without being assaulted by the Boston *a*. In Britain, whatever losses have occurred, language in recent decades has become a skirmish line in literature, especially in Scotland. If dialect is the most subtle form of treason, the United Kingdom is threatened partly by the quiet rejection of standard English.

Kathleen Jamie is one of a group of younger Scottish poets who don't take English as the natural valence of the tongue. Just when she has allowed you to grow comfortable in the language you know, she'll throw in a "smirr of rain" or a "place hained by trees"; and you'll realize how tentative our treaty with dialect is. (Scots began as a dialect of Middle English, but whether you think it a dialect now or a separate Anglic language may depend on which side of the border you're on.) *Waterlight*, a selection of Jamie's poems, introduces American readers to her modest, insinuating voice, one often with a surprising sting to it.

> *When I pause to consider*
> *a god, or creation unfolding*
> *in front of my eyes—*
> *is this my lot? Always*
> *brought back to the same*
> *grove of statues in ill-*
> *fitting clothes: my suddenly*
> *elderly parents, their broken-down*
> *Hoover; or my quarrelling kids?*

This sounds like a poem Larkin might have written, had he been a woman. So many young poets on both sides of the Atlantic fall into dotty blandness or the dementia of accusation (the difference between the School of Blah-Blah-Blah and the School of Wah-Wah-Wah), it's a pleasure to read a poet with the courage of her grumpiness.

Most of Jamie's recent poems limit their attention to nature. Often they start with some casual thing she's observed—molted feathers washed ashore, a peregrine that returns to the quarry where it fledged. Taut, closely rendered, the poems mark out a moral territory by negating almost everything outside it.

> *First come the jellyfish:*
> *mauve-fringed, luminous bowls*
> *like lost internal organs,*
> *pulsing and slow.*
>
> . . . .
>
> *It's as though we're stalled in a taxi*
> *in an ill-lit, odd*
> *little town, at closing time,*
> *when everyone's maudlin*
>
> *and really, ought just to go*
> home.

These poems are local in the best sense, true to the torsions of the poet's experience, a chronicle of the way nature rubs against the human. It's not surprising that Jamie is attracted to places filled with *disjecta membra*: secondhand shops, dumps, shorelines.

The poems she casts into Scots, unfortunately, offer only beauties borrowed or begged—perhaps that's the result when a language once robust becomes largely literary, learned with half an ear in childhood or only later from books: "I'd raither/whummel a single oor/intae the blae o thae wee flo'ers/than live fur a' eternity/in some cauld hivvin." That may be the language of Burns and MacDiarmid; but, "wee flo'ers" and all, the lines might just as well have been inscribed in whatever passes for a Hallmark card north of Hadrian's Wall. When a Scots poem doesn't work, you feel you've woken up in the middle of a haggis-throwing contest. Tom Scott's versions of Baudelaire and Dante almost fifty years ago and William Laughton Lorimer's more recent translations of the New Testament and *Macbeth* promised more than Scots poetry has delivered.

Jamie's English poems, however, offer a mind with a mortal view. There's nothing preplanned about their architecture—they seem accidental, full of the random imposition of the ordinary. She loves long, implicating sentences that take time to catch her restless intelligence—like Amy Clampitt, she treats syntax as the machine of thought. If many poems seem slight or offhand, Jamie is a poet defined by her limitations as well as determined in them. She's a poet of senses as well as sensibility, interested in the sculpted presence of the world but in little she cannot see. (Scotland has a long tradition of skeptical thought, though Hume would not have written these poems.) The poems look better the more you know of them and the more of them you know—they live halfway in the shadows, like a predator waiting to strike.

Robert Hass

Robert Hass is the most intellectual poet of his generation, but he's intellectual in a curious way. The poems in *Time and Materials* usually start in a sort of post-Buddhist, post-meditative fog. Shadow-dappled woods, scudding streams, the stippled haze off the coast (not for nothing was his first book titled *Field Guide*)—these make you think what follows will be the California version of emotion recollected in tranquility; but the gestures of lyric, the invocation of Wordsworth, may plunge darkly into an anecdote of wartime:

> *The other man, the officer, who brought onions*
> *and wine and sacks of flour,*
> *the major with the swollen knee,*
> *wanted intelligent conversation afterward.*
> *Having no choice, she provided that, too.*
>
> *Potsdamerplatz, May 1945.*
>
> *When the first one was through he pried her mouth open.*
> *Bashō told Rensetsu to avoid sensational materials.*
> *If the horror of the world were the truth of the world,*
> *he said, there would be no one to say it*
> *and no one to say it to.*
> *I think he recommended describing the slightly frenzied*
> *swarming of insects near a waterfall.*

Are those American soldiers? Russians? (The soldier pries open the raped woman's mouth to spit in it.) It's surprising how horrifying this flatly composed scene is—yet the poet's contrast with lyric innocence, the limitation of language in the face of monsters, seems to condemn poetry for being poetry. Are Shakespeare's sonnets culpable for not mentioning the Spanish Armada?

(The one supposed allusion is likely anything but.) Or Pound's lyrics worse for not conjuring up Passchendaele? Lyric is not the villain here.

Hass wants to say the unsayable; yet his poems imply that happiness must always be guilty, because someone somewhere is dying. (The cynic would say that, if someone somewhere is dead, someone else must be happy.) Hass's poems are often novel in conception, full of wrenching juxtapositions for which the term *discordia concors* might have been coined—after a while, though, you recognize that he possesses a rigid set of mannerisms: if he mentions poetry, it's to belabor the self-consciousness of it; if a woman, to spring into bed with her (there's a lot of heavy breathing in this book); if war, to condemn the inhumanity of it. No one would deny him his tastes, but why does he think they're in any way remarkable?

The most disturbing poems in *Time and Materials* are prosy narratives:

> *When I was a child my father every morning—*
> *Some mornings, for a time, when I was ten or so,*
> *My father gave my mother a drug called antabuse.*
> *It makes you sick if you drink alcohol.*
> *They were little yellow pills. He ground them*
> *In a glass, dissolved them in water, handed her*
> *The glass and watched her closely while she drank.*
> *It was the late nineteen-forties, a time,*
> *A social world, in which the men got up*
> *And went to work, leaving the women with the children.*

This is cruel, even excruciating, though Hass seems to believe his readers so doltish they know nothing about families in the 1940s. The father here is a vague figure full of phony bonhomie; but, just when the poet might say a word about his mother's drunken benders, he calls up the scene of Aeneas escaping the flames of Troy with his father astride his shoulders (he's a burden, see). Then:

> *Slumped in a bathrobe, penitent and biddable,*
> *My mother at the kitchen table gagged and drank,*
> *Drank and gagged. We get our first moral idea*
> *About the world—about justice and power,*
> *Gender and the order of things—from somewhere.*

And that's the end. *Justice and power? Gender?* What was a harrowing family portrait finishes as a lecture on gender. There's no pity for the father, guilty of that terrible crime, not wanting to leave his young son with a lush.

Poetry, for Hass, has increasingly become a conscienced prose, but not necessarily good prose—the syntax is often wobbly; you'd pay a ransom for a few semicolons; some of the modifiers dangle until hell freezes over; and, when the poet attempts to distinguish between *O!* and *Oh!,* he botches it. Hass is too clever and dry a writer for the "poetry of witness," that most deadly of contemporary genres—instead he writes the "poetry of lecture." A long poem called "State of the Planet," commissioned by a famous observatory, starts with one of his gorgeous pastoral set-pieces:

> *Through blurred glass*
> *Gusts of a Pacific storm rocking a huge, shank-needled*
> *Himalayan cedar. Under it a Japanese plum*
> *Throws off a vertical cascade of leaves the color*
> *Of skinned copper.*

Soon, however, he's droning on about chlorofluorocarbons; by the time he's done preaching about the destruction of the ozone layer, you're counting the tiles on the floor. One poem offers a potted history of aerial bombardment in Vietnam; another, a sandbox account of the Korean War. The facts are numbing, but they're too eager to become parables. Most people learned these things in tenth-grade textbooks, or from Al Gore.

Hass's taste for Horatian state-of-the-nation poems too easily becomes moral hectoring—after all the idealism, you long for a little *Realpolitik.* It's one thing to be nervous about what the lyric ignores, another to blame poetry for the horrors of the world. These poems of genial guilt overwhelm poems far more intriguing: a Pinteresque conversation between lovers, a tale about watching a thirties movie with the sound off, or the many lavish poems about eating (though Hass can't devour a piece of Parma ham without letting the reader know that somewhere a city is getting sacked—food all too often makes him think of mass murder). In these new poems, you get rueful intelligence by the bucketful, a welcome suspicion about the nature of language, and stunning renderings of the natural world, as well as a lot of scolding. I doubt I'll like a book of American poetry better all year; but it's a pity Hass has become a lyric poet with a conscience, because he can't make the conscience shut up.

Verse Chronicle

Valentine's Day Massacre

Ted Kooser

Back in 1986, Ted Kooser wrote a poem for Valentine's Day, printed it up on a postcard, and sent it to women he knew. He did this the next year, and the next, adding a name or two, each year shipping the cards over to Valentine, Nebraska, for the postmark. After two decades of this sweet, facetious nonsense, he decided to call it quits—by then the mailing list had grown to twenty-six hundred names, and the printing and postage exceeded the annual budget of Omaha. *Valentines* collects these poems, pieced out with black-and-white drawings of farmhouses, prairie landscapes, and an alarming number of dead trees. Perhaps they're just waiting for spring; but it does seem odd to illustrate a book of love poems with a lot of leafless shrubbery.

Joseph Brodsky wrote a poem every year at Christmas; more poets might adopt a holiday, preferably an obscure one like Liberty Tree Day or National Mustard Day, commemorating it year by year until they have a tidy chapbook. It would keep a lot of poets out of trouble, at least until the holidays ran out. *Valentines* would have made a wonderful book had the poems been any good.

> *If this comes creased and creased again and soiled*
> *as if I'd opened it a thousand times*
> *to see if what I'd written here was right,*
> *it's all because I looked too long for you*
> *to put it in your pocket.*

This, you can't help but feel, is what most people want poetry to be. A poem should be like a greeting card—with a point so blindingly obvious that reading it is like getting hit by a lead pipe. The poem should tell a little joke, per-

haps shout *Ba-da-boom!* and skip offstage. If it can't make a joke, it should try
to squeeze out a few cheap tears.

> *If you feel sorry for yourself*
> *this Valentine's Day, think of*
> *the dozens of little paper poppies*
> *left in the box when the last*
> *of the candy is gone, how* they
> *must feel, dried out and brown*
> *in their sad old heart-shaped box.*

Well, you say, as you sit around the pot-bellied stove, *I bet them paper wrap-
pers don't feel too good, now, do they?* (I'd be sorrier for those discarded wrap-
pings if the poet didn't go on to write that there's "not even / one pimpled nose
to root and snort / through their delicate pot pourri.")

Kooser must have been told that poems have musical language, because
at times he tries out a jingly phrase ("high in the chaffy, taffy-colored haze").
He must have heard somewhere that poems use metaphors, because he tosses
a few in, higgledy-piggledy: "those solemn Sunday / sacraments of Clorox
in the church / of starch" or, considering some refrigerated celery, "Surely it
misses those long fly balls of light / its leaves once leapt to catch." Technique
doesn't matter much to a poet whose versified prose, sometimes beaten out on
a bongo drum, is used mainly to say something whimsical or twinkly. The po-
ems are short (they had to be short to fit on a postcard) and uplifting, though
they don't have a lot to lift and don't try to lift a lot.

What's curious about *Valentines* is how vacant and insipid the poems are.
Surely a poet who sets himself up writing love poems ought to have suffered a
passion or two; yet the language is as generic as a pair of blue jeans. Just when
you think the poet might be making a point, he begins to gush; and then it's
sentiment all the way down, enough to fill a lard bucket. If you want poems of
thwarted love, try Hardy. If you want passion, read Donne. *Valentines* is the sort
of gift book you'd buy for your sweetheart if you had no imagination but some-
how knew that, on Valentine's Day, women like flowers, and chocolate, and . . .
and poetry. Should you be too cheap for the first two, poetry would have to do.

In the House of Fame, there's no doubt a broom closet for Ted Kooser.
Such a poet won't ruin poetry—if poetry can survive Jimmy Stewart and
Jimmy Carter, it can survive anything. Kooser lives on borrowed capital, in
this case the capital accrued by Robert Frost. Frost was a complicated man, so

complicated that sometimes he tried to seem simple—he contained as many multitudes as Whitman, and perhaps a few more. Most Frost imitators have tried to get away with just being simple. Frost's backwoods manner was too good to be true, but not too true to be good; when he said something wise, often it *was* wise. Kooser rarely says anything wiser than a wisecrack.

Just when I thought that Kooser didn't have a brain in his head, however, he surprised me. The last poem in the book, written for his wife, has all the fierce, stubborn Frost-like humor the rest of the volume lacks.

> *The hog-nosed snake, when playing dead,*
> *Lets its tongue loll out of its ugly head.*
>
> *It lies on its back as stiff as a stick;*
> *If you flip it over it'll flip back quick.*
>
> *If I seem dead when you awake,*
> *Just flip me once, like the hog-nosed snake.*

There might be life in the old snake yet.

Melissa Green

Twenty years back, Melissa Green published a striking debut volume, *The Squanicook Eclogues,* and then more or less vanished. Full of gorgeous detail, blowsy with observation, the verse flaunted the giddy excesses of a young poet coming to terms with her talent. Then there was silence, apart from a scarifying memoir on mental illness more than a decade ago.

Last fall Green reappeared in a quiet way, publishing a limited-edition chapbook that quickly sold out. The poems in *Fifty-Two,* each consisting of six lines, are abrupt, hard bitten, and revealing in a discomfiting way. They have little of the appetite of her early work; some terrible nemesis changed her life and altered—indeed, for a time almost destroyed—her gift.

> *I was lovely once. The semester I was twenty-eight.*
> *After, scalpel-thin, my shocked soul shut down. A century, a hundred*
> *pounds later,*
> *I woke. Why do my roses bloat into bud, blush, die unopened?*

The landscapes and gardens once splashily decorative now torment her with loss. The eclogues have become elegies.

The form Green has chosen might easily have gone unrequited. Of the half-dozen lines, the third and fourth are always half lines, with a sharp pause or breach between, the other lines long and prosy. This broke-back stanza rewards the snapshot, the intake of breath—the poems are cuttings, postscripts, musings that must be spoken with purse-lipped brevity. They exist in a world of Greek gods, the Old Testament, and fine art:

> Paul César Helleu used to borrow pen nibs from his friend Singer Sargent
> and do dry point portraits of society women in the belle époque. One
> inexplicably turned up in our cellar.
>   I live in a big black house.
> Whoever heard of a black house? I ought to laugh—and sometimes do.

Helleu was an artist who outlived his time. The tone here moves quickly, deliciously, through matter-of-fact narrative, mild surprise, self-mockery, solemnity—are we to take the black house as fact and symbol both, house and the house of plague? Is the self-portrait meant to be dry as drypoint? Does the beauty of the society women make more cruel the poet's loss of beauty? From such tentative, teasing amputations are these poems made.

The most explicit poems, those that confront her severe depression, are the most shocking, but also the most familiar. After Plath, after Sexton, there's only so much ground to cover when a poet says, "I forgot to let myself be loved" or "Someone else is living the life I thought I'd get." (Men often recount their bouts of madness in a robust and even jocular way, as if they'd been off stalking a lion. Women tend to be braver in their bereavements, and more honest.) The stark revelations, though they verge on self-pity, are merciless:

> The latest in a series of sunset-colored dogs,
> our tall sons, their stair-step children stamping off snow, the holiday table
>   groaning
> with our work: vegetables, poetry, merriment.
>   It never happened, the house, the oeuvre,
> the husband holding me, older. Illness married me.

This is a poet learning to make art of her losses but finding that the loss remains despite the art.

Fifty-Two is a difficult book, often unappealing, at times overwritten ("Raise, oh lift me from this barrow. / Breathe into me a flux of wonder. Rinse my phosphorescent palms and kiss.") The tone and diction veer wildly from pre-Raphaelite fustian to the delirious slang of "fuck-me pumps"—in one poem the flaying of Marsyas gives way to "I want flamenco, / two beaded McEwan's Ales, a friendly fuck." It's no surprise that the *Metamorphoses* sustains this poet—she calls herself a "middle-aged Daphne caught in Dante's silvery, arthritic, suicidal wood."

This book of barely three hundred lines is a relief from the stultifying manners of contemporary verse, even if writing offers only a secondhand salvation:

> *A fusillade of blossoms blows from the sour plum, a siege of horizontal hail*
> *riddles the garden's infantry dense with bleeding hearts, the lilac bush*
> *hammered by the east wind into a scythe.*

These rueful, damaged poems present the uncomfortable portrait of a woman who has been to the edge.

Elizabeth Spires

Elizabeth Spires is in love with ordinary things. The best poems in *The Wave-Maker*, her sixth volume, are quiet, unprepossessing, filled with wonder at the mortalities and fleeting beauties of the world. Like many connoisseurs of the small, she tries to make the familiar unfamiliar again, as it was for those innocents in the Garden of Eden.

> *There was intricate machinery involved & a powerful desire*
> *to make it all move. It had been easy then to stand waist-deep*
> *in the waves & will the world into existence, sea, sky, & cloud,*
> *the ever-changing elements, moving & robed, like characters*
> *on a stage delivering their lines. Or so she had thought at the time.*

Spires never tries to overwhelm the reader—she has placed herself in the tradition of Elizabeth Bishop, whose faux innocence she has shamelessly borrowed. We are so used to our makeshift world, at times it takes a scientist

of happenstance to see anything unusual there. Yet while contenting herself
with the homely fact, no less transcendent for being true, this poet lives in the
dangerous intersection of religion, linguistic tact, and the bald-faced lie. It
makes poetry no more morally abrupt if you call religion philosophy.

Spires is never afraid of abstractions (she's rare in being able to write ab-
stractly without sounding ridiculous); her poems consider the degradations of
age, the loss of beauty, the shadows rising slowly around her.

> *The road is dust,*
> *and the town is dust,*
> *and even my mother*
> *is dust. But here,*
>
> *set back among the pines,*
> *a teahouse long and low*
> *where we sit like ancients,*
> *cradling lacquered cups.*
>
> *Outside, the storm of afternoon.*
> *The dust of existence.*
> *Then the storm passes.*
> *The bamboo shines.*

The simple lines, effortlessly compact, have abraded some of the verbs into
nothingness. This confident elegance suffers a shimmer of doubt at that shin-
ing bamboo, as if there the poet wanted too desperately to affect the reader.
Soon a cherry tree blooms, autumn is blazing, and the poem collapses into a
chummy plea for sympathy: "My friend, sit with me / for a little while. / Let us
cleanse ourselves / of the dust of existence."

These shy, religiously tinged meditations often stop in the middle of an or-
dinary day to ask questions (Spires's question marks are more unnerving than
her exclamation points, of which there is a bumper crop). The poems show
how much can be written from nothing, without the jazzed-up heartiness of
a Frank O'Hara, so concerned with trivia he misses the moments between
incidents when life takes place. Spires's poems are loveliest in the mildness of
their ambitions. She looks at a snail (she may be more interested in snails than
even snails are), or a fish, or an insect, or perhaps just stares out a window—at

times you wish she'd get out a little more. Not much happens, and not much is meant to happen except a woman coming to terms with herself.

Spires once kept her sentimental side in delicate balance with the brooding skeptic, but the sentiment has begun to win out. Her new poems are often infiltrated by the magical awe of children's tales, tales where anything might happen and, alas, anything does, tales where you can suffer only so much innocence before you want to push the poet into an oven and bake her the way the witch should have baked Hansel.

> Sometimes   I cannot   bear the world
> the beauty & perfection of a snail   created
> by the same Creator   who created   me

It's hard to feel such things, but even harder to make poetry of them. When Spires contemplates the mute world, the poems suffer from their self-conscious soulfulness. What might have been the rage of natural history becomes something closer to prayer, without the haunted bearing of religious supplication. As she writes of Advent, "We felt its approach, / peered like curious children / into the bright cave // where the miracle happened."

Like Bishop, like Moore, Spires has the courage of her modesty, which is no less than faith in her procedure (she lacks Bishop's cheerful apprehensions and Moore's disarticulating eye, the eye of a taxidermist); yet it's often in the depths of technique that her poems break down—they are winsome rather than unbearable. There's a struggle in her soul between a conventional poetry of superficial instinct and a darker one more wounded, more unlikely, more indomitable.

Campbell McGrath

Campbell McGrath loves the world's bewildering variety (you might mistake his poems—gaudily colored, artificially flavored—for a candy shop), and like most gods he can't bear to leave a single thing out. He has an eye for the natural world, particularly the shell-strewn beaches of south Florida, and a sculptor's understanding of nature's forged, damascened surface:

> Ocean like beaten metal removed from the cooling pail,
> mark of the hammer and tongs, the smith's signage,

grain revealed as by pressure of the burin in a Japanese print,
substantial, bodily, color of agave, color of bitter medicine . . .

Such gorgeous, insistent language suffers only a touch of self-congratulation;
yet McGrath has trouble knowing when to stop—the poem soon breaks down
into pointless and exhausting profusion:

the frilled lips and spooned-out tails of horse and queen conchs,
sponge tubes, varieties of seaweed and uprooted coral,
tiny broken elkhorn infants, torn fans, punch cards,
serrated disks and tribal ornaments, teeth, dismembered ears
and bleached stone knuckles of a skeleton seeking restitution.

Whew! a critic once wrote. Hiroshige has his endless views of Edo, and
McGrath his endless views of Miami sand and Miami sky; but such jerry-
built lines seem far too much like the rampant property development he com-
plains about.

    Seven Notebooks is a pell-mell jaunt through one poet's calendar year, di-
ary entries interrupted by poems, poems abandoned for long quotations—this
catchall lacks any noticeable pressure toward concision or hint of deep-browed
introspection. Accumulation is all. Some of the notebooks claim a presiding
form (the ode, the haiku), some an artistic familiar (Neruda, Whitman, Hiro-
shige), and some a theme (rhetoric, disorder), though few possess all of them.
At times, McGraw shows how an acorn of prose becomes a poem—freshly
sawn and sanded in the workshop, the poem is often less attractive than the
rough oak of prose with which he began.

    Because we're still in the great Age of Confession, the notebooks tell you a
lot about the poet's wife and his sons and his planar fasciitis, tales that might
be gripping in a Christmas letter but are of little interest outside the imme-
diate family. It's a pity that suburban lives and suburban worries are rarely
riveting—not every man is a Larkin. It would be all right if McGrath's nattering
were an excuse for poetry, though the poetry seems an excuse for the nattering.
He can write a musing, probing line that suggests all the virtues of curiosity:

Then the imagination withdraws, drifts across the table
to investigate the glass flowers rolled in cloth tape.

It hovers, probes the petals, some like galaxies,

some like figs or seashells. Dutiful and penitent,

it shimmers back across the gulf of air,
without a metaphor, to doze away the afternoon.

Then just as reasonably, just as artfully, he can write lines of fatuous self-absorption or ponderous mumbo-jumbo: "The opposite of sunlight/is not darkness but anti-light,/a mass of ionic occlusion,/seams of which riven/ with purple fire illuminate/the parataxis of butterflies." That sounds like Isaac Asimov on a bad day.

McGrath takes himself seriously, which means too seriously. He writes a lot about "cognitive manipulation," "rhetorical posture," "ethics of stimulus," "harmonies of fulfillment"—trying to make poems of such things is like trying to build a Ferrari from spit and cardboard. ("Ideas that burn in the mind!" he exclaims at the end of one poem. *Good luck with that,* you want to reply.) Too often the poems seem like a freshman philosophy seminar wrestling with a chapter on epistemology. It's nice to have a loose baggy monster as a form, but not if what you get in the end is a loose baggy monster.

Whitman is the dominating presence here; but it's a mistake for a poet without the gift for blather or much warmth of spirit to quote the good gray poet so lavishly. Whitman *thought* about things (later readers condescend to him at their peril), where McGrath just writes agreeably about them in his sun-addled way. The modern poet wants to make 9/11 his Civil War, but he sounds like William Jennings Bryan—he won't stop the rhetorical roar until the apocalypse comes to town:

And I beheld a city
where blood ran through streets the color of raw liver,
stench of offal and kerosene and torched flesh,

tongueless heads impaled on poles and severed limbs
strung on barbed wire beneath unresting surveillance cameras . . .

On and on it goes, like some PG-13 version of *Howl.* Poetry has to be more than a mass of images presented without taste or judgment, or pretentious witterings about language ("If language is a circulatory system of symbols . . ."). McGrath never notices when the reader's eyes have glazed over.

Marie Howe

The long line in poetry requires a page too narrow—if you designed a book as wide as the longest line in *Leaves of Grass*, the lines would seem mere prose, or typography run amok. Though it might seem counterintuitive, a poem's long lines need the runovers imposed by a rational margin. Such lines reveal their character in a continual breach of manners.

Marie Howe makes her lines fabulously long—twenty or thirty or even forty syllables can go by before she feels obliged to call it quits. The poems in *The Kingdom of Ordinary Time*, her first book in ten years, have a lot to say. Angry, foulmouthed at times, she writes as if she were thrashing her enemies with a club.

> *The thing about those Greeks and Romans is that*
> *at least mythologically,*
>
> *they could get mad. If the man broke your heart, if he*
> *fucked your sister speechless*
>
> *then real true hell broke loose:*
> *"You know that stew you just ate for dinner, honey?—*
>
> *It was your son."*
> *That's Ovid for you.*

Poets have looked to Homer and Virgil and Ovid for a lot of things, but rarely for permission to get mad. Angry poets are almost always angry *at* someone—usually parent or spouse or lover (how many poets have ever been angry at their kids?), but you wonder if they would have been any less angry if the wife or father or boyfriend had never existed.

Howe is better than most poets in this vein—it's unfair to call them Confessional Poets, because they have so little to confess. They might better be christened the Memoir School, poets so wrapped up in the truth of their lives (though truth is the first victim of memoir), the poems seem claustrophobic. The trouble with such poets is that their lives become an end in themselves, rather than a needle's eye used to interpret the world. Shakespeare's sonnets are memoirs of a sort, probably drawn from hard experience—but they tell us about the modes of love, not the manners of his life.

Howe's poems are always a little more honest than you would expect and a little funnier than you could hope for. She's gloomy, to be sure, and unappealingly dramatic, on occasion jabbering on witlessly; but her sardonic humor comprehends her limitations.

> I don't want to offend anybody but I never did like
> fucking all that much. Like I always say
>
> the saw enjoys the wood more than the wood enjoys
> the saw—know what I mean?

These remarks are laid at another woman's doorstep; but such things are rarely said and even more rarely hilarious. Howe has a way of making you think—she's a bully at times—and then making you sorry for it. That's what good art does.

Howe's life seems too privileged for her to ask for so much sympathy; but she listens to the irritable part of her soul, and sometimes her ironies are more visible when you read the poems again. The weakest poems here are meditations in the voice of the Virgin Mary—the idea is too self-important and the sequence too pious to let in Howe's compromised vision. She's far better in a horrific poem about her drunken father, who in the middle of the night orders his children to clean the kitchen, then the basement, then the garage. Her small acts of defiance explain a lot in the poems that follow—they're the aftereffects of a Catholic girlhood.

Howe has a knack for finding the small inscrutable moments in life and leaving them inscrutable. (Airless as contemporary poetry often is, it could gain a lot from the short stories of Flannery O'Connor and Grace Paley.) In my favorite poem here, the poet has been ordering her daughter to hurry here, hurry there, to keep up. Then:

> Today, when all the errands are finally done, I say to her,
> Honey I'm sorry I keep saying Hurry—
> you walk ahead of me. You be the mother.
>
> And, Hurry up, she says, over her shoulder, looking
> back at me, laughing. Hurry up now darling, she says,
> hurry, hurry, taking the house keys from my hands.

There's a recognition of mortality in those lines. Not all Howe's poems cohere; sometimes they're collections of bits and stunts that make a discordant whole, if they make a whole at all. Though she rarely does more than C. K. Williams (she must be president of the Manhattan chapter of the C. K. Williams Fan Club), though at times she's so intense she holds eye contact too long, these bitter, bittersweet poems offer the woman's half of an unanswerable equation. Howe has learned how not to be ordinary about ordinary time.

Jorie Graham

When Jorie Graham has a message, it's a very big message; and it couldn't be any BIGGER if it were plastered on a BILLBOARD. Things MATTER, they matter a LOT, no REALLY, they matter this VERY SECOND. Graham wasn't always a poet reduced to pouting and pontification; but the reader can keep track of her now only by how loudly she's shouting:

> blues, you know the trouble at the heart, blue, blue, what
> pandemonium, blur of spears roots cries leaves master & slave, the crop
> > destroyed,
>
> water everywhere not
> drinkable, & radioactive waste in it, & human bodily
> waste

Graham's poems in the past two decades have forgotten the cunning deployments of language her earlier poems knew by heart. The not-so-quiet point in *Sea Change* is that time is running out—the waters are poisoned, the ground is polluted, and it's all our fault. Messages are very difficult in poetry if you're not witty and Augustan or you don't work for Western Union.

Poetry is a graveyard of talent destroyed by ambition, yet ambition is rarely ruined by talent. Graham has long taken the medium for the message, shifting her style from book to book, adopting a new punctuation mark or changing the movement of her lines (peculiar mid-word enjambments are the hallmark here). *Sea Change* alternates lines very, very long with lines very, very short; this drama of displacement might be effective if the reader didn't suspect there was a secret purpose behind it. Graham bared all in a recent issue of *Poetry*:

> *[The poems] marry the long line of Whitman to the short line of Williams, two poets convinced that their extreme lines—very long, very short—were generative instruments for a music that would explore and enact the idea of, and sensation of, "the democratic experience." Of course these are poems being written at a time when much of what might have been imagined to be "a democracy" has failed. These utopian poetics . . .*

but perhaps I should leave her in full flow. What such lines have to do with democracy (and Williams didn't always use very short lines) is beyond me.

Whatever the change of form, the style of thinking is exactly the same, a fretful record of the mind's hesitations and repetitions (call it the idling of consciousness)—we used to refer to it as dithering. The poems are busy with their own business, flighty, intensely and doggedly and wearyingly serious, with a breathless delivery full of its own importance:

> *& what*
> *is the structure of freedom but this, & grace, & the politics of time—look*
> *   south, look*
> *   north—yes—east west compile hope synthesize*
> *   exceed look look again hold fast attach speculate drift drift recognize*
> *   forget—terrible*
>
> *gush—gash—of*
> *form.*

Having made your way through the thickets of style, often you discover that Graham is saying something rather banal—the great maze has only a mouse in the middle.

If ecology is the subject, more or less, some of these poems become lectures by a latterday Mr. Wizard ("which also contains / contributions from the Labrador Sea and entrainment of other water masses, try to hold a / complete collapse, in the North Atlantic Drift, in the / thermohaline circulation"). However worthy the sentiments, the poem is no more interesting than a pile of scrap metal or a mound of compost, fascinating though these might be to the chemist or the art critic. It's hard for Graham to complete one thought without being distracted by another, as if she suffered some form of poetic ADHD. The gushing is awful enough; but, every time I think she has written as badly as she can, she exceeds my expectations: "breathing into this oxygen which also pockets my/looking hard," the "very fact of God as/invention seems to sit, fast, as in its saddle."

The disparity between what Graham believes she's doing and what the reader sees on the page is enormous. Perhaps these rambling, doddering, lifeless poems *are* "crucial," as she claims; yet it's as if all their imaginative energy went to "enact the idea of, and sensation of" writing the poem itself. I'm not sure aesthetic choices should be justified in philosophic terms, because it makes matters of taste seem conditioned or inevitable (taste can have philosophical carriage, but perhaps it takes a century or more to discover it). Her language, so slack and unbearable now, doesn't possess the resources of Williams or Whitman, whose arguments lay in language, not the length of line. Graham can chatter in the latest philosopher's mode but can't compose a good metaphor.

It's hard to say to a poet that her career has gone off course, especially when she has been showered with awards for just the things that seem disastrous. Graham was once a poet of magnifying charm and an appealing wildness; but her editorials are so at odds with the evenhanded articulation of thought, she has lost almost all the graces of language that once graced her work. The poems have become elegies to their own progress. Some poets are born dull, some achieve dullness, and some have dullness thrust upon them.

The Forgotten Masterpiece of
John Townsend Trowbridge

John Townsend Trowbridge (1827–1916) was born two years after the opening of the Erie Canal and died during the First World War. The friend of Longfellow and Holmes and Whitman (at a time when Longfellow and Holmes refused to meet the author of *Leaves of Grass*), he wrote gouts of poems, a string of popular plays, and at least forty novels, including more than one best seller. Having started with hack work in New York, with hack work he continued, growing so impoverished in the Grub Street of the day that at one point he took to the business of engraving gold pencil-cases.

The literary odd-job man, who turns his hand to whatever a hand can be turned, has long been nearly extinct (perhaps the sole example remaining, like a last elegant dodo, is John Updike). From such a writer, poems and stories and plays and novels come, now like a freshet, now like a flood—many of them bad, or bad enough, some of them good, or good enough, and perhaps in a life one or two with the flare of brilliance.

Born in a cabin in the wilderness west of Rochester, which was soon to be a boomtown, Trowbridge grew up a plodder, a dull student who all his life suffered from chronic eye-inflammation. He might have become a hardscrabble farmer like his father had he not been shocked into curiosity at about fourteen, according to his autobiography, by a "list of foreign words and phrases" in the back of his spelling book. He turned himself into a lover of Byron and Pope and Shakespeare (however much he liked the Bard's tragedies, however, he was never able to get through *Love's Labour's Lost*) and eventually taught himself Latin, Greek, and French. Some of his earliest verses were composed behind a plow.

Having come from almost nothing, Trowbridge cast a critical eye on the foolishness and self-deceptions of the social world of New York and Boston, the city where he eventually settled; and he was deeply roused by injustice.

The *American Sentinel*, the paper of which he was temporary editor in 1851, may have been hurried into failure by his satirical leader on the Fugitive Slave Law. His pseudonymous novel *Martin Merrivale*, published the same year as *Leaves of Grass*, remains one of the rare back-alley accounts of the antebellum writing trade. A few of Trowbridge's poems betray a rueful view of literary fame.

> *"BRILLIANT SUCCESS!" the play-bills said,*
> *Flaming all over the town one day,*
> *Blazing in characters blue and red,*
> *(Printed for posting, by the way,*
> *Before the public had seen the play!).*

The lines were based on experience.

Trowbridge's poetry, like Trowbridge's work in general, suffers from all the literary sins of the mid-nineteenth century—the ready-to-wear adjectives, the sentimental climate, the shelf of sympathies and pieties that look like so many dusty knickknacks now. If there was a right side, however, he was on it—years before the Civil War, he wrote an abolitionist novel compared to *Uncle Tom's Cabin*. After the war, he toured the broken battlegrounds and wrecked cities of the South and reported on the appalling devastation. Yet such gifts as he had, deformed or coarsened by the demands of his readers, produced a row of works more or less successful to the degree they were untouched by a hint of original imagination.

All this provided enough for the applause of his time, if too little for a later century to hear it. The sharp ear for grievance, a confidence in his critical judgment, a willingness to back the long shot (as with Whitman), and a highly developed sense of amusement at human weakness suggest that a more reckless talent lay largely untapped. Had he given way to his taste for mocking the hypocrisies around him, he might have written something less dependent on melodrama or moral authority, something that whispered of the psychology of a world in argument with itself.

Perhaps once he did give way. In 1878 a Boston firm published an anthology titled *A Masque of Poets*, its contributors all anonymous. Publication in disguise was the rage—it might have seemed, from the four-columned three-page list of pseudonyms published in the *Literary World* that year, that more authors than not were appearing incognito. *A Masque* was published in the "No Name" series (there was a rival called the "Round-Robin" series), which otherwise consisted of novels "written by eminent authors," according to the publisher, the "authorship of the work . . . to remain an inviolable secret." Advertisements for A Masque of Poets teased the prospective reader by suggesting that Christina Rossetti and William Morris might be among the masked crowd. Though the latter did not appear, there were poems by Henry David Thoreau, Louisa May Alcott, Sidney Lanier, Austin Dobson, and James Russell Lowell. The anthology is now remembered (and rendered hugely expensive in the rare-book trade) because of a single poem by Emily Dickinson, one of the handful published before her death. The disguises proved successful—the reviewer in the *Literary World* guessed at the authors of a dozen poems and was wrong all but once. Indeed, he thought the Dickinson poem had been written by Emerson.

At the end of the volume, taking up almost half the whole, was a "novelette in verse" called *Guy Vernon*, dashingly Byronic in character, the tale of a marriage conceived in haste, full of secrets, with a fair damsel tempted to betray her vows. The poem opens:

> *He was as fair a bachelor as ever*
> *Resolved to take a wife at forty-five.*
> *Indeed, how one so amiable and clever,*
> *Good-looking, rich, et cetera, could contrive*
> *Till the high noon of manhood not to wive,*
> *Was a vexed theme, and long remained a mystery*
> *To those who did not know his early history.*
>
> *And none knew that among his bride's relations.*
> *At Saratoga, where you meet all grades*
> *Of well-dressed people spending short vacations,*
> *Manoeuvring mothers, marriageable maids,*
> *And fortune-hunters on their annual raids,*
> *He saw her waltz, and spite of every barrier*
> *Of years or influence, inly vowed, "I 'll marry her!"*

The swaggering confidence here is quite unlike the plowed-up lines Trowbridge usually favored. The rhyme royal dragged something spirited from him, a something evident particularly in the three-syllable rhymes that close these stanzas—*barrier* and *I 'll marry her* honors the wilder shores of Byron's rhyme, which included *intellectual / henpecked you all* and *that horrid one / pastor Corydon.* (To a modern ear, *wive* and *inly* sound archaic; but they were apt to the period—Byron used *wive* in *Beppo* and Emerson *inly* in one of his poems.)

Guy Vernon may well announce to himself that he will marry the girl, whose name is Florinda; but there is an impediment on each side—in him, the puzzle of his having remained a bachelor; in her, another lover, one rather younger:

> *Rob Lorne, a journalist, and sort of poet;*
> *A fellow so unthrifty and so witty,*
> *That honest people said it was a pity*
> *A needle of such point should have a head*
> *Too fine to take a strong and useful thread.*

Florinda! Rob Lorne! We are in the land of comic pastoral. (Poor Lorne, whose name is twice lorn.) Trowbridge was considered a fair hand at plot (much of his later career was spent writing juvenile novels, which could be said to depend on little else), and his other poems at times show a mordant wit that suited narrative more than lyric. Soon the younger suitor unselfishly withdraws his suit, though not without tears; and the mismatched lovers are betrothed—she church-mouse poor, he handsome, rich, but . . . et cetera.

> *For though the bride was penniless, and brought him*
> *Her beauty for sole dower (that proud array*
> *Of lace and diamonds was his gift, they say),*
> *A multitude of friends conspired to render*
> *The wedding feast a perfect blaze of splendor.*

> *She did not know, before, she had so many*
> *Rich and enthusiastic friends: the snob,*
> *Who never would have sacrificed a penny*
> *In bridal gifts for one who married Rob,*
> *Made haste to join the fashionable mob,*
> *Since Vernon was the man, and would have given his*
> *Last dime to buy her something nice at Tiffany's.*

These "friends" appear here and there through *Guy Vernon*, eager to approve whatever fashion approves, eager to disdain what propriety disdains—

they're a Greek chorus composed of harpies. Yet who would not applaud a gorgeous young woman decked in Tiffany's finest? (Founded in 1837, the firm was well established.) The preposterousness of the rhyme is reason enough to delight—it would have charmed Byron, not just for its own sake, but because he was himself not at all shy about product placement: as he says in *Don Juan,* "In virtues nothing earthly could surpass her,/Save thine 'incomparable oil,' Macassar."

The plot of *Guy Vernon* is a mock-heroic mixture of speed and lassitude: the poet lingers over small events, while large ones race by in a stanza or two. The disappointed young journalist-poet is dispatched to foreign climes, a traveler "writing verses for the magazines,/Newspaper sketches, stories, correspondence, he/Struggled with his hotel-bills and despondency." The new couple, against all odds, prove deliriously happy:

> *The wedded pair went off to Louisiana,*
> *Where Vernon owned a very large plantation,*
> *And wintered in New Orleans and Havana,—*
> *A season of delightful dissipation,*
> *Sight-seeing, dining, driving, conversation,*
> *And—best of all—the infinite variety*
> *Found in each other's ever-fresh society.*

The only shadow over this wedded bliss is cast by Vernon's manservant, a high-yellow mulatto and fop of the worst kind. Rumored to have been Vernon's slave, he is now, though servant still, wealthy and insufferable. Florinda loathes him, even renaming him at whim: though he is "so superb and exquisite a dandy,/Resplendent in all sorts of gaudy things,/Florinda called him Saturn, for his rings." (The joke is typically keen-witted—and Saturn, of course, ate his children.) Her reaction suggests that, long after the war, a northern prejudice lingered against blacks too ambitious or successful, blacks who had risen above their station—hers are not merely the resentments of good taste, though good taste is part of it:

> *Of all unfeathered bipeds,—Feejees, Negroes,—*
> *In any clime, of race refined or rude;*
> *Where crawls the crocodile, or where the tea grows;*
> *Pale, swarthy, tawny-skinned, or copper-hued;*
> *Turbaned or pigtailed, naked, furred, tattooed;—*

> *The queerest yet turned out from Nature's shop*
> *Is your complete, unmitigated fop.*

Florinda asks for the servant's dismissal, yet her husband flatly refuses. She's taken aback by this suddenly revealed limit to his devotion, but the author doesn't spare her—he can be as ruthless as Pope. She bursts into tears, "and for five minutes she was broken-hearted."

Though Vernon remains in every way attentive, thereafter she finds herself practicing her affections and concealing her hurts. Soon she notices a change in her husband—he grows moody, agitated, and when gently asked about this unhappy transformation brutely sends her to the detested servant for explanation.

> *He smiled, bowed, hand on waistcoat: "'Pon my honor!"—*
>   *Quirking his eyebrows, he stood leering at her,*
>   *Like some bedizened, over-civil satyr,—*
> *"Extremely sorry—news from our attorney—*
> *In short,—hem!—madam, we must make a journey."*
>
> *"Where?" cries Florinda.—"Back to our plantation."*
>   *"Tell me at once! what is the dreadful news?"*
> *"The business scarce admits of explanation;*
>   *For ladies, altogether too abstruse!"*
>   *"When do we go?"—"Ah, madam! please excuse*
> *The cruel circumstance, the—what you call*
> *Necessity,—you do not go at all."*

That Dickensian pause—that "hem!"—is masterfully placed. Trowbridge excelled in versifying dialogue (there's a touch of Browning in him), which, while never forgetting its satirical intent, here reached notes of cruelty in the hesitations and reversals meter supplies.

All Florinda's fears—is the problem money? a duel? another woman?—are blandly dismissed by this Iago, who stands, in what is just short of a racist portrait, "Grimacing, shrugging, lynx-eyed, white-toothed, woolly." Falls short, perhaps, until that last adjective. The simpering and insinuating character of Saturn troubles these passages. Here you begin to think that Trowbridge intended to recast the Othello story with the races of Othello and Iago reversed. As if in confirmation, only a few stanzas later, when Florinda rushes back to question her husband, he does nothing but glare at her with "strange, awful eyes. // Othello's thus on Desdemona burned."

Guy's actions remain an enigma. Poor Florinda imagines the worst, and worse than the worst; in a clever figure, the poet compares her fears to the Brocken specter, that meteorological phenomenon in which the giant shadow of a mountain climber is cast upon the clouds, his head surrounded by a rainbow corona.

> *So Fear has oftenest but itself to fear.*
> *But though imagined ills are still the worst,*
> *To troubled souls this truth is never clear;*
> *When evil lowers we deem the rule reversed,*
> *And fancy blacker woes about to burst*
> *Upon our heads than any yet conceived.*
> *So now Florinda, right or wrong, believed.*

This has a marked psychological point. The reviews of character are drawn with admirable economy, even if they're in thrall to the conventions of period fiction.

Florinda and her maid are to be dispatched back to New York by ship—to be sent away by her husband without chaperone was, by the manners of the day, a great insult. As she lingers in Havana, however, she stares out the window and sees her rejected beau, Rob Lorne. This is one of those coincidences beloved by Victorian novelists, and the narrator—though himself responsible for this unexpected turn—cannot help but ridicule ideas of love. Poor Lorne, instead of remaining forever downcast by his failed romance, has become quite carefree.

> *He had not died of love,—that heart-disease*
> *Which proves but seldom fatal, to my thinking.*
> *Defeated hope, sick fancy, if you please,*
> *Often induce a sentimental sinking,*
> *Drive some to suicide and some to drinking,*
> *But stop far short of any such forlorn*
> *And dismal end, with high, brave hearts like Lorne.*
>
> *He had come down at first as far as Florida,*
> *And seen the alligator and flamingo;*

Then, passing on to regions somewhat torrider,
  Reached the French-negro side of San Domingo,
  And learned a little of the curious lingo
The people speak there, but conceived no mighty
Love for those Black Republicans of Hayti.

Not only is it far-fetched to find Lorne in Havana, but he and Florinda happen to choose the same moment to glance at each other, she down from her window and he up from the street. Of such absurdities melodrama is made, though Trowbridge remains alive to the necessity of retarding the plot through hindrance and digression—the recognition having occurred, the author dawdles through a florid description of the city, a description not without its comic relief:

The place is picturesque with blacks and coolies,
  Peasants and panniered beasts: there's nothing odder
Than the slow-paced, half-hidden, peering mule is,
  Beneath his moving stack of fresh green fodder.
  It would be better if the streets were broader,
The windows glazed,—of that, though, I'm not sure,—
The hotels better, and mosquitoes fewer.

Afterward, half afraid he will see her again, the rejected beau bolts for the interior.

Trowbridge is adept at moving the mild comedies of character through this musty drama, making of the traveler's scene what Pope made of a card game. Though the descriptions can be lush with the evocation of tropical depths ("And flowering forests through whose wealth of blooms,/Like living fires, dart birds of gorgeous plumes"), Trowbridge had a taste for the prefabricated phrase, lazy and formulaic (*ardent wooer, abject woe, billowy verdure, indolent desire*)—he was often that sort of poet, given to unrolling the bolt of whole cloth and covering everything in sight with it.

What's more remarkable is how cannily he eyes the social character and how easily he rises into a mode of model intelligence when encouraged. The light verse acted like an acid that bit into the copperplate of period manner. The light verse, and the light comedy—for Rob, trying to flee the vision of his former lover, ends up on the same steamer back to New York. Having said good-bye to the island where he had found her again, and still ignorant of her presence on shipboard, he hears a call for supper.

> *With excellent appetite, if one must know it,*
>   *Which at the long, well-lighted cabin table,*
> *Crowded with hungry passengers, our poet*
>   *Was solacing as well as he was able,*
>   *When, glancing round the clattering, chattering Babel,*
> *He paused, aghast,—a slice of tongue half swallowed,—*
> *Seeing the Fate which, flying, he had followed!*

> *Florinda! pale but lovely still; enrapt in*
>   *The delicate discussion of cold chicken,*
> *And some engaging topic with the Captain.*
>   *Just then, amid loud talk and teacups clicking,*
>   *Over the wing she happened to be picking*
> *She looked—and there was Lorne, quite dazed and pallid,*
> *Staring at her across a dish of salad.*

A *slice of tongue half swallowed*! The old lovers move slowly toward a rapprochement, though here and there interrupted by the author's droll metaphysical speculations ("Evil, perhaps, being nothing more nor less/Than good in disproportion, or excess")—indeed, it takes some dozen stanzas after that glance over the salad for them to say hello. Trowbridge lets his lovers bow to a fate wholly authorial, but that is one of the satisfactions of satire. Having reminded us of the artifice of fiction, the author also sends up the overwriting to which his poems were often devoted.

> *O dear, inconstant Seraph of Repose!*
>   *Wing to the homes of woe thy downy flight;*
> *Visit the couch of wretchedness, and close*
>   *The aching sense that wearies of the night!*
>   *But when immortal Freshness and Delight*
> *Sail with the enraptured soul the glorious deep,*
> *What have we then to do with thee, O Sleep?*

I take this as having comic intent; sometimes with Trowbridge it's hard to tell. He loses his satirical touch in the stanzas that lead to reconciliation; but, just when you think the poem might be heading toward an overdose of sentiment, he breaks into a paean to the steamship!

> *When I behold this little peopled world,*
>   *Large as an asteroid, in the nether blue,*
> *Its flashing wheels, proud decks, and flags unfurled;*
>   *Then fancy that ancestral savage who*
>   *First pushed from shore with paddle and canoe,—*
> *I'm forced to the Darwinian conclusion*
> *That here's a masterpiece of evolution.*
>
> *From the first skiff of sutured skins or bark*
>   *To the three-decker with its thundering guns,—*
> *From Jason's classic junk, or Noah's ark,*
>   *To the grand steamship of five thousand tons,—*
>   *The thing developed: just as Man was once—*
> *Well, not a monkey; that he never was—*
> *But something less, evolved through Nature's laws.*
>
> *Allah il Allah! great is Evolution,*
>   *And Darwin eminently is its Prophet!*
> *Out of primeval chaos and confusion*
>   *It massed the nebulous orb, and fashioned of it*
>   *The sun and planets; one whereof it saw fit*
> *To finish off with most attractive features,*
> *And make the abode of curious living creatures.*

To joke at Darwin's expense, and use Islam to do it, suggests how complex a humor Trowbridge possessed—twenty years after the publication of *The Origin of Species* (1859), he had absorbed its lessons and was arguing dryly with it. (He himself believed, or feigned to believe, that a "vast unoutlined Presence" stood behind the "puppet-show of Evolution.") Trowbridge was hardly the first poet to do so, but the other examples I've found are minor stuff.

The old lovers grow intimate on shipboard—she needs a friend and he needs whatever men need. This does seem fatally indiscreet of her, as, despite the servant's reptilian manner, Guy Vernon's disappearance may amount to nothing. We see here the flaw in Florinda—once her belief in her husband is shaken, she's vulnerable to her jilted lover, though Rob Lorne in a gentlemanly way tries to convince her that her husband's absence is meaningless. After a tremendous storm (allowing the poet to rhyme *something seemed the matter as* with *Cape Hatteras*), the steamship docks in New York.

The novelette still has a long way to travel—there is the pitching and tossing of the two lovers' affections; the shock to her aunt and her friends when she returns without her husband; her temporizing explanations, which call forth from the author some unkind thoughts about women and truth; and then, well, a lot more plot. Florinda is feted on her homecoming to Brooklyn; but, when her husband's absence is prolonged, doubts rise among her friends (after indiscreet remarks by her maid, some even drop her acquaintance). It takes only another 150 more stanzas for all the mysteries to stand revealed. In the end, no one is quite what he seems. Many of the best stanzas are devoted, not to the working out of the creaky drama, but to the author's sidelong comments on manners, mores, and writers. Indeed, though Rob Lorne has gone back to a New York garret, he continues to compose his traveler's notes:

> *He plunged in work: his Southern notes he winnowed;*
> *And, much as he a mean deception spurned,*
> *In corresponding with the press, continued*
> *To date from countries whence he had returned,*
> *If he indeed had seen them; and so learned*
> *The art—imaginative and dramatic—*
> *Of writing foreign letters from an attic.*

Rob's friends "marvelled why such genius should remain/A beggar in a barren garret, when/He might, like many far less able men,/Become a lawyer, or a politician,/And strike for office, fortune, and position." *Plus ça change.*

Such observations, such attitudes struck or stricken, have their insistent pleasures, as do Trowbridge's lines—worthy of Pope—on society's Pecksniffery: when Guy belatedly arrives in New York, "once more Good Society/Inclined to take Florinda into favor./Those who had wronged her graciously forgave her." Trowbridge turns the screw deeper:

> *Society is full of politic,*
> *Smooth people, courteous, shunning all dissension,*
> *Who, should they find even Judas in their clique,*
> *Well-dressed, would treat him with polite attention,*

And hardly think it worth the while to mention
That most unfortunate misunderstanding
He is reported to have had a hand in.

The later sections of *Guy Vernon* never quite regain the energy and reck-
less insouciance of the first half—there's a slackening of detail, and the lines
are more infected by the sins of Trowbridge's minor work. (Many a reader
who has started *Don Juan* has failed to finish it—something in rhyme royal
and ottava rima encourages authors to go beyond their measure.) Neverthe-
less, Trowbridge often cleverly wrong-foots the reader, finding some twist of
plot truer to human relations than to the necessities of drama.

It is hard to imagine a serious novel with a heroine named Florinda—she's
the joke of her own name—and yet, however often he mocks her imprudence,
her silliness, her pretensions ("All in accordance with her utmost wishes,/
Even to the monogram upon the dishes"), the poet takes her seriously; her
sorrows are not cobbled up to make her a figure of comic humiliation. She is
perhaps unfairly dismissed in the finale (I'm enthusiastic enough about the
poem to obey the author's wish that the ending not be revealed), but she has
collaborated in her fate—and fates are often undeserved. *Guy Vernon* shows
in half-light the social exactions and suffocating restrictions deemed permis-
sible by mid-nineteenth-century society—the symbol Trowbridge uses is, al-
most inevitably, the lady's corset.

What Trowbridge has borrowed from Byron, he has borrowed cleverly,
down to the narrator who insinuates himself, anticipating our questions, tell-
ing the story partly for his own delight, professing ignorance of certain mat-
ters, and never quite receding into the background—the poet is the correl-
ative of his own invention, the devious servant Saturn. Trowbridge is even
at times Byron's equal as a student of human behavior—his description of a
madman, for example, seems a clinical diagnosis of manic depression:

"*Sometimes for several years he is exempt;*
Then the old indications: first, a strange
Irritability; then perhaps the attempt
To hide even from himself the coming change
In a forced gayety; then the symptoms range
From moody melancholy and fitful sadness
To deep despondency and downright madness!"

This "novelette" was, in length and form, unlike anything Trowbridge attempted before or after (his next-longest poem was not a quarter the length); its sly protest against social mores, its whirl of melodrama and comedy, its carelessness about the proprieties of poetry, its subtle intuitions of psychology, and its delirious and preposterous rhymes make it one of the most interesting descendants of *Don Juan*—it's the poem of a man who had gotten drunk one night on Byron and never recovered. (Unfortunately, at this period the reputation of Byron and *Don Juan* were at an ebb.)

The use of rhyme royal rather than Byron's ottava rima, whose every stanza requires a terrifying density of rhyme (*abababcc*), meant that Trowbridge didn't have to grope about for rhymes quite as manically, or maniacally. English is notoriously poor in its rhymes, though that's no fault of Byron, who relished the two- and three-syllable rhymes to which his invention was goaded. Rhyme royal, which rhymes *ababbcc*, would be merely a series of couplets if not for the second line in each stanza; that single interruption creates a form in which, however much they would like to move forward, the stanzas are forced to pause and recover. The trouble with rhyme royal and ottava rima is that the onrush of narrative often stumbles over the closing couplet of each stanza, where the poet is pressed to make a witty turn. Byron and Trowbridge used that hindrance to their advantage.

Trowbridge echoes Byron's ottava rima without going quite as far—indeed, you could say rhyme royal always comes up a line short. It was a great stroke, nevertheless, for the later poet to see the possibilities of the form in modern English. Rhyme royal had been out of favor since Drayton abandoned it when revising the book that became *The Barons' Wars*—when William Morris used it in "The Earthly Paradise," a decade before Trowbridge, he could make nothing better than a piece of taxidermy. If *Guy Vernon* reaches back to *Don Juan* and the heroic couplets of *The Rape of the Lock*, it reaches forward to Auden, who cast "Letter to Lord Byron" in rhyme royal.

Most poets are deservedly forgotten. Reputations are unmade even faster than they are made (for every poet who, like Byron, woke up famous, the reputations of a thousand died with them). Very few poets slip into anonymity only to be rediscovered later—the exceptions are usually those who, unpublished in their time, like Thomas Traherne and Emily Dickinson, left manuscripts behind. Byron offered Trowbridge a way out of the popular poetry in which he was mired (often poetry must move backward to move forward, retreat in order to advance), yet *Guy Vernon* proved a dead end. If there are other poems by Trowbridge half as good, I have been unable to discover them, though he showed an extraordinary facility with rhymed forms (including ottava rima—his poems have all the eclectic weariness of the nineteenth century) and just as astonishing a gift for mediocrity. He was always a little too quick to dip into the Gladstone bag of stock phrases.

Trowbridge never again picked up his pen for such corrosive satire. His later verse—he wrote for another ten years and then almost gave up poetry— returned to the country-bumpkin-come-to-the-city manners with which he began (the poet he most resembles is Whittier). Yet in its Southern and Caribbean scenes, *Guy Vernon* joins the books of the American outback—*Martin Chuzzlewit, The Confidence Man, Huckleberry Finn*—with its vision of a nation filled with forward-looking go-and-get-'em types and genial frauds, while the few stanzas devoted to New York society have the razor's edge of *The Bostonians*. The poem's cynical view of human existence (and especially of that most tenuous of gambles, hope) allowed a more sculptured line and a resistance to the treacle-coated sentiment that otherwise disfigured Trowbridge's verse. In *Guy Vernon*, for unknown reasons, he wrote savagely—I'd trade the whole of "Aurora Leigh" and "Enoch Arden" for the best passages in it.

Some of the authors in *A Masque of Poets*, it's said, entered into the diversion by masking their styles—but a few soon acknowledged their contributions or republished the poems under their own names. Not until his autobiography a quarter of a century later did Trowbridge publicly admit his part. *Guy Vernon* must have cost him long labor—why did he not claim this out-of-wedlock child sooner?* Perhaps that was not the sort of poet he wanted to be. Perhaps he felt the poem a failure—the reviewer in the *Literary World* called it "easy verse of no very high order"; yet the *Boston Transcript*, according to an early advertisement for the book, said *Guy Vernon* was "one of the cleverest literary productions of the last half-dozen years." The poem pointedly did not appear in Trowbridge's *Poetical Works*, published, like his autobiography, in 1903. Though he lived into his eighty-ninth year, John Townsend Trowbridge never reprinted *Guy Vernon*.

---

* Curiously, the *Arlington Public Library Catalogue-Supplement, 1881* has an author entry under Trowbridge for *Guy Vernon*. Trowbridge lived in Arlington and was one of the library's trustees. Perhaps as early as three years after *A Masque of Poets* he wanted to make a quiet out-of-the-way acknowledgment of his achievement.

Frost at Midnight

When the flesh departs, when the reader can no longer ring up the author to badger him about an obscure line or quiz him on his influences, there are only the material remains of his workshop. For Shakespeare we have virtually nothing—no foul papers (apart from the scraps of *Sir Thomas More* and what might be the palimpsest of revision in his own plays), no letters, only tittle-tattle from years after his death and the elegies of his friends: in other words, so little matter that speculation conquers all. Other poets, whether by accident or design, have been less stingy with their *disjecta membra*—Milton left the drafts to "Lycidas" that so shocked Charles Lamb; Coleridge enough trunkfuls to overturn the myths he told about himself; and many modern poets warehouses of overdue bills, tattered school-essays, and airline tickets, so many aisles of flotsam and jetsam that scholars get lost and never emerge.

To go behind the scenes of the poems, to find out how they came to being, gratifies impulses contrary and even conflicting. There is the simple curiosity to know how brilliant things began (few readers want to examine the drafts of a hack), to see if they are in reach of the ordinary grinder or the pure result of inspiration; there is the scholar's hunger to discover, in the backwaters of the poem, the source of the Nile; there is the critic's itch for context and explanation (the same longing that would ferret out the "original intent" of the authors of the Constitution rather than settle for the homely ambiguity of words on the page)—these motives share an exhaustion of means, of wanting to know all that can be known. (The metaphors of scholarly attention derive from gluttony rather than other deadly sins.) More darkly, consider the village gossip's appetite for the dirty secrets of composition, the suspicion that there is less than meets the eye, the prurient desire to tear off the fancy dress to show the poem's shabby underdrawers.

The draft of a poem can reveal too much but is always doomed to reveal too little. Poets sometimes consider wild alternatives, reject weak phrases even while scribbling them down, complicate by ambiguities they did not intend—looking at the trace evidence of drafts and notebooks may give the critic too much confidence in devising a meaning of his own. Drafts are always what has been rejected, the *pentimenti* of abandoned hope; and the crooked path to meaning may, in its course, leave only a trail of bread crumbs a poet wanted to brush from the page. W. H. Auden loved to disturb a line simply by tossing in a *not*, as a man faced with a quiet pool might throw in a rock—that doesn't mean he was equivocal. Like most great poets, he wanted to see what happened when he played with words. Sometimes a reversal of meaning betrays a deeper meaning.

Robert Frost was the most American of American poets after Whitman. When poets love their country, their poems usually suffer from nickel-plated patriotism (even good poets go bad in time of war) or a taste for writing down myths and calling them history; but you forgive Whitman and Frost their moments of naïveté and touches of sentiment because they saw squarely, un-mistakably, the figures in that imagined landscape. If every trace of the con-tinent were to vanish, you could almost reconstruct America from the clues left in *Leaves of Grass* (1855) and *North of Boston* (1914). These poets saw their country through an alien eye, with a sympathy few foreigners have granted—and it is through those few, like Alexis de Tocqueville and Frank Marryat and Isabella Bird, that we have known America for what it was.

Frost relished the country he found and lamented the country ways al-ready vanishing—he was an adopted New Englander but became more of a Yankee than most Yankees. Even now, almost half a century after his death, when people reach for a poet plainspoken and plain dealing, who says what he means and says it rare, they reach for Frost—yet Frost was never as simple as he seemed. His poems are full of anger, betrayal, wrenched pride, foolish-ness, all the frailties of men; and he brooded upon weakness like a philoso-pher. You have to drag younger readers to Frost today—in part because he's so badly taught, represented in anthologies by some of his most egotistical and kitsch-befouled verse. Even his darker poems, rubbed into lessons by genera-tions of high-school teachers (something there is that doesn't love a symbol), have lost their murderous underthoughts. A few of his best poems leave a sour aftertaste, because there's nothing worse than poetry gnawed down to meaning. (Frost famously said, "Poetry is what is lost in translation"; but it's usually forgotten that he added, "It is also what is lost in interpretation.") In the fluorescent light of the classroom, even "Stopping by Woods on a Snowy Evening" can seem genial as Whittier, a buggy ride with a cup of hot eggnog at the end. It's a poem that should be read only at midnight, and in freezing temperatures.

Frost was a dull, generally unrevealing letter writer who guarded his workshop door by destroying most of his rough drafts. From the days when he was a young man, however, he kept tablets and memo books in which he scrawled the private thoughts he worked into public speech. The raw sources for *The Notebooks of Robert Frost* form a seventy-year exhibit of American stationery—according to the descriptions, there are stitched pages in black buckram, loose-leaf binders, various strip-bound pads, a clothbound notebook that includes a calendar for 1910, a record book, a diary book bound in green canvas and another smaller than a man's palm, theme books, and spiral notebooks of the kind you can still pick up at Wal-Mart, some forty in all surviving, with scatterings of loose pages besides. Frost not only failed to destroy these homely volumes but, for reasons that are unclear, gave some of them away; even so, many have pages torn out, and a scattering of stray sheets comes from notebooks now lost or destroyed.

Frost picked notebooks up and threw them down as it suited him, used and abused them, wrote sideways or upside down, skipped pages, started at the rear and worked his way back—the poet, in other words, has not cooperated with those after his secrets. (You could say that Frost's brilliance in poems was where he refused to cooperate.) The editor, Robert Faggen, has made informed guesses in dating these worn survivals; but, as in all cases where the author is not by nature compelled to order, the difficulties quickly become impossibilities. An occasional date, a datable draft, a drafted occasion—these are rare anchor posts for the editor's conjectures. Some of the books must have stayed within reach for decades, so the editor can only throw up his hands and say, "1890s–1950" or "1910–1955."

What we find in this stolid volume are notes on teaching (the only things the editor has suppressed are lists of students and a grade roster, though even these might have proved of interest); notes toward lectures of the poet-takes-the-podium type, a genre that has almost died out; a mass of tedious philosophizing on man's place in society, from which the weaker strain of Frost's poems descends; much pointless noodling in prose, or whatever interim form the poet's thoughts assumed before they were pressed into verse; a few half-worked, pretentious dialogues (between, for example, a pair of Romans soon to be short-lived emperors); and the usual detritus and waste matter of notebooks—potential titles, addresses of acquaintances, scraps of conversation. Only rarely, amounting to perhaps a quarter of the whole, are there drafts of poems, some of them unpublished. (It's good to see Frost sawing away at half an idea for a poem without much chance of succeeding—it makes his best poems seem the more remarkable.) Every twenty or thirty pages the poet says something extraordinary, something you don't quite find in the poems—the stray and straying thoughts emphasize the governors Frost put on his poetry, or the filters he found there. The best of his poems, those dark and divided affairs, must have emerged from the same slovenly rumpus seen in the notebooks, their internal disorders intact.

We consider Frost a modern for dragging speech out of the preciousness of the *fin de siècle* and the studied airs of the Georgians into an idiom that a century later still sounds colloquial; except in his plastic and conversational handling of meter, he was the most formally conservative of the moderns, one who could call Pound, with a devilish wink, "Bertran de Bornagain." Frost sought a language that captured his own rhythm and intonation, and it took him a long while to find it. At the turn of the century, at an age when Keats was already dead, he was writing humdrum and decorative verse, prettily rhymed, that said nothing a florist doesn't say when he tries to sell you wilted flowers. A *Boy's Will* (1913) contains a good deal of such verse ("Thine emulous fond flowers are dead, too, / And the daft sun-assaulter, he / That frighted thee so oft . . ."); but Frost already understood that the American character could not be recorded in diction so tearstained and thumbed-over—it had to come from the "real language of men," as Wordsworth had called it more than a century before. However different their temperaments, in the depth of Frost's notice of the poor he was Wordsworth's heir (he preferred a vocabulary "not too literary; but the tones of voice must be caught always fresh and fresh from life"). In that first book, published when Frost was almost forty, there is already a scheme of human attention amid a naturalist's observation, though he has not yet purged the outdated syntax (the "laborers' voices late have died") or the stock ballad-figures of "maidens pale" and the "bravest that are slain."

Even the earliest notebook displays an ear for American English that obeys a rhythm Frost found superbly adaptable to pentameter.

I preached a sermon on him once He didnt come

Dont preach it now

He says dont preach it now.
Hes listening to us—every word we say [. . .]

Im feeling better since I had my spell.

Thats probably his son. He's state police

He said we were as good as under arrest.

Frost was listening to the voices around him and shaping them into verse. (Here and in the quotations that follow, for reasons that will become plain, I've made corrections to the editor's transcripts after consulting copies of the notebooks.) It's unfortunate that we cannot date such lines precisely; though they probably come from the period of *North of Boston* or later, they show how easily he molded homely speech into meter.

Once he had freed himself from the stale perfume of the nineteenth century, Frost created a vernacular flexible within the limit of his expectation—the limit of what he wanted the poem to provide. He was capable of vivid description—a woodsy altar's "black-cheeked stone and stick of rain-washed charcoal," a man's hand "like a white crumpled spider on his knee"—but he never let himself be lavish with metaphor. He parceled out his figures like a Yankee his nickels. Frost was not attracted, like Pound, to the romantic argot of the troubadours (hence "Bertran de Bornagain") or, like Eliot, taken with tormented metaphors of the soul. The New England poet is unsettling more than he admits to being unsettled: compare "Desert Places," a slightly terrifying poem, with "Hysteria," where Eliot seems, as elsewhere, frantic and overemotional—the differences of temper are instructive.

Some of the best passages in Frost's notebooks are a register of overheard conversation—we can make inferences from what he set down, because poets record what they fear to forget. (Frost was always on the lookout for cheating clerks and calculating egg-salesmen.) If his eavesdropping reminds us how sharp-eared the poems were, in the notebooks you have to wade through a lot of woolgathering and pot-bellied-stove philosophizing to get to it. Frost thought a lot about man and society; he read Darwin, Marx, and Freud while claiming to be an anti-intellectual; he wrote many lectures and essays that might have been herded together under a heading like "Civilization—What Is It?" or "Man! Has He a Future?" He spent decades at this and managed almost never to say a memorable thing. It's a pity these notebooks are largely the repository for Frost's musings on government, social justice, the idea of America, the problems of rich and poor, the experiment of Russia—his analysis and commentary are tedious to the extent that they are virtuous. You wish he could have seen what prose did to him; it turned him into the dullest of town councillors—garrulous, petty, a little mean-minded, but keenly interested in the improvement of the town curbstones. This side of Frost didn't make him a thinker; it made him a bore. If the poems came from such necessary tedium, we are the worse for being exposed to it; if such passages prove irrelevant to the imagination that so often exceeded them, we are no wiser for having read them.

Frost knew a lot about making poems but as little as most people about political philosophy. He mulled over the same questions a long while, coming to no conclusions, or far too many conclusions—in part because he didn't have the right intellect; in part, more sadly and humanly (the self-delusion in Frost makes him likable), because he fancied himself something of a backwoods philosopher. Being able to settle the antique questions of mind and matter is difficult even for a brain of a philosophical turn, which most poets lack—of the moderns, only Eliot could write convincingly about such things, and he had been trained in graduate school at Harvard. (Frost's virtues lie outside his thought—there's nothing here about government or society that couldn't have been written better by an educated garage mechanic.) Frost may have felt Eliot his rival philosophically as much as poetically—Eliot's sophistication and originality in writing about the designs of verse make him, on long acquaintance, all the more compelling as a poet.

Frost's insights are psychological, not philosophical—his philosophy is of the Yankee "good-as-most, better-than-some" variety. You feel that, ten minutes after meeting him (the Frost of the poems), you'd be chewing his tobacco and he'd be chewing yours. He was canny about people as no poet of his day except Eliot, who looked at others the way an entomologist looks at bugs, a little hungrily. Eliot scrutinized people with bland curiosity and the gifts of subtle analysis, though he never forgot that they *were* bugs, as in a way were Prufrock and Sweeney and Phlebas and the rest. (You might say that from the start Eliot suffered a condition common to people ripe for conversion— the men and women around him seemed hollow, flawed creatures, sinners all. But then at the start he was drawn to sinners.) Eliot was interesting as an anatomist only in the dissection of the soul—this makes *Four Quartets* one of the most mournful instruments of precarious faith. Frost, who had in him a touch of the Jeffersonian Deist, took sad delight in men because of their foibles—he recognized their defects and registered their small triumphs. He presented the human side of men as only a skeptic can, but a skeptic can be very hard to live with.

"Does Wisdom Matter?" was a fond topic for Frost's lectures, the editor reminds us, though it's hard to think of a subject more antithetical to the poet's gifts. His genius came, not in offering what might be called homespun horse-sense, but in rendering the quarrels with self that complicate, and even destroy, the characters in his poems. Frost is the great poet of human failing, limitation, stoicism, bleak outlook, frustration, and blind pride. Though he was not as bleak as Hardy, that acid-bitten pessimist, you read Frost on men and shake your head sadly and say, "It's so. It's so." He wanted to think well of men, but he flinched a little from them (consider the professor in "A Hundred Collars," who was perhaps a crude and knowing self-portrait)—he knew their limitations and through them, at least in his verse, something of his own. Then you read Frost on women and wonder what other poet since Shakespeare knew women so well. (Frost is the master-mistress of American verse.) There's a lot of hokum in Frost; but it's dry, wrenched-from-the-heart hokum—sometimes it's mere playacting, as in the sentimental poems (these represent the Frost Frost wished he were, or for a moment thought he was). His best poems come when the poem distracted him from the way he thought.

One of the early notebooks has a long list of titles, probably for articles in a farm journal to which the poet contributed, though you wish he'd written poems on them instead: "The Thankless Crime," "Ace & the Pigs," "The Philosophy of Potato Bugs," "The Moral Struggles of My Home Neighbors," "Nothing Lost in Sod," "Lives for a Poet in Business," "Crows & Potatoes," "The Worst Chicken," "The Question of a Feather." (Frost did write an essay with the last title for *Farm-Poultry*, as the editor neglects to mention; so it's likely that other titles were used as well.) You can detect, in the etiology of such titles, the pressure toward lesson, example, and homily that drives the poems and that produces the occasional maxim that keeps the reader in hope through deserts of philosophizing. Frost possessed an aphoristic intelligence—he was a splendid composer of epigrams and apophthegms and the like, perhaps too good for his own good, because once he settled on an idea he found it hard to get rid of (he was rarely, however, in the league of Heraclitus and Pascal, to whom the editor compares him). Frost would rub the old coin over and over until it shone, like the neighbor in "Mending Wall," who, against all evidence, keeps muttering, "Good fences make good neighbors." If a maker of sayings and saws believes his own wisdom, he becomes hidebound, because aphorism prevents more thinking than it provokes—fortunately most aphorists suffer from wit more than wisdom.

Frost's humanity was half invented by language; but the other half lay in the length he hauled a thought as it formed itself—he liked to go a furlong or two farther than expected. (Curly brackets enclose words Frost wrote in superscript.)

If its a good thing to be dead it must be half as good to be half dead

In unicellular life what is the difference between eating each other and marrying

Whenever I doubt if my letters {to a friend} are numerous or long enough I am sustained by the thought that it was not at a friend of anybody that Luther threw ink by the bottlefull.

I wouldnt trust a preacher any further than I could throw a church by the steeple.

Paints cost more than ink.

His night thoughts on writing, on the other hand, aren't disappointing so much as accidental and unconvincing—they seem mused upon, left-handed, not untrue but not quite true, either, as if the plumb hadn't dropped straight.

A poem is a triumph of association

A poem is a run of lucky recalls

You can always get a little more litterature if you are willing to go a little closer into what has been ~~considered~~ *left unsaid as unspeakable just as you can always get a little more melon by going a little closer to the rind or a little more dinner by scraping the plate with a table knife.*

Such thoughts seem not to derive from long meditation or profound insight— they're chance occurrences or "lucky recalls." The poet was brilliant almost despite himself (Frost's knowledge of self was always his insight into others);

his cracker-barrel cheeseparing got in the way of that black-browed, unre-
mitting Frost from whom the major poems came; and yet the major poems
needed a little of the cheeseparing in order not to descend too far into despair.
Frost's lesser self helped his great to be greater. In these notebooks, perhaps
only when he wrote "How many pains make an agony?" or "Mercy is illogical
kindness" did he reveal, or seem to reveal, something that lay troubled be-
neath the surface of the verse.

Occasionally, very occasionally, you see in the prose that instinct for the
half-articulated that animates the poems:

> *The saddest is not to see the poor longing for what they cant have: but to*
> *see a poor child happy in the possession of some thing too trifling for any-*
> *body else to want.*

> *Story of the blind old gardener. I guess them _____ aint a going to bloom.*
> *We'd a heard from them* ~~fore~~ *before this if they was.*

The blindness catches at the anecdote—you might say such blindness is more
metaphysical than physical (hearing would be the blind man's most trusted
sense, even as metaphor). I'd trade five hundred pages of these notebooks for
two more pages where the poet noticed people in so quirky and broadhearted
a fashion.

Frost's aphorisms almost never work unless dramatically rendered, which
makes "Something there is that doesn't love a wall" gnostic and shrewd, its
mysteries not expunged but exposed in syntax, while "The saddest thing in
life / Is that the best thing in it should be courage" is static, a dead fish of
wisdom, and not that interesting *as* wisdom. The younger Frost knew how to
give such sayings a darker face, how to invest them with the same frailty that
led to his monologues and dialogues, those playlets he called poems—the
older Frost was too busy saying important things. The memorable quotations
here are so obscurely buried, it might reasonably be asked whether a selection
a quarter of the length would not have served the reader better.

Some of the aphorisms are malicious when they mean to be wry, as when
Frost suggests that both rich and poor are a bad business; but the poet had
a meanness in him he knew (and makes calculated use of in his most deso-
late verse) and a meanness he did not know. Vain, selfish, jealous, Frost was
a nasty piece of work to his family; and all the Yankee warmth in his poems
could turn jellied and cruel toward those around him. (In the days she lay dy-

ing after a heart attack, his wife pointedly never asked to see him.) Yet think
of the other moderns—Eliot the cold fish whom Virginia Woolf accused of
wearing green face-powder; Pound iffy about Jews (Eliot, too); Stevens a mon-
ster to his underlings; Williams the small-town philanderer; and Moore an
emotionally stunted terror who used racial slang like "coon" and called her
American Indian students gnats and sluggards, according to her biographer.
You might think great poetry was a side effect of personality disorder.

Frost was not much possessed by a sense of humor—he could be mordant,
yes, with a Yankee distrust that sometimes reads like humor. He could man-
age a gruesome pun, but that's as far as humor usually took him (this makes
a reader wonder about the forms of attention Frost preferred). It adds a layer
to that mysterious onion Frost to find the notebooks pierced by doggerel and
light verse, though his light verse comes in any color you want, as long as it's
black. There are some sixty lines in boisterous couplets, unfortunately too
scrawled over and revised to quote, spoken by a Columbus four hundred years
at sea, and a draft of couplets in the voice of a dead Roman, which begins:

> A thousand years ago in Rome
> And I was in a catacomb
> Stretched out upon a stony shelf
> I had entirely to myself.
> I lay apparently becalmed
> From having died and been embalmed
> With toes upturned, arms composed,
> And you would never have supposed
> What I lay there a-thinking of—
> Of everything but mostly love.

(To make this and the next three quotations more readable, I've removed
canceled words and supplied punctuation where necessary. In the penul-
timate line here, I've also removed an extraneous "they," which must have
been an error of anticipation Frost neglected to delete.) These lines remind
us how strangely tender Frost could be. He saw just how weak men were, and
knew how weak he was himself; all that imperfection, all that taut resistance
to apology and amelioration—the unction, in other words, of walking around
and being a man—makes his crustiness likable. What he knew about men
who wanted to be certain about things produced one of his most ambivalent
poems, "The Strong Are Saying Nothing," which admires the stoic's philos-

ophy but understands the limitation of hope it imposes. There are also, from the notebook, these unpublished lines:

> *Aries, Taurus,*
> *Gemini, Cancer,*
> *Arise in chorus,*
> *What's the answer?*
>
> *Tell, oh, tell us,*
> *If it be a*
> *Blend of Hellas*
> *And Judaea.*
>
> *Who and what'll*
> *Solve the poser,*
> *Aristotle*
> *Or Spinoza?*

Frost cast a wary eye upon religion, the eye of an atheist who refuses to blink, all the while professing to be an orthodox believer (some think him as much an Arminian heretic as Milton). How hard he wrestled with the invisible—this was an old Yankee inheritance, to be sure, but we simplify the past by forgetting its subtleties; and in Frost there is at least as much religious conscience and torment as in Donne, or Eliot, or Geoffrey Hill. The notebooks allowed him to be a little more unbuttoned on the subject than in print, especially as he grew famous and became ROBERT FROST in capitals big as tenpins. He was willing to ask the metaphysical questions, the questions to which there are never answers (he was in any case a poet more suited to questions than answers); but the poems didn't always find that a diet of philosophy agreed with them.

Frost was not a systematic thinker—thank goodness, I'm tempted to say—though there are a few places in the notebooks where he tries to categorize experience in the manner of Auden or Kierkegaard. Frost had a curiosity about science (he seems to have taken his ideas from popular articles), which is not surprising, when science offers so much to a poet for whom homily mediates between scientific hypothesis and the certitudes of faith. There are numerous notebook pages that puzzle over some scientific notion or try to mold it into poetry, as he did in "Desert Places." Such poems remind us, not just how rarely poetry borrows from science now, but how reluctantly it is drawn to homily. Frost was interested in what the individual revealed to the general, not how each peculiar soul suffered his torments. The public record exceeded the private case—you can see Frost's crippled private life, but darkly.

Sometimes the darkness was too dark. It's tempting to think that Frost could write poems so gloomy even he couldn't publish them, their sourness shot through with a sardonic glee at how awful the human condition can be:

> *There were two brothers come home from their trial.*
> *They took of[f] their coats with a terrible smile,*
> *And one of them calmly said to the other,*
> *"The court says we didn't kill father and mother.*
>
> *The court's word in such things is final for men.*
> *Our neighbors can never accuse us again.*
> *The worst they can say to us under the laws*
> *Is Som[e]one was guilty: if we weren't, who was?*
>
> *With the judgement of God, we may still have to cope,*
> *But not for a good many years, let us hope."*

There are many such amusements in the notebooks, places where Frost unbuttoned his vest, or took the road less traveled, or rattled on endlessly—and then abandoned such things to the dead matter of the spiral pad or the buckram-covered pages. You sense that in the notebooks Frost felt he was milking himself, as Milton's daughters milked Milton. (Notebooks are where a Protestant confesses—or were until poetry became the confessional.) Little of this, however, gets us much closer to Frost the poet, so it is fortunate that these books house substantial drafts of two long poems he never published, "A Bed in the Barn," which was meant for *Steeple Bush* (1947), and "Old Gold for Christmas," which struggles through a few incomplete drafts and discards fragments elsewhere.

"Old Gold for Christmas" begins on a freezing night, when a stranger helps an elderly man who has fallen to the icy pavement. The good Samaritan, who serves as narrator, has little to do but listen to the old man's tale:

> *"You stand and let me lean on you a minute*
> *Till I can think. Don't ask me who I am.*
> *I'm all mixed up from having been retired."*

> He rued a bloody knuckle in the street light
> As a girl gloats on her engagement ring.
> I helped him shoulder one of his suspenders.
> "I've been down on some ice and lost my coat.
> The empty busses at this time of night
> Are so insane to get home to their car barns
> They'd as soon knock you down as pick you up.
> I must have thrown my coat away at one.
> The place I've got to get to is a farm
> That's out here on a side road with two rows
> Of sugar maples leading up to it—
> The air, lit up by seven burning maples,
> In case you had a mind to take me there
> Or rout out someone else to do it for you.
> You're on foot walking so you can't yourself.
> It's where I live and claim my residence
> To vote at when there's any need to vote.
> The house is not much, but the barn is standing.
> There! midnight I suppose or one o'clock!"

This is from the second draft we have; but no doubt there are drafts missing, as the opening lines in the initial draft have been neatly transcribed. Frost begins the story with all the confidence of the poems in *North of Boston*. The details have that roughed-up pathos that makes his characters seem party to the injury that is the world—the old man looking at his knuckle with pride, the way a "girl gloats on her engagement ring"; the furious, fruitless gesture of hurling his coat after the departing bus (a horse-drawn trolley bus, perhaps, or one of the electrified sort that still run on the streets of Boston); the foxy Yankee rectitude of "It's where I live and claim my residence / To vote at when there's any need to vote." And then the farm with its "burning maples" (seven of them, and *burning*, details unsettled by the bush of Moses, the seven branches of the menorah), yet modified by the old man's disarming modesty, a modesty almost proud: "The house is not much, but the barn is standing."

Frost was agile at hard-grained details—his characters live, not just at the mercy of the trivial, but through its quiet, insistent force. The poem is the observation of distress and rock-bound pride found in "The Death of the Hired Man" or, more pertinently, "Snow," where a local preacher stops at a house and then, against the pleas of the couple there, pushes on into a blizzard—he does it because he has to, because it's a sort of calling. Frost loved such characters—you sense he tried to find stories for them. The tale in "Old Gold for Christmas" starts so well, it's a mystery why the poet couldn't finish it. The delicacy of Frost's judgment lies in the observation "I'm all mixed up from having been retired." The confusion of meaning is part of the old man's confusion; but you feel he has it right, that retirement had made him lose his bearings—and he has *been* retired, as he says. It may be just an acknowledgment that time has passed, but it sounds involuntary. There's a mark of attentive charity in "I helped him shoulder one of his suspenders," where the disheveled man's awkwardness, his slight haplessness and hopelessness, make him the more vivid. He isn't beyond anger at his plight, at his treatment by the buses. Partly this is a poem about the future. The old man has been turned out of his job, or turned himself out; and the world rushes onward, in the progress of those buses that will not stop and the street lights (now electric, because they go out "on one sudden breath") to which the old man objects. Frost handles the symbols so quietly, you hardly notice—the lights *are* going out for the man; and the poet has the right simile, "like candles on a birthday cake." Frost knew a lot about being old, even when he was young.

Once you start noticing, it's hard to stop. I love the old man's selfish practicality: "The thing for us is to stay propped together"—it's good for him, but he tries to make it seem good for the stranger, too. And the narrator, though he wants to get away from this grasping elder, can't quite resist him (the narrator is the wedding guest and the old man the Ancient Mariner). The stranger wants to bring the man to a house nearby, the only one with a light still on. The old man knows who lives there:

> "No one I'd care to introduce you to.
> He's a church preacher and a baseball pitcher—
> Combined. He pitches for us Saturdays
> And preaches to us Sundays. He can pitch.
> Only they claim he's too wild for his strength.
> Catchers cant hold him, or he'd make the league.["]

These lines were deleted from the first draft. You feel that the two occupations are reciprocal and collusive, pleasure one day, preaching the next, strikeouts then sermons. "He can pitch," the old man says mildly of the preacher—he's silent about the preaching. The very thing that spoils the pitching probably makes the preacher overzealous at the pulpit (he's the kind of preacher who might turn the Devil into Casey at the Bat). No wonder the old man doesn't want to be dragged to the house. When we do meet the preacher-pitcher, or pitcher-preacher, it turns out that the old man was once his catcher, "in the bare handed days before the mitt." That pushes their acquaintance back to the 1870s or thereabouts (the first major-league player to wear a glove was in 1875, and he was embarrassed to do so).

Frost's method, so far as method reveals itself here, is to drive the action of the poem forward until the lines grow fragmentary, then start again, not necessarily at the beginning, trying to consolidate passages as he goes along or striking off into a later passage that might be included. (Frost formed his lines into pentameter as he wrote—you sense this even in the shattered phrases where narrative breaks down.) He seems to have felt that "Old Gold for Christmas" was too digressive; but the character of Frost lies in digression, and he should have given way to his impulses.

Something goes wrong with the story, and the drafts begin to thrash about trying to find a solution. Part of the problem is the old man. He's a little "touched," and there turns out to be no farm. He worked for forty years firing the furnace at a local factory, given a wage so paltry, the entire sum could be paid once a year in gold—probably with a single coin, a double eagle. He never asked for a raise; indeed, he became proud of his status, as though aristocratic, of being paid just once a year at Christmas. Frost can't seem to settle on a way to tell the old man's story, how much to render through other characters (in "The Death of the Hired Man," the other characters do all the talking). Once it's revealed that he's partly mad, something must happen— but nothing much *can* happen, other than the inevitable tragedy. Perhaps the revelation of madness, handled with Frost's usual judgment of the off-center center, would have proved enough to set the tragedy in motion. Instead, he plunges into further drafts, changing the story slightly but getting further away from what made the earliest draft affecting. Frost tries various shifts: in the first draft, the preacher tells the old man's story, while the man sits doltishly by; in the second, the old man himself tells it, and the preacher-pitcher and his wife become simply "some people in the nearest house" and then are written out entirely. A son, silent in the first version, does duty in the second— but he's a less interesting character than the Billy Sunday–style preacher.

There's an ending, the right ending—some weeks later the old man fools another passerby into taking him out to the farm he claims to own ("The place I'm trying to get to all my life"—it *is* a kind of Paradise, but it's also death) and freezes to death. There's the ending, but Frost can't quite get there from where he is. The third draft is even more fragmentary than the second. Frost returned to the poem briefly in a later notebook, but then seems to have given it up.

The reader who watches closely as the poem emerges from the ruck of composition (emerges, only to sink back unfinished) will know much more about Frost the craftsman, about how feelingly he manipulates the lines and how what he sought was the force of plainness, not the vigor (or waste, a favorite theme) of decoration. Poetically speaking, he was a clapboard Presbyterian, not a gilded Catholic. The notebooks, though they are not at all devoted to poems, at least in the surviving pages, nevertheless give a sense of how the poems were assembled. Perhaps, in a way, all the dead matter of these notebooks proves merely what the poet needed to discard or discharge before he could write poetry. It would be a mistake to view them as waste without purpose (Eliot, Frost's *bête noire* at times, once referred to a poet's "necessary laziness"). The poet's task is to find a purpose for what others call waste, and to the poet all chronicles are chronicles of wasted time.

Robert Faggen deserves every credit for taking on a difficult, unenviable task, the sort for which thousands of small successes go unpraised but every slip is damning. The paleographer is the drudge of academic scholarship, though the most useful book for a reader is a good edition of a poet's letters, drafts, or fragments—most volumes of theory will be out of date by the week after next, but the editions of Coleridge's notebooks or Dickens's letters may never be superseded. Faggen is one of the leading figures in "Frost studies," as they are amusingly called (leading to meteorological phrases like "new directions in Frost studies" and "possible futures for Frost studies"), an editor with long practice reading Frost's difficult, geometric hand. He should be a trustworthy guide to this crabbed, private, willful poet; but in just about every way possible the edition goes wrong.

The reader's confidence is shaken by the strained reading, on the first page of the introduction, of Frost's comparison of his poems to a child's "ordinaries," meaning toys and small possessions. Faggen calls this an "extraordinary use of 'ordinary' as a noun"; but it's not extraordinary at all, though the meaning has fallen out of use. He then compares the word to religious ordinaries— devotional manuals or long-headed ecclesiastics—which is hardly what Frost had in mind (you might as well say it "resonates" with other old uses, the ordinary as courier, or customary meal, or lecture, or part of a fleet laid up and not in commission). One can ignore the blather the editor feels obliged to spout ("Robert Frost's poetry has long compelled readers with its clarity, dramatic tension, and vocal presence. Its pleasure arises from the promise of cognitive order") but not the plague of typographical errors that infects the text, so many the reader begins to doubt that all the misspellings in the transcription are Frost's. (At one point the editor refers to a "jllegible phrase," though it isn't "jllegible" at all.)

From the start, there are problems of pagination. The notes and index refer to page numbers notebook by notebook, so "1.1r" means Notebook 1, page 1 recto. Unfortunately, there are two pages known as 1.1r; wherever Frost included some loose sheets or jumped to the back of a notebook and soldiered forward, similar confusions occur (in addition, the numbering of Notebook 26 starts over halfway through without explanation, and there is a bad case of misnumbering in the middle of Notebook 31). The group of loose and miscellaneous sheets called, somewhat unhappily, Notebook 47 has no fewer than fifteen pages that could be termed 47.1r—but the editor is too canny for that. When reference is required, he blithely refers to "47," which means the poor reader must paw through thirty-seven pages of text to find the passage he seeks. (Worse, this "notebook," for no good reason, collects sheets from two different libraries—best of luck to the researcher who doesn't notice a footnote to that effect, buried in the middle of the text. Worse still, some pages allegedly at Dartmouth are either missing or at some other location.) The editorial practice is baffling in other ways. Frost sometimes skipped a page while scribbling down his thoughts (perhaps the following page was filled already or contained some pertinent digression). The editor rarely points out where the passage continues a couple of pages later, leaving the reader mostly to fend for himself.

The index is helpful as far as it goes, and it goes only as far as being unhelpful—the reader will soon discover that it is very difficult to find anything. Frost mentions a man named Bently or Bentley, but the notes offer no assistance, and the index fails to include him; context suggests this is simply Richard Bentley, the cantankerous seventeenth-century classicist. Where is the entry for the poem "The Bed in the Barn," or for one of Frost's earliest poems, "The reason of my perfect ease," or for the essay notes titled "Education Seventy Years Afterward"? If you want to look at all the pages containing drafts of "Old Gold for Christmas," the index refers to some lines in Notebook 35 that seem from another poem altogether, while there are half a dozen or more pages in Notebook 1 that belong to the poem and go unrecognized. Where are the index entries for Lenin and Quisling, Josiah Royce and Mary Wollstonecraft, Benedict Arnold and Aaron Burr, among a crowd of other unhappy absentees? Indeed, where are the entries for Athens and Sparta (there's one for Greenwich Village); or Dartmouth, Vassar, and Chapel Hill; or Jove, Jesus Christ, and God? Or the Bible? In notebooks that speak so much of religion, these last are unforgivable omissions. There are incomplete entries for Chesterton, Einstein, Emerson, Freud, Job, Jonah, Keats, Lindbergh, Wordsworth, and far too many others. Worse, Walter Pater appears as William Pater; but by this time that's hardly surprising.

Say you recall reading an anecdote about Agassiz. The index and one of the notes steer you confidently to 6.24r (Notebook 6, page 24 recto), a page that does not exist. Or, should you be curious about Frost's notion of Kipling, the index entry reads, in part, "Kipling, Rudyard, 4.33r; 66r, 25r; 6r; 15; 17.32r. (Entries in the same notebook are separated by commas, different notebooks by semicolons.) The first and last of these references are perfectly clear and happen to be correct. The notation "66r" is a mystery; "25r; 6r" should be "7.25r, 6r"; and "15" should be "15.11r." Even if the middle pair were corrected, you might start thumbing through Notebook 7, find that page 6r is blank, and give up—but you should have kept thumbing, because there's a second "6r" further on. It might have seemed precise to adopt this mode of reference; but the many ambiguities of pagination should have suggested the folly being indulged. (The editor seems not to have considered that convenient device, the page number of the volume itself.) Two other index entries for Kipling steer the reader into the thirty-seven-page swamp of Notebook 47, without compass or direction.

Many of the notes are splendidly well informed. Faggen has nosed out inviting connections and provided much of the basic matter for understanding Frost's stray references and allusions, without ever being the sort of editor who condescends to the reader. Nonetheless, after a while I wondered if he possessed the basic cultural knowledge necessary to interpret Frost. How could anyone of even modest learning transcribe one line in these notebooks as "Sog Magog Mempleremagog" and then, to compound ignorance with inattention, fail to make note of it? Gog and Magog famously appear in Ezekiel; though Frost's capital *s* resembles his capital *g*, there is no excuse for this. (*Memphremagog*, the word Frost actually wrote next, is the name of a glacial lake between Vermont and Quebec.) What should the reader think when Frost writes "Co ex co ex co ex"? Or, in some light verse,

> *To sit there on a waterlog*
> *And with your Breck a Re ok co ex*
> *Ventriloquize the tranquil bog?*

He should think *Aristophanes*! These lines imitate the famous chorus of frogs in *The Frogs*, "Brekekekex koax koax"; but they go unnoted.

If ignorance of the Bible and Aristophanes is no bar to being an editor, perhaps some acquaintance with the historical and cultural milieu in which Frost flourished might be considered an advantage; yet the editor misses an obvious reference to FDR's attempt at court packing and fails to note that a "tumbledown dick preacher" alludes to Tumbledown Dick, the nickname given Richard Cromwell, Oliver Cromwell's son and hapless successor. Frost says he reads obituaries, according to the transcription, in the *Times* and the *Tribute*—that should, of course, be the *Tribune*, as a look at the notebook page confirms. And how does an editor with any knowledge of eighteenth-century printing manage to transcribe a sentence as "No one ever took a wife for wise except by mistake in reading old print Wife Wife"? This makes no sense. Frost has in fact *painfully* printed out, to make the distinction clear, "wife wiſe" to show that printer's type for the old long s was easily mistaken for ſ, as any first-year grad student knows—the title page of *Paradise Lost* looks like *Paradiſe Loſt*. No editor is perfect, but such errors suggest a level of incuriosity fatal to a good one. (The blindness to typography, for which the carelessness of the editor and the complacence of the publisher should be roundly scolded, means that initial apostrophes are habitually reversed.)

Given the hard labor such an edition requires, a tolerance for mistakes might be the price of gratitude. There are few jobs more thankless than that of an editor tasked to decipher a dead man's hand. Faggen has slaved thousands of hours over writing often snagged like old fishnet. Frost usually wrote with a fountain pen, his script stiff, juddery, hairpin angled; and he did his editor no favors (though who in the privacy of his notebooks would think to do such favors?) by occasionally dropping a letter while writing at speed or malforming letters, especially at the end of a word. His terminal *r* can be mistaken for *s*, his *d* confused with *cl*, his *a* with *ci*, and his *p* identified with no letter known in this world (it looks like the design for a billhook). He failed to cross *t*'s or dot *i*'s and left punctuation for the most part to the imagination. These are just the things, however, that bring torments of joy to the paleographer's heart. There are lines where the editor has made sense of what to most readers would look like chicken scratches.

Editorial procedure, however it is understood, must aim for clarity of description and accuracy of transcription, both of which this edition fails to achieve with a certain consummate brilliance. Obliged though readers must be for this unknown Frost, the transcription is a scandal. To read this volume is to believe that Frost was a dyslexic and deranged speller, that his brisk notes frequently made no sense, that he often traded the expected word for some fanciful or perverse alternative. Even a casual comparison of the text with the five photofacsimiles included in the introduction shows a discomforting degree of inaccuracy. I would not normally stake my eyes against those of an editor who had spent years in company with these notebooks; yet, having requested a dozen or two photocopies from the Dartmouth library, where most of the books are housed, I shook my head in wonder at the editor's wild suppositions, casual sloppiness, and simple inability to set down what was on the page before him. (I ordered another dozen, and another dozen, and kept going.) Words are added or subtracted, punctuation missing where it is present and present where it is missing, canceled words unrecorded, and sense rendered nonsensical. In this long volume, there are typographical errors that suggest a failure to proofread the final text against the notebooks and enough highly inventive misreadings to fill a phone book. Frost wrote in a rush and was not a perfect speller ("literature" comes out at least three different ways), but he was not the maniac speller the editor makes him. He suffered, as many writers do, the occasional stretch of wayward syntax; yet, in most of the cases where Frost's words seem deranged, a glance shows that it was not Frost but his editor who was mad.

Take, for example, a passage Frost jotted down for "Education Seventy Years Afterward." The editor offers this transcription of a few lines:

> *Thus there is another rule of life I ~~never~~ {always think of when} I see a player serving two or three bats once before he goes to the plate to fan pitcher with one bat. Always try to have arranged that you were doing something harder and more disciplinary [~~illegible~~] than ~~what you~~ the picktie exhibition you ~~have before you~~ are about to make of yourself.*

This has a jostling, out-at-elbows, stenographic air, the syntax going wherever the thought drifts. The batter metaphorically serves up his bats before, by some topsy-turvy turn of phrase, he fans the pitcher; and there is a country redolence to the "picktie exhibition," whatever that might be—no doubt some blue-ribbon event at a county fair. Unfortunately, this is nothing like what Frost wrote, which I would read as follows (the underlining notes the differences):

> *<u>Then</u> there is another rule of life I ~~never~~ {always think of when} I see a ~~m~~ player <u>swing</u> two or three bats <u>at</u> once before he goes to the plate to fan <u>the</u> <u>pitches</u> with one bat. Always try to ~~ha~~ have arranged that you were doing*

something harder and more disciplinary ~~that~~ than ~~what you~~ the <u>public exi-bition</u> you ~~have before you~~ are about to make of yourself.

In the course of two sentences, the editor has committed three comical mis-readings, overlooked two words and a misspelling ("exibition"), and left strike-outs untranscribed or wrongly transcribed—ten errors, four of them serious. The editor fails even to mention the ruin of a poem drafted at the top of the page. A large part of the page has been torn out, mutilating the draft; but about forty words remain legible at the beginning of the lines and perhaps an-other dozen on the reverse. Given how rare Frost's drafts are, you wonder why in the notes the editor did not even allude to such lines. The transcription is not much better later in the passage: what the editor abandons as "someone who said in [illegible]" is actually "someone who said in Latin."

Or take these relatively simple and cleanly written paragraphs from Note-book 22. Here is Faggen's version:

That ~~was are reason~~ Middlebrow! that was a new one to me and I am afraid it was mean to be for my embarrassment. It was as much as to say ~~invidi-ously~~ you old [illegible] what of ~~at~~ the level of intellect so to call it where you at which you vote and peddle rhyme sheets. It was invidious perhaps. Anyway ~~I was chastened~~ it was all to the good. I was chastened {brought up dull in my slang} and put in my place. But I it was better than good: it furnished me a new refrain for a poem some day.

> *High brow*
> *Low brow*
> *Middle brow*
> *And no brow*

With acknowledgments to Polybius and Pound {the poem} it would the story of the girl Hannof the Carlingian captured on the coast of West Af-rica outside the Gates. It would begin:

> *She had no brow but a mind of her own*
> *She wanted the sailor to let her alone*
> *She didn't like sailors she didn't like men*
> *They had to shut her up in a pen.*
> *She was quite untractable quite contrary [b.i.]*

Hannof the Carlingian? That mysterious "[b.i.]" gives a sense of what has gone wrong—it's the editor's note to himself that the line was written in black ink. He has somehow forgotten its purpose and, instead of using a footnote to record the change in ink, as elsewhere, mindlessly included it as part of Frost's passage. The lines above might more accurately have been transcribed thus:

> *That ~~was a new on~~ Middlebrow! <u>That</u> was a new one to me and I am afraid it was <u>meant</u> to be for my embarrassment. It was as much as to say ~~invidiously~~ {<u>you,</u>} you old <u>skeezicks</u> what ~~at~~ {<u>of</u>} the level of intellect so to call it ~~where you~~ at which you vote and peddle <u>ryhme</u> sheets. It was invidious perhaps. Anyway ~~I was chasened~~ it was all to the good <u>if</u> I was <u>chasened</u> {brought up <u>to date</u> in my slang} and put in my place. But it was better than good: it furnished me a new refrain for a poem <u>someday</u>.*

> > *High brow*
> > *Low brow*
> > *Middle brow*
> > *And no brow.*

> *With <u>acknowledgements</u> to Polybius and Pound ~~it~~ {the poem} would <u>be</u> the story of the girl <u>Hanno</u> the <u>Carthaginian</u> captured on the coast of <u>west</u> Africa outside the Gates. It would begin*

> > *She had no brow but a mind of her own*
> > *She wanted the <u>sailors</u> to let her alone*
> > *She <u>didnt</u> like sailors she <u>didnt</u> like men*
> > *They had to shut her up in a pen.*
> > *She was quite <u>intractable</u> quite contrary*

That the editor provides an erudite note on Hanno the Carthaginian makes his initial error mystifying (*Hannof the Carlingian*, indeed). I have again noted the differences by underlining—here the editor has fobbed off on Frost misspellings he did not commit and overlooked the misspellings he did (*ryhme* and *chasened* here—in previous paragraphs the editor accuses Frost of writing *ofr*, *tow*, and *palin* where the poet plainly wrote *for*, *two*, and *plain*). Faggen has been unable to read a couple of difficult phrases that did not take long to puzzle out; has missed strikeouts, capitals, and terminal *s*'s; has failed to record where phrases are written in superscript; and has made Frost's start at a logical phrase like "a new one" into "are reason." (The editor also has a bad habit of throwing the phrases revised in superscript before rather than after the draft phrases they replace.) I counted some two dozen errors in the three paragraphs leading up to this passage, so the problems are not local. The editor seems to have worked in haste (though not yet repented at leisure). Two sentences later, we find:

> They they hung it up in the temple of Ashtaroth as hide [linigue] for har-riners. Tunique ought to be rhymed somehow with Runic—Runique.

Linigue? Harriners? Tunique? Runique? This should read:

> ~~They~~ _They_ hung it up in the temple of _Astaroth_ as _a_ hide _unique_ for _hairi-ness. Unique_ ought to be rhymed somehow with _Punic-Punique._

And on it goes, page after page of appalling errors and flat misreadings, twenty or thirty per page at times, some trivial, most trying, too many disastrous. Frost is a much clearer and more sensible writer than Faggen's transcripts suggest. Two pages after the passage above, we discover this:

> It runs poor spirited to wonder if sometimes when half gods go if cant quar-ter godst that arrive and so on down to no gods at all.

That should read:

> It _seems_ poor spirited to wonder if sometimes when half gods go _it isn't_ quarter _gods_ that arrive and so on down to no gods at all.

Or, early in the notebooks:

> History that coming / I [illegible]

Every word of this is wrong. Frost in fact wrote:

> _His son thats coming's / ~~Is~~ State Police_

Passages have been so mangled, they bear only dim relation to Frost's thought. In one of my favorite lines—it's almost mean to quote it—the editor offers, "I know someone who has been given money to consider bear one year," which sounds suitably woodsy. Alas, Frost wrote "to consider *fear* one year" (fear had been mentioned in the sentence just preceding). It's as if the editor had forced some grad student to type up the rough notes, given them a cursory glance, and then dispatched them to print—how else explain places where a query meant to remind him of a suspect reading became a question mark never made by Frost's pen?

The editor does no better with a tangled draft of poetry. Here is his version of a passage in Frost's rollicking doggerel on Columbus:

> *My name is Christopher Columbus*
> *I cant be moved by ~~all this~~ {?threat} and rumpus*
> *Put up your knives and go below*
> *We're members of the O. {HO Hi Ho} O. Hi.O*
> *A stock exchange affiliate*
> *I ~~know~~ {see}* **who** *you are!*
> *~~Lets hear some more~~! Vociferate!*
> *For such a husky ~~lot~~ {herd} of boys ghostly noise*
> *You make a ~~very husky~~ {very [illegible]} noise*
> *~~It does you fools us good to strike~~ {you strike and strike and strike and*
> *   strike}*
> *I end by sailing where I like.*

The word in bold type has wandered in from the editor's imagination. I would transcribe these lines as follows:

> *My name is Christopher Columbus*
> *I cant be moved by ~~all this~~ {threats and} rumpus*
> *Put up your knives and go below*
> *We're members of the [two letters illegible: ?O I.] O. {HO Hi ~~O~~ Ho O. Hi. O}*
> *A stock exchange affiliate*
> *~~Lets hear some more~~ {I ~~know~~ {see} you are}! vociferate!*
> *For such a husky ~~lot~~ {herd} of boys*
> *[in margin: ~~you know~~] You make a ~~very husky~~ {very ~~feeble~~} noise {ghostly*
> *   noise}*
> *[in margin: ~~You see You see~~ {~~know~~}] ~~It does you fools~~ ~~no~~ ~~good to strike~~ {you*
> *   strike and strike and strike and strike}*
> *I end by sailing where I like.*

It's hard to know which are worse, the misreadings, the omissions, or the out-right inventions. Here, even more hilariously, is the last couplet on the page, followed by some marginal couplets, first in the editor's transcript:

> *Colundres! Christophes! No less!*
> *What no one left alive but you*
>
> *He boards again*
> ~~*Columbus boards*~~ *in I [illegible]*
> *Till someone comes up over [side]*
>
> *The meekly [?vaunt] single file*
> *Columbus brooch alone awhile*

This, however, is what Frost wrote:

> <u>*Columbus*</u>*!* <u>*Christopher*</u>*! No less!*
> *What no one left alive but you*
>
> ~~*Columbus broods*~~ *{He* <u>*broods*</u> *again} in* <u>*Spanish pride*</u>
> *Till someone comes up over side*
>
> <u>*They*</u> *meekly* <u>*vanish*</u> *single file*
> *Columbus* <u>*broods*</u> *alone awhile*

"Columbus brooch alone awhile" ought to have given the editor pause. On the following page, he has "They've named it for Americas," which is pretty obviously "Americus."

In places above, the editor has given an inaccurate idea of when Frost is revising by superscript and when he's starting a new line (he can't even de-scribe his own practice accurately in his pages on editorial procedures). To show how complicated it is to render poetic revision, here's a complex line in the editor's version:

> *But that* ~~*you*~~ *{brute} at [illegible]* ~~*in the*~~ *{our}* ~~*way.*~~ *{[illegible]} {*~~*desert*~~ *{sea-coast} bars our way}*

The editor notes that the last bracketed phrase falls below the line, and the word "seacoast" below that; but he has disfigured the draft in all sorts of ways.

Frost originally wrote "But that *great [?lump]* is in our way," then substituted "brute" for "great" and tried, successively, "reef" and "coast" for "[?lump]" and then "desert bars our way" and finally "seacoast." A more accurate transcript, using the editor's sigla, might be rendered thus:

> But that ~~great~~ {brute} [?~~lump~~] {~~reef coast~~} ~~is in the~~ {our} ~~way~~ {desert {seacoast} bars our way}

The problems continue—on one page, the editor substitutes "Who are you marring with now?" for "Who are you *marrying me to* now?"; on others, "And if I did today" for "And if I *died* today," "Lets not be personal!" for "Lets not be *personal*," "And put in y in some fold of her dress" for "And put *it by* in some fold of her dress," and, amazingly, "In colleness or in the quest of fruit" for "In *idleness* or in the quest of fruit." He's at times willing to put down any old rubbish, however nonsensical, rather than stare long enough to see the homely meaning. It's a pity that the editor has apparently misidentified the location of certain pages in Notebook 47, because I'd bet the farm that what the transcript has as "The use of lipstitch and howdy . . . in public should be forbidden" is the much less inventive "*lipstick* and *powder*."

These transcriptions are full of errors so basic, it's difficult to see how they escaped the attention of the editor or *his* editors. Many are trivial; but it makes a difference whether Frost wrote, as the editor has it, that he "may be so attracted to Russian" instead of "*Russia*," or that players "got know down" instead of "got *knocked* down," or that there was frozen ground men might "dig your rave in if your dead" instead of "dig your *grave* in if *you died*." Or, to continue this sad catalogue, Frost wrote, not "all he is parinian" but "all he is *poor man*"; not "wild hearths and deserts" but "wild *heaths* and deserts"; not "go to wrack and mine" but "go to wrack and *ruin*"; not "two rows of rock samples" but "two rows of rock *maples*"; not "He might have arrested the thinking folk" but "He might have *parroted* the thinking folk." I would be surprised if the errors in the whole volume numbered fewer than ten thousand. Not a page of transcription can be considered trustworthy; and Harvard University Press, if it has any regard for its reputation, should withdraw this edition and subject the transcripts to microscopic examination—and the final text to the hawkeyed copyediting and proofreading it somehow failed to enjoy.

These notebooks are not for the casual reader. But is Frost's poetry for the casual reader any longer? Is there even a casual reader to attract? Here you have the most technically restrictive of the modernists, who reformed the pentameter line until it became expressively vernacular. (You might think reformers were a dime a dozen, but the list is short: Marlowe, Shakespeare, Milton, Pope, Wordsworth, Browning, and few others.) Sometimes the Whig narrative of modernism emphasizes only the breaches and ruptures of form, which consoles us in our fallen free-verse ways. This tends to strand Frost as a fuddy-duddy, a man who couldn't play tennis without a net. Eliot and Pound, however, thought of *vers libre* as a temporary breach in the manners of poetry. They kept the free and the metrical in constant creative tension, Pound writing lines with the memory of meter, Eliot flexibly using tradition where it bore upon his matter (or where it simply suited him). Wallace Stevens's elegant pentameter is usually ignored in favor of his exotic language and absurdist instinct—free verse earned him forgiveness for his galumphing manner and symbolist mannerism. Marianne Moore used a scaffolding of syllabics and rhyme to construct her poems but years later in revision sometimes cheerfully (or distractedly) abandoned them. Only William Carlos Williams came to free verse as if it were home and stayed there contentedly, though the ease and consciousness of rhythm in the later meditative poems suggest that, however much he desired a linoleum-like prose, the subtlety of his ear wouldn't quite let him. Where does this leave Frost? More in the middle of a group trying out certain tensions in the verse line, tensions between meter and prose unimagined in French *vers libre*, in the earlier essays at free verse by W. E. Henley and Stephen Crane, or in the long philosophizing line of Tupper and Whitman.

Frost would not be the first poet to require form to order his imagination. Is the scattered and unhappy organization of his lectures due to a routine of mind the notebooks reflect, a habitual dislocation or relocation of focus, or to the patchwork, crazy-quilt character of the notebooks from which he drew (in which case he lacked some essential integrating faculty in prose)? A notebook is an aide-mémoire, an act of self-education, a way to stem the tide of trivia that passes through the writer's mind, a jump start for poems, the grave of failed expression, and much else—in notebooks, the poet is often waiting for lightning to strike or the sewers to overflow. It doesn't diminish Frost that his notebooks are less interesting than those of other writers, just as it doesn't diminish Beethoven that his rough drafts are less fluent than Mozart's— indeed, you might say that the clutter of sawdust and brown wrapping-paper that composes the notebooks ennobles Frost, because in the poems he rose so far above them.

Interview by Garrick Davis

When did you begin writing criticism? Did you see it as an inevitable task—an obligation—of your poetry?

I was drawn to criticism blindly and without regard for the justice or ethic of the role. There may be artists born to criticize (and those whose every poem is a review)—my own criticism is no more than a shout from the back of the room. A sort of "Yeah, yeah," a double affirmative that reads like dissent.

As a critic I began with little except passion and an ornery nature. I spent my late teens and early twenties reviewing records for a grimy and now forgotten rock magazine, a suitably depressing place to learn a little, a very little, about critical prose. Such Grub Street reviewing had its moments—my opinion once so offended a record executive the next records I received were lovingly and individually vandalized. I had an absorption in music that at times approached the pathological and was the more delicious for that.

On a whim, at the Writers' Workshop at Iowa, I reviewed a novel for the student newspaper; with that callow introduction, I began reviewing fiction for the *Chicago Tribune*. My opinions were sharpened by putting them in ink—no doubt this is a common experience. At least, I'd like to think I'm not the only critic who discovers his mind (not the impulse of taste but the very words) in the act of writing. Those early reviews look hollow and ill at ease now. It wasn't until I started reviewing poetry that my criticism showed an act of imaginative sympathy, a deeper dwelling as a reader. Perhaps I was more cruelly affected (or more irritated) by poetry, or perhaps as a poet I felt something more critical at stake.

I don't think poets owe a penny to criticism (though I'd support a law making every poet write a review as the price for writing a poem). I admit that some years after I innocently began I felt, if not a calling, at least a whispering. Criticism is an act partly moral; but it contains the devious and immoral pleasure of putting words on the page, of being forced to think about books.

What do you think the role of the poet-critic should be? What critics or poet-critics do you consider exemplary in this regard?

Some of the gestures of my reviews have paid homage to Randall Jarrell— I've alluded or mimicked, because his criticism *is* so often exemplary. Reviewing is a trade, even at times a rough trade; and Jarrell was the roughest and most cunning of traders. His distant forebears were Francis Jeffrey and Edgar Allan Poe. I owe deeper debts of inspiration to R. P. Blackmur, perhaps the most brilliant critic of verse in the past century; to Eliot, the critic most sensitive to the poet's interior view of his art; and to countless others. If such a list seems to dress me in clothing that doesn't fit, let me say that my criticism can never repay those debts.

I'm not sure a "poet-critic" has a role, or should have one—I'm not even sure what a "poet-critic" is, though it sounds like a mythical beast, part goat and part hyena. The term implies an equality or balance I doubt most poets feel when they descend to criticism (it's not poet=critic). At least, I've never felt the contentment of such balance. Perhaps it is no accident that many of the best critics of poetry have been poets, since poetry matters so much to them and so little to anyone else—but isn't this rather strange? (Critics of poetry have rarely been poets of the first rank. Coleridge, Eliot, Pound, and Auden are exceptions, not a norm.) The rough-and-tumble of criticism in other arts isn't usually carried on by the artists.

To call myself a "poet-critic" would be to give myself airs. My own imaginative life is lived almost entirely in poetry. I could give up criticism tomorrow with only minor regret, so to dwell in this interview on criticism is to represent myself in a way amusingly prejudicial. I'm merely a poet who has opinions and has sometimes been paid to publish them.

What do you think of the present situation of poetry? Of its current health as an art?

I distrust the motives of the question. Much of what we dislike about the poetry around us won't bother readers of the future, because it will have been forgotten. I doubt even the Pulitzer Prize winners of the past two decades will have many poems in anthologies half a century from now. This isn't simply a problem with the prize, though it's a scandal that Amy Clampitt never won it and another that Gjertrud Schnackenberg has yet to win it.

Our poetry is healthy, if the sole measure is that there's a hell of a lot. Much is mediocre, but most poetry in any period is mediocre. What bothers me, as a reader, is how slim current ambitions are—too many contemporary poems start small and end smaller. They don't bite off more than they can chew—they bite off so little they don't need to chew. They're content to be trivial or frivolous, without remembering that frivolous poetry (the light verse of Carroll, Housman, Auden) has exceptionally high standards.

Poetry is now too often a minor art, an art of the margins. No matter how many buses and subway cars carry poems (always little bite-sized poems), no matter how many poetry months there are (October could be declared a second poetry month—then look out!), no matter how many poets laureate we have (and how easy their poems are to understand), it takes labor and education to read most of the poetry of the present and almost all poetry of the past. I have students who find it difficult to read Robert Frost—Robert Frost! In thirty years teachers may be moaning about students who find it hard to understand Seamus Heaney. Or Billy Collins! When poets are tempted to moan about the irrelevance of poetry, we might remind ourselves that playwrights and photographers and composers are worse off—poets can publish and be damned, but in other arts young artists have more trouble being seen or heard.

What do you think of the present situation of poetry criticism? Of its health?

It's despicable that, too often, magazines have to fill what little space they leave for reviews with transparent forms of logrolling and back patting, the slouch of minor corruption (as well as the emollient cant of bad taste). Editors often complain that poets hate to review their contemporaries, because they're afraid of making enemies. Perhaps this is cowardice at its most genial. When poets lather their reviews with nothing but diplomatic flattery (or criticism so mild it wouldn't kill a fly), criticism has failed its readers.

Jarrell thought his reviews had cost him a Pulitzer, and maybe they did. But perhaps he was just unlucky. He lost to three poets anyone would have been delighted to lose to—Elizabeth Bishop, Marianne Moore, and Robert Frost (though he wouldn't have shared the judges' high opinion of *A Witness Tree*). It must have been irritating to lose to Richard Eberhart, however, and galling to lose to Peter Viereck and Phyllis McGinley. Worse, the year Jarrell published one of his best books, *Little Friend, Little Friend*, the judges gave no award at all. It would be hard to say that such missed chances were a cost of the criticism. (When Jarrell expressed his disappointment about the Pulitzer, he had already won the National Book Award.)

Reviewing is not a dangerous trade if the worst that can happen, even to a poet as good as Jarrell, is to be deprived of a few honors. What was Shaw's remark about the critic? "His hand is against every man and every man's hand is against him." Any critic should give up the idea of winning awards. He shouldn't want to win awards in the first place (it would suggest he isn't doing his job—he hasn't offended enough people). That doesn't mean he shouldn't accept an award—it's rude not to accept gifts.

Eliot believed the poet-critic criticized poetry in order to create it, so that his views were often partial and dogmatic. Allen Tate said that the poet-critic "is not concerned with consistency and system, but merely with as much self-knowledge as he needs to write his own verse." Whereas Randall Jarrell's criticism does not seem so intimately linked to his poetry. The critic in him was an ideal reader, who rarely expounded ideas or clarified the intentions of the poet. The two roles seemed to exist in him separately.

Do you see your own criticism as that of a poet's, partial and dogmatic, or an ideal reader's? Is there a vital connection between your own poetry and prose?

Within the narrow terms offered, I feel a stranger to both camps. I haven't written criticism in order to clear a path for my own work, and I'm not sure my poems would have been different had I not written a critical word. I know what Eliot meant—criticism often seems not self-exculpatory or self-explanatory (in the sense that an artist explains himself to himself) so much as self-condemning. Criticism is written in a fallen condition—and perhaps allows the critic, as a soiled act of grace, an occasional glimpse into how language works. If there's a connection between the labor of criticism and the languishing pleasures of art, it is that in both, at fifty, one can still be a student.

I certainly don't have a system, and to that extent *must* criticize as a reader—not an ideal reader, surely, merely an imperfect and partial one. Perhaps in longer essays, where there's room to wrestle with an artist's intentions (rather than merely praising or scolding the execution of those intentions), I've developed certain crippled ideas. I object to the characterization of Jarrell, who got under the skin of Whitman and Frost and Moore and Bishop in a way few critics have. He offered taste and a sensibility, and those have proved, not only more useful than much systematic criticism, but more lasting. It's important to remember that we go to Eliot and Jarrell for different things, and that poetry would be poorer for the loss of either.

If one considers, as a body of writing, the poetry criticism written in the first half of the twentieth century to that written in the second half, then clearly there was a marked deterioration. What caused it?

I'm not the only reader who likes to pick up issues of *Partisan Review* half a century old. The criticism there and in *Sewanee* and *Kenyon* and earlier in *Southern* and *Hound & Horn* seems thrilling now, yet these were just the sorts of little magazines Jarrell complained of in "The Age of Criticism." However odd or awful our own age, things can get worse. Much of the brilliant criticism in those journals was written by academic critics, many of them devotees of New Criticism (a label for a tendency, not the heading of a manifesto)—at this distance New Criticism seems to have been immorally suited to a poet's habits of mind. The shame is that academic criticism now, so jargon ridden and unreadable, is of such little use to poets. Postmodern criticism impoverished and corrupted, when it did not drive from the university entirely, a generation of serious readers—those who loved literature enough to study for the doctorate.

But what has caused the deterioration, the near bankruptcy, of that poor cousin of criticism, the poetry review? Cowardice, if you like. Laziness, perhaps. Jarrell stopped reviewing poetry at forty-two yet felt his career was shadowed and perhaps poisoned by it. (And yet wouldn't we give up all but a few of his poems for his reviews?) I'm no less cowardly and no less lazy than other poets, but I was fortunate to review poetry in drowsy innocence until I was hardened in my ways. I wrote to please myself, and my criticism met only silence. Perhaps it was the silence of compassion.

There was an age, certainly, when poets felt it necessary to respond to contemporary poetry. But when was that age, exactly? The major Romantics were not critics, apart from Coleridge. Nor were the major Victorians. (Poe is an exception among American poets, but Poe was not a major poet.) Much of our modern sense of a poet's duty as a critic comes from Pound and Eliot (both in the shadow of Arnold). The poets of the following generation, Auden and Empson superbly, extended and complicated that achievement. And there is the lonely and brilliant example of Blackmur (followed and echoed, in an odd way, by Geoffrey Hill, another idiosyncratic and difficult critic). Weren't Pound and Eliot just magnificent exceptions? The course of poetry criticism may be more dependent on the venues open, the fees paid, than on the lack in poets of a predatory instinct. Would we have more lucid critics if the *New York Times Book Review* paid $2,000 for a review? Or would we just have wealthier cowards?

Is there some way to account for the fact that the vast majority of American poet-critics have been, and continue to be, politically conservative? From the New Critics to the New Formalists, many of the important poet-critics have been denounced for their political allegiances as much as their aesthetic ideas.

Eliot and Pound were founders of our avant-garde, and it's easy to forget they had conservative principles—yet calling them politically conservative might be an error of tact as well as category (Pound was drawn to Roosevelt's progressive politics, though Eliot might have given his write-in vote to George III). But what of Williams, in opposition? New Critics like Ransom and Tate certainly longed for a vanished South, the south of mules and Old Hickory (their poems are steeped in the whiskey of antique desire)—but you couldn't say all the New Critics were conservative. The *Partisan Review* crowd were good Trotskyites, Jarrell was entranced by Kennedy, Lowell was a conscientious objector, and he and Berryman marched against the war in Vietnam. I don't know the politics of most of the contemporary critics whose work I admire, and I certainly hope readers aren't interested in mine. I write for magazines in all shades of the spectrum, so I am complicit with failed politics of violently opposed sorts.

What do you think of the yoking of politics to poetry, such a fixture of recent American poetry?

Those oxen rarely pull in the same direction. A politic poetry, as well as a political poetry, is tedious because it advances upon us with its motives scrawled on banners. It wears its slogans on its sleeve. Socialist painting, communist drama, political poetry—in such oxymorons there are only dustbin arts. I don't say a poem can't be political (among our contemporaries, Seamus Heaney has avoided or averted the difficulties—or suborned them in the service of art); but a poem whose purpose is political usually rouses a reader's distrust, unless he loves the chill of propaganda, as some readers do. Poetry may succumb to such designs, but it's not the purpose of art to make people comfortable in their prejudices. It takes a Heaney or an Auden to arouse our suspicions and seduce us anyway.

Besides, isn't part of the pleasure of poetry admiring poets whose politics you find despicable? It's fortunate that we can't always predict a man's politics from his poetry. Many New Formalists are New Deal liberals, and I am told that one or two avant-garde poets vote Republican. It would be amusing, if so.

Much has been made in recent years of the proliferation of creative writing programs in the United States. Do you think this academicization has had a beneficial or baleful effect on poetry?

Probably a little of both. The collapse of artistic culture in big cities, the disappearance of warrens of young writers who criticized each other's work (the writers are there, but social cohesion vanished with the literary jobs that supported it), created a need for artificial Sohos. Informal groups, inside or outside the university, have often aided the hothouse growth of young poets. (Weren't the University Wits such a group, four centuries ago?) Writing programs are still rare in Britain; but poetry there is as numbingly conformist as in America, so MFA programs aren't entirely to blame.

Such programs are rarely academic or rigorous enough—they tend to be cordial and undemanding. I must declare my interest, having taught in an MFA program a long while and given some thought to its construction. In a workshop, the students often take means for ends. A poet may set his students a form and perhaps a theme, to give their imaginations skeletal structure (not necessarily traditional or metrical) and the ghost of a logic, just as quattrocento apprentices were asked to copy drawings by their master. The best students exceed the cost of those lessons. Less gifted students think writing a villanelle or a sestina or some cobbled-together form an end in itself. I'm all for occasional poems, and I don't think every poem needs to be inspired—but it should come to its inspiration along the way. Much recent poetry reads as if it didn't want to be written—it lacks any necessity or nemesis. And workshops often move toward consensus, grinding away a young writer's originality, the burrs of his gift.

Would American poetry have been worse had Pound made good his plans for an Ezuversity? Or had Auden continued to teach? It may be no bad thing to spend a short apprenticeship under poets who know something about the art. (I make no claims here for my own teaching.) We have almost all been affected, inspired, transformed by a good teacher (I will pay my debt here to two teachers who, late in my undergraduate career, taught me much I needed to know—David Milch and Richard Howard). Of course, many MFA programs are full of mild and middling professors, timeservers, the almost-weres and never-wases. And there are students who travel nomadically, program to program, summer workshop to summer workshop, looking for advice to set in order the disordered houses of their imaginations. Still, I would be wary of condemning an institution that produced, or provoked, poets as diverse as

W. D. Snodgrass, Donald Justice, Philip Levine, Robert Bly, William Stafford, Mark Strand, Charles Wright, and Jorie Graham.

What do you think of the vast subsidized system of grants, prizes, and awards that poets currently compete for?

Is it so awful that poets are patronized? I'd rather throw my taxes at crop after crop of poets than crop after crop of tobacco. You don't want poets to get settled and lazy, so perhaps such awards and grants should be rare and capricious. Only recently have we freed ourselves, in our democratic way, from the notion of private patronage (a notion still current in John Quinn's generosity to Pound and Eliot). But the world was not better when poets had to bow and scrape before lords—think of Shakespeare's weaselly dedications, and the tone of his first sonnets, which make my flesh crawl. Apart from some odd examples like Pope (who grew rich from translation) and Byron (who hardly needed the money), poets have not written their way into fortunes. Before the twentieth century many poets were, if not wealthy, at least able to escape daily labor. When you read the biographies of most of the great poets from Milton to Lowell, you think, didn't any of these folks have a steady job? (I don't mean to denigrate Milton's work as Latin secretary to the Council of State.) Williams's medical practice and Stevens's insurance work were dedicated but oddball exceptions.

The cant of "arts administration" is creepy and dispiriting, and applying for grants a dreadful trade, though perhaps a necessary check to a poet's pride. Poetry is such a difficult art, often such a minor art, these small emoluments create no sense of privilege in the recipients. The ordinary reaction is relief—at having gained an hour or a month or a year for indulgence in the art. Perhaps the Croesus-like awards given (for "lifetime achievement," whatever that might be) to poets long into cozy retirement should be scattered like seed corn among poets under thirty—that would be a start.

Governments have patronized the arts without destroying them, or destroying themselves, though our sentimentalities blind us to the examples. The art of trecento Siena was bought by state patronage, not the riches of counts or dukes. Not long ago the Works Progress Administration proved that government is not always the enemy of art. Maya Lin's Vietnam War monument is one of the most beautiful and stirring of public sculptures. And yet the money for "public" art worked into the budget of every federal building is a feather bed for mediocrity. Where is the Semtex when you need it?

Which contemporary poets do you read with pleasure?

A critic should answer that question with his reviews, and I hope I've answered it in mine.

Which contemporary critics?

I've recalled at length, in the interview at the end of *All the Rage,* my fondness for the criticism of Geoffrey Hill, Christopher Ricks, and George Steiner. Let me mention a few critics less well known. I think Michael Hofmann the most distinguished of the younger critics. I must declare an interest again, because he is my colleague at Florida; but his collection of essays, *Behind the Lines,* is thorough and original. James Fenton has written thoughtful left-handed pieces on poetry, most still uncollected; and Craig Raine is as cheerfully combative and learnèd as Jarrell. These critics have written mostly for British journals. Among younger American critics, Adam Kirsch and Christian Wiman are both worth attention and argument.

Are there any books of poetry published in the last few years that you would particularly recommend to readers?

Let one stand as an example—Gjertrud Schnackenberg's luminous and insufficiently appreciated *The Gilded Lapse of Time.*

Can poets regain the common readers they once had? Will poetry ever exert itself again in American culture as it did a century ago? Does criticism have a role to play in this?

No, no, and alas no, but we can hope to keep the uncommon readers we have always had—the dispossessed, out-at-elbows readers, ones who would rather curl up with a book than watch football or play a computer game. Perhaps these readers will grow fewer and unhappier (which means that most poetry books will sell their five hundred or a thousand copies, just as they did when the country was much smaller). Surely the worst way to create readers is by praising everything under the skies—I've read many a review, perfectly convinced by the logic of its praise, only to laugh out loud when I came to the poems themselves. (The worst criticism can't even lie convincingly.) Expecting poets to review their friends harshly (or even their enemies), expecting those who judge contests or awards to be impartial, is no doubt naive. The fault is no less despicable—or disappointing—for being human. When we have a criticism that does nothing but praise, readers know poetry critics are idiots.

Some argue that the poems of Sharon Olds or Billy Collins attract readers who will graduate, by slow and childlike steps, to a poetry more demanding. Perhaps there have been a few such readers, scarce as glass slippers. But readers satisfied by such poetry are not likely to look beyond it, and not likely to be satisfied when they do. Poetry must fall on prepared ground, and most readers have not read enough poetry to be prepared. A poetry like Robert Frost's or Emily Dickinson's, with a high level of craft and cunning as well as plain moral values (though not always simple values), is very rare. It measures our distance from Browning that we'll never need a Sharon Olds or Billy Collins Society. Perhaps we're the luckier for that. (Sometimes readers love very difficult poetry if it's charged with enough mystery—or publicity.)

We aren't going to regain the lost readers of the nineteenth century, those who didn't know radio or television or the Internet, who were educated in French and Latin, who as children read Milton and Shakespeare and could bash out a decent verse themselves (one that scanned and rhymed effortlessly, if without originality). Those common readers of poetry are long in the grave, and they were readers differently trained and with different expectations from readers now (they expected moral virtues from poetry, or at least moral suasion). Even if we could have those old-fashioned readers again, would we want them? The embedded question is not, "What sort of poetry would gain those readers now?" but "What sort of poetry would attract more readers than we have?" The probable answer is an uncomfortable one—a poetry that catered to the sentimentalities of its audience. Criticism is likely to grate against such sentimentalities.

What do you think of the recent revival of performance poetry—the so-called poetry slams?

It costs little to be tolerant of such a goofy form of entertainment. I doubt any lasting poetry will emerge from it—I'm still waiting for lasting poetry to come from rock lyrics.

Do you think your criticism has hurt the reception of your poetry? Have your reviews cost you anything?

I certainly hope so. Why write criticism if it's so trivial it doesn't have a cost? I've been warned, often enough, that writing criticism is suicide (that would make a pleasant story by Borges); yet I can't say my poetry has suffered in reviews, can't say I've faced real disfavor. Because criticism rouses passions, because it has more currency (and is sometimes easier to understand), there are readers who think of me only as a critic. The poet mildly objects.

There has been a certain baying after me on the Internet, I understand. I'm not sure such readers have the best objections to my reviews; but to reassure them perhaps I should say that, unlike Housman, I don't store up witty sayings in a notebook, to use as occasion arises (though I might wish I did); that I don't review books to call attention to myself (too much attention is likely to make me stop writing criticism altogether); that my harsher criticism isn't motivated by envy, as far as I can tell (envy is what makes me write good reviews, not bad ones); and that I'm amused by readers who say so violently that I should be more mild. Readers who assume I don't praise other poets, and who have failed to discover long essays of appreciation on Pound, Frost, Auden, Bishop, Wilbur, Hill, and others, have not read very deeply.

If criticism has cost my poetry something, it can be only a thing of limited value. I'm not trying to be high-minded—my poetry must make its own way. Poets are always complaining they haven't received their due—that they deserved this prize, were cheated of that grant, that X got it first, or Y when he was younger. Most writers get more than their due.

Permissions

"The Bowl of Diogenes; or, The End of Criticism": *Poetry*, February 2006.

"Out on the Lawn": *New Criterion*, December 2003.

"Stouthearted Men": *New Criterion*, June 2004.

"The Most Contemptible Moth: Lowell in Letters": *Virginia Quarterly Review*, Fall 2005.

"Forward into the Past: Reading the New Critics": *Virginia Quarterly Review*, Spring 2008. Foreword to *Praising It New: The Best of the New Criticism*, ed. Garrick Davis (Swallow Press/Ohio University Press, 2008).

"One If by Land": *New Criterion*, December 2004.

"The Great American Desert": *New Criterion*, June 2005.

"The State with the Prettiest Name": *Parnassus* 28, nos. 1–2 (2005).

"Elizabeth Bishop Unfinished": *New Criterion*, April 2006.

"Elizabeth Bishop's Sullen Art": *New Criterion*, March 1997.

"Jumping the Shark": *New Criterion*, December 2005.

"Victoria's Secret": *New Criterion*, June 2006.

"Attack of the Anthologists" (Lehman): *New York Times Book Review*, April 16, 2006. Copyright 2006 by the New York Times Company. Reprinted by permission.

"Attack of the Anthologists" (Strand): *Wall Street Journal*, July 21, 2005.

"The Lost World of Lawrence Durrell": *TLS*, July 28, 2006.

"Hart Crane Overboard": *New York Times Book Review*, January 28, 2007. Copyright 2007 by the New York Times Company. Reprinted by permission.

"On Reviewing Hart Crane": *Poetry*, October 2008. "Postscript": *Poetry*, December 2008.

"The Endless Ocean of Derek Walcott": *New York Times Book Review*, April 8, 2007. Copyright 2007 by the New York Times Company. Reprinted by permission.

"The Civil Power of Geoffrey Hill": *New York Times Book Review*, January 20, 2008. Copyright 2008 by the New York Times Company. Reprinted by permission.

"God's Chatter": *New Criterion*, December 2006.

"Let's Do It, Let's Fall in Luff": *New Criterion*, June 2007.

"Pynchon in the Poetic": *Southwest Review* 83, no. 4 (1998).

"Back to the Future": *Virginia Quarterly Review,* Summer 2007.

"The World Is Too Much with Us": *New Criterion,* December 2007.

"Valentine's Day Massacre": *New Criterion,* June 2008.

"The Forgotten Masterpiece of John Townsend Trowbridge": *New Criterion,* April 2008.

"Frost at Midnight": *Parnassus* 30, nos. 1–2 (2008).

"Interview by Garrick Davis": *Contemporary Poetry Review* (online) (2002).

Books Under Review

Verse Chronicle: Out on the Lawn

Billy Collins. *Nine Horses*. Random House, 2002.
Rosanna Warren. *Departure*. W. W. Norton, 2003.
Howard Nemerov. *The Selected Poems of Howard Nemerov*. Ed. Daniel Anderson.
  Swallow Press/Ohio University Press, 2003.
Sherod Santos. *The Perishing*. W. W. Norton, 2003.
Carolyn Forché. *Blue Hour*. HarperCollins, 2003.
James Fenton. *The Love Bomb, and Other Musical Pieces*. Faber and Faber, 2003.

Verse Chronicle: Stouthearted Men

George Oppen. *Selected Poems*. Ed. Robert Creeley. New Directions, 2003.
Franz Wright. *Walking to Martha's Vineyard*. Alfred A. Knopf, 2003.
Tony Hoagland. *What Narcissism Means to Me*. Graywolf, 2003.
Spencer Reece. *The Clerk's Tale*. Houghton Mifflin, 2004.
Charles Wright. *Buffalo Yoga*. Farrar, Straus and Giroux, 2004.
Philip Larkin. *Collected Poems*. Ed. Anthony Thwaite. Farrar, Straus and Giroux,
  2004.

The Most Contemptible Moth: Lowell in Letters

Robert Lowell. *The Letters of Robert Lowell*. Ed. Saskia Hamilton. Farrar, Straus
  and Giroux, 2005.

Verse Chronicle: One If by Land

Gary Snyder. *Danger on Peaks*. Shoemaker and Hoard, 2004.
Rita Dove. *American Smooth*. W. W. Norton, 2004.
Derek Hines, trans. *Gilgamesh*. Anchor, 2004.
Stephen Mitchell, trans. *Gilgamesh: A New English Version*. Free Press, 2004.

Derek Walcott. *The Prodigal.* Farrar, Straus and Giroux, 2004.
Czeslaw Milosz. *Second Space.* Ecco, 2004.

Verse Chronicle: The Great American Desert

John Ashbery. *Where Shall I Wander.* Ecco, 2005.
Dean Young. *Elegy on Toy Piano.* University of Pittsburgh Press, 2005.
Jorie Graham. *Overlord.* Ecco, 2005.
Kevin Young. *Black Maria.* Alfred A. Knopf, 2005.
Ted Kooser. *Delights & Shadows.* Copper Canyon, 2004.
——. *Flying at Night: Poems 1965–1985.* University of Pittsburgh Press, 2005.
——. *The Poetry Home Repair Manual.* University of Nebraska Press, 2005.
Richard Wilbur. *Collected Poems, 1943–2004.* Harcourt, 2004.

Elizabeth Bishop Unfinished

Elizabeth Bishop. *Edgar Allan Poe & the Juke-Box: Uncollected Poems, Drafts, and Fragments.* Ed. Alice Quinn. Farrar, Straus and Giroux, 2006.

Elizabeth Bishop's Sullen Art

Elizabeth Bishop. *Exchanging Hats: Paintings.* Ed. William Benton. Farrar, Straus and Giroux, 1996.

Verse Chronicle: Jumping the Shark

Kim Addonizio. *What Is This Thing Called Love.* W. W. Norton, 2004.
Billy Collins. *The Trouble with Poetry, and Other Poems.* Random House, 2005.
Kay Ryan. *The Niagara River.* Grove, 2005.
Mark Doty. *School of the Arts.* HarperCollins, 2005.
Jack Gilbert. *Refusing Heaven.* Alfred A. Knopf, 2005.
Geoffrey Hill. *Scenes from Comus.* Penguin (UK), 2005.

Verse Chronicle: Victoria's Secret

Seamus Heaney. *District and Circle.* Farrar, Straus and Giroux, 2006.
Louise Glück. *Averno.* Farrar, Straus and Giroux, 2006.
Don Paterson. *Landing Light.* Graywolf, 2005.
Tess Gallagher. *Dear Ghosts,.* Graywolf, 2006.
Anne Carson. *Decreation.* Alfred A. Knopf, 2005.
Geoffrey Hill. *Without Title.* Penguin (UK), 2006.

Attack of the Anthologists

The Oxford Book of American Poetry. Ed. David Lehman. Oxford University Press, 2006.

100 *Great Poems of the Twentieth Century.* Ed. Mark Strand. W. W. Norton, 2005.

The Lost World of Lawrence Durrell

Lawrence Durrell. *Selected Poems.* Ed. Peter Porter. Faber and Faber, 2006.

Hart Crane Overboard

Hart Crane. *Complete Poems and Selected Letters.* Ed. Langdon Hammer. Library of America, 2006.

The Endless Ocean of Derek Walcott

Derek Walcott. *Selected Poems.* Ed. Edward Baugh. Farrar, Straus and Giroux, 2007.

The Civil Power of Geoffrey Hill

Geoffrey Hill. A *Treatise of Civil Power.* Yale University Press, 2007.

Verse Chronicle: God's Chatter

Natasha Trethewey. *Native Guard.* Houghton Mifflin, 2006.
Mark Strand. *Man and Camel.* Alfred A. Knopf, 2006.
A. R. Ammons. *Ommateum, with Doxology.* W. W. Norton, 2006.
Louise Glück. *Firstborn.* New American Library, 1968.
Franz Wright. *God's Silence.* Alfred A. Knopf, 2006.
Paul Muldoon. *Horse Latitudes.* Farrar, Straus and Giroux, 2006.

Verse Chronicle: Let's Do It, Let's Fall in Luff

John Ashbery. A *Worldly Country.* Ecco, 2007.
Frieda Hughes. *Forty-Five.* HarperCollins, 2006.
Cathy Park Hong. *Dance Dance Revolution.* W. W. Norton, 2007.
Frederick Seidel. *Ooga-Booga.* Farrar, Straus and Giroux, 2006.
Robert Lowell. *Selected Poems: Expanded Edition.* Farrar, Straus and Giroux, 2006 [2007].
Henri Cole. *Blackbird and Wolf.* Farrar, Straus and Giroux, 2007.

Pynchon in the Poetic

Thomas Pynchon. *Mason & Dixon*. Holt, 1997.

Back to the Future

Thomas Pynchon. *Against the Day*. Penguin, 2006.

Verse Chronicle: The World Is Too Much with Us

Les Murray. *The Biplane Houses*. Farrar, Straus, 2006.
Robert Pinsky. *Gulf Music*. Farrar, Straus and Giroux, 2007.
Sandra McPherson. *Expectation Days*. University of Illinois Press, 2007.
Charles Wright. *Littlefoot*. Farrar, Straus and Giroux, 2007.
Kathleen Jamie. *Waterlight: Selected Poems*. Graywolf, 2007.
Robert Hass. *Time and Materials*. Ecco, 2007.

Verse Chronicle: Valentine's Day Massacre

Ted Kooser. *Valentines*, University of Nebraska Press, 2008.
Melissa Green. *Fifty-Two*. Arrowsmith, 2007.
Elizabeth Spires. *The Wave-Maker*. W. W. Norton, 2008.
Campbell McGrath. *Seven Notebooks*. Ecco, 2008.
Marie Howe. *The Kingdom of Ordinary Times*. W. W. Norton, 2008.
Jorie Graham. *Sea Change*. Ecco, 2008.

Frost at Midnight

Robert Frost. *The Notebooks of Robert Frost*. Ed. Robert Faggen. Harvard University Press, 2006.

Index of Authors Reviewed

Biographical Note

William Logan has published eight volumes of poetry and five volumes of essays and reviews. *The Undiscovered Country* won the National Book Critics Circle Award in Criticism. He lives in Gainesville, Florida, and Cambridge, England.